YERBURY

A PHOTOGRAPHIC COLLECTION

1850 - 1993

YERBURY

A PHOTOGRAPHIC COLLECTION

Trevor E. R. Yerbury   Malcolm Cant

Foreword by Richard Demarco

MERCAT PRESS EDINBURGH

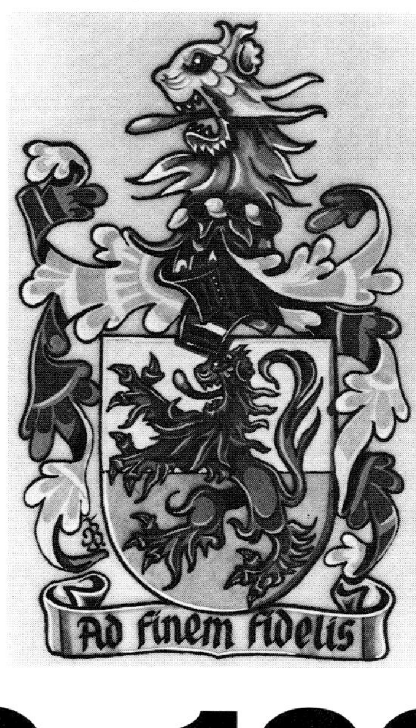

1850 - 1993

First published 1993 by Mercat Press
James Thin, 53 South Bridge, Edinburgh EH1 1YS

ISBN 1873644248

This book is dedicated to
Blanche, Faye and Rachel

Typeset by Quorn Selective Repro Ltd
Design by Keith Kail, Type Area, Falkirk
Printed by Butler & Tanner Ltd, Frome and London

CONTENTS

Foreword by Richard Demarco 7
Acknowledgements 8
Introduction 9

1 The Yerbury Family 11
2 The Old Town 22
3 The New Town 42
4 Suburbs South 64
5 Other Suburbs and Locations 93
6 Royal Visits 114
7 Sport and Leisure 129
8 Portraits 147
9 Portraits by Trevor Yerbury 176

Index 191

FOREWORD
by Richard Demarco

TREVOR YERBURY is a photographer essentially concerned with portraiture. What is more, his portraits are inspired by the long tradition of portraiture associated with his family's photographic business which has recorded the Edinburgh scene since 1850. It is probably impossible to document the precise number of images bearing the Yerbury name, especially those associated with the beginnings of the family business. The Yerbury collection must surely represent one of the richest photographic archives in the British Isles. All these images seem to be the preparation for the work which Trevor Yerbury has set for himself, because undoubtedly he uses a camera not only with a photographer's eye but with an artist's eye, adding to that indefinable and essentially perverse dimension which makes a photograph much more penetrating than any other method of recording the natural world.

He has created his own world; one populated by a cast of personalities which he chooses to focus upon with remarkable intensity, often emphasising the sensual, particularly in relation to the female face and figure. He creates a *mis en scene* suggesting that his subjects are capable of playing a dramatic role within a setting of heightened tension. By preferring black and white photography he makes manifest his delight in texture and the stuff and substance of surfaces inherent in the forces of nature and in landscape. In his celebration of the sensual life-enhancing human presence he also manages to suggest the mortality inherent in all earthly beauty.

He has dared to add a dimension to the image of Edinburgh not normally associated with a city of Protestant moral rectitude. Particularly over the past five years he has to be congratulated for his unerring sense of reality which has enabled him to create this world which lies beneath the surface of Edinburgh's everyday life. He protects it, enlarges upon it and rejoices in it. It is a world 'born on the edge of reverie', to quote Gaston Bachelard, the French phonomenologist. The human presence through his camera's lenses exists halfway between a world observed in full wakefulness and a world of dreams.

ACKNOWLEDGEMENTS

I AM INDEBTED to a large number of people who have assisted with various aspects of this work. In the interests of simplicity and impartiality I have listed the names of individuals alphabetically in one group, and the names of various institutions in another group, remembering always, of course, that the institutions can operate only through the dedicated individuals who work there. To everyone I extend my thanks and appreciation:

James Allan; Archie Baird; Miss Joyce M. Barrie; Maurice Berrill; John Cameron; George R. Campbell; Ian Colville; Mrs Helen Davidson; Peter Heatly; Robert Herkes; D. L. G. Hunter; Mrs Agnes G. MacKinnon; Rev Dr J. S. Marshall; Sandy Noble; Mr and Mrs Robert Orr; Mrs Jane Paris; C. R. G. Paul; Mrs Margaret B. Ritchie; Lord and Lady Rosebery of Dalmeny House; James N. Savage; Sheriff David B. Smith; Douglas F. Stewart; Harry D. Watson.

The Advocates' Library; The Balmoral Hotel; The Bruntsfield Links Golfing Society Limited; The Caledonian Hotel; The Company of Merchants of the City of Edinburgh; The Court of the Lord Lyon; The Doune Motor Museum; The Edinburgh City Archivist; The Edinburgh Room of the Central Library; Edinburgh University Library; The Glasgow Museum of Transport; The Grange Cricket Club; Melrose Motor Museum; The Mitchell Library; Murrayfield Golf Club Limited; The North Berwick Golf Club; The Royal Archives, Windsor Castle; The Royal Company of Archers; The Royal Scots; Scottish Rugby Union.

There is a final group whose involvement in the project has been so close and involved that they deserve a special mention. Mrs Blanche Yerbury, and Trevor and Faye Yerbury have spent many hours looking through old photographs and researching the family history. I also thank my wife Phyllis for typing the script, and members of my own family for their support and encouragement. Morag Sinclair has again checked the proofs with great accuracy.

MALCOLM CANT
EDINBURGH, 1993

INTRODUCTION

THE NAME Yerbury, in Edinburgh, is synonymous with photography and has been so for well over a century. Indeed there can be few people brought up in the city who do not have a Yerbury photograph of themselves, or a friend or relative, taken whilst at school, university, club or association annual dinner, or sports occasion. The photographic tradition in the family spans four generations starting in the 1860s and continuing to the present day. Researching and writing the historical text for *Yerbury: A Photographic Collection 1850–1993* has for me been a departure, albeit a pleasant one, from my previous efforts to put pen to paper. I hope I have provided a commentary which is sufficiently interesting and detailed to match the excellence of the photographs.

One hundred and thirty years of photography in one family has produced a formidable number of negatives and prints, some of which have been lost over the years, whilst others have not been returned by would-be researchers. Despite these losses more than a sufficient number of pictures remained under the control of Trevor E. R. Yerbury to enhance the pages of an illustrated book on aspects of Edinburgh and its surroundings. A few of the pictures have appeared with the permission of the Yerbury family in books on Edinburgh over the last decade. Until now, however, no comprehensive attempt has been made to show a major part of the collection still in private hands. Recently Trevor Yerbury and his mother, Blanche Yerbury, agreed to release the pictures for further research, as a result of which it was found that most of the collection fell naturally into the groups covered by the following chapters. Whilst all the pictures included form part of the Yerbury family collection, it is acknowledged that many of the Edinburgh street scenes are the work of J. C. H. Balmain whose firm was incorporated into E. R. Yerbury & Son many years ago. In the chapter on portraits and groups some of the work of William Crooke and J. Moffat is also included. It remains now to give a brief description of each of the chapters included.

The first chapter is a collection of photographs pertaining to the Yerbury family. It opens with a portrait of each of the four generations and includes family groups, weddings and engagements, along with a light-hearted look at some of the family as children.

Chapter 2 is devoted to a series of pictures of the Old Town, mainly by J. C. H. Balmain, starting with four of the oldest views dated between 1850 and 1860. They show the appalling state of housing in Edinburgh around that time. Thereafter, the photographs are arranged more or less by locations, from the Castle to the Palace of Holyroodhouse. Where known, the date has been included in the caption. Of particular interest are the surviving photographs of the street characters and traders in the Royal Mile at the end of the nineteenth century — Coconut Tam, the Hokey Pokey Man and Polly the Fortune Teller. The chapter concludes with a group of pictures around South Bridge and Tollcross.

By contrast, Chapter 3 follows the development of the New Town across the first North Bridge opened in 1772. The development of the Bridge is shown and its replacement with a new structure, begun in 1896. Views of the area around the General Post Office, the Balmoral Hotel and Calton Hill are included, before progressing along Princes Street towards the West End. Many classic views of Princes Street are shown, taken either from the North British Hotel (as it was then) or from the Scott Monument. The West End of Edinburgh is also given full coverage, including a unique picture of St Cuthbert's Church bell about to be hoisted into position, watched by the ministers and the architect, Hippolyte J. Blanc.

Chapter 4 consists mainly of the work of J. C. H. Balmain and illustrates his great interest in the buildings and street scenes of the south of Edinburgh, where he lived. It is not difficult to imagine that many of his photographs would be taken during fairly long walks from his home in Salisbury Place out into 'the countryside' of the Grange, Liberton, Craigend, Cameron Toll, Peffermill and Craigmillar. The chapter includes

Tunny's Photographic Rooms in South Clerk Street in 1850; the Coach Office belonging to David Adamson in Newington Road, 1886; and Mr and Mrs Balmain with a group of American friends on a cycling holiday. Graphic accounts of the poor quality of housing in Causewayside contrast sharply with the elegant villas of Hatton Place.

The photographs assembled in Chapter 5 provide an opportunity to see other suburbs of Edinburgh and locations outside the city, notably Queensferry, Cramond, Newhaven, Portobello, Fisherrow, Musselburgh, Roslin and North Berwick. There are several early transport scenes — a horse bus at Levenhall and a horse-drawn tram at Murrayfield — and a series of photographs showing some of the passenger ferries which plied the Forth at the end of the nineteenth century. Some much more recent pictures portray Portobello in its heyday as a seaside attraction.

Chapter 6 is devoted to Royal Visits to Edinburgh, dealing mainly with two great events: first, the visit of King Edward VII and Queen Alexandra in 1903 and secondly the visit of George V and Queen Mary in 1911. These pictures are confined generally to the area around Princes Street and the processional routes throughout the city, where a variety of triumphal arches was erected for the occasion.

In Chapter 7, on 'Sport and Leisure', the lighter side of the Edinburgh character is shown. There is a strong golfing contingent including historic pictures of 'Gowffing in the 1850s', the Open Champions Braid and Vardon, and the weather-beaten countenance of 'Fiery' the Musselburgh caddie. The first Scottish XV v. England team is photographed at Raeburn Place in 1871, to say nothing of the Heart of Midlothian Football Club as winners of the Scottish Cup in 1956. Tennis, cricket, curling, skating and other pursuits complete the picture.

Chapter 8 has a vast array of portraits and groups, many by Edward Reuben Yerbury (grandfather of Trevor) and William Crooke. They have been chosen from a much bigger collection, hopefully showing as wide a variety of subjects as possible, without sacrificing quality for novelty. Unfortunately many of the portraits have not been individually dated and therefore do not appear in strict chronological order. Almost every name could be mentioned, but a few will suffice: General de Gaulle; Sir James M. Barrie; Andrew Carnegie; Sir William Y. Darling; and many other award-winning studies.

The final chapter has been included to show the work of Trevor E. R. Yerbury whose individual style sets him apart from other photographers today.

Taken together the photographs are essentially a private collection: they are reproduced for the enjoyment and appreciation of everyone with an interest in Edinburgh and its environs.

MALCOLM CANT

CHAPTER 1

My great-great-grandfather, Edward Reuben Yerbury, was born in London on 2 November 1816, where he lived for most of his life. He married in 1842, but died a comparatively young man in 1864, a few days after his forty-eighth birthday. His eldest son, my great-grandfather, also Edward Reuben, began his working life in London at the age of fourteen. He later attended the London School of Photography from 1862 to 1864. In 1864, when he had completed his photographic training, my great-grandfather travelled to Edinburgh and set up in business with a partner at No. 3 South Hanover Street, under the name *Yerbury & Stewart, Photographers*.

Nothing is known of Mr Stewart's origins, but the partnership did not last long, and my great-grandfather soon became the sole proprietor of the firm *E. R. Yerbury*, providing 'photography in all its branches'. In October 1875, eleven years after his arrival in Edinburgh, my great-grandfather married Emma Tyrrell, the youngest daughter of Walter Tyrrell, goldbeater, of 74 Rose Street. The wedding ceremony was conducted by the Reverend Thomas McEwan of Hope Park Church at the house of the bride's father in Melville Terrace, a practice not uncommon at that time.

My great-grandfather worked all his life as a portrait photographer, building up the business in

A Victorian drawing room of the family in the 1890s.

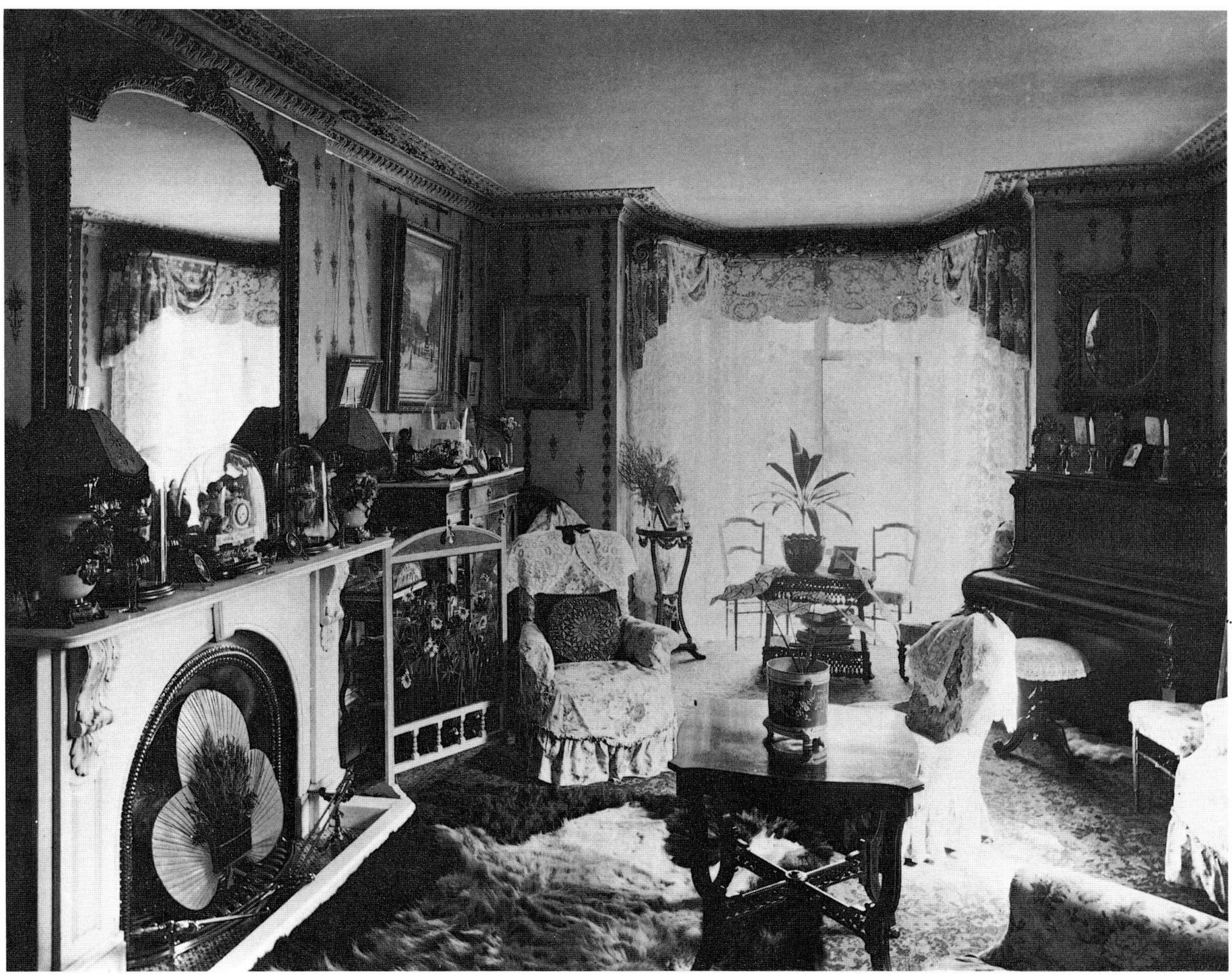

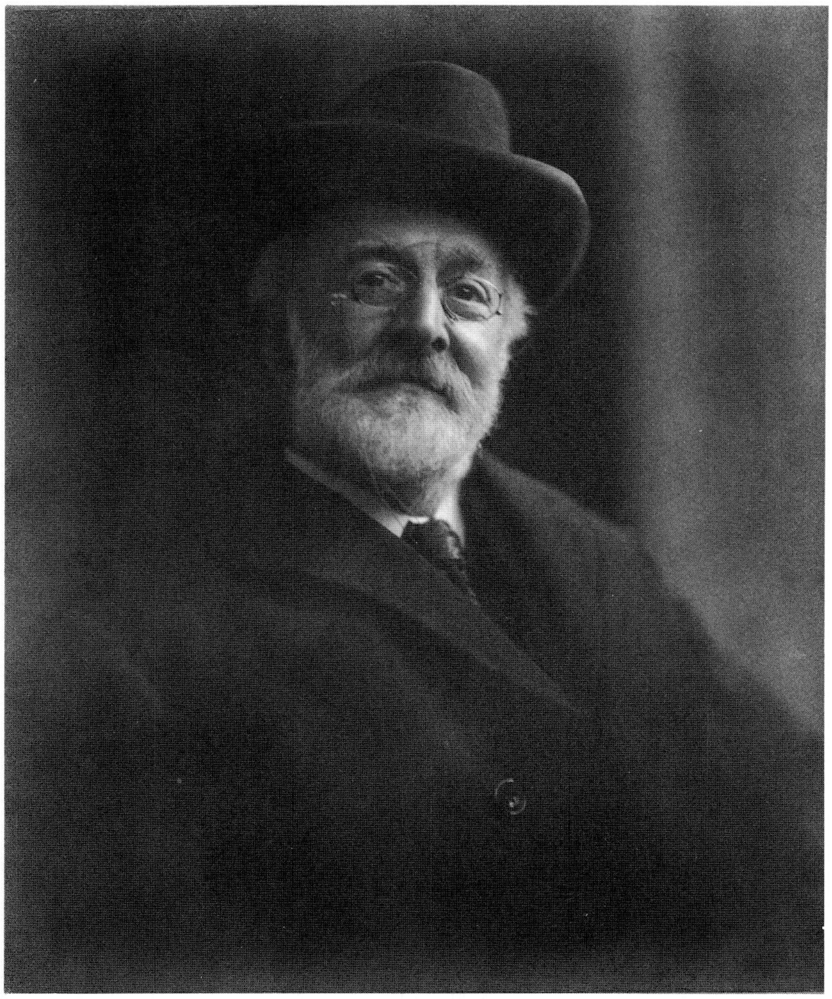

Edward Reuben Yerbury 1843–1933.

LAURENCE YERBERIE OF BATCOMBE D.1509

THOMAS YERBERIE = ALICE HORTON
WILL PROVED 1573. BOTH BURIED IN
TROWBRIDGE CHURCH

ELDEST SON
JOHN YERBURY OF BRADFORD
WILL PROVED 1614

2ND SON OF JOHN
WALTER YERBURY = ELIZABETH EDWARDS

3RD SON OF WALTER
FRANCIS YERBURY = ANN

3RD SON OF FRANCIS
THOMAS YERBURY b.1630

WALTER YERBURY b.1660

WALTER YERBURY b.1707

RICHARD YERBURY b.1748

JOHN YERBURY b.1777. d.1856

EDWARD YERBURY b.1816. d.1864
= ELEANOR LIEF

EDWARD b.1843
= EMMA TYRRELL

ELEANOR b.1845

ELIZABETH b.1853

EMMA b.1876

ELIZABETH b.1879

EDWARD b.1881

ELEANOR b.1883

EDWARD

DAVID

TREVOR

PETER

LAURA

MY PHOTOGRAPHIC FAMILY TREE

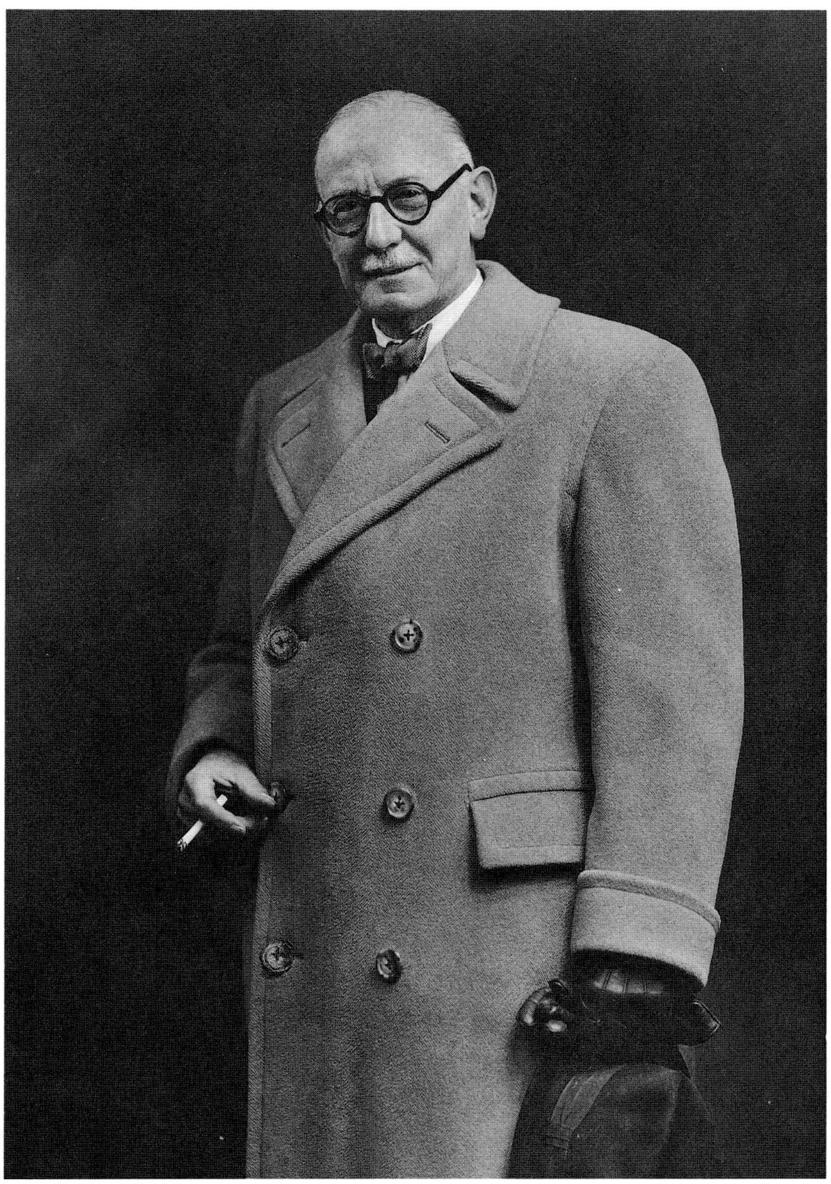

Edward Reuben Yerbury 1881–1952.

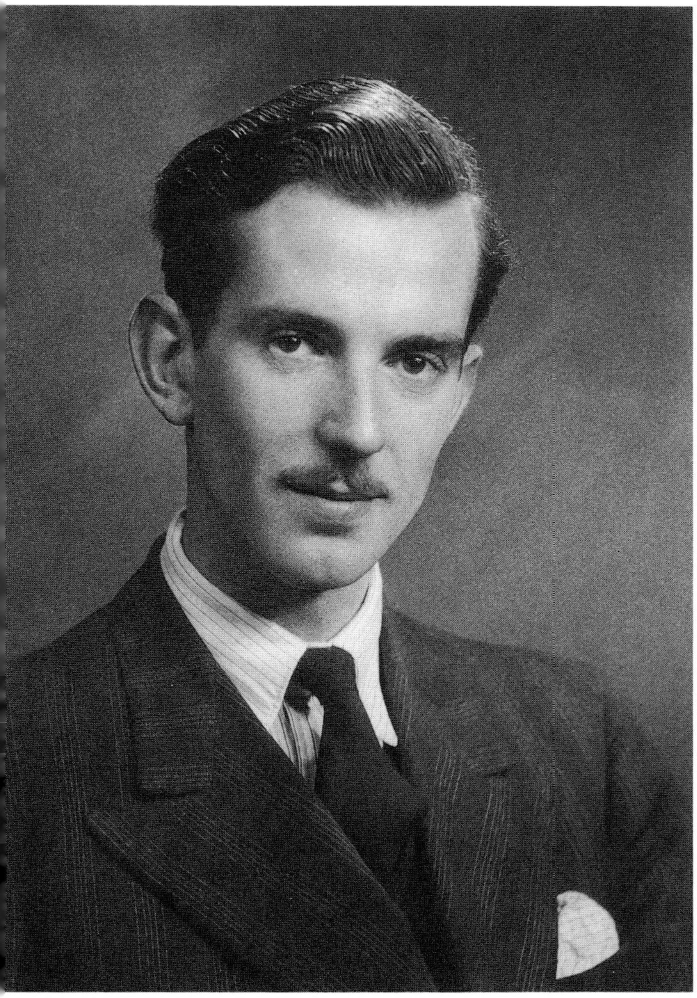

David Stenhouse Yerbury 1925–1980.

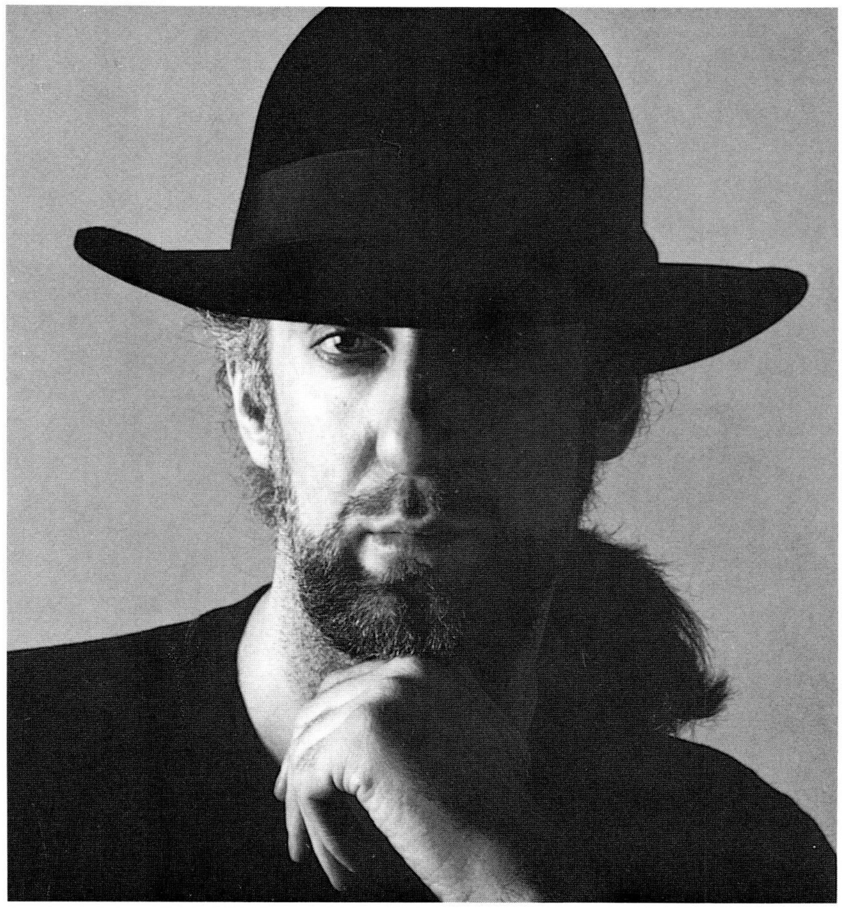

Trevor E. R. Yerbury 1951–

Hanover Street and then planning and organising the move to new premises at 90 and 92 Morningside Road, Church Hill, where he continued to maintain an active interest until his death in his home, at 121 Dalkeith Road, in 1933, a few weeks short of his ninetieth birthday. He was buried in the Dean Cemetery.

The third generation, my grandfather, also Edward Reuben, was born on 23 June 1881. He entered the family firm under the guidance of his father at about the time of the move from Hanover Street to Church Hill, which took place in 1905.

Grandfather was married by the Reverend Canon Dawson at St Peter's Church in Lutton Place to Grace Philip Stenhouse, the second daughter of the late David Martin Stenhouse (formerly Managing Director of Stratheden Linen Works of Cupar) and Mrs Stenhouse, then residing in Edinburgh. In her early years my grandmother was a talented singer and dramatic recitalist, but there is no evidence that she ever took a prominent role in the business of photography. On the other hand, my grandfather launched himself into the photographic world with a fervour which was unequalled in Edinburgh at that time. He exhibited on an international level and won many awards for his work. He specialised in portraits and nude compositions of the female form. This latter work, carried out in an age when photography of the nude was not commonplace, appears to have enhanced grandfather's reputation as a photographer rather than detracted from it. In 1930 he exhibited at the All British Exhibition of the Professional Photographers' Association at the Suffolk Street Galleries in Pall Mall, London, where his photograph *Master, Treasurer and Assistants of the Merchant Company of Edinburgh* won the highest accolade and was named as 'Picture of the Year'. Similar success followed throughout the 1930's for grandfather and he collected awards from salons throughout the United Kingdom and at international salons in South Africa, Czechoslovakia, France, Spain, Switzerland, Belgium and many other countries.

As well as leading the apparently glamorous life associated with national and international photographic exhibitions, grandfather and his staff spent many long hours in the studio and work rooms at Church Hill preparing the works to be exhibited. Yerbury's reputation in Edinburgh was such that a constant stream of clients arrived at the studio, either to sit for a portrait or to have the latest addition to the family photographed. Other sources of business included society wedding photographs taken at the church or the studio, and

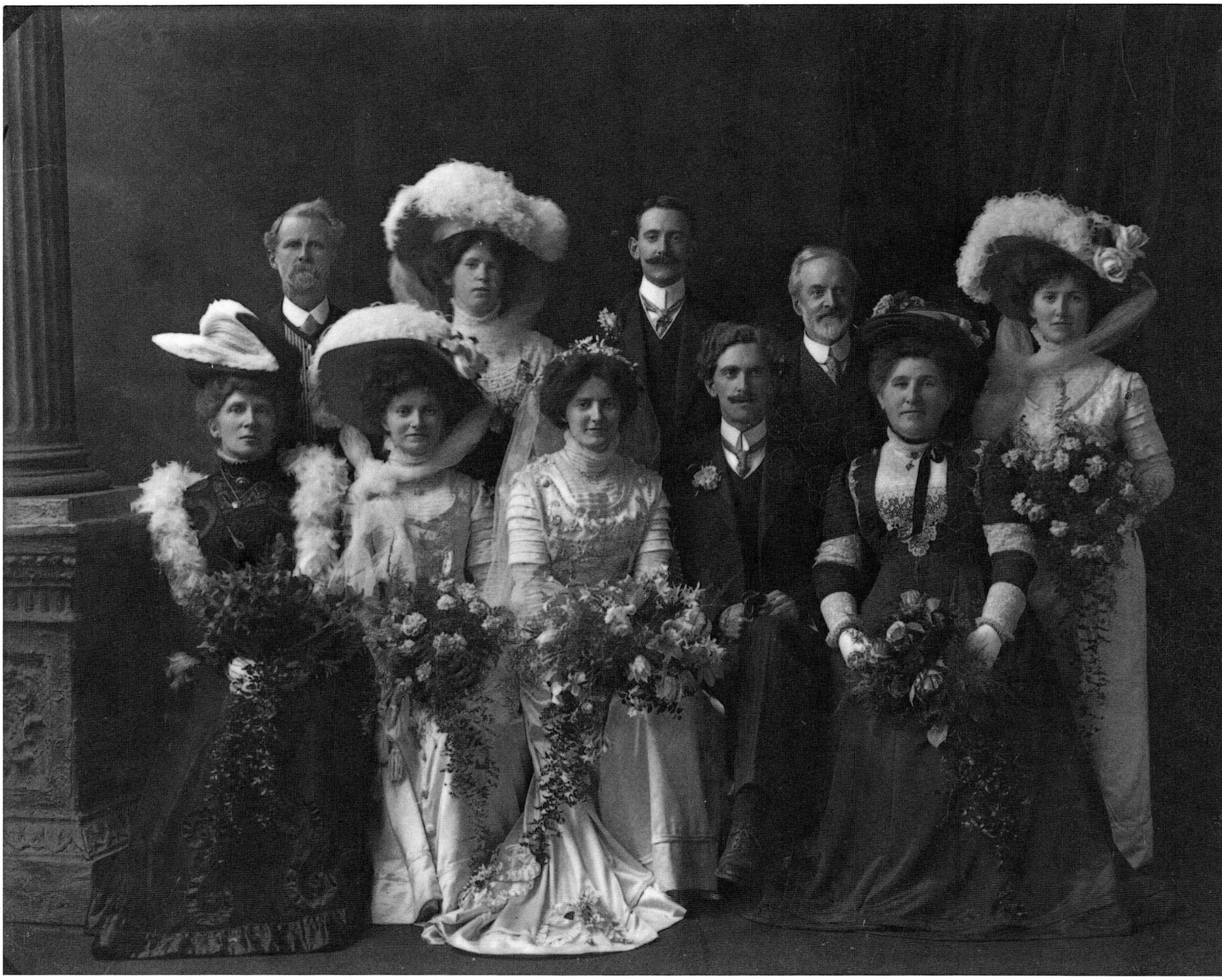

A family group at the wedding of Elizabeth Yerbury and Reginald J. Kingston Russell. The bride's father, E. R. Yerbury, and the bride's brother (also E. R. Yerbury), are beside one another in the back row. Mrs Yerbury (*née* Tyrrell), the bride's mother, is seated to the right of the groom.

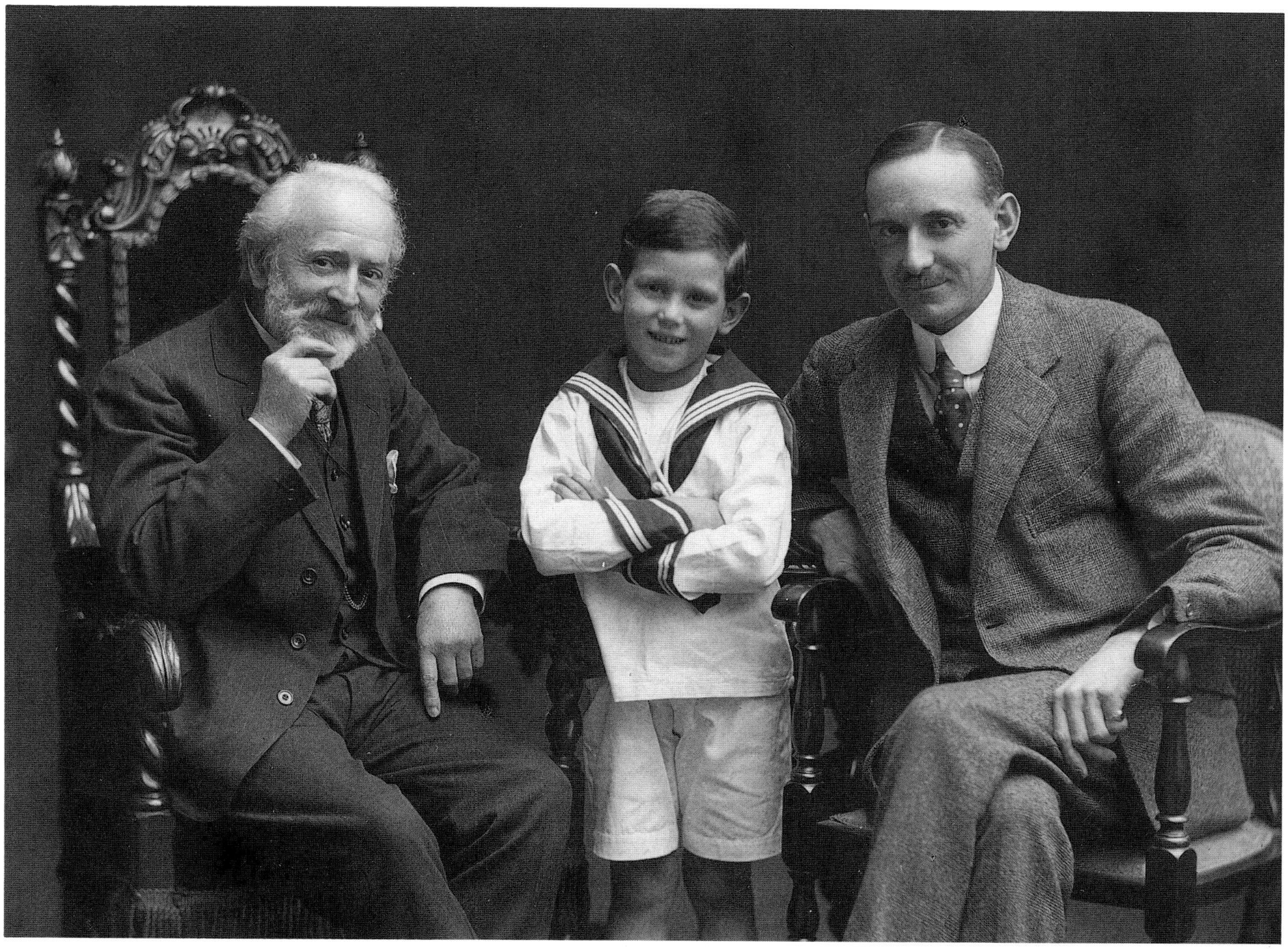

Edward R. Yerbury — times three
— all photographers, born 1843, 1881 and 1915.

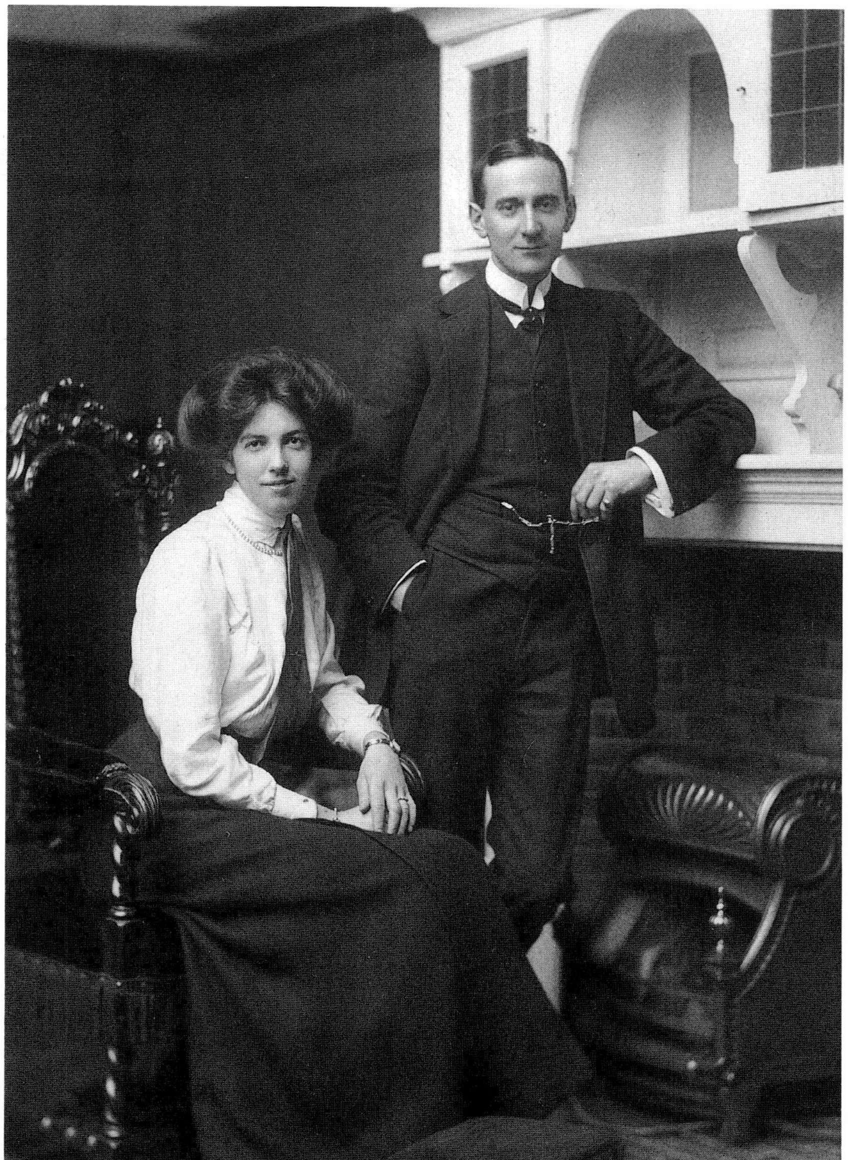

Edward Reuben Yerbury and Grace Stenhouse on the day of their engagement.

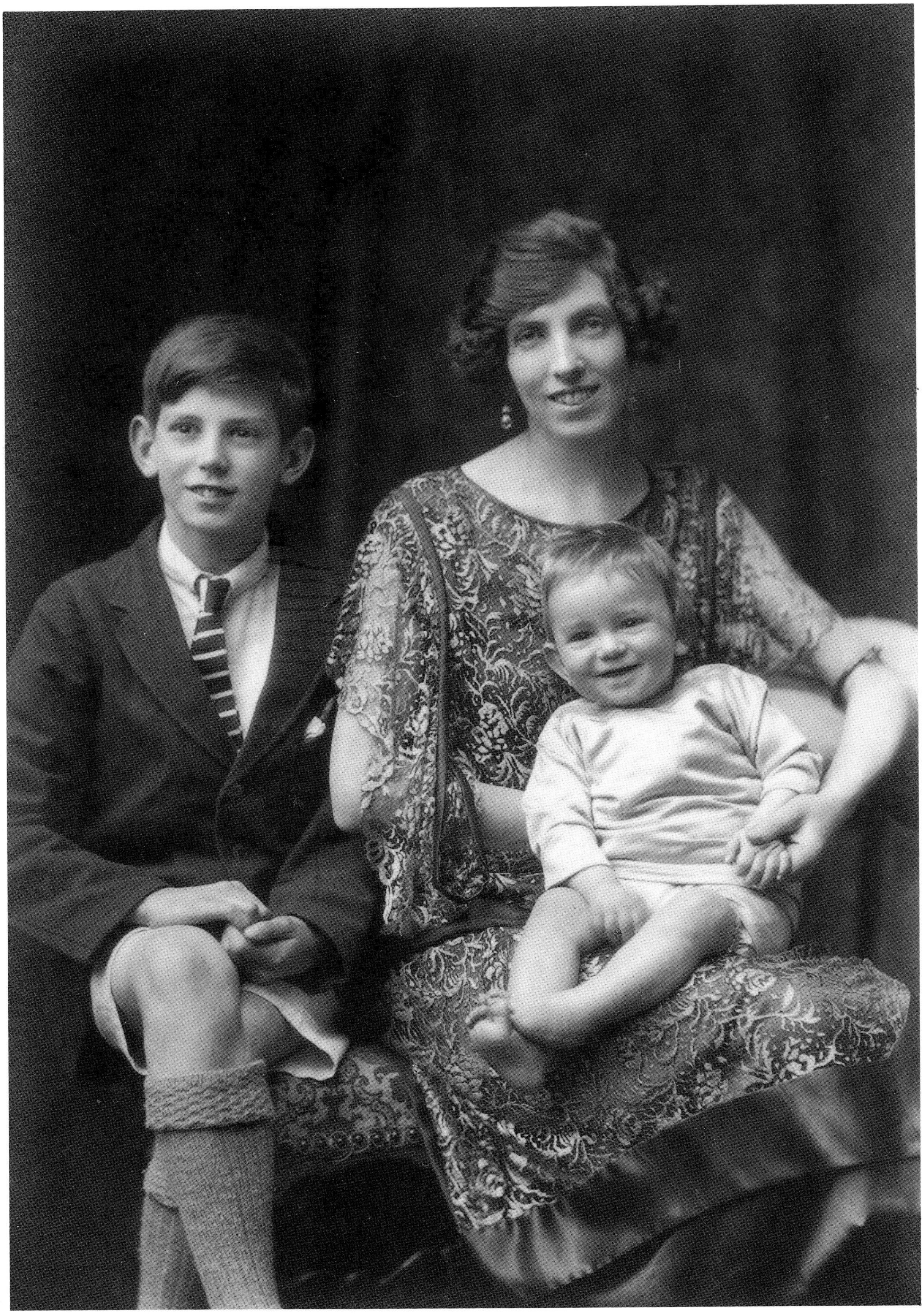

Mrs Grace Yerbury (*née* Stenhouse) and Edward, with David on her knee.

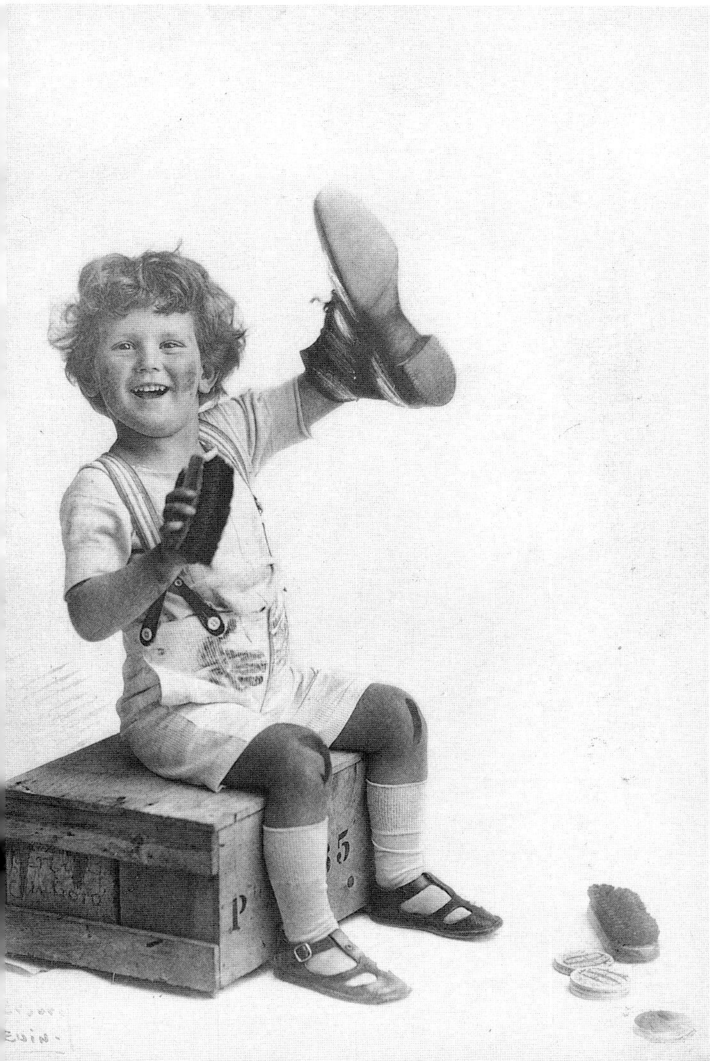

All young men like to acquire a polish — Edward Roper Yerbury, c. 1918.

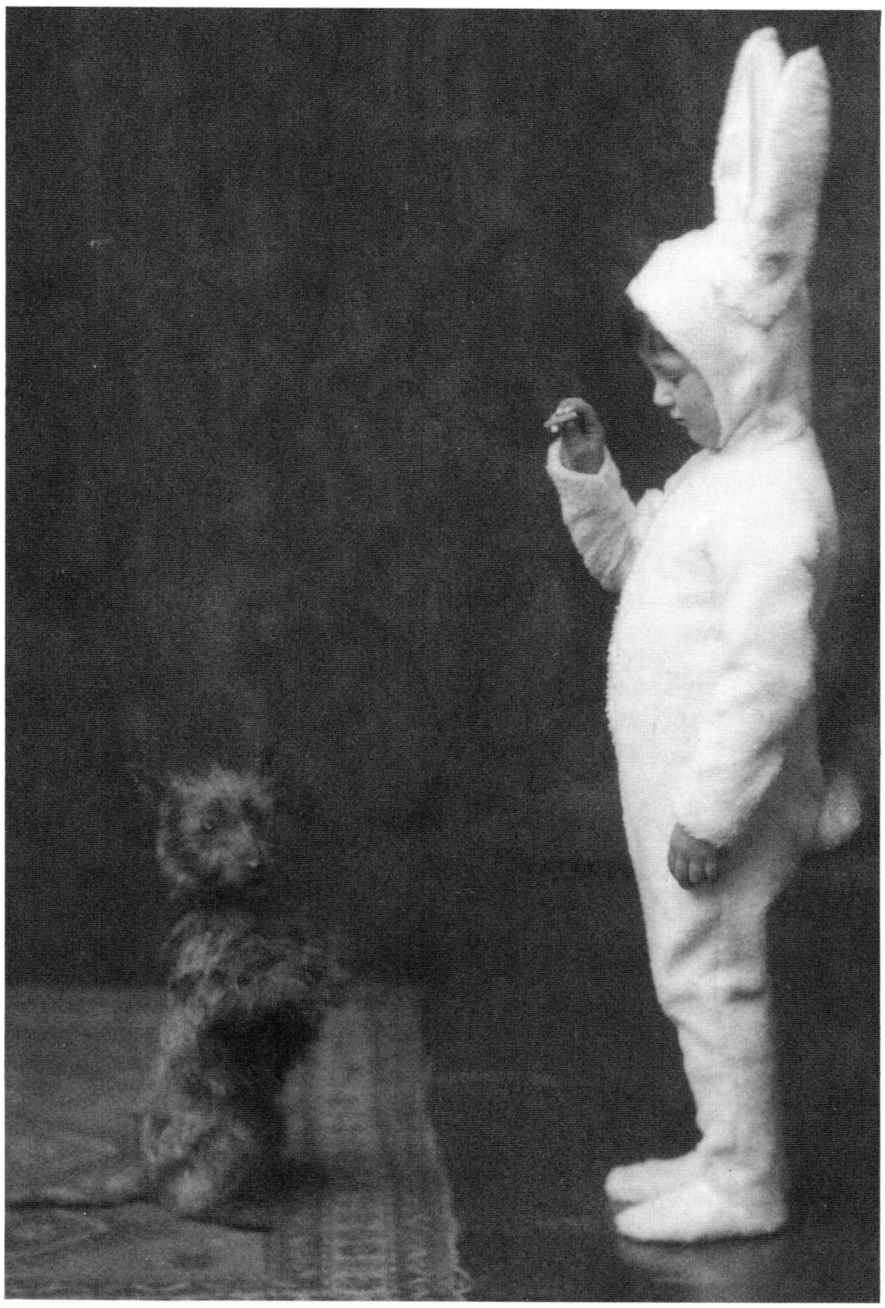

David Stenhouse Yerbury as White Rabbit at a fancy dress party given by Mrs McCallister.

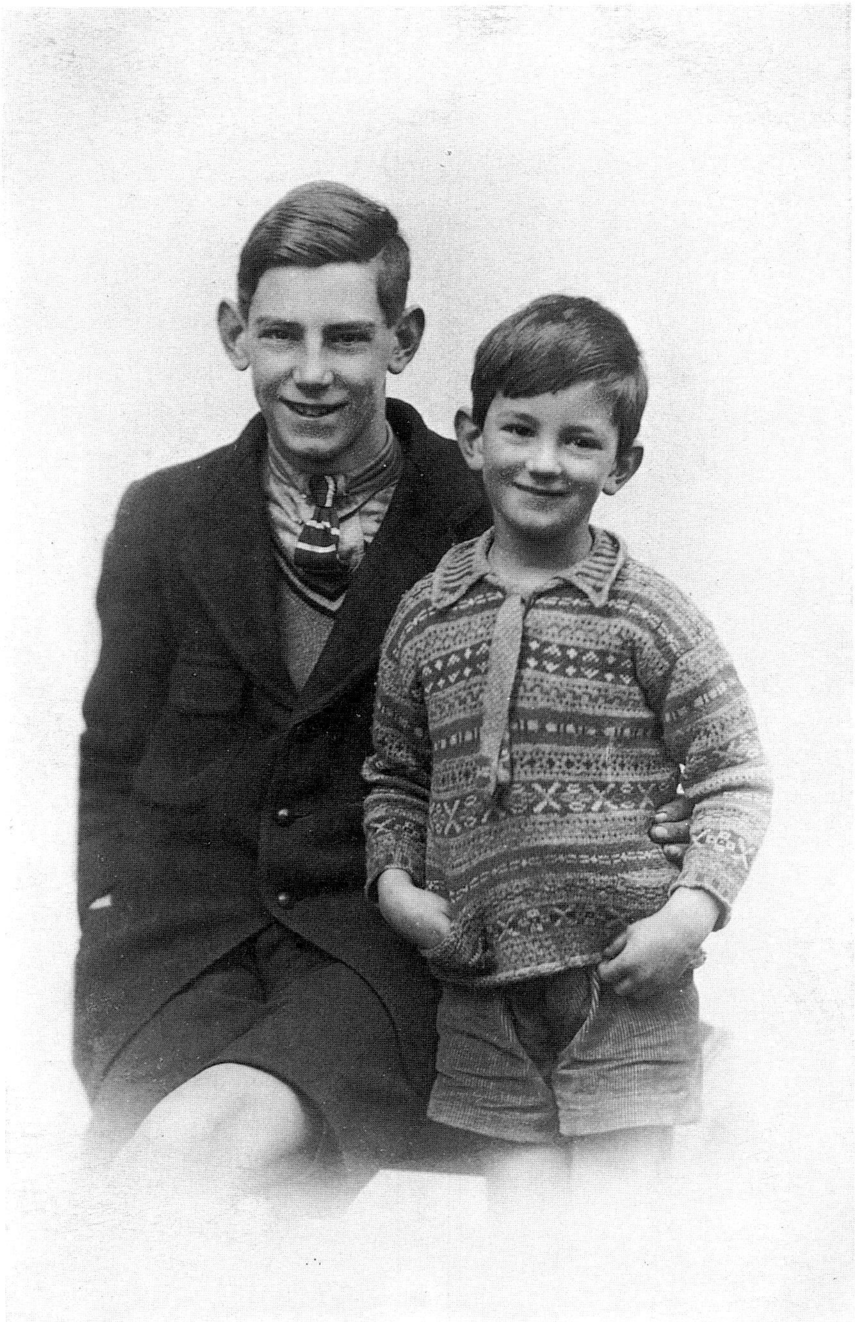

Edward Roper Yerbury and David Stenhouse Yerbury, 1930.

graduation portraits for clients who, as children, had perhaps sat in the same seat several years earlier. Much of the work was also tied to annual events, including regimental and association dinners, sporting occasions, class and sports photographs for most of Edinburgh's private schools and indeed for some as far away as Glenalmond and Strathallan, the General Assembly of the Church of Scotland and the Royal Garden Party at the Palace of Holyroodhouse. Towards the end of grandfather's long and distinguished career he received what, for him, was perhaps the highest accolade — a return invitation to Paris to photograph General Charles de Gaulle. When De Gaulle visited Edinburgh in 1942 grandfather, through his great friend Baron de Marchand, made several excellent portrait studies of the Free French leader. In 1945, at the invitation of the French government, grandfather flew to Paris, staying for a week, and produced several superb studies of De Gaulle.

In 1945, grandfather was 64 years old, and nearing retirement. His eldest son, Edward Roper Yerbury, my uncle, born in 1915, had entered the firm for a short while but then had decided to travel and had journeyed to Rhodesia, where he worked for Kodak, intending to return to Edinburgh to take over the reins of Yerbury's. He became engaged on Christmas Eve 1938 to Patricia Taylor, niece of the Governor of Rhodesia. They married on 9 September 1938. Tragically my uncle was seriously injured in a road accident in May 1940 while riding his motor cycle in Queen's Drive, Bulawayo. He died as a result of his injuries a few days later.

Meanwhile my grandfather's younger son, my father, David Stenhouse (born 28 May 1925) was at the time of my uncle's death serving with the Royal Air Force. At the end of the Second World War Father agreed to take my uncle's place and join the family business in partnership with my grandfather, rather than pursue his first ambition to become an architect. Father worked closely with grandfather learning the business, maintaining existing contracts and extending into new and challenging areas. My grandfather retired in 1949; the following year David married Blanche Daniels at St Oswald's Church, Edinburgh. I was born in 1951, my brother Peter in 1954 and sister Laura in 1960.

My grandfather died, aged seventy, on 7 March 1952, after more than forty years in the family business. By this time all the work was concentrated at the studio in Church Hill, the studio at 28 Comiston Road and the branch office at South Clerk Street having been closed some years earlier. Father maintained the family tradition and entered works — a portrait and an architectural study — in the 1954 Exhibition of Professional Photography in London. He was elected an Associate of the Institute of Photography and held the presidency of the Scottish centre of the Institute of British Photographers. He also sat on the national council of the Institute in London. Among the many annual contracts father undertook were the official photographs for the Scottish Rugby Union, and the annual portraits of

June, 1932

The Yerbury Studio in Edinburgh

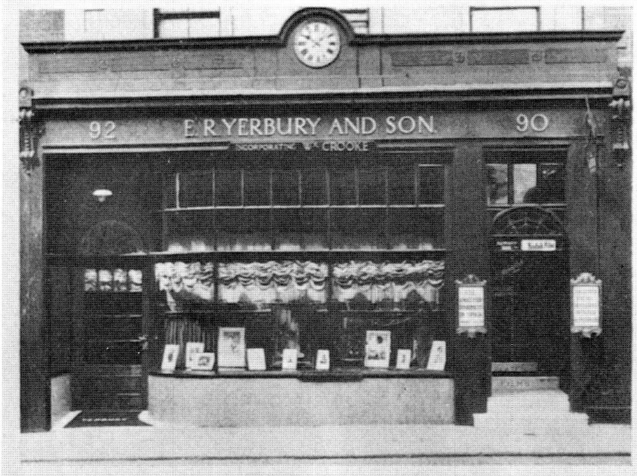

Front facia, from plans by the late Mr. Drinkwater Butt. Showing electric clock controlled by a master clock inside the studio. This clock is the best advertisement we ever had. It controls the time of our district and is referred to, and depended on, by residents, with the result that we get more publicity from this source than one would imagine.

Note separate entrance for amateur department.

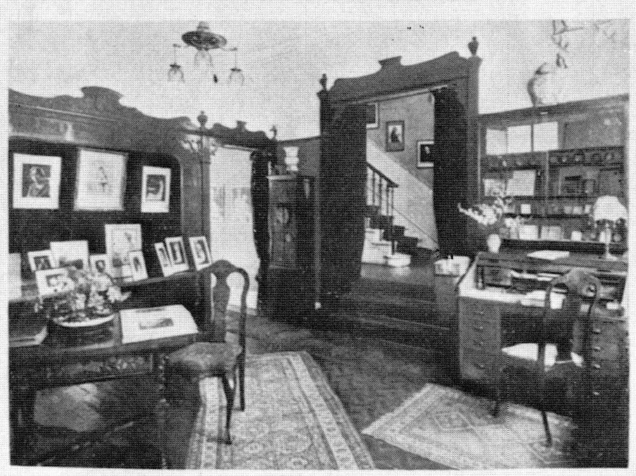

A corner of the reception room

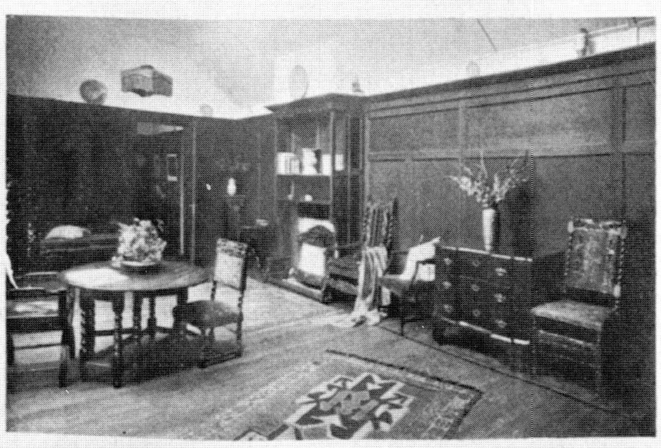

Another view

The premises of E. R. Yerbury & Son at 90–92 Church Hill, Edinburgh from 1905 to 1972.

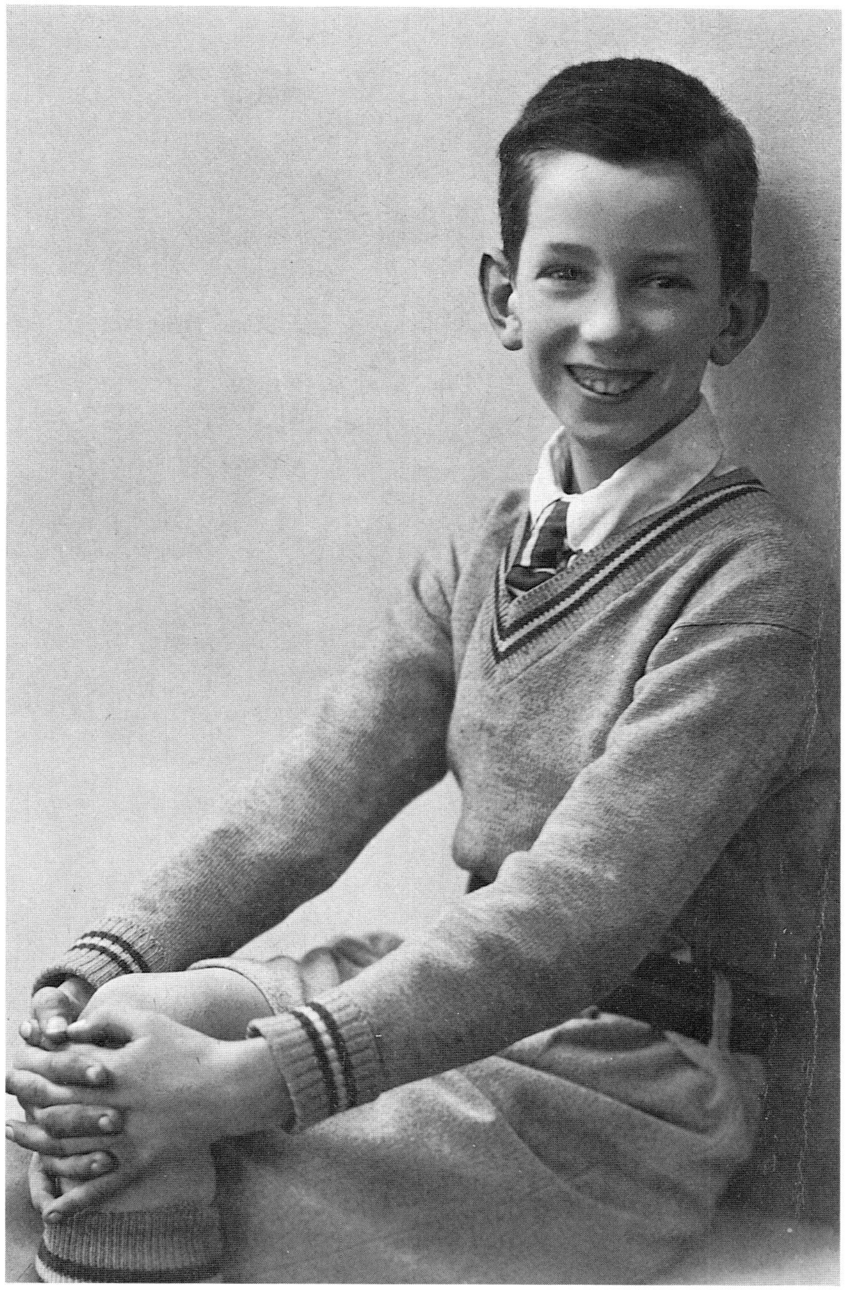

David Stenhouse Yerbury at age ten.

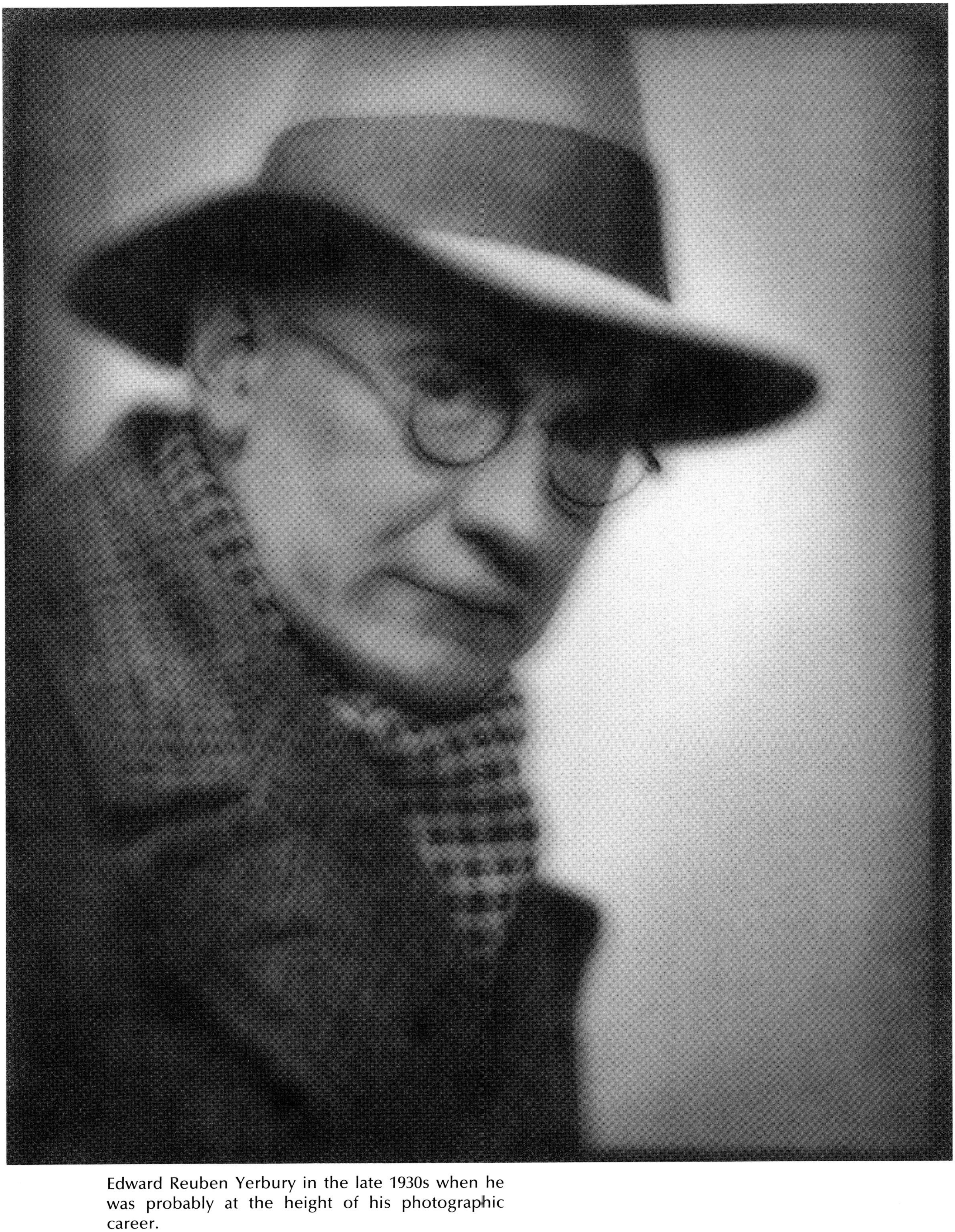

Edward Reuben Yerbury in the late 1930s when he was probably at the height of his photographic career.

the Moderators of the Church of Scotland; he was also the official photographer to the University of Edinburgh; and perhaps the most prestigious of his tasks were the annual photographs of the Lord High Commissioner and his guests at the Palace of Holyroodhouse during the week of the General Assembly of the Church of Scotland. He photographed several members of the Royal family during their many visits to Edinburgh. He was acclaimed as one of the leading photographers of society weddings.

In addition to the photographic work undertaken by the family for over a century, Father and Mother extended the business into the acquisition and sale of original paintings by Scottish artists. Many of these paintings graced the windows at 90 and 92 Morningside Road during the 1960's and 1970's.

The firm continued at Church Hill during the 1960's, and in 1968 I joined the business, as the fourth generation, straight from boarding school. Unlike my father, whose ambition was to become an architect, I had never wanted to be anything but a photographer and I entered the photographic profession with enthusiasm. With the advent and popularity of colour photography the need for large darkrooms and workrooms was greatly reduced and Father decided in 1972 to close the Church Hill studio and transfer the business to new premises in Edinburgh's New Town. The studios at 38 Howe Street were ideal, and Father and I continued the family tradition for twelve years until tragically in 1980, he died at the early age of 55. My mother and I continued to run the business in Howe Street until 1984 when we decided to close the studios. I then spent several years working on my own projects, including holding many successful exhibitions and developing my interest in portraiture and the classic female nude, all very much in keeping with the work of my grandfather back in the 30's. This work has attracted interest from all corners and I have collectors of my work in this country and overseas. I have recently undertaken a series of portraits of Scottish personalities which I hope will form the basis of another book in the years to come. Several of these are included in this book.

During 1993 I was interviewed and filmed by the B.B.C. for the arts programme 'The Bigger Picture' while making a portrait study of Billy Connolly.

My wife Faye and I have recently opened new studios in a beautifully restored Georgian town house at 71 and 73 East Claremont Street, Edinburgh. From here we will continue to follow the photographic traditions of the Yerbury family. Perhaps my daughter Rachel will take the dynasty into its fifth generation and the 21st century.

TREVOR E. R. YERBURY
Edinburgh, June 1993

CHAPTER 2

The Old Town from Princes Street

In 1859 the full horror of the decaying Old Town of Edinburgh was laid bare by the camera lens in this panoramic view, taken from near the Scott Monument. The original Waverley Bridge sweeps across the valley of the old Nor' Loch from Market Street, which runs from left to right across the picture. The construction of Cockburn Street makes a deep incision in the body of the Old Town, leaving the nerve endings severed and ragged. The skyline is dominated by the steeple of the Tron Kirk, the high square buildings of the City Chambers, St Giles' Cathedral and the Bank of Scotland. On the site of Waverley Station three railway companies operated: the small building on the extreme left was the Edinburgh, Perth and Dundee Railway Company; the larger one with

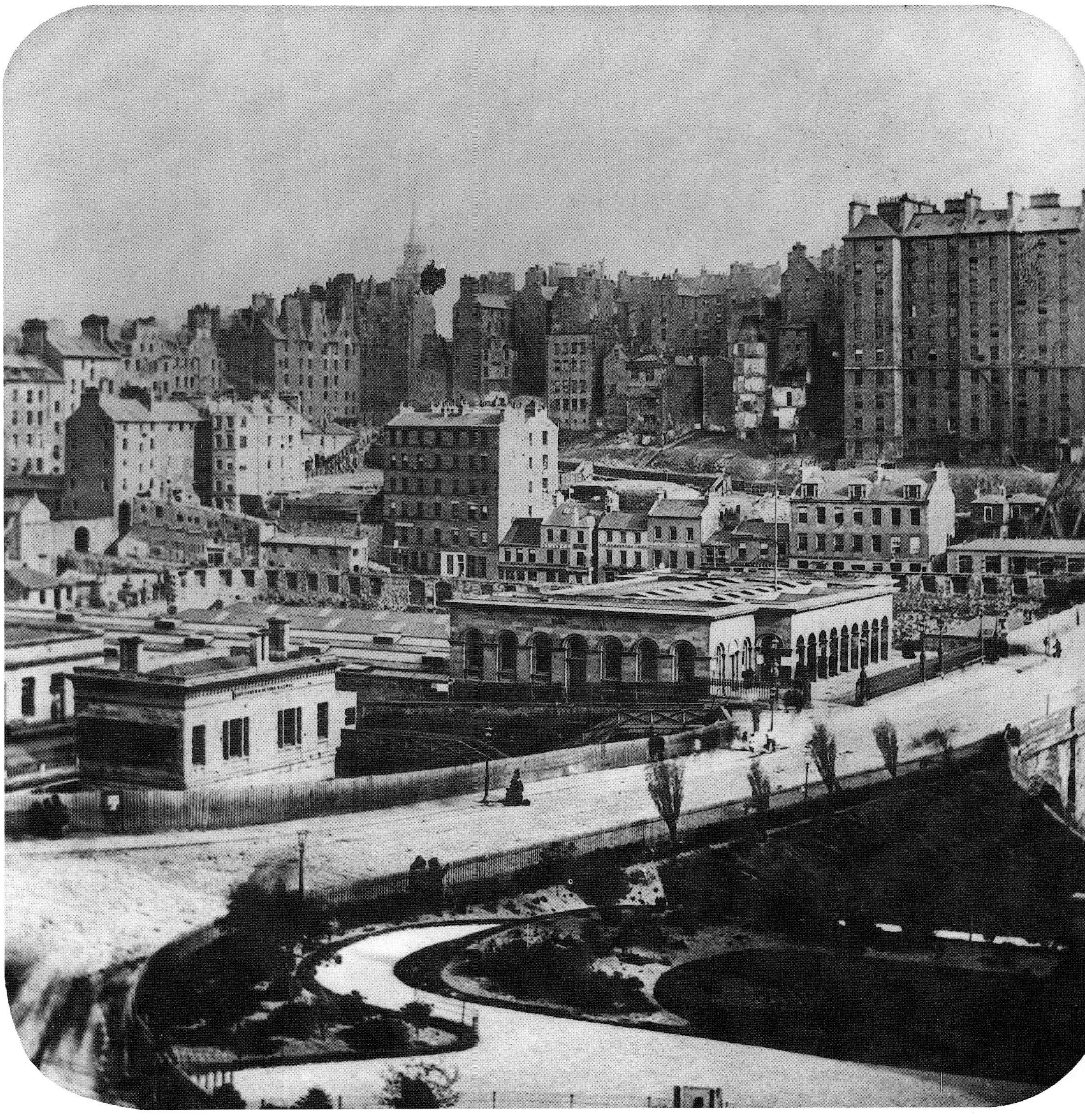

the arcaded frontage was used jointly by the North British Railway Company and the Edinburgh and Glasgow Railway Company. Between these two buildings is Canal Street in the position of the present-day entrance ramp. In contrast with the old closes in the High Street, the east section of Market Street is in good condition, and housed several hostelries, including the Northern Tavern, the North British Hotel and Tavern, St Boswell's Railway Tavern and the Argyle Tavern. The west section of Market Street is equally interesting: the three-storey building in line with the spire of St Giles' is the Railway Station Hotel, to the right of which is St Mary's Roman Catholic School with the open belfry. Behind these two buildings is Advocates' Close, looking derelict but for the washing and the smoking chimneys. The big square building beside the factory chimney is McLaren and Oliver, forerunners to McLaren, Son & Co., silk and dress retailers of No. 329 High Street. Finally, the Bank of Scotland on the Mound is yet to be embellished by David Bryce's additions made between 1864 and 1870.

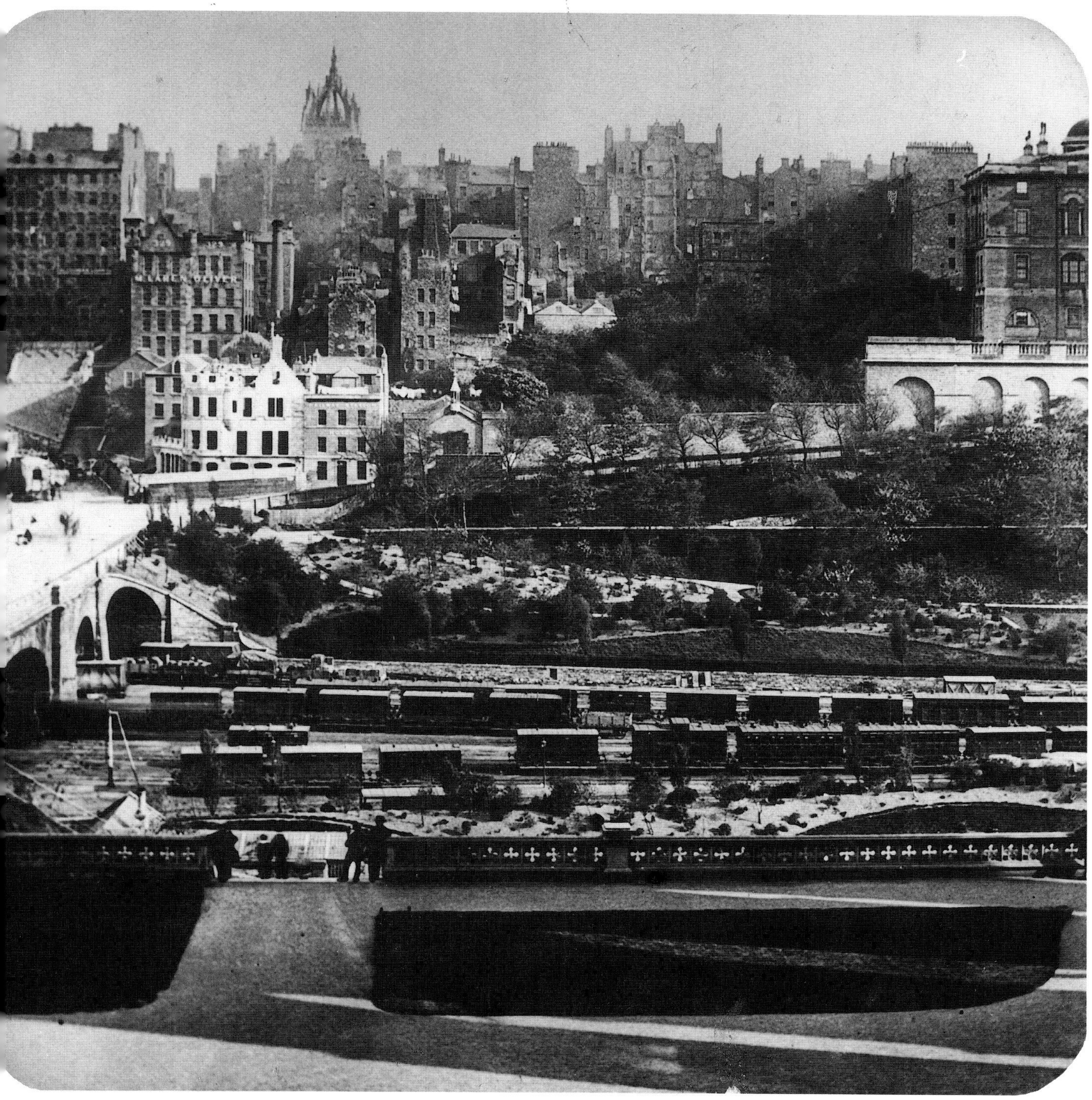

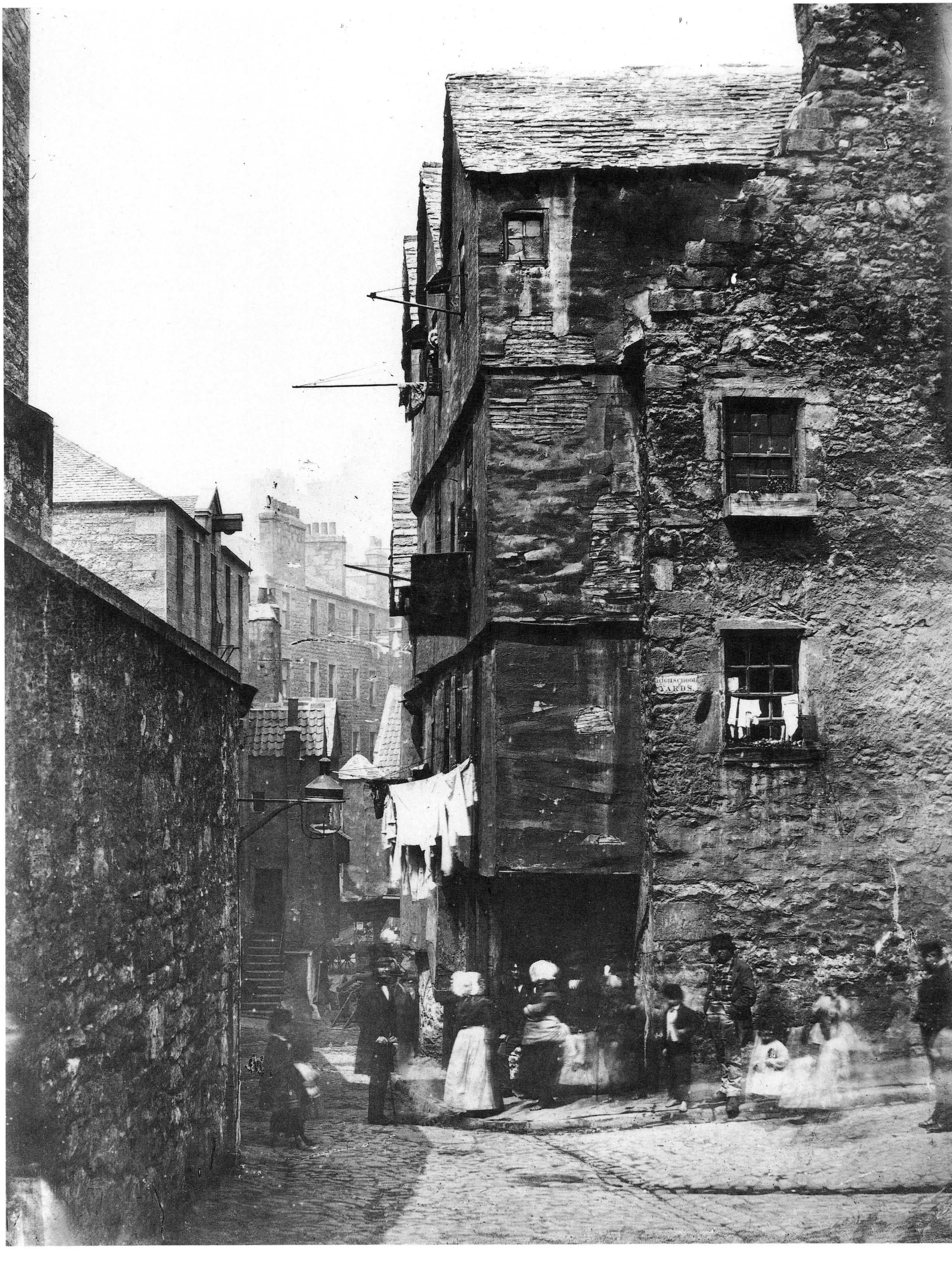
HIGHSCHOOL
YARDS.

High School Yards

This dilapidated building, partly of lath and render construction, stood on the corner of High School Yards and High School Wynd in 1850. The name is derived from the Royal High School built there in 1777 and in use until the opening of Thomas Hamilton's Grecian building in Regent Road in 1829. At the foot of the Wynd, to the right of the cart wheels, is the distinctive corbelled house of Cardinal Beaton, born in 1494 and murdered at St Andrews on 29th May 1546. On the far side of the Cowgate the tenement building is at the foot of Blackfriars Street.

The Cowgate

The Cowgate, looking west to the Grassmarket, in 1860, is flanked by rundown properties and 'brokers' who dealt in second-hand furniture and general goods. The huge arches of George IV Bridge cross the Cowgate at what was Excise Office Close. On the extreme left of the picture the sign projecting from the first-floor window says 'Lodgings', and the shop front with the semi-circular doorway was last used as a provision and spirit merchant's. Today, the south-east bridge pier has a plaque commemorating James Connolly who was born in the Cowgate and was executed by the British in Dublin for his involvement in the Irish troubles of 1916.

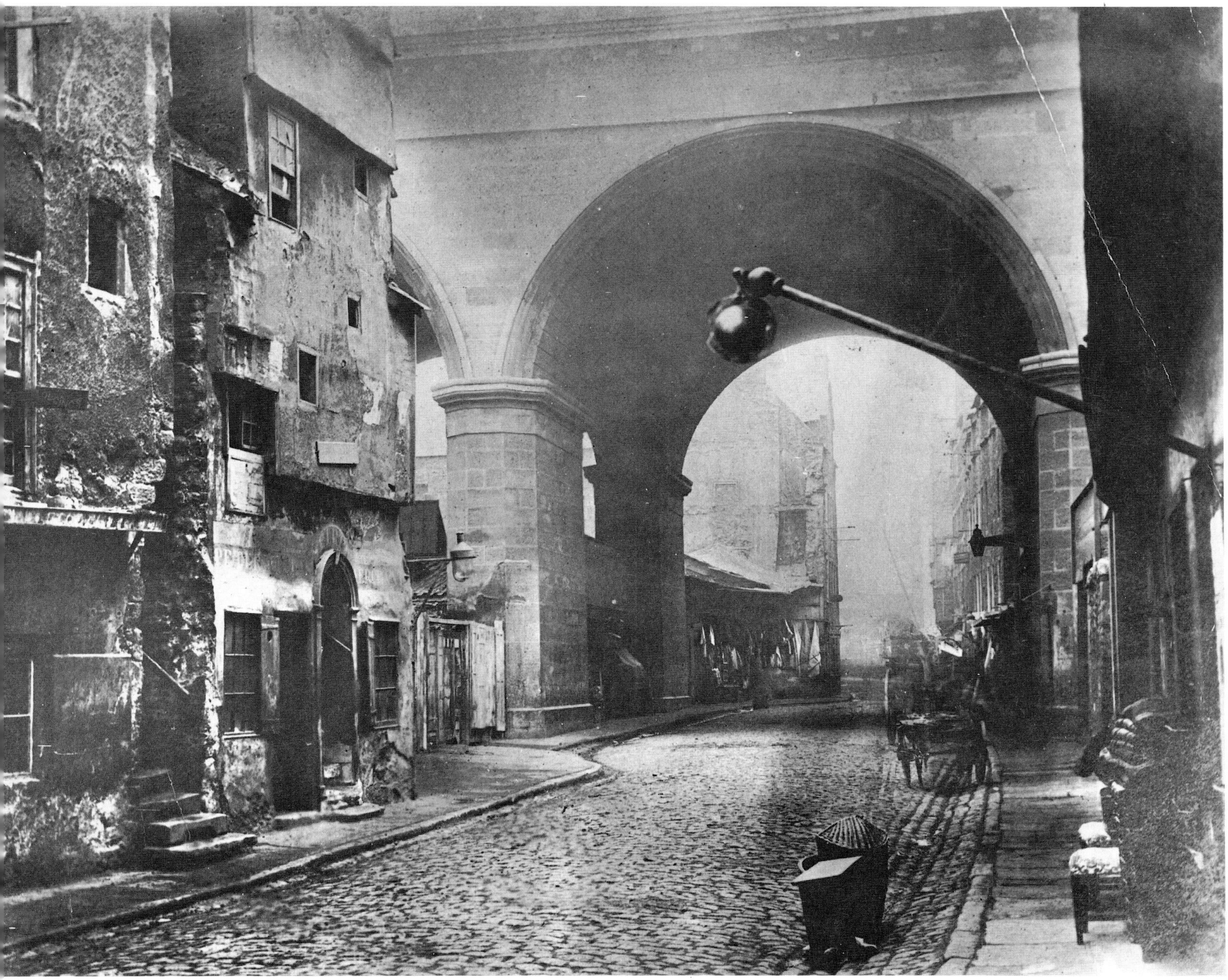

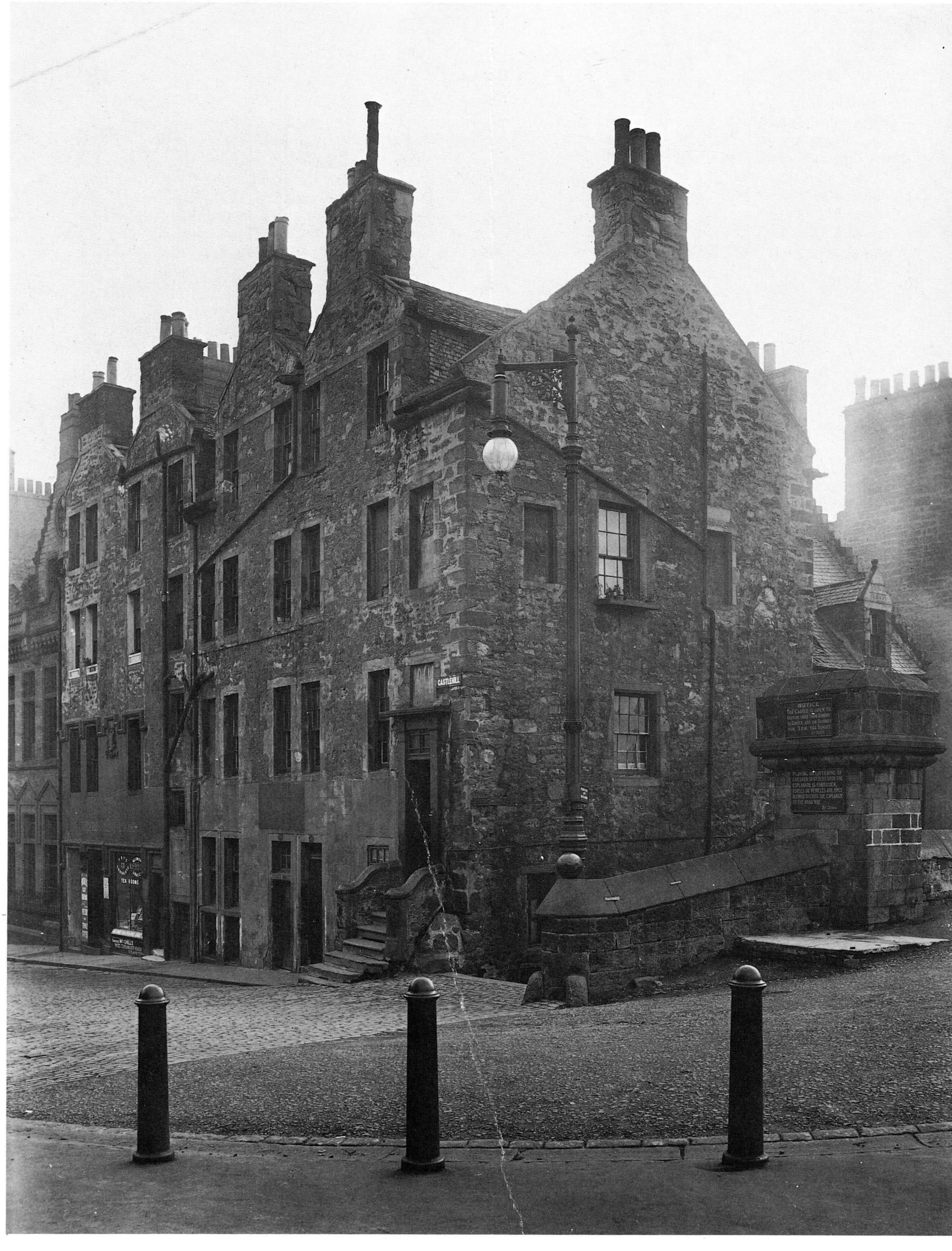
CASTLEHILL
NOTICE
TEA ROOMS

Cannonball House

Cannonball House at the head of Castle Hill, c. 1900, derived its name from the cannon ball embedded in its west gable, seen in the picture below and to the right of the window with the plant tray. How the cannon ball got there is a matter of conjecture, but the theory that it was fired from the castle can be safely discounted. A more practical suggestion, but not proved conclusively, is that the cannon ball was placed in the building to mark the height to which the town's original water supply would rise, through pipes laid from Comiston Springs. On the extreme left of the picture is Castle Hill School, recently converted into the Scotch Whisky Heritage Centre.

Upper Bow

This photograph of one of the Old Town's most interesting corners was taken c. 1875. It shows the junction of the Lawnmarket and the Upper Bow or upper part of the old West Bow. The corner premises are occupied by T. Sword, Woollen and Rag Store, and the smaller shop down to the right is James Nixon's, the furniture dealer, at No. 8. Above Sword's name is a sign advertising 'Swimming Baths', and the newsagent's has the *Courant* and the *Review* for sale.

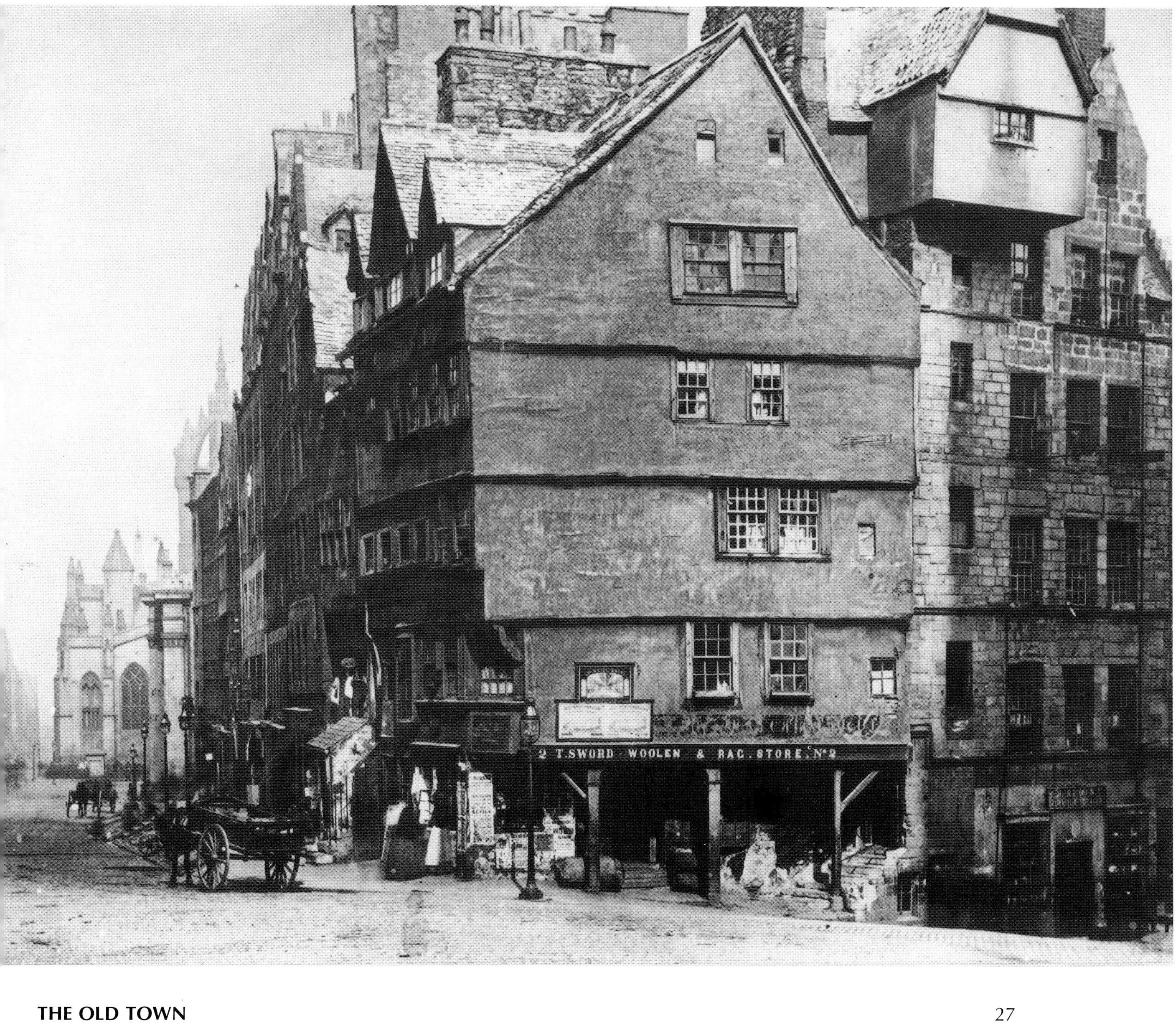

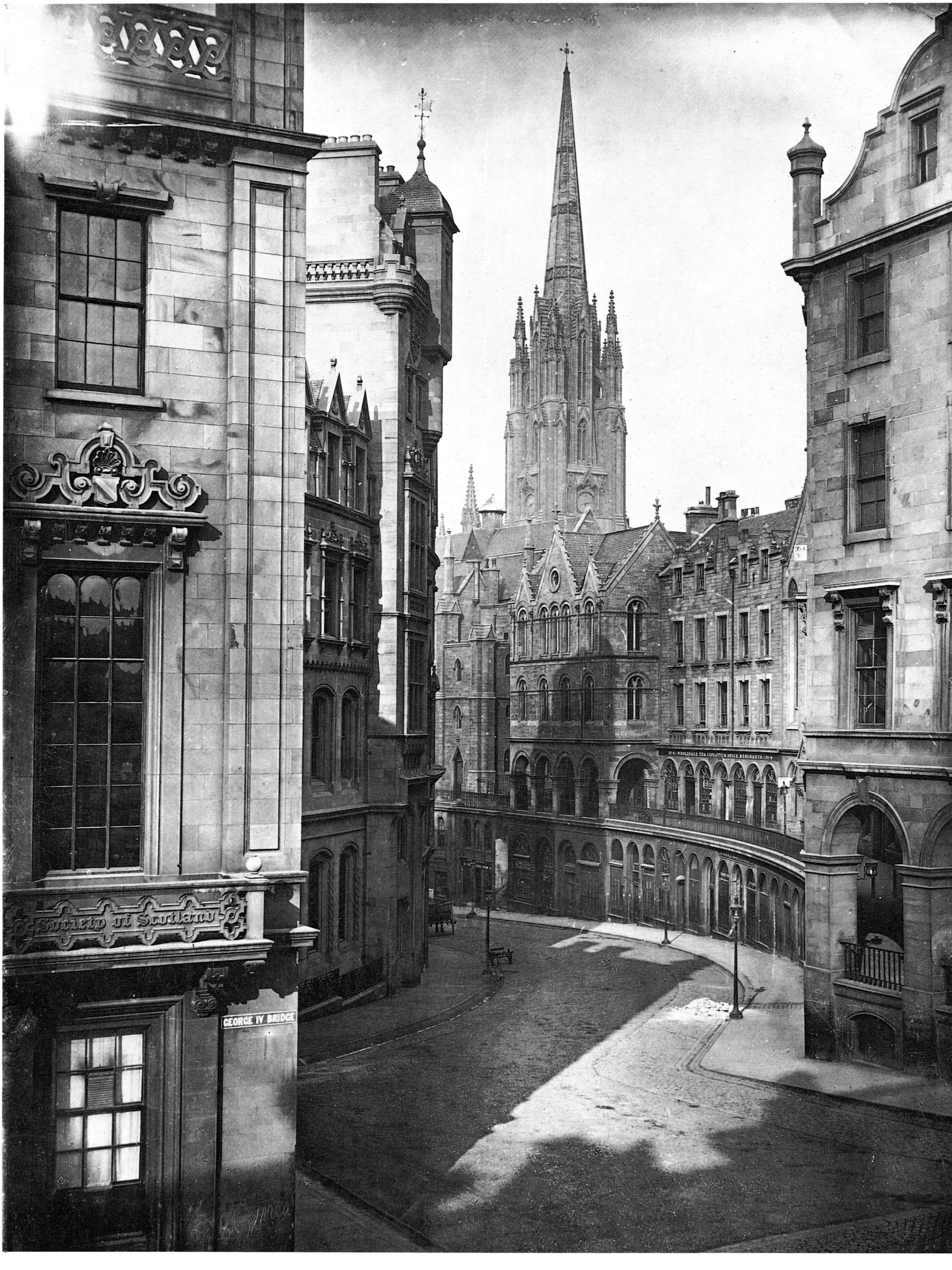
Society of Scotland
GEORGE IV BRIDGE

Victoria Street

The huge Gothic spire of St John's Tolbooth Church (formerly a meeting hall of the General Assembly of the Church of Scotland) towers over Victoria Street and Victoria Terrace. The arcaded building in the centre of the Terrace is the Original Secession Church built in 1865. Between it and the arcade on the right of the picture is the Edinburgh Mechanics' Library, which was at Victoria Terrace from 1855 to 1890. On the left of the picture is the corner of George IV Bridge, showing the former offices of the Highland and Agricultural Society of Scotland.

Polly the Fortune Teller

In St Giles' Street (with the Scott Monument in the background) Polly the fortune teller draws an eager audience — for those old enough to understand — *c.* 1880. The notice on the birds' cage reads: 'CHARMING BIRDS — Ladies and Gentlemen for the small sum of one penny these innocent birds will select from this box a planet telling you your past or future life. Try for yourselves'.

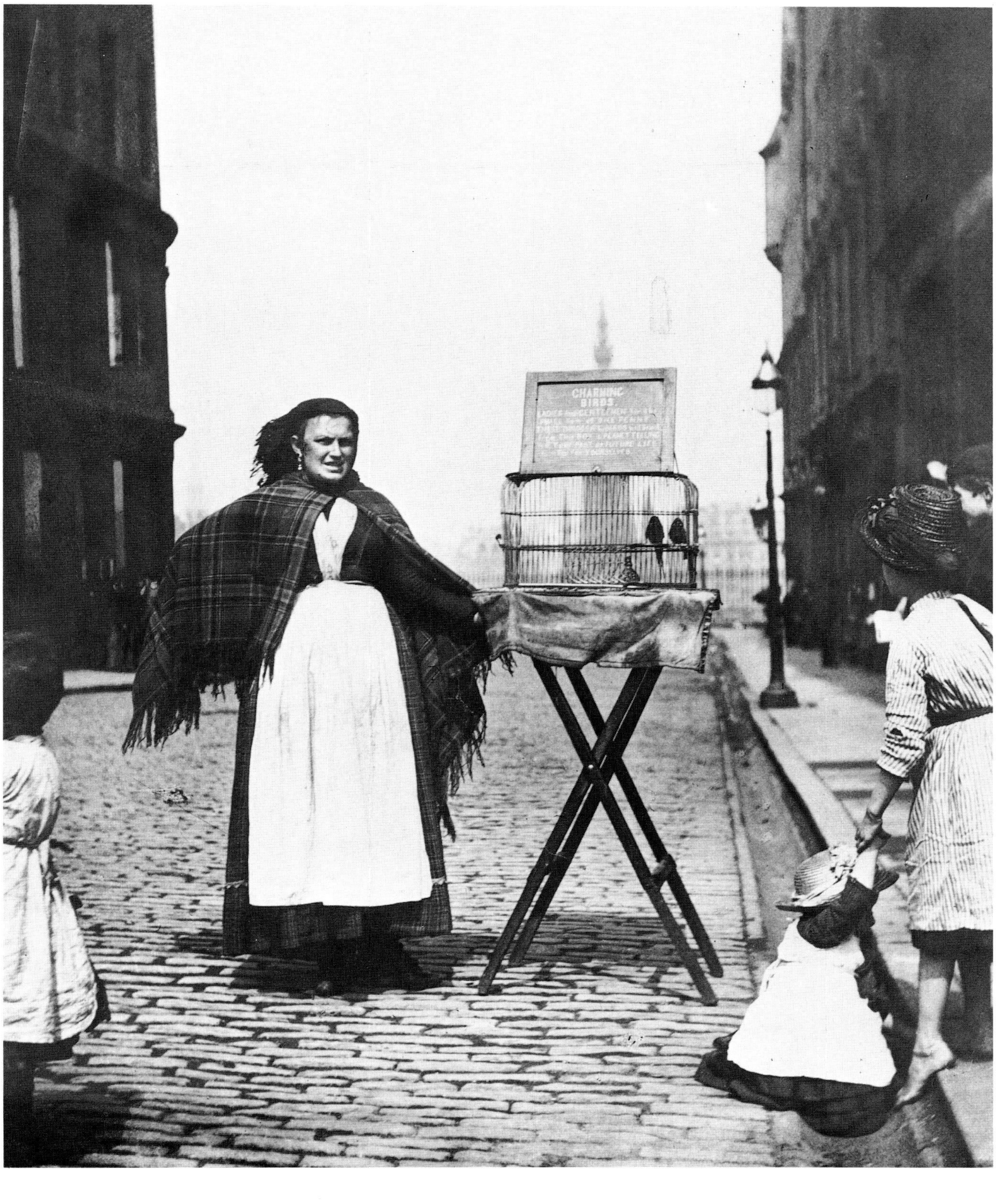

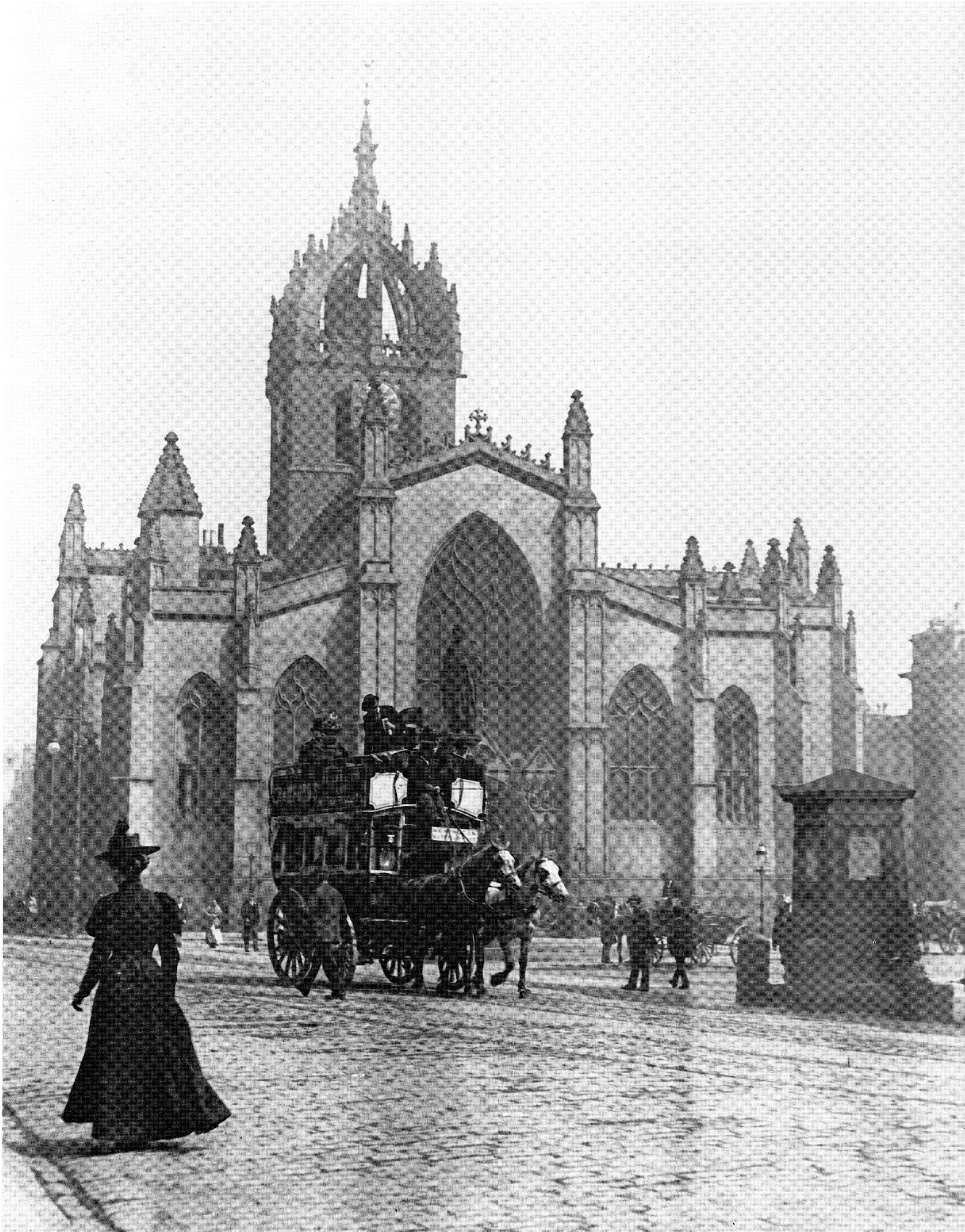
CRAWFORD'S
OATEN WAFERS
AND
WATER BISCUITS

St Giles' Cathedral

Beside St Giles' Cathedral the photographer captures a study in Victorian elegance c. 1885. The horse bus operates from Newington and Mayfield Road, and one of the advertisements on the side is for Crawford's Water Biscuits. The Heart of Midlothian and the ornamental plinth of the statue of the 5th Duke of Buccleuch (1806–84) are obscured by the horse bus as it makes its way up the High Street. Behind the public well, in Parliament Square, is a stance for carriages.

The Fruitseller

Towards the end of the nineteenth century the Old Town of Edinburgh had many street traders who operated from very basic carts or barrows. The fruitseller is photographed c. 1880 at her usual stance, believed to be on the south side of the High Street between the Tron Kirk and St Giles' Cathedral.

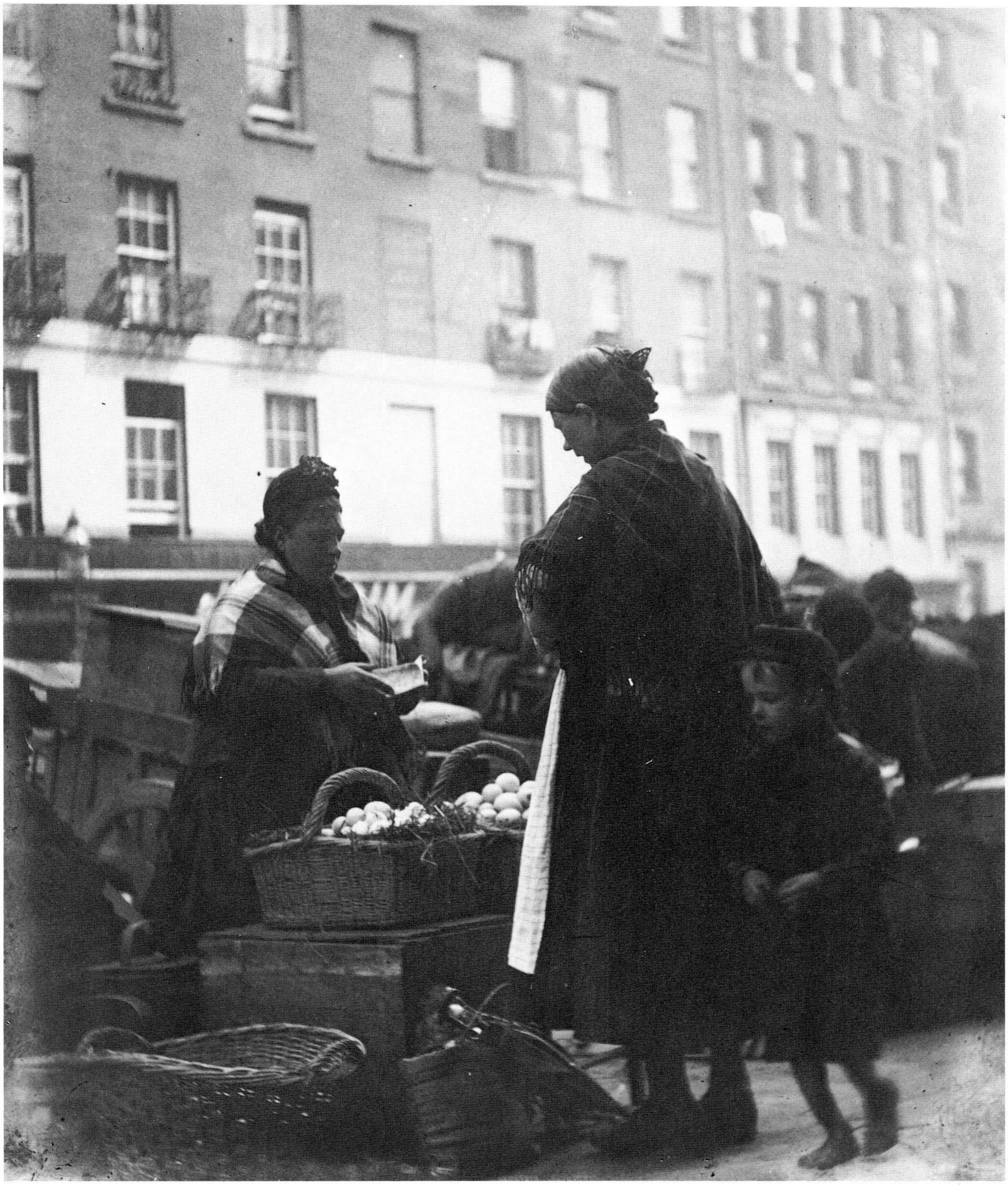

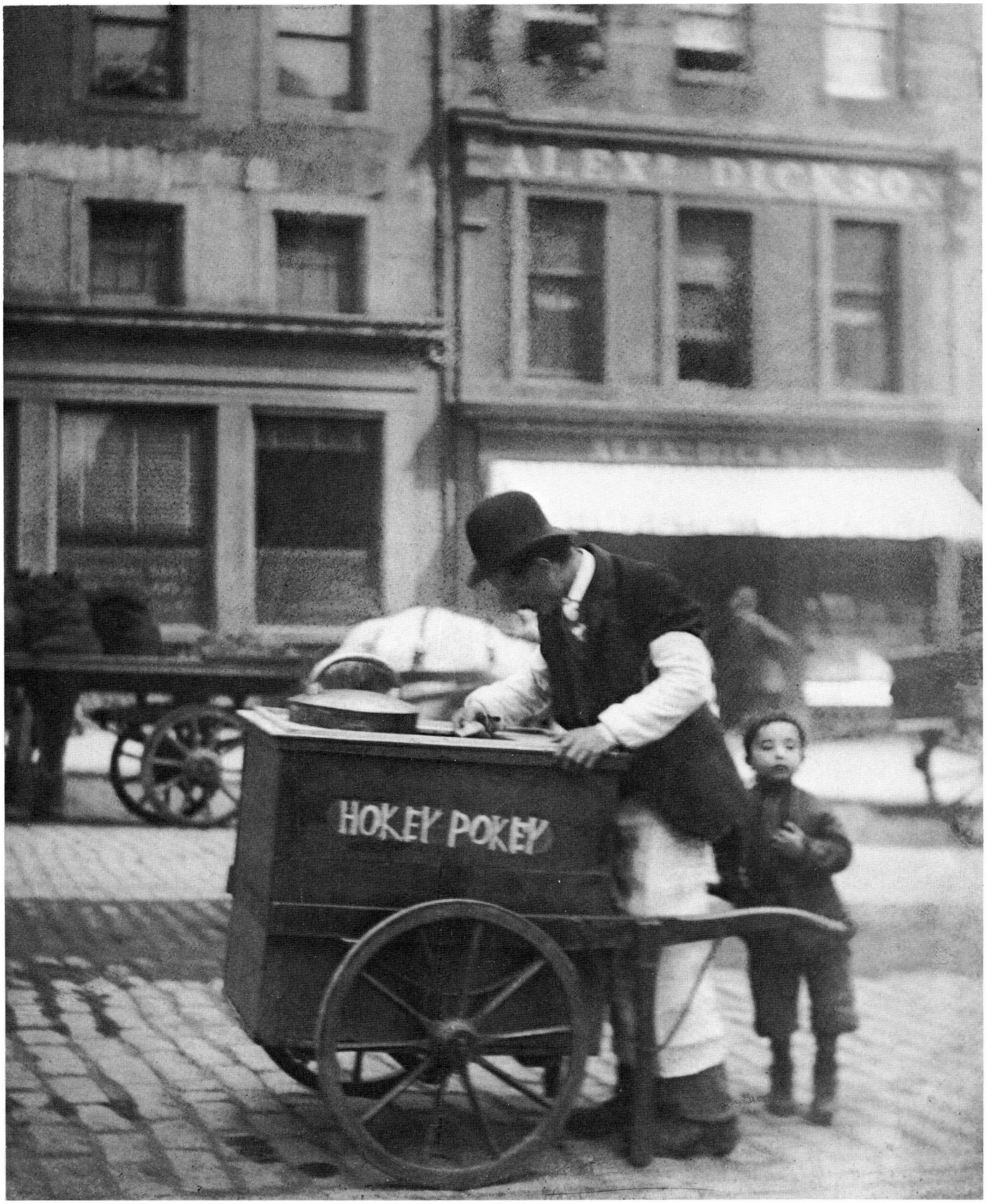

Hokey Pokey Man

Another regular street trader was the Hokey Pokey man, who sold frozen flavoured ice, always a favourite with the young children of the High Street when they had something to spend. His distinctive street cry came straight from the heart, albeit sometimes via the stomach:

> Hokey Pokey, a penny a lump,
> The more you eat, the more you jump!

He is photographed here, *c.* 1880, opposite Alexander Dickson, the grocer, at No. 175 High Street. The tenement seen in the picture was demolished for the construction of the shops on the north-west corner of the High Street and North Bridge. In recent years the upper storeys were converted into Royal Mile Mansions.

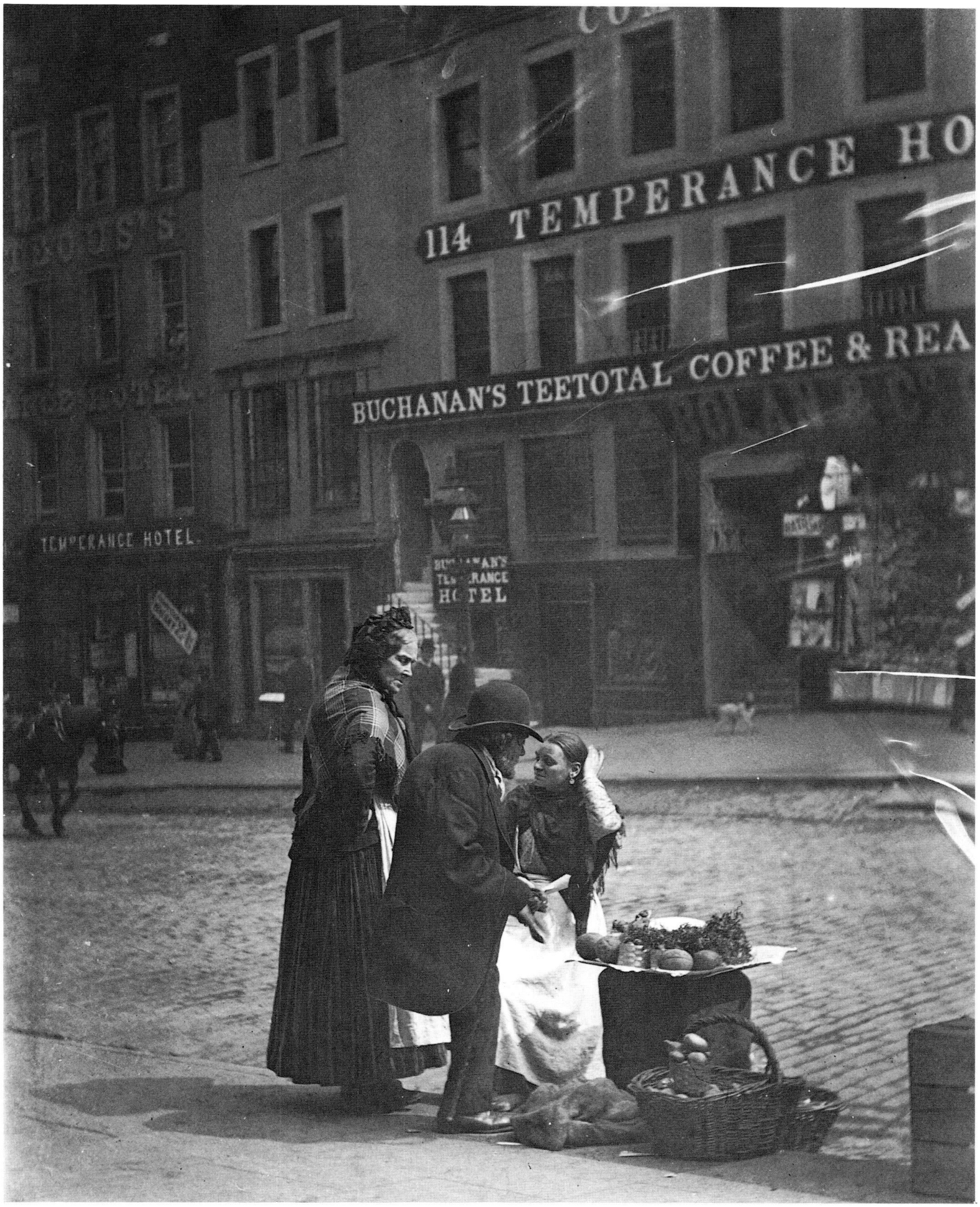

Coconut Tam

The doyen of all the street traders was undoubtedly Coconut Tam, who lived and worked in the same part of the High Street for many years, until his death in 1894 at the age of seventy-one. His diminutive figure and unusual attire – a long black jacket and a billycock hat — marked him out as one of the Old Town's real characters. The photograph, taken in 1880, shows Coconut Tam at his stance on the north side of the High Street, a few yards down from the junction with North Bridge. The opposite side of the street includes Cant's Close at No. 108; William McEwan the baker at Nos. 110 and 112; Buchanan's Teetotal Coffee House and Hotel at No. 114; and Dickson's Close at No. 118. On the left of the picture is another Temperance Hotel, run by James Porteous, but to get to it, it is necessary to pass the shop advertising whisky, at 2/6d (12½p) per bottle. In the 1960s the site became one of Edinburgh's famous 'holes in the ground', before being redeveloped as the Scandic Crown Hotel in 1990.

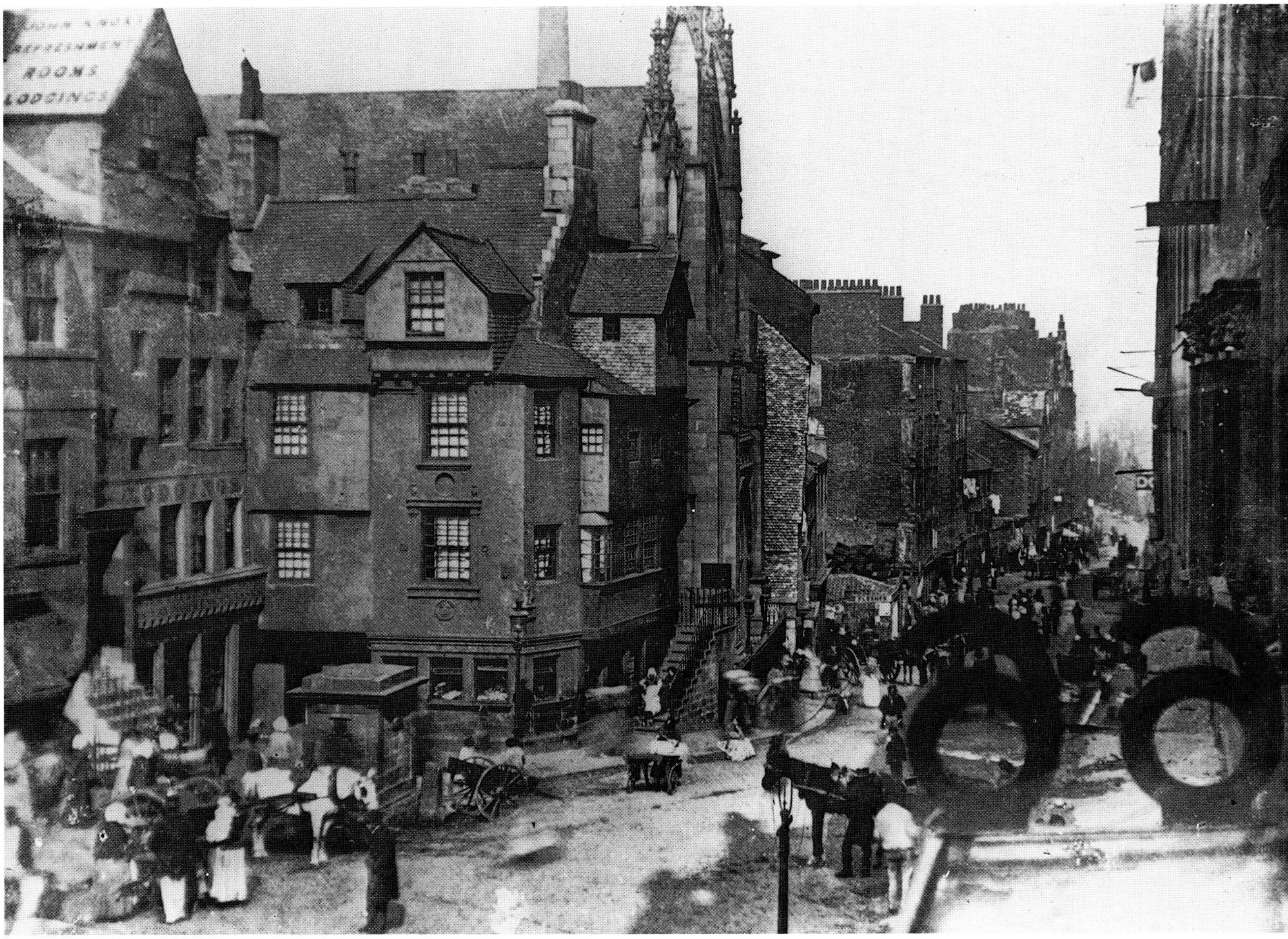

John Knox's House

There is considerable controversy over Knox's exact association with this house, but the tradition is so strong that it is unlikely to be seriously weakened. The house dates from the early sixteenth century, although it has been altered on many occasions. Of almost equal interest is Moubray House, *c.* 1630, which can be seen to the left of the picture, somewhat reduced in importance by the roof sign which reads 'John Knox's Refreshment Rooms and Lodgings'. Beyond Knox's House is the Moray-Knox Church dating from 1853 and demolished for the construction of the Netherbow Centre in 1971. The photograph obviously pre-dates 1867 when the City Improvement Act was passed for the construction of Jeffrey Street. The site is covered with dilapidated buildings, the single-storey shop with the pantiled roof being Andrew Knowles, the flesher. Nearest to the camera is the projecting shop sign 66.

Whitehorse Close

Despite its abysmal condition in this 1850 picture, Whitehorse Close exudes great charm and character — from the nesting boxes in the roof space to the flagged and guttered courtyard below. Its exact age is uncertain, a date stone of 1523 having been recut in the 1930s to read 1623 in an effort at historical accuracy. Tradition has it that the close once formed the stable yard of Queen Mary. According to Storer (writing in 1820), the close was known as Davidson's Land 'after the name of the present proprietor'. During its long history, including the time when it was a coaching inn, the building has been altered and renovated on several occasions, most recently in 1962.

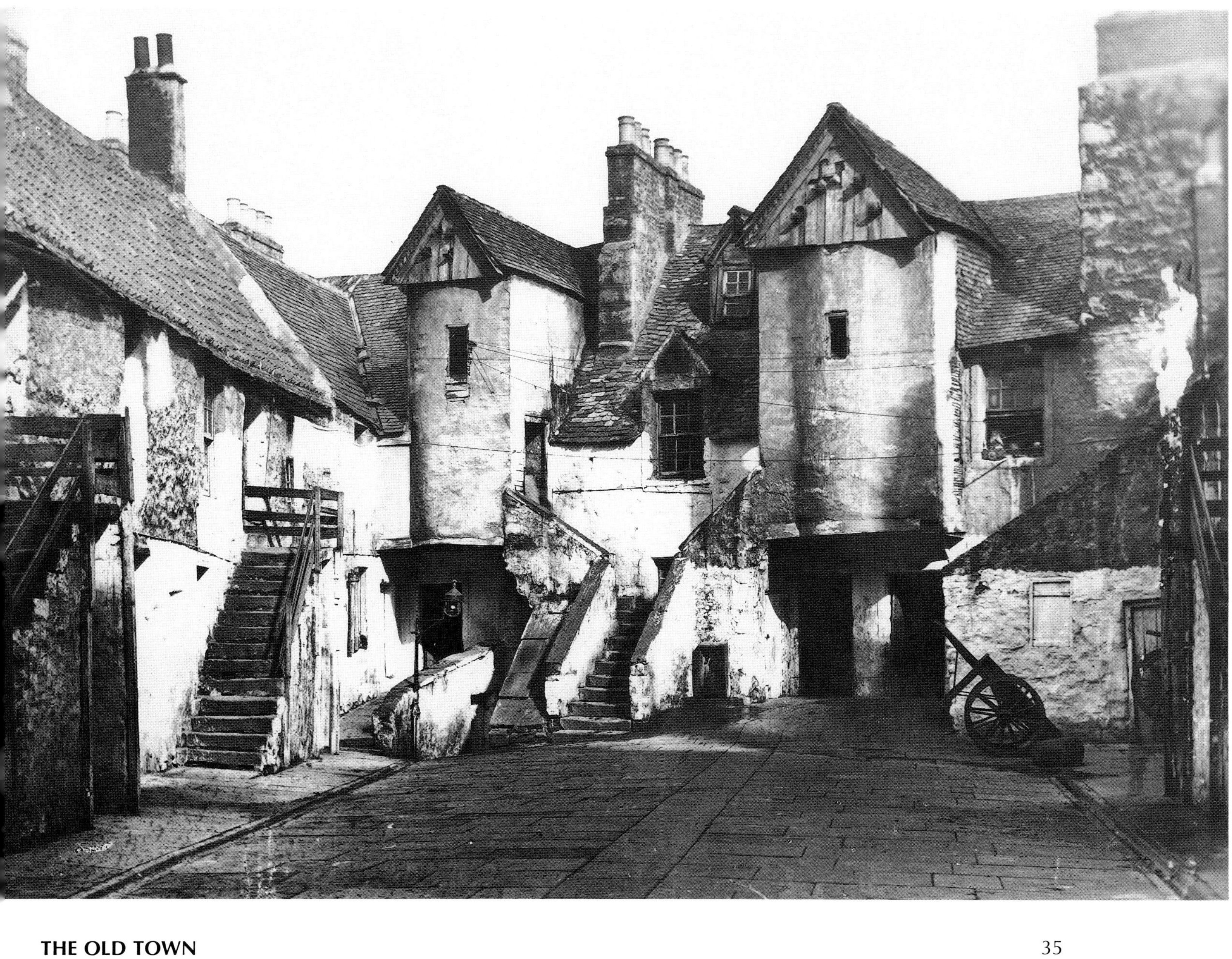

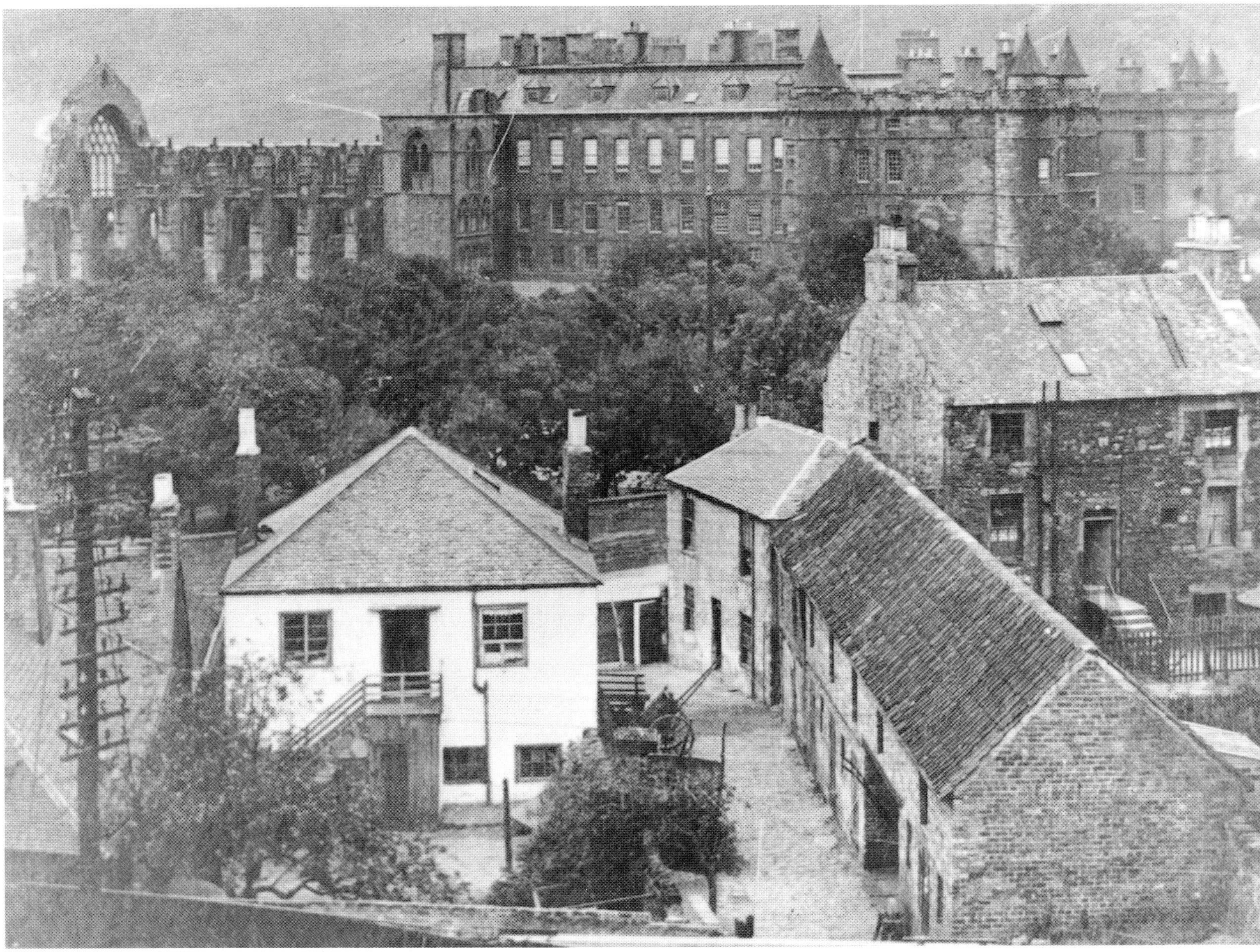

Old Houses at the Palace of Holyroodhouse

Modest housing sits cheek by jowl with its royal neighbours at the south end of Abbey Hill, previously known as Watergate, at the foot of the Canongate. According to Maitland (1753), the Canongate 'suffered more by the Union of the Kingdoms, than all the other parts of Scotland: for having, before that period, been the residence of the chief of the Scottish nobility, it was then in a flourishing condition; but being deserted by them, many of their houses are fallen down, and others in a ruinous condition; it is in a piteous case'. After the Act of Union in 1707 Holyroodhouse 'became a tenement of exclusive flats for noblemen who had acquired grants of lodging there'. At the present day the Palace of Holyroodhouse is the main royal residence in Scotland and is used by the Queen during her visits to Edinburgh.

Holyrood Abbey, seen in ruins in the top left hand corner of the picture, was founded by David I in 1128. It was extensively damaged during the Earl of Hertford's invasion of 1544, and again at the Reformation. Restoration schemes, as recently as 1906 and 1945, were rejected because too much new stonework would have been required to maintain authenticity.

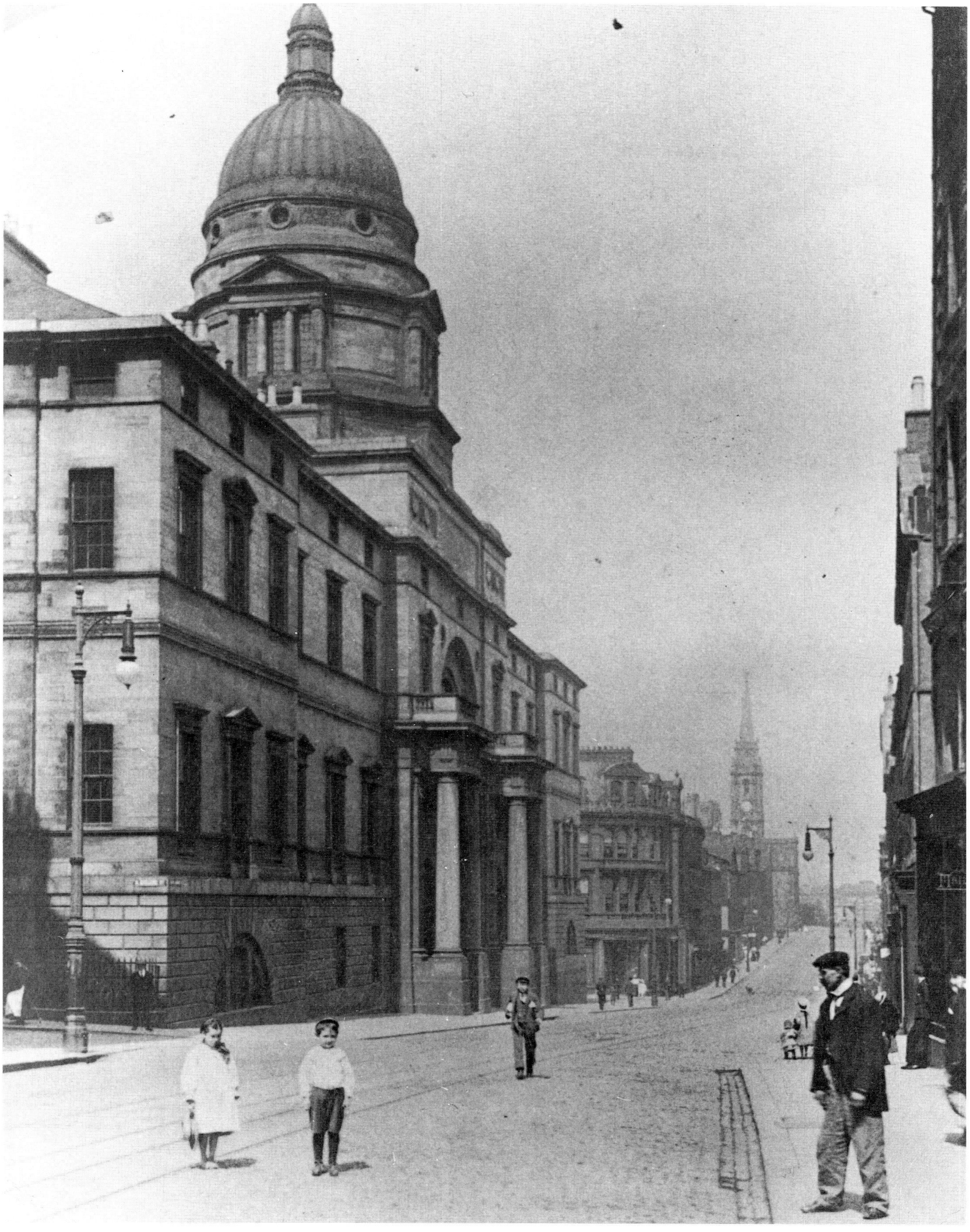

Edinburgh University Old Quad

Of all the grand buildings of Edinburgh, the Old Quad of the University has one of the least appealing situations, hemmed in along its magnificent frontage by tenement and commercial buildings. The grand architecture of its exterior, usually photographed at a very oblique angle, is the work of Robert Adam in 1780. The inner quadrangle is by William H. Playfair between 1819 and 1827. The dome was added in 1879 by R. Rowand Anderson, with a figure of Youth bearing the torch of Learning, by John Hutchison. When the foundation stone was laid on 16th November 1789, by Principal William Robertson, the University had already been in existence for more than two centuries, founded in 1582 by James VI.

Cockles and Mussels

Even if the trade is not brisk, at least the fare is being appreciated by this young customer at the stance for cockles and mussels in St Patrick Square, *c.* 1880.

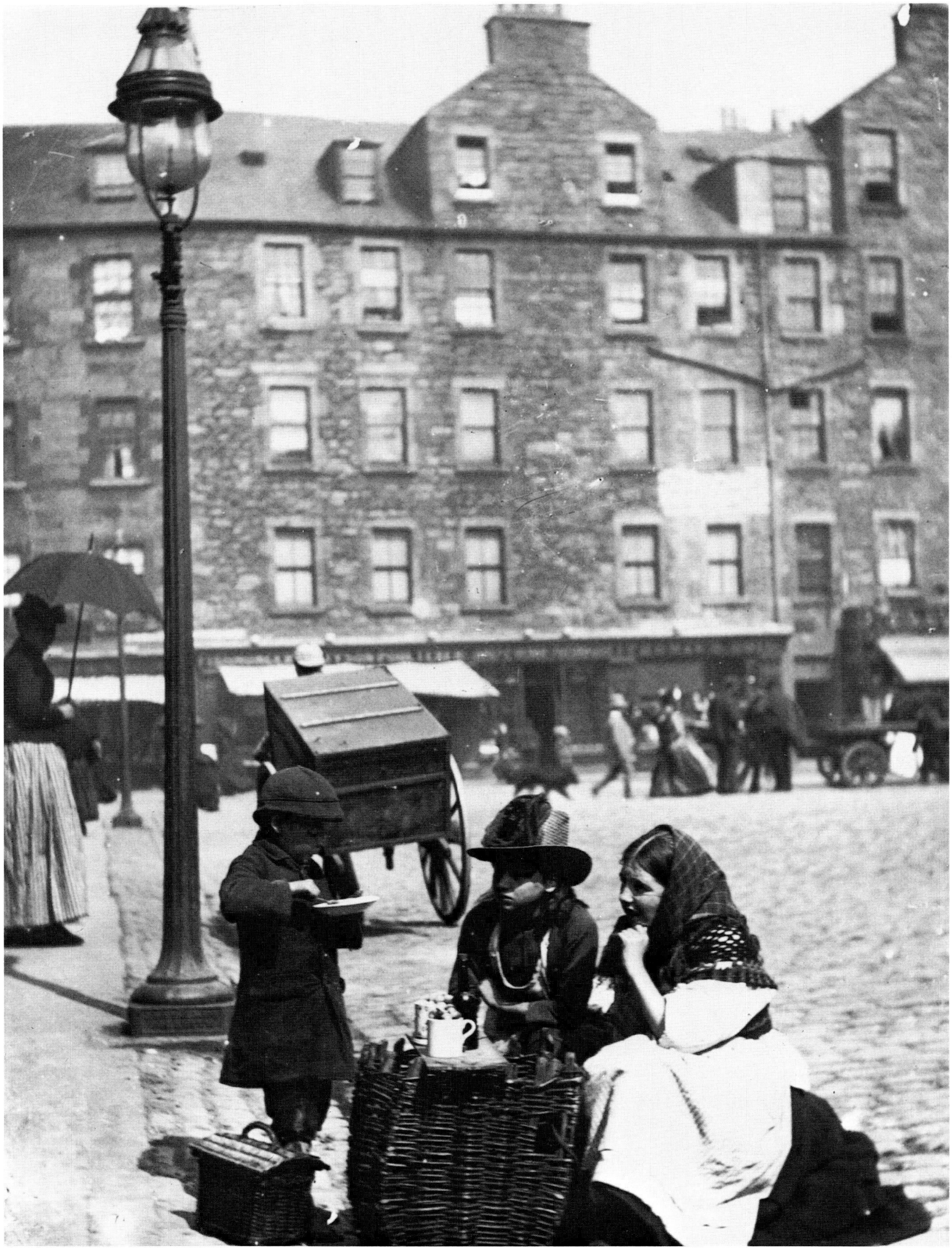

Leven Street

Tollcross has always been an area famous for its small traders. In the early 1900s the corner of Leven Street and Tarvit Street had many small shops with bargains in fruit, flowers and groceries. The corner shop is a branch from Covent Garden, Leith, with a side window heaped with sweet oranges at 40 for 1/- (5p). Above the Cut Flower Depot (which is advertising items for Easter) are the grain stores of James Thomson & Son, whose oatmeal built the bones of the nation. Next door, T. J. Malcolmson seems to be on 'a half day', but Schnitzler is open for picture framing and fine arts. The group of delivery boys in front of the fruit shop are well dressed and well shod, envied, perhaps, by the barefoot lad near the horse and carriage.

The entire corner was demolished for the construction of the King's Theatre designed by J. D. Swanston and James Davidson and built by W. S. Cruickshank & Son of Lower Gilmore Place. The foundation stone was laid on 18th August 1906 by Sir Andrew Carnegie and the opening performance was the pantomime, *Cinderella,* on 8th December 1906.

Waverley Station and Jeffrey Street *(over page)*

This view of the east side of the Old Town, c. 1902, taken from the clock tower of the old North British Hotel, gives some idea of the number of domestic and factory chimneys which were contributing to Auld Reekie's reputation. Most of the centre of the picture is taken up by the glass roof construction of the Waverley Station, redesigned for the North British Railway Company by Charles Jopp in 1866, and built between 1868 and 1874. Beyond are Market Street, and Jeffrey Street on the higher level, with the pedestrian access bridge (now demolished) to the Waverley Station. New Street is dominated by the Edinburgh Gas Light Company's Works, replaced in 1927 by a bus depot. Despite its name, New Street, or Young Street, dates from c. 1760 when it was built as 'a curious sample of fashionable modern improvement, prior to the bold scheme of the New Town'. The name Young Street was taken from Dr Thomas Young, who lived there in the mid-eighteenth century.

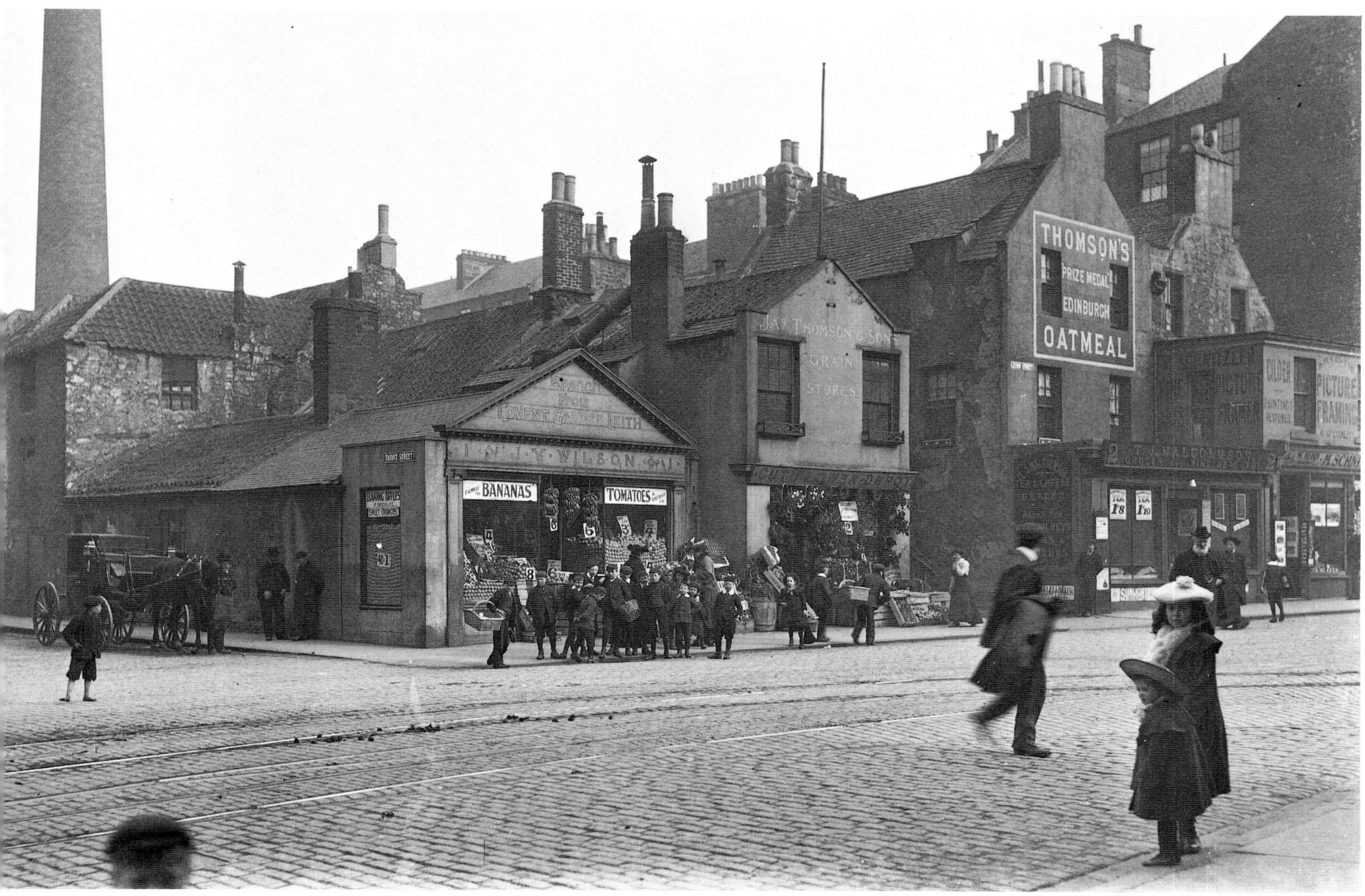

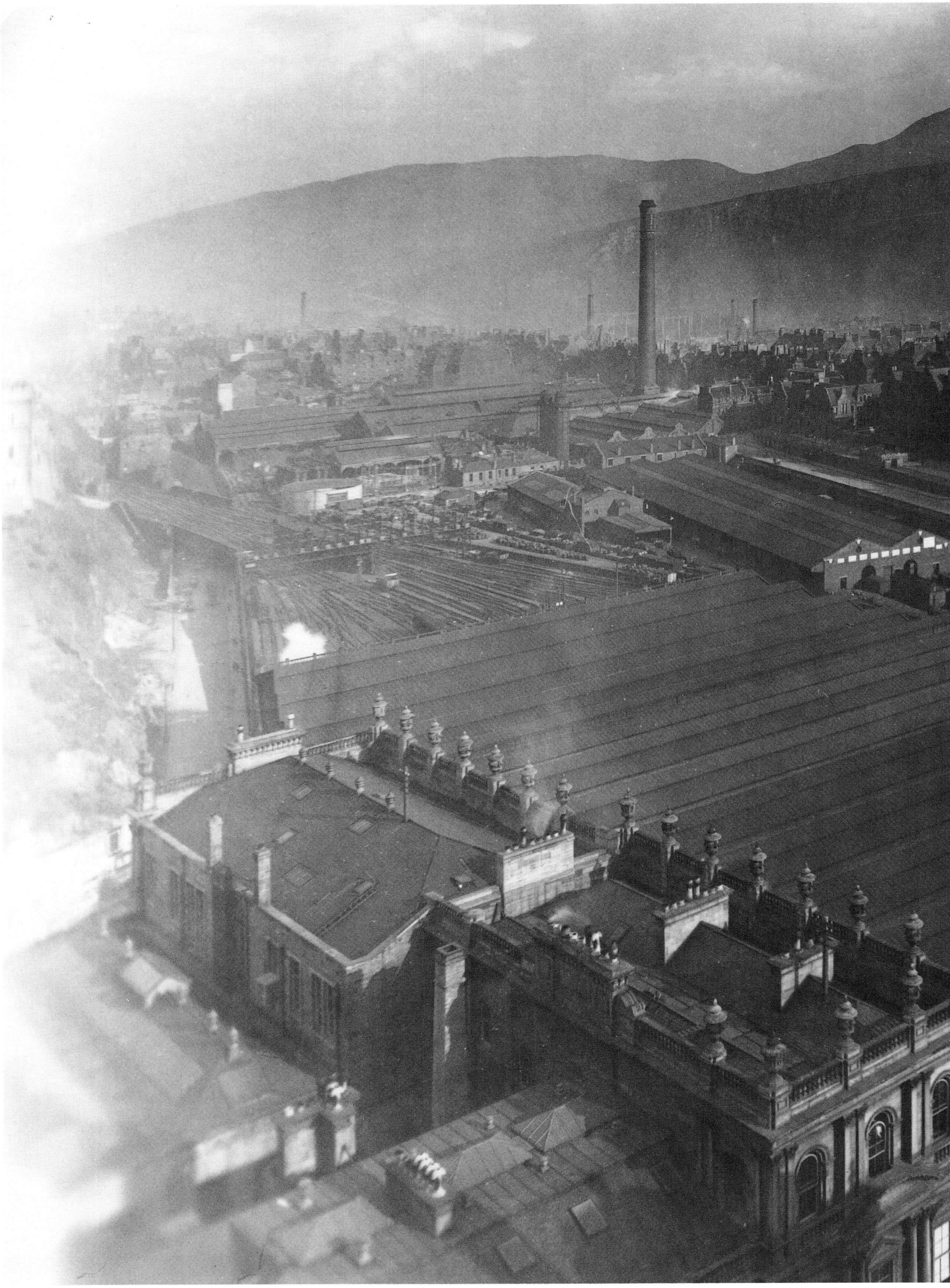

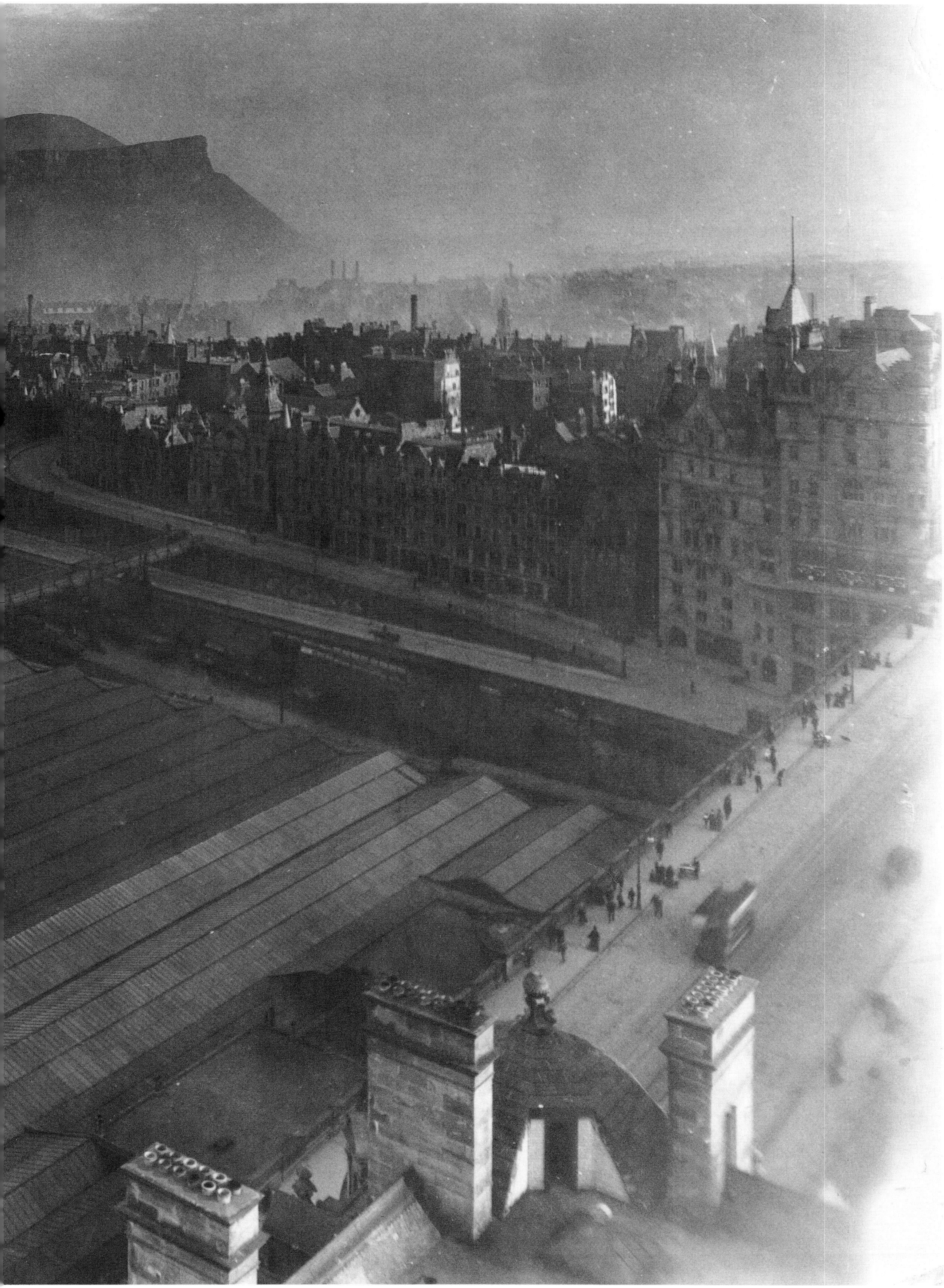

THE NEW TOWN

CHAPTER 3

The First North Bridge to the New Town

As early as 1732 there was serious discussion about building a bridge from the Old Town of Edinburgh, across the valley of the Nor' Loch. It was not until 21st October 1763, however, that the foundation stone for the first North Bridge was laid by Lord Provost Drummond. Two more years elapsed before contracts were signed, based on an estimated cost of £10,140 for a five-arch bridge, 1,134 feet in length, to be completed by Martinmas 1769. All went well until August 1769 when an arch at the south end of the bridge collapsed, killing five people. After considerable delay the bridge was actually opened in 1772, at a total cost of £17,354. As well as being of immense value to the citizens of Edinburgh as a direct link to the north, the bridge was put to a rather unusual use. In 1774 the Magistrates proclaimed that all beggars found in the streets 'would be imprisoned in the dark vaults beneath the North Bridge and there fed on bread and water'. The photograph shows North Bridge, *c.* 1850, with Register House at the north end, and the rear of the Theatre Royal on the right. The North British Hotel (now the Balmoral) had not yet been built, and most of the site was occupied by Charles C. Young & Co., Iron Gate and Bridge Manufacturers. A terrace, with railings, gave access to the Rainbow Coffee House and Tavern below street level.

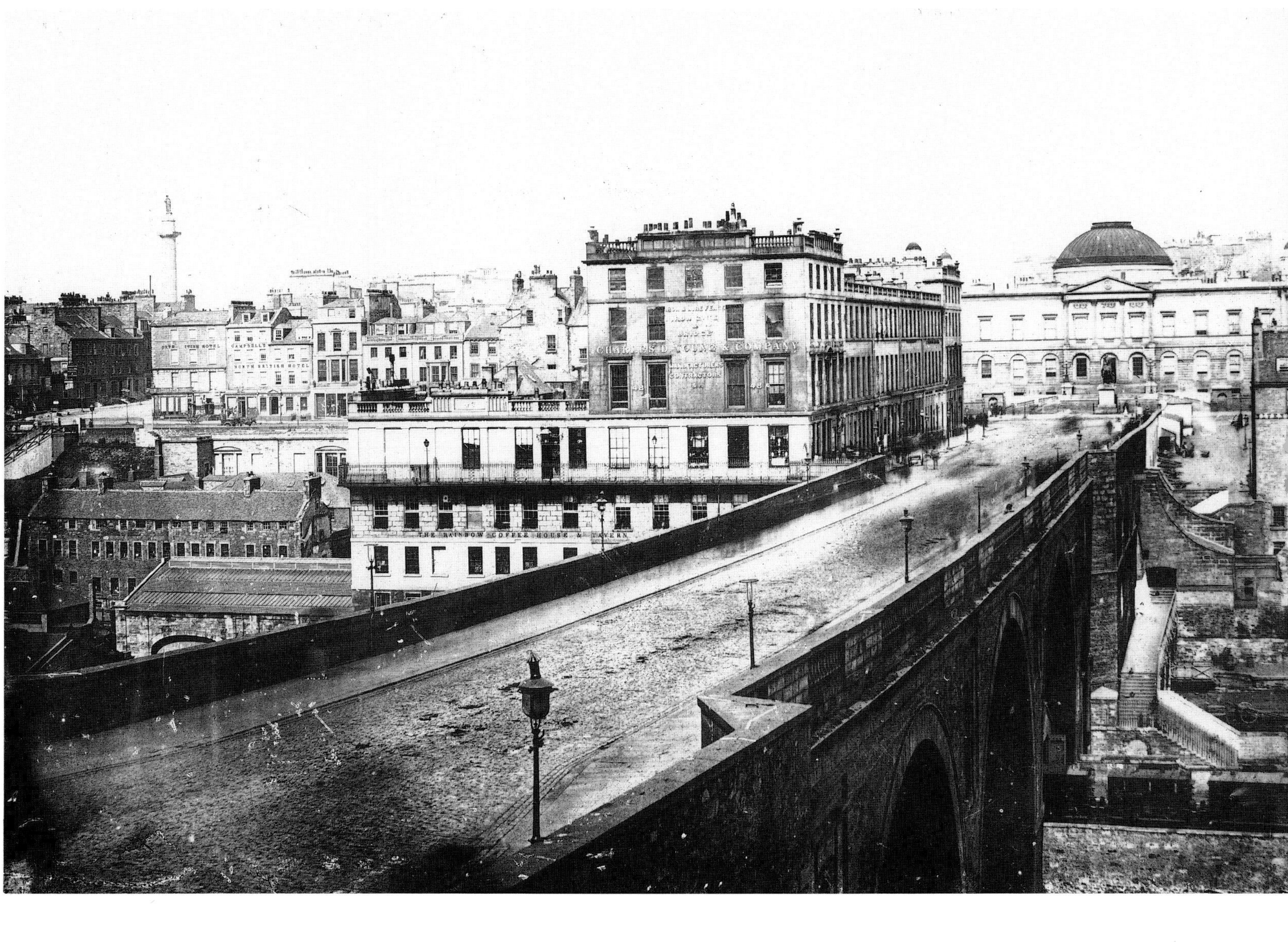

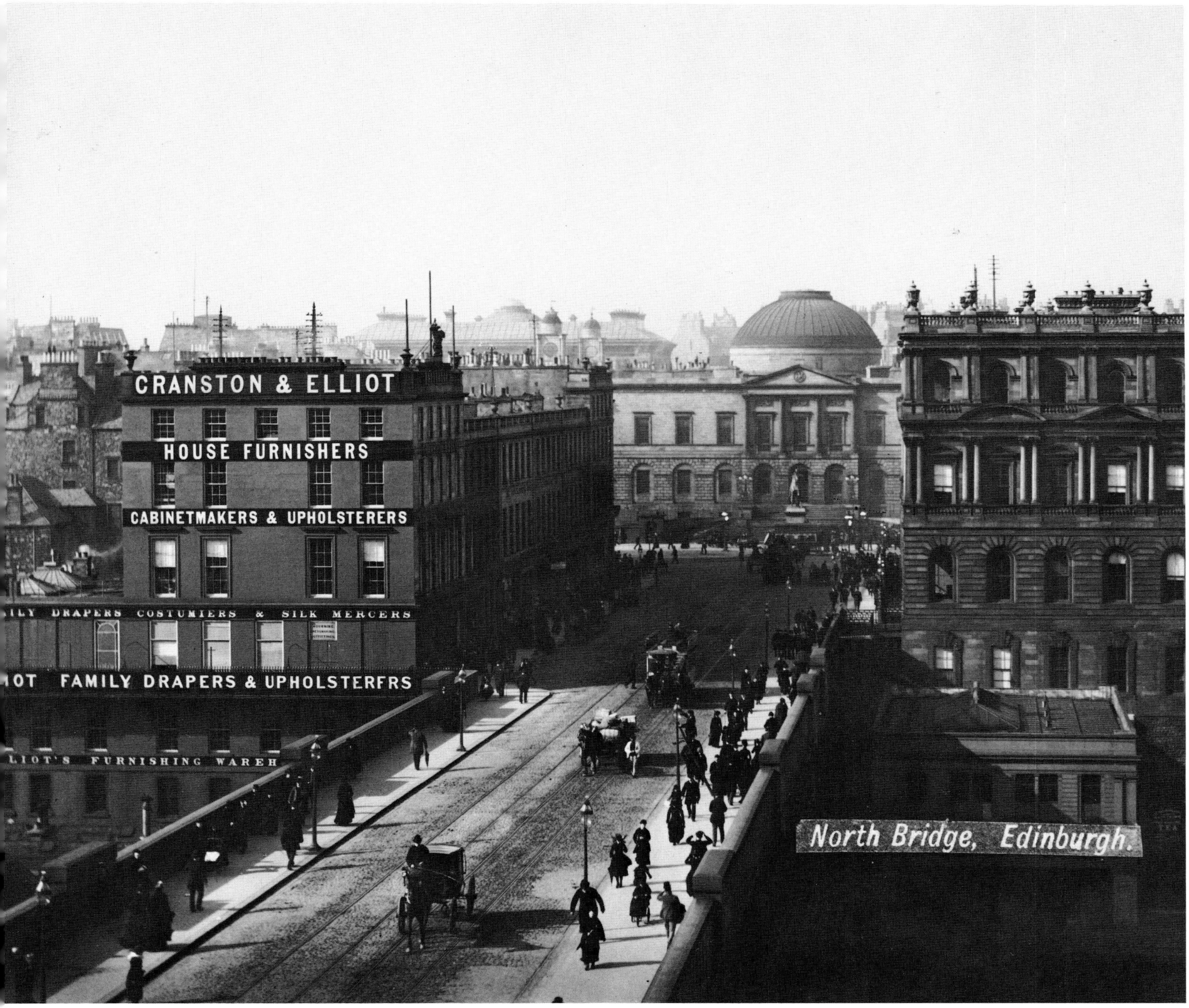

Alterations to the First North Bridge

By 1873 increased traffic, and the laying of tram rails, meant that the original bridge needed to be widened to 54 feet 'by the throwing out upon each side of massive iron brackets and box girders'. The improved appearance of the bridge is clearly evident in this photograph taken in 1885. Register House appears timeless, but the Theatre Royal has been demolished and replaced by the General Post Office, built between 1861 and 1866. On the opposite corner the entire building has been taken over by Cranston & Elliot, House Furnishers. Robert Cranston, founder of the firm, was Lord Provost of Edinburgh from 1903 to 1906.

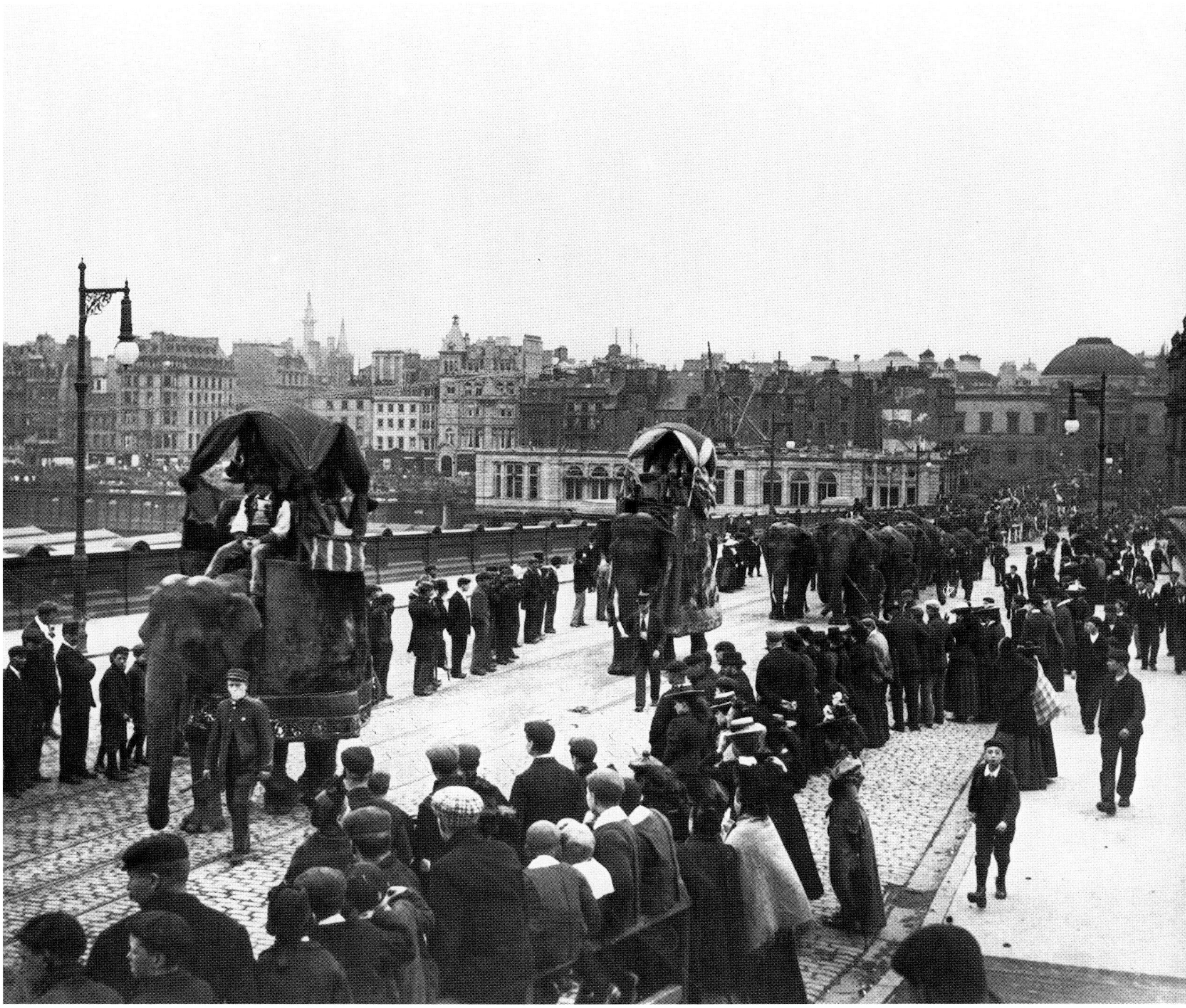

The New North Bridge

In the early 1890s the North British Railway Company was keen to reconstruct Waverley Station, but was restricted by the bulky piers of the old North Bridge. The Company agreed to contribute £30,000 towards the cost of a new bridge (£90,000) provided the piers were resited. Work started in 1894 on a new bridge with three spans, each 175 feet long, and 75 feet wide, between the parapets. The foundation stone was laid on 25th May 1896 by Lord Provost McDonald. Never averse to blowing their own trumpets, the civic leaders announced that each day the new bridge carried 100,000 pedestrians, 2,000 vehicles — and sometimes several elephants. Taking up the rear ground is the North British Station Hotel under construction; it was opened in 1902.

Duke of Wellington Statue and North Bridge

The 'Iron Duke in bronze by Steell' appears to be on his mettle, directing traffic from North Bridge to Leith Street in 1885. The destination board on the side of the horse-drawn tram says 'Bernard Street, Leith and Newington', and the advertisement above it is for Mackenzie's Cod Liver Oil Emulsion, 'pleasing and efficacious' — in every way. At the top of North Bridge *The Scotsman* office has not yet been built, the site being occupied by Marshall and Aitken, military outfitters and army contractors, at Nos. 27 and 29. On the other side of the road Patrick Thomson's Cash Drapery Stores and the old Carlton Hotel have not yet been built. The old building is occupied by Mackintosh & Co., hosiers, with Lawrie and Mitchell's Portrait Rooms on the top floor. A board announcing another photographer, Cumming Bros., at No. 63, can be seen to the right of Wellington's head.

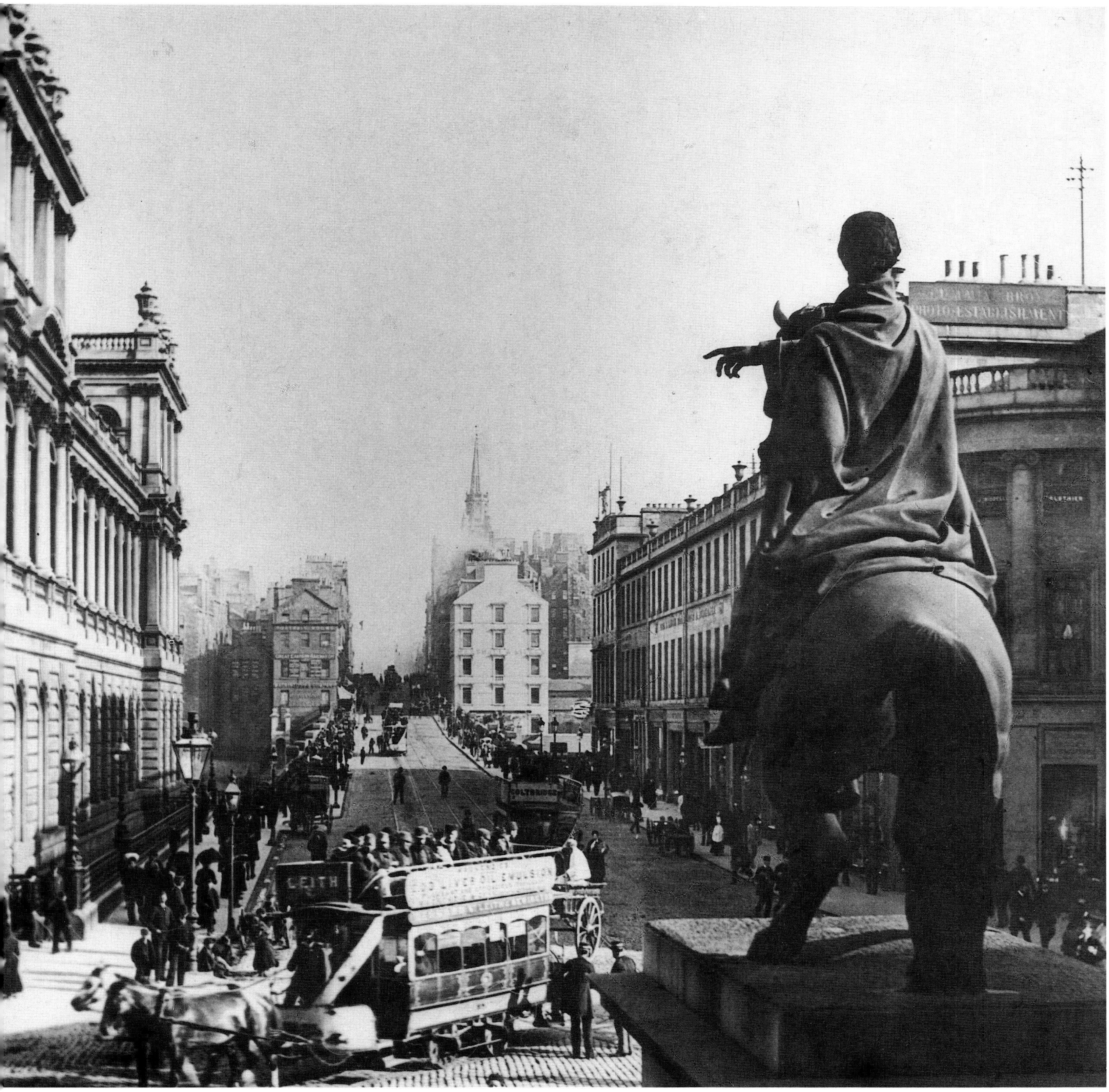

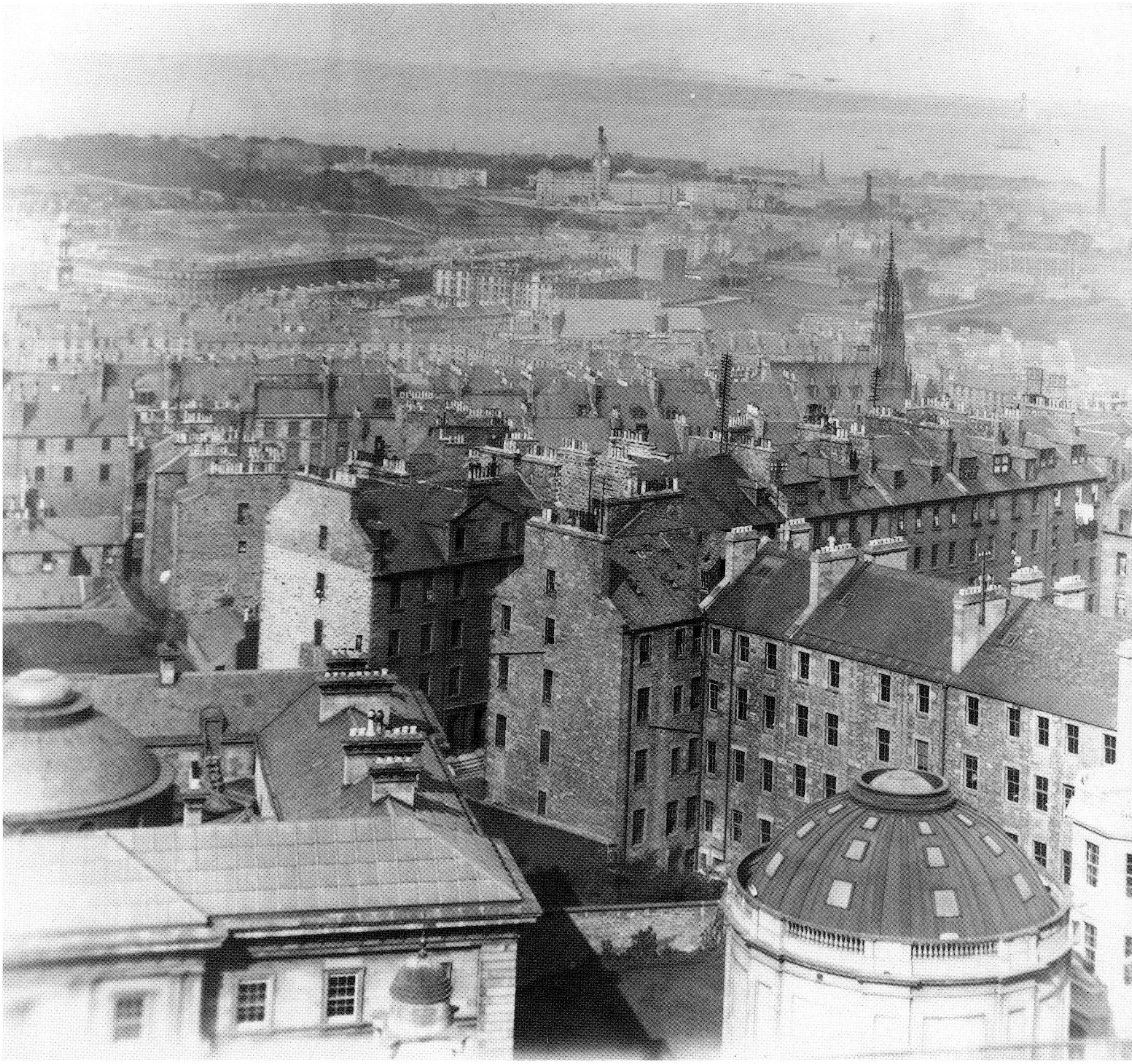

St James' Square Looking North

The domed roof of Register House in the foreground contrasts sharply with the tall tenement buildings of St James' Square, demolished for the construction of St James' Centre in 1965. In the middle ground three churches are prominent. On the extreme left are the clock and tiered columns of the Burgh Church, St Mary's, in Bellevue Crescent, designed in 1824 by Thomas Brown. In the centre is the Catholic Apostolic Church (containing murals by Phoebe Traquair) by R. Rowand Anderson in 1872, and on the right, St Mary's Free Church which stood on the corner of Albany Street and Broughton Street. In the background the clock tower, partly hidden by the factory chimney, is part of Chancelot Flour Mills, Bonnington, now demolished.

Calton Jail

When the Tolbooth in the Canongate became too small to accommodate Edinburgh's prison population, the Magistrates considered several sites for a new jail, including Forrester's Wynd and the south side of Princes Street. The latter plan was abandoned because 'the exhalations arising from the North Loch . . . must be detrimental to the health of the prisoners'. A site on Calton Hill to the west of the Bridewell was chosen and the foundation stone laid in September 1815. The completed building (as seen in the photograph) was divided into several compartments, each with its own exercise area, for different classes of prisoner. There was also an infirmary, a chapel and a school. The Bridewell was an earlier 'house of correction' established in 1791 for 'strolling poor, lazy beggars, idle vagrants and common prostitutes'. It had 134 sleeping closets each with a bed and a bible, and 52 working cages containing implements suited to the capabilities of the occupant.

St Andrew's House was built on the site of Calton Jail and the Bridewell between 1936 and 1939.

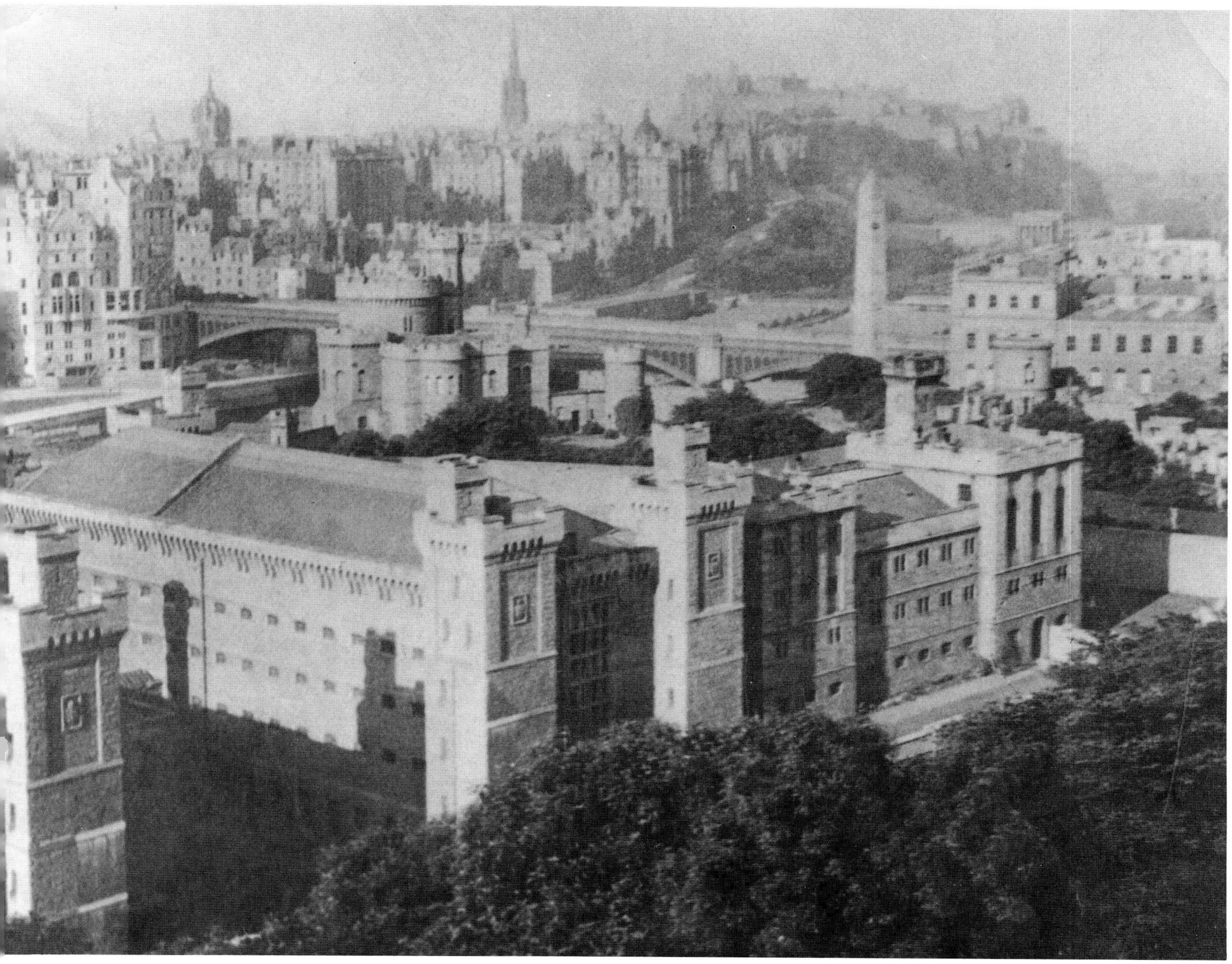

Princes Street and Waterloo Place

The East End of Princes Street is clearly a centre of activity *c.* 1887 with all the public and commercial buildings formed as they are at the present day. The projecting sign at the General Post Office appears to read 'Great North Railway East Coast . . . to England'. Although some of the merchandise being carried through the streets looks rather unusual, no-one is taking very much notice. Above the Ionic columns on the left-hand side of Waterloo Place is an advertisement for W. Sutherland, Wine Merchants, at No. 3 Waterloo Place.

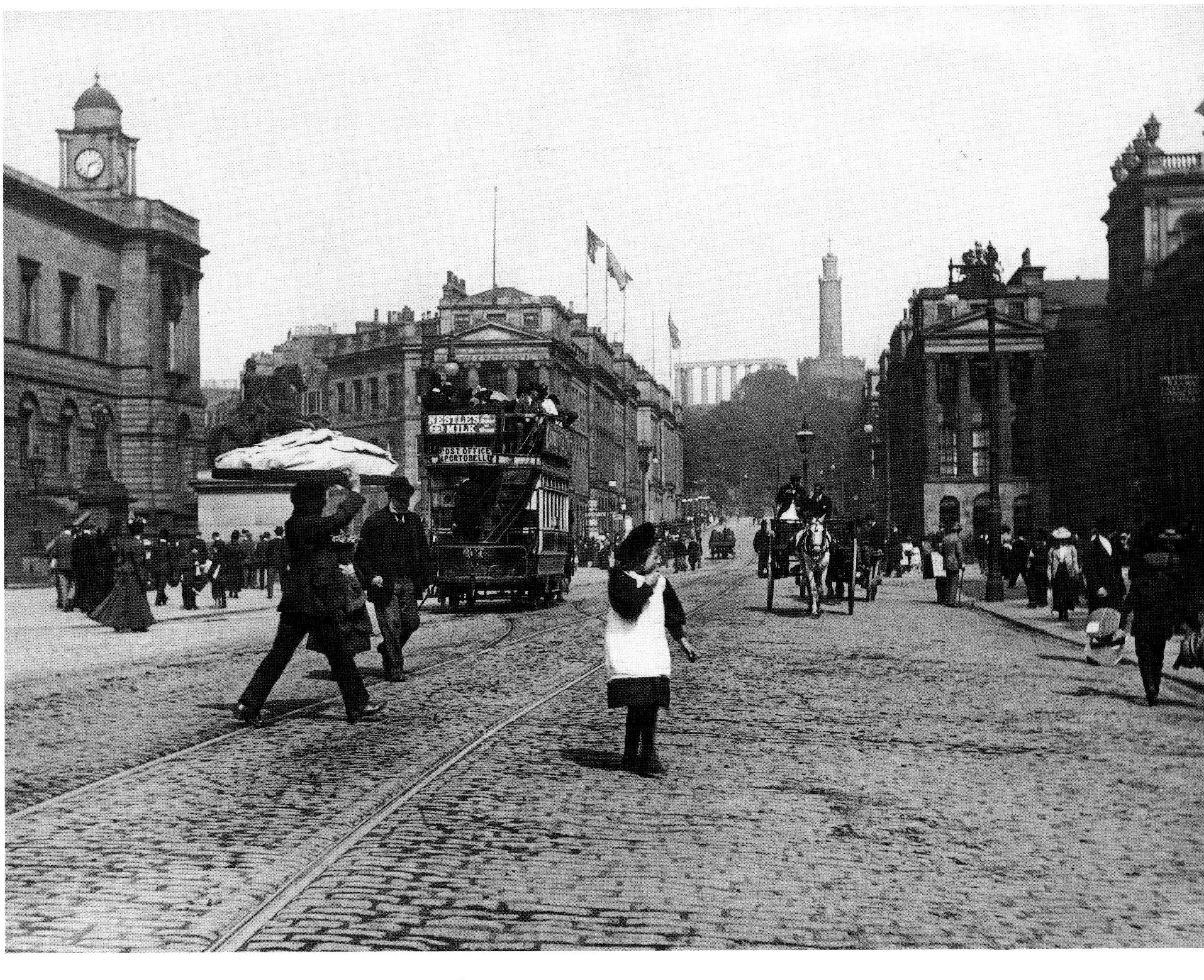

A decade later public transport is much the same. Is the bowler-hatted gentleman about to travel to Gorgie Road or is he just trying to cross Princes Street? On the upper deck of the open-topped tram, ladies' hairstyles need a little protection from the wind (or perhaps the sun!).

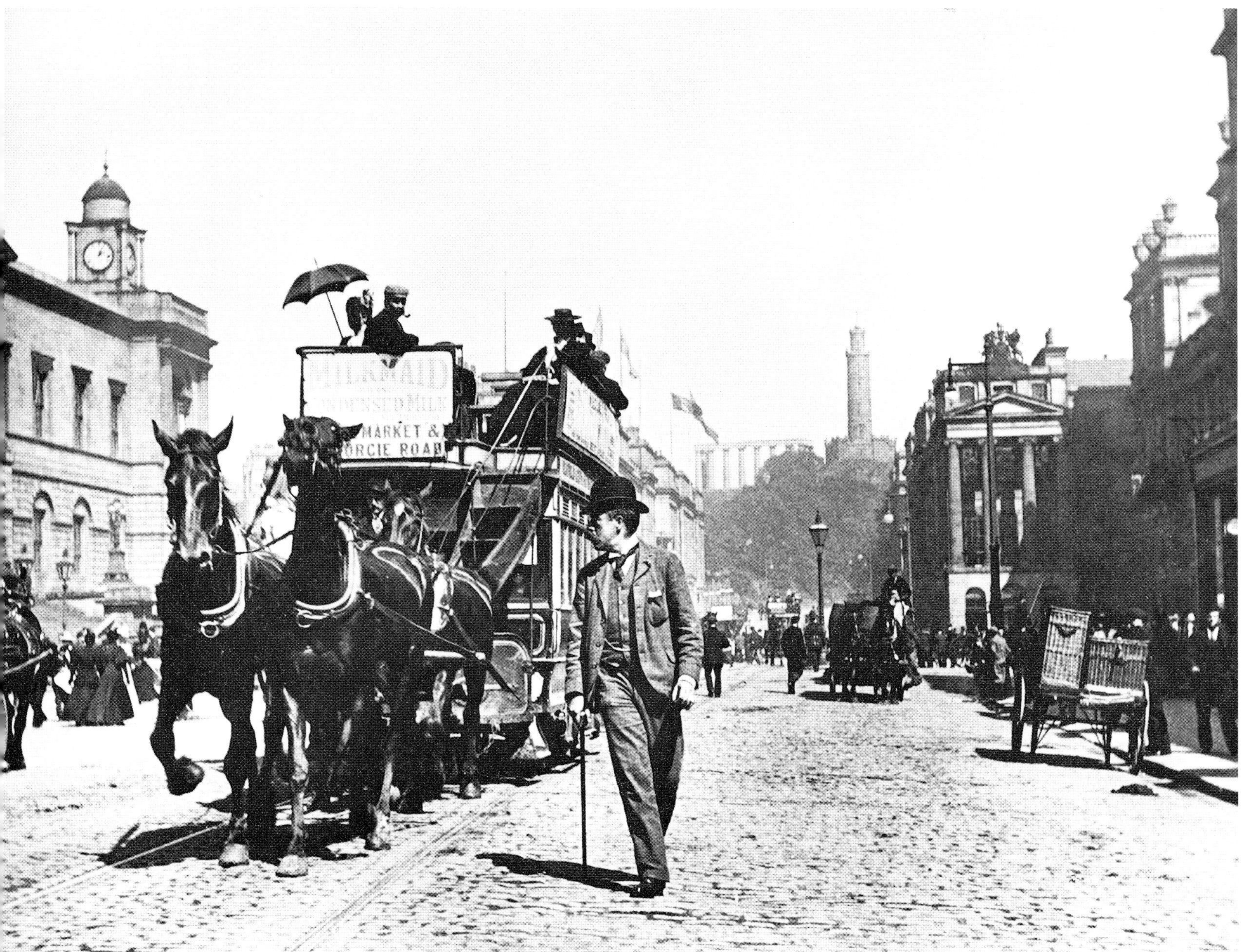

Princes Street Looking West at Waverley Bridge

By 1850 the structure of the south side of Princes Street had been formed for several years, although the Waverley Market site was largely undeveloped. The north side of Princes Street had become commercialised with numerous shops and hotels. South St Andrew Street is flanked by the North British Hotel and Harvey's Royal Bazaar, selling French china, Bohemian glass ornaments, toys and cricket bats. On the left corner is John Millar's China and Glass Ware, with statues and mythical beasts over the shop front. Most of the buildings have steps down to basement stores below the level of Princes Street.

Princes Street Looking East at Waverley Bridge

Almost the same section of Princes Street is photographed here, c. 1850, looking east to Calton Hill. On the left, the building with the ornate pillars and balcony is the Star Hotel. Horse-drawn vehicles are numerous, the entire road surface is laid in setts, and the pavements are built high with projecting stones to facilitate getting into the carriages. Neither the General Post Office, nor the North British Hotel, has yet been built. The site of the present Balmoral Hotel is occupied by Graham's Hotel on the upper storeys, and Potts, Cairnie and Ray, Cabinetmakers and Upholsterers, at pavement level. The General Post Office site is occupied by the Theatre Royal which held its last performance on Wednesday 25th May 1859, with a programme which included *Masks and Faces, Cramond Brig,* and *A Farewell Address.*

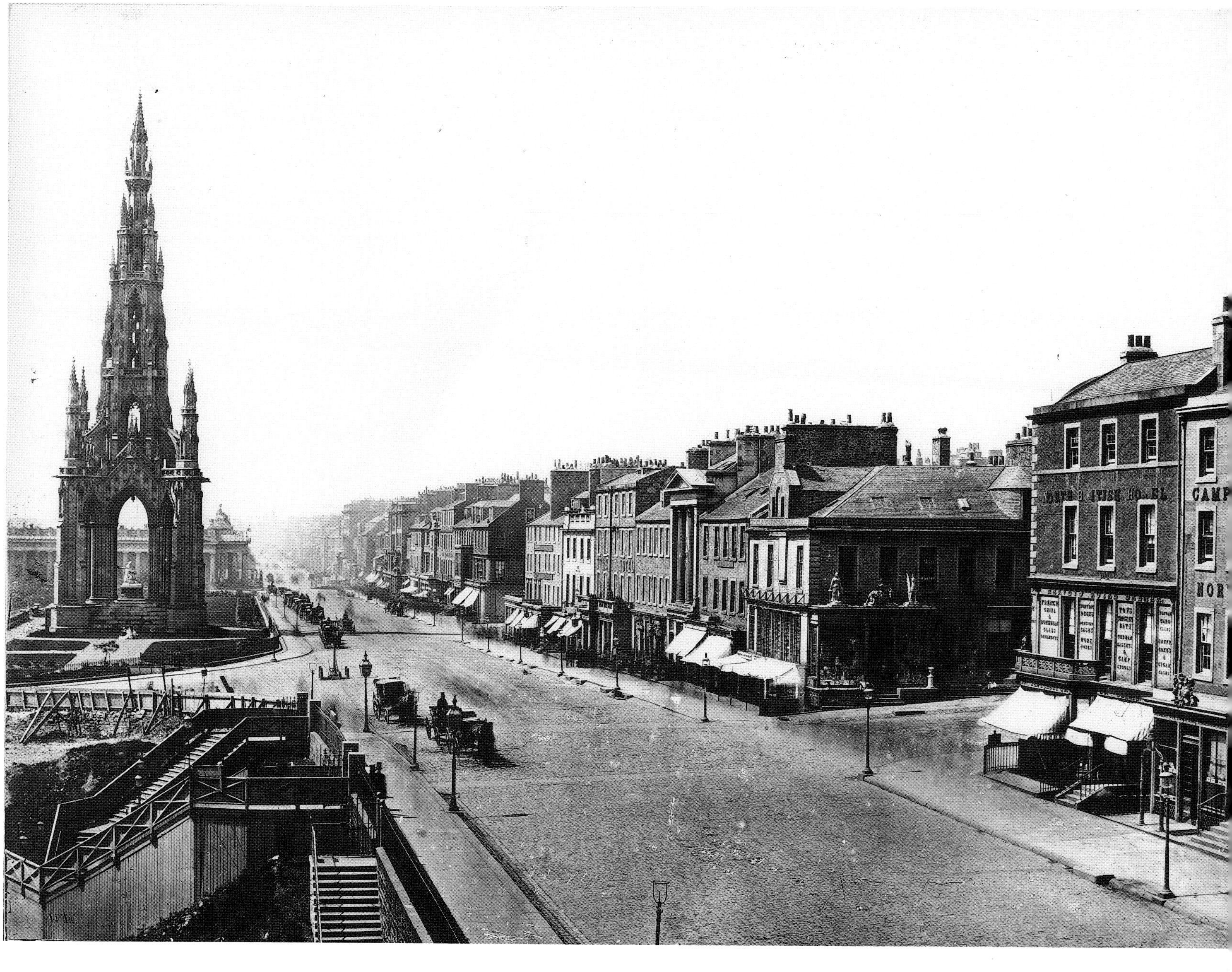

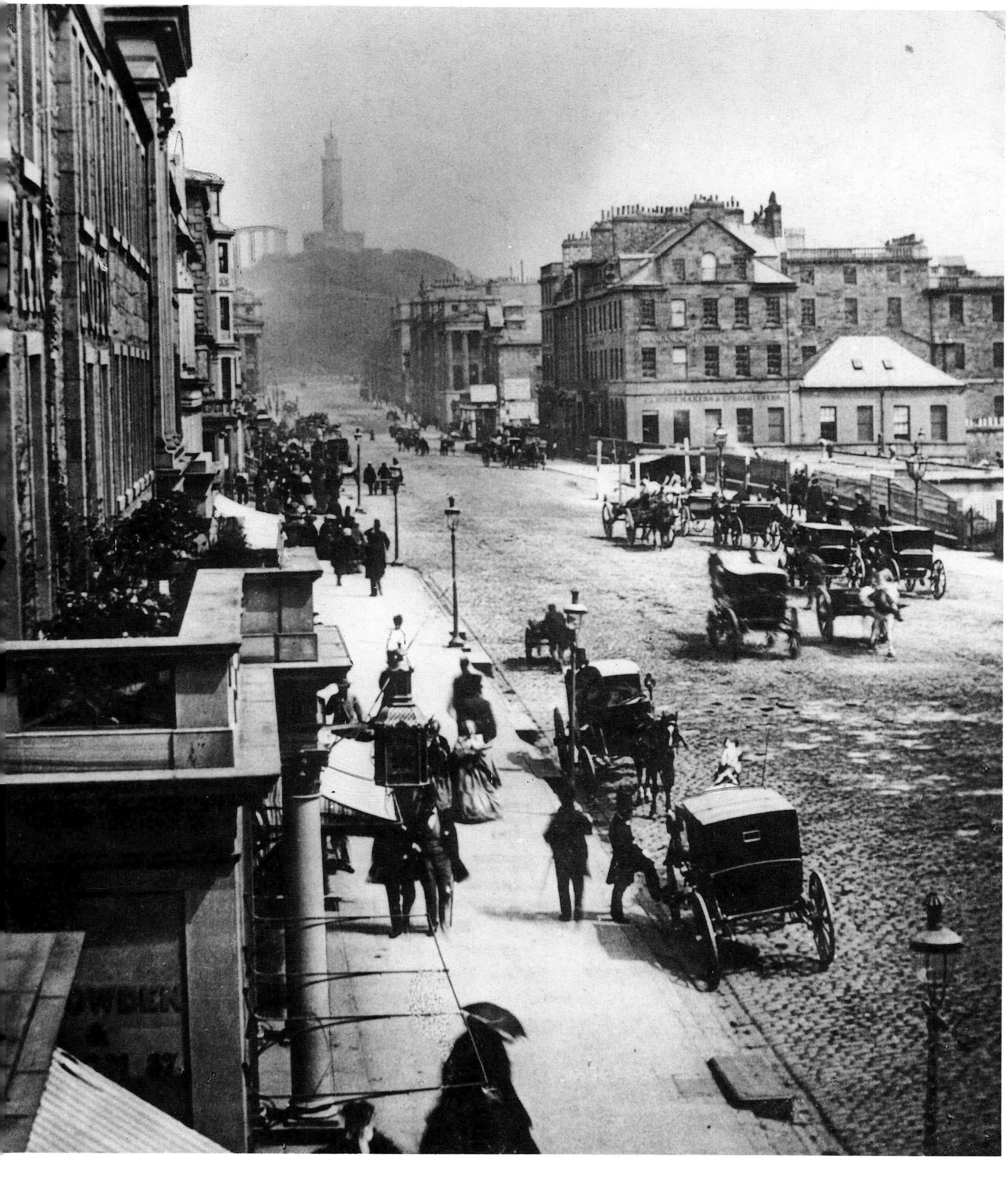

Waverley Market and Princes Street

A cluster of ornamental lamps dominates the junction of Princes Street and Waverley Bridge, c. 1875. The road surface is criss-crossed with rails for horse-drawn trams, although carriages are still very much in evidence. Waverley Market is still completely uncovered, showing the Waverley Steps and stabling for horses used to pull the trams. Above the steps (on the site of the present Balmoral Hotel) are the offices of the Midland Railway Co., and the East Coast Railway Companies. Topping the lot is Dunlop the hatter, whose premises were at No. 64 North Bridge.

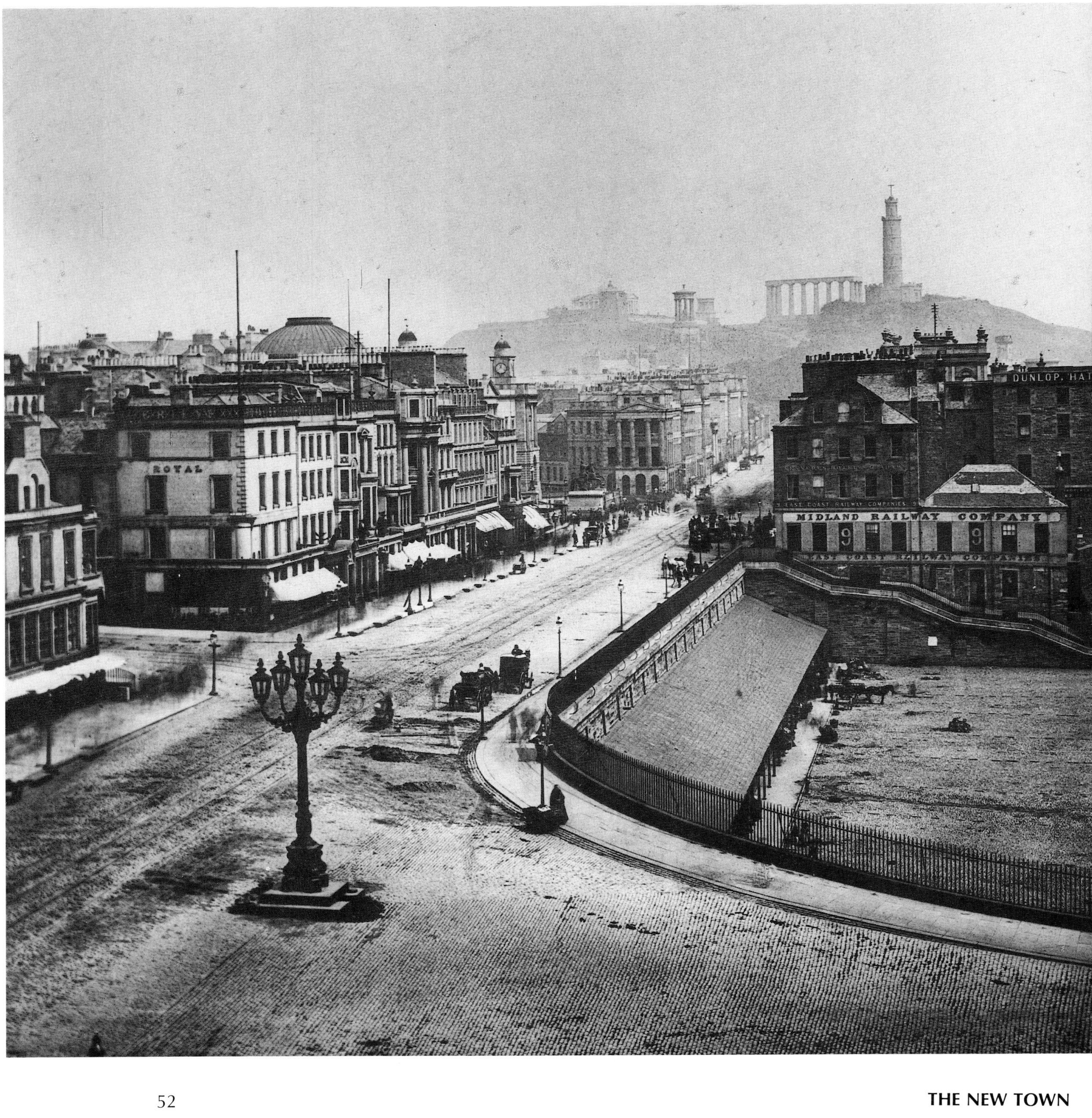

Princes Street at Waverley Market

A decade later (c. 1885) the same scene provides a more sophisticated impression of Princes Street. The ornamental lamps at the junction with Waverley Bridge are arranged more like a chandelier, and many of the basement shops have been built over. An ornamental garden was constructed over the open-air Waverley Market in 1877 and the north pavement has been realigned without the stepping-on blocks. A grand new building has appeared on the west corner of South Saint Andrew Street, occupied as the Richmond Hotel, to the left of which is Dow and Fender, hosiers, at street level, and above it the National Property Investment Co. Ltd.

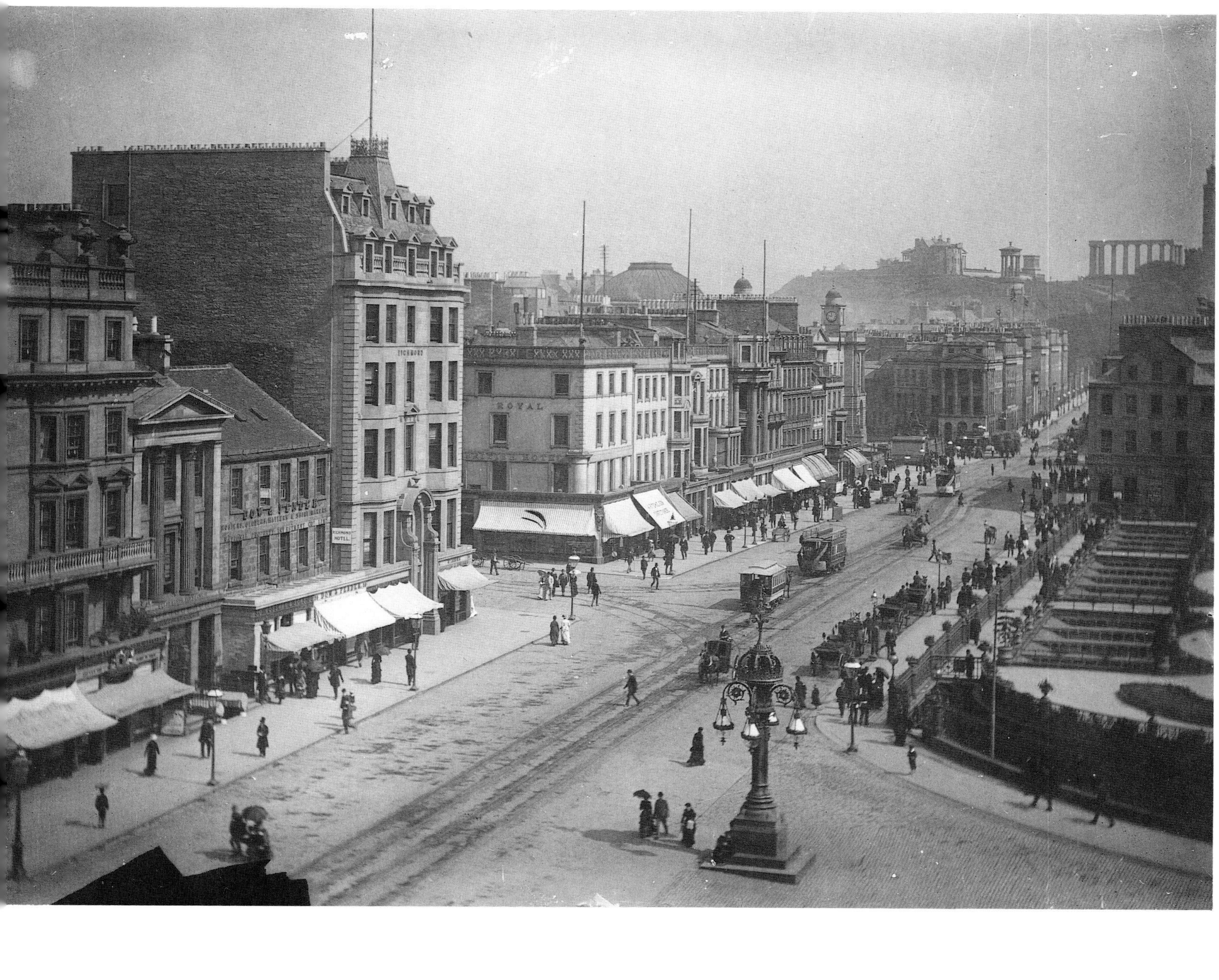

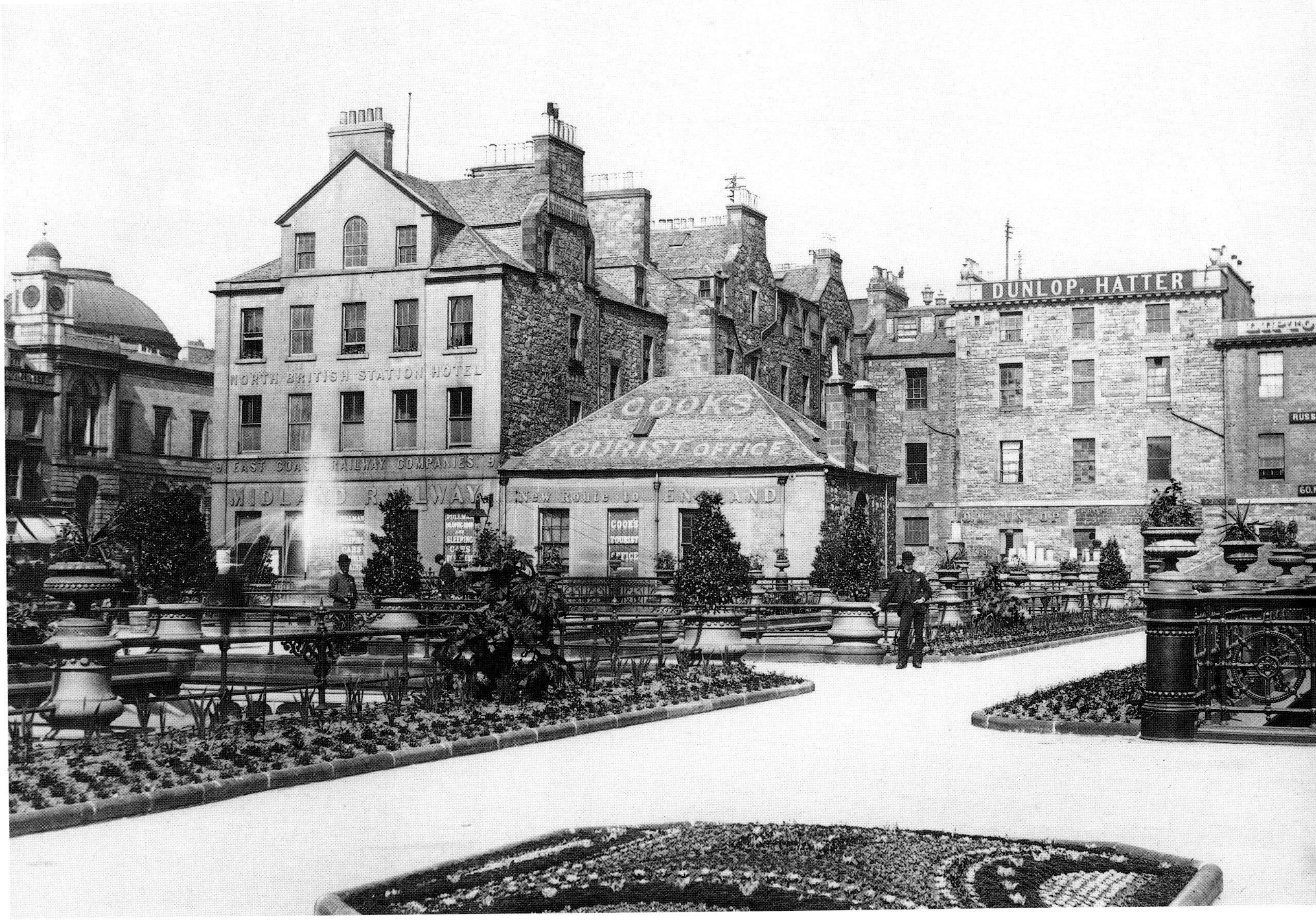

Waverley Market and the North British Station Hotel

The roof of the old Waverley Market was laid out in a series of paths, fountains, flower beds, urns and ornamental ironwork. The photograph was taken c. 1886, ten years after the open-air market was roofed over. The picture gives a fascinating close-up of the group of buildings swept away for the construction of the North British Hotel (now the Balmoral Hotel) completed in 1902. The building on the extreme left is Robert Adam's Register House begun in 1774. To the right of it is the original North British Station Hotel with the offices of the East Coast Railway Companies and the Midland Railway on the ground floor. The single storey building in the centre of the picture is Cook's Tourist Office with a 'New Route to England'. On the right is the rear view of several business premises on North Bridge: D. M. Dunlop, the hatter at No. 64; Scottish Property Investment Company at No. 62; and Liptons, the provision merchant at No. 59.

Scott Monument

This early view of the Scott Monument was taken c. 1850, a decade after the foundation stone was laid on 15th August 1840, at the 69th anniversary of Scott's birthday. The monument, a Gothic extravaganza in Binny sandstone by George Meikle Kemp, rises 200 feet above ground level and sits on a solid rock foundation 52 feet below Princes Street. In addition to the principal statue of Sir Walter Scott seated with his favourite dog, Maida, there are sculptures of 16 Scottish poets, including Burns, Fergusson, Hogg and Ramsay, and 64 statuettes in various niches representing characters from Scott's novels. In 1990 a long awaited programme of stone-cleaning and renovation was considered but delayed pending further reports. Whatever happens the cleaning is not likely to affect the words of Lord Jeffrey buried deep in the foundation stone:

THIS GRAVEN PLATE

Deposited in the Base of a Votive Building
On the fifteenth day of August, in the Year of Christ 1840,
And never likely to see the light again
Till all the surrounding structures are crumbled to dust
By the decay of time or by human or elemental violence,
May then testify to a distant posterity that
His Countrymen began on that day
To raise an Effigy and Architectural Monument

TO THE MEMORY OF SIR WALTER SCOTT, BART.

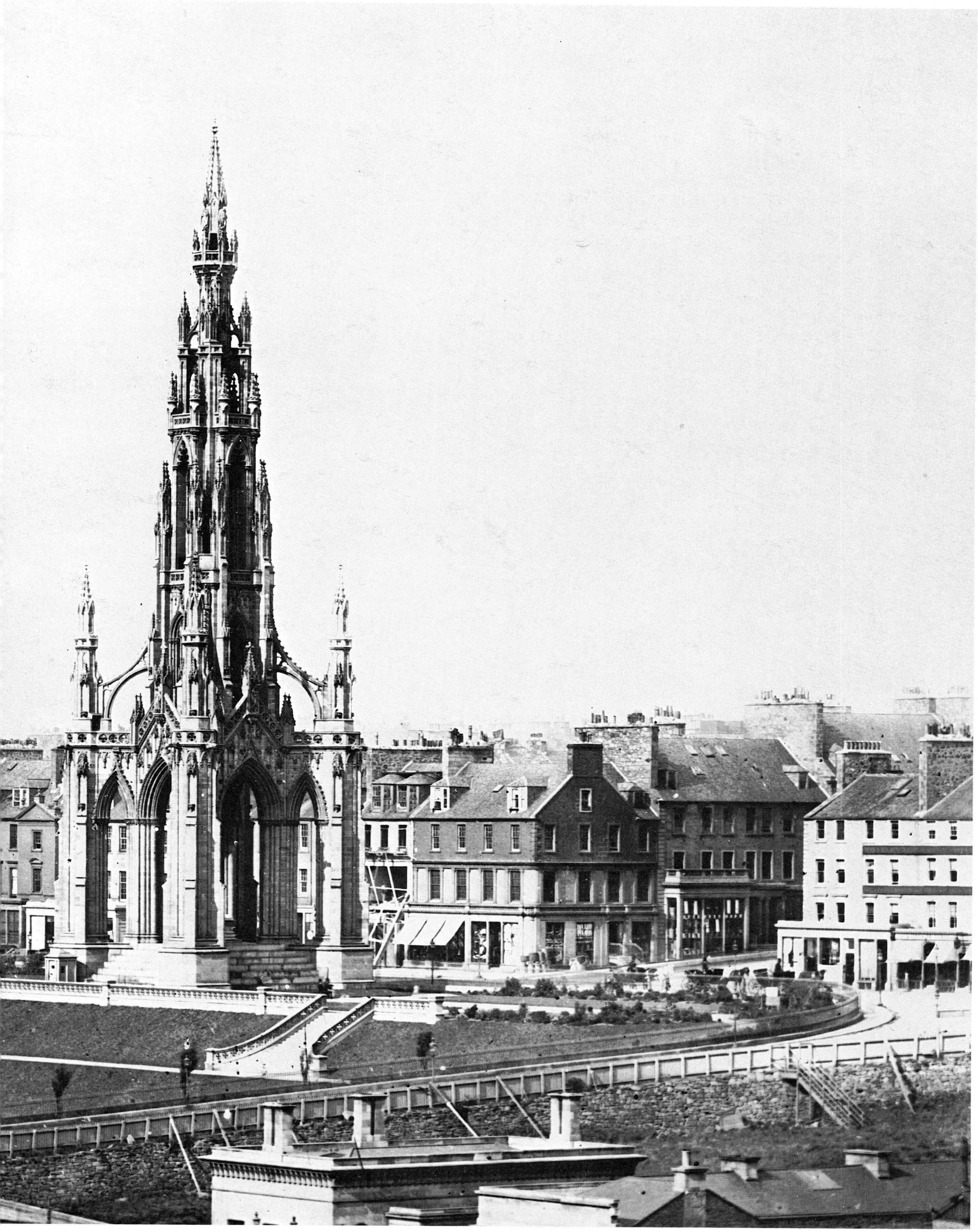

Princes Street Looking West from the Scott Monument

From the Scott Monument the view westward along Princes Street, *c.* 1880, closed with the single spire of St Mary's Episcopal Cathedral in Melville Street, the smaller west spires being added between 1913 and 1917. On the north side of Princes Street, nearest to the camera, is the Royal Hotel; the photographic studio of James Howie Junior; Romanes and Paterson; John Dickson & Son, gun makers; and the North British Insurance Co. To the west of the junction with Hanover Street is Thornton & Co., 'waterproof, airproof and India rubber manufacturers', and the Life Association of Scotland.

The Mound

The Mound has always been a challenge to public transport, particularly for a fully laden cable car *c.* 1904 hooked precariously to the central running cable — which had a tendency to fail suddenly.

The art galleries have changed little in appearance over the years, other than from the effects of stone cleaning to remove decades of railway grime. In fact, the building at the foot of the Mound (now the Royal Scottish Academy) was first designed in 1822 by William H. Playfair and was greatly extended by him in 1831. The gallery nearest to the camera is the National Gallery of Scotland, also by Playfair, completed in 1850 after several design alterations.

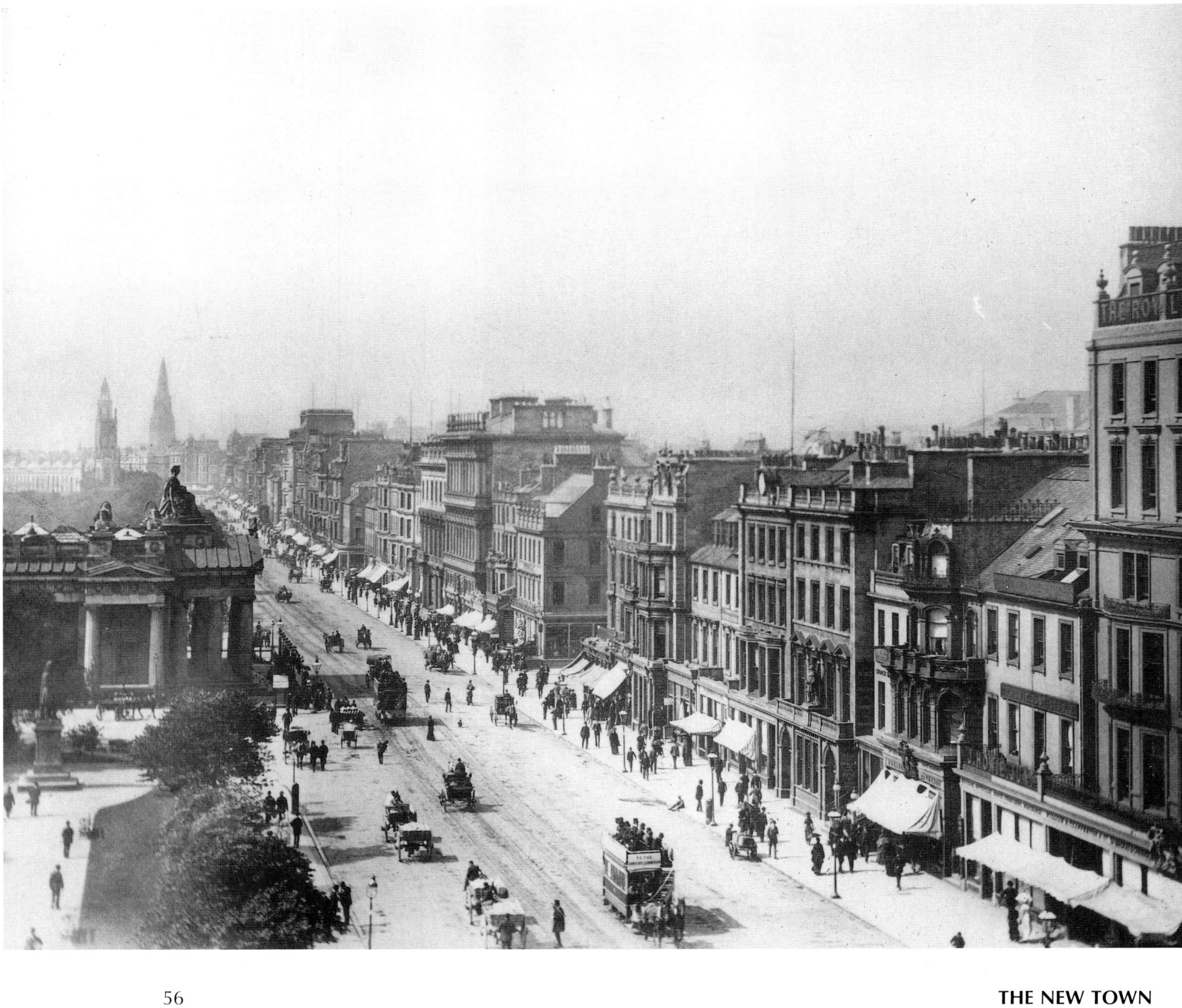

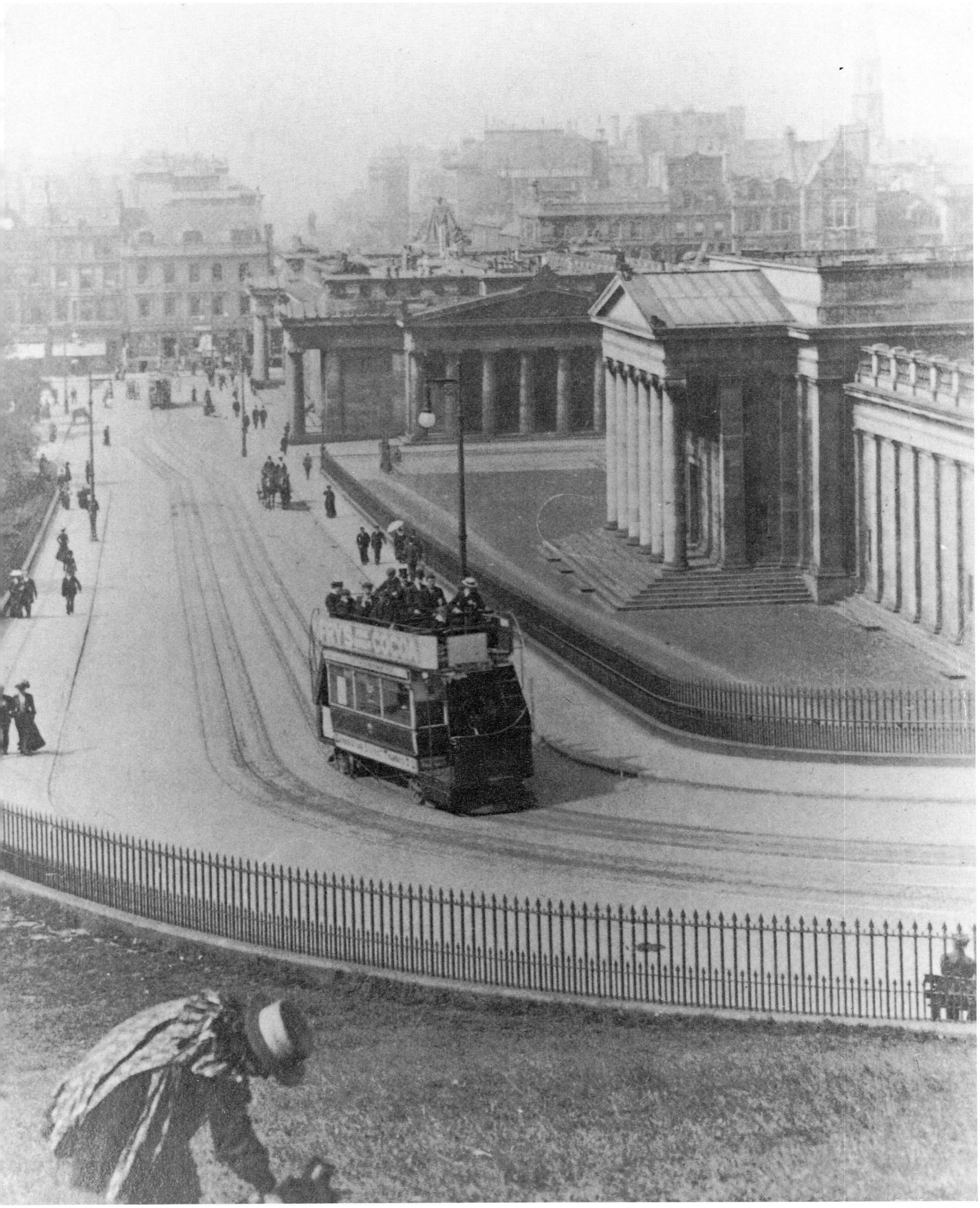
FRY'S COCOA

Edinburgh Castle and Princes Street Gardens

This panoramic view, from the Bank of Scotland, of Edinburgh Castle and Princes Street Gardens in the 1950s looks almost timeless (apart from the available parking spaces). It could yet be altered dramatically if a recent proposal is ever implemented to build an amphitheatre for the Edinburgh Military Tattoo on the sloping rough grass area in the centre of the picture.

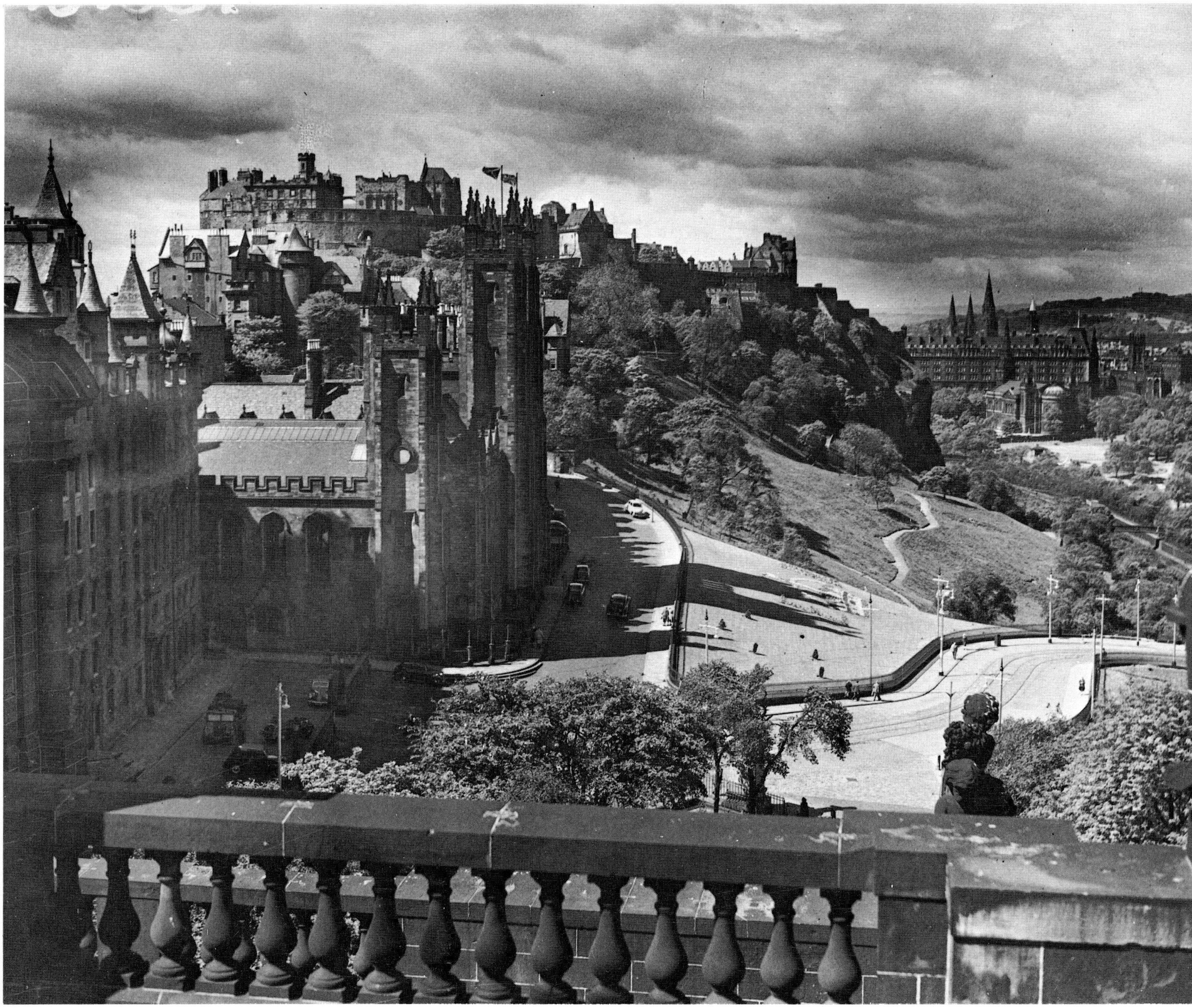

The Royal Institution

This Doric masterpiece by William H. Playfair, now the Royal Scottish Academy, was built between 1822 and 1826, and then extended in 1831. It is shown here with an imposing decorative obelisk flanked by open columns on each side. A similar arrangement, probably intended for one of the Royal visits, can be seen on the right of the picture at the foot of the mound.

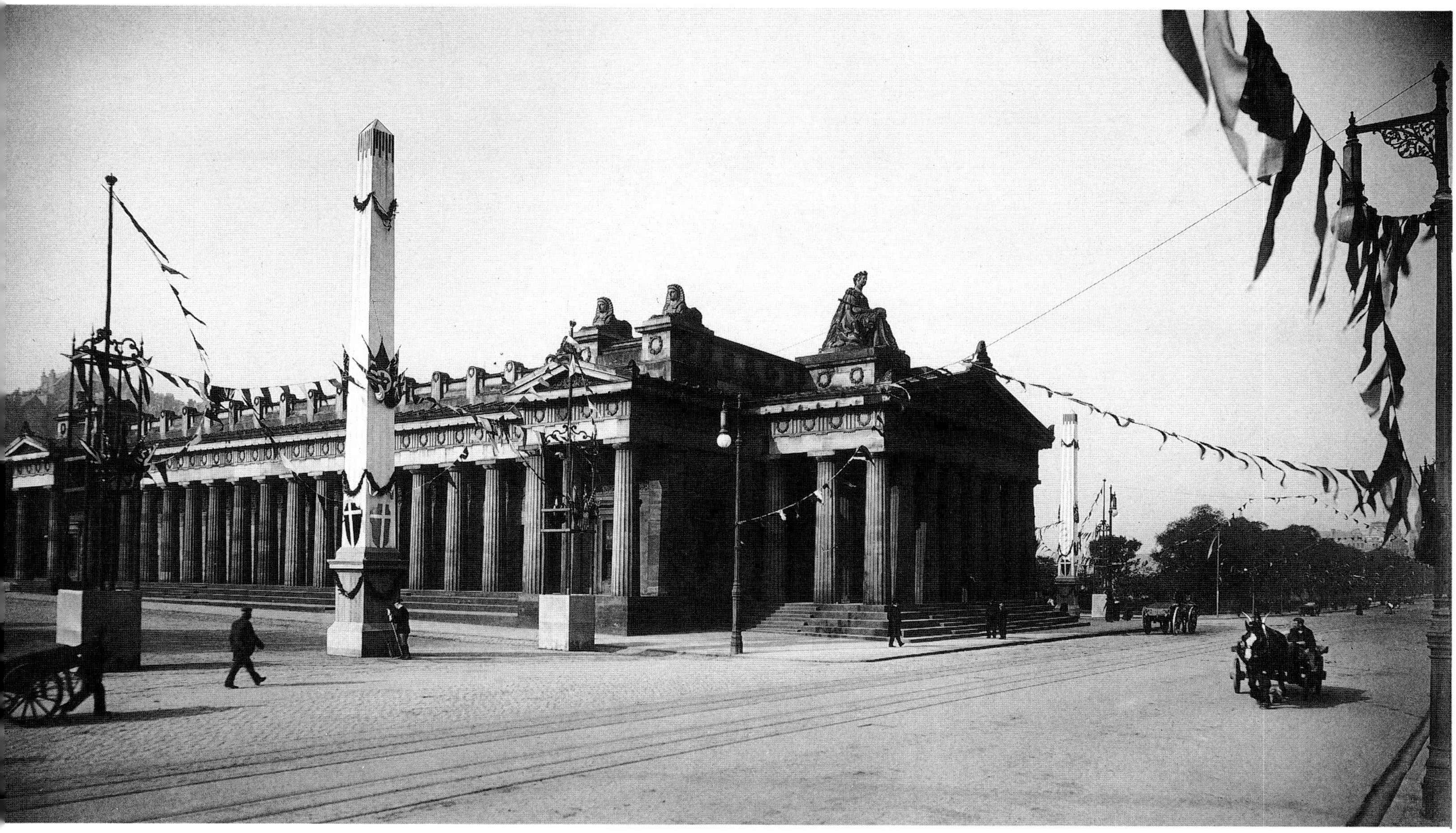

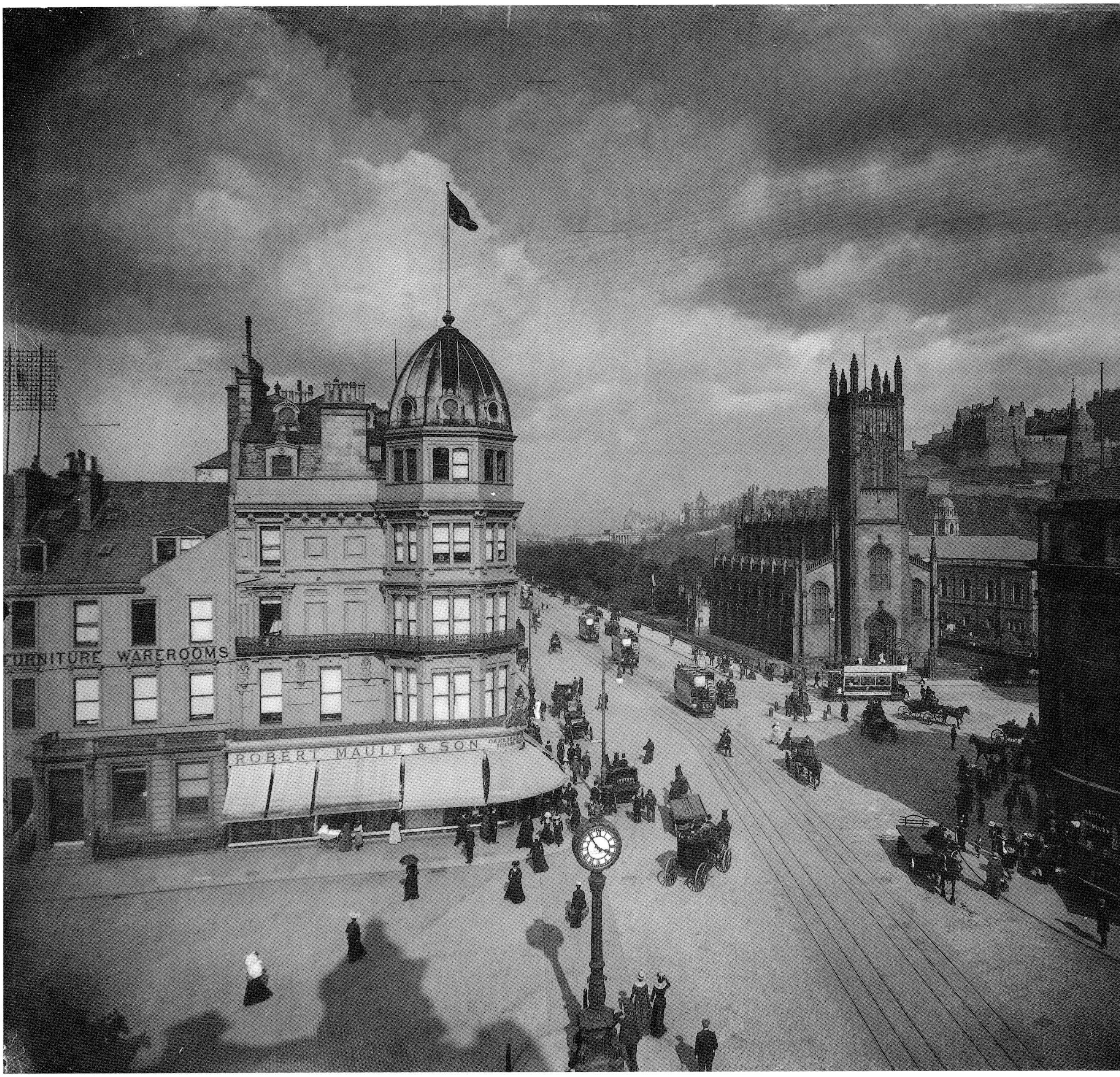
FURNITURE WAREROOMS
ROBERT MAULE & SON

Maule's Corner

This distinctive and instantly recognisable view of the West End of Princes Street was photographed *c.* 1902 — at six minutes to four. Maule's were furnishers, drapers and removal contractors, whose corner site was later occupied by Binns and then Frasers. After several traffic experiments in the late 1950s and early 1960s the West End clock was moved to its present position in Leith Walk. The two main churches, St John's and St Cuthbert's, are as yet uncluttered by overgrown trees. However, the roofline and skyline are beginning to bear the brunt of the telephone era, before the lines were put underground. In true West-End fashion the corner shop on the right advertises on the window 'fruits and primeurs'.

St John's and St Cuthbert's

This photograph, taken *c.* 1903, shows St John's Episcopal Church and St Cuthbert's Parish Church, with Edinburgh Castle and the spire of the Tolbooth Church in the background. In Princes Street the upper floors of many of the buildings have not altered greatly, but at pavement level the scene is quite different to the present day. Public transport is by open-topped cable cars run by Edinburgh and District Tramways Co. Ltd.

St John's Episcopal Church, designed by William Burn, was built between 1815 and 1818, and St Cuthbert's Parish Church was re-designed by Hippolyte J. Blanc between 1892 and 1895, retaining the steeple of the former church on the same site.

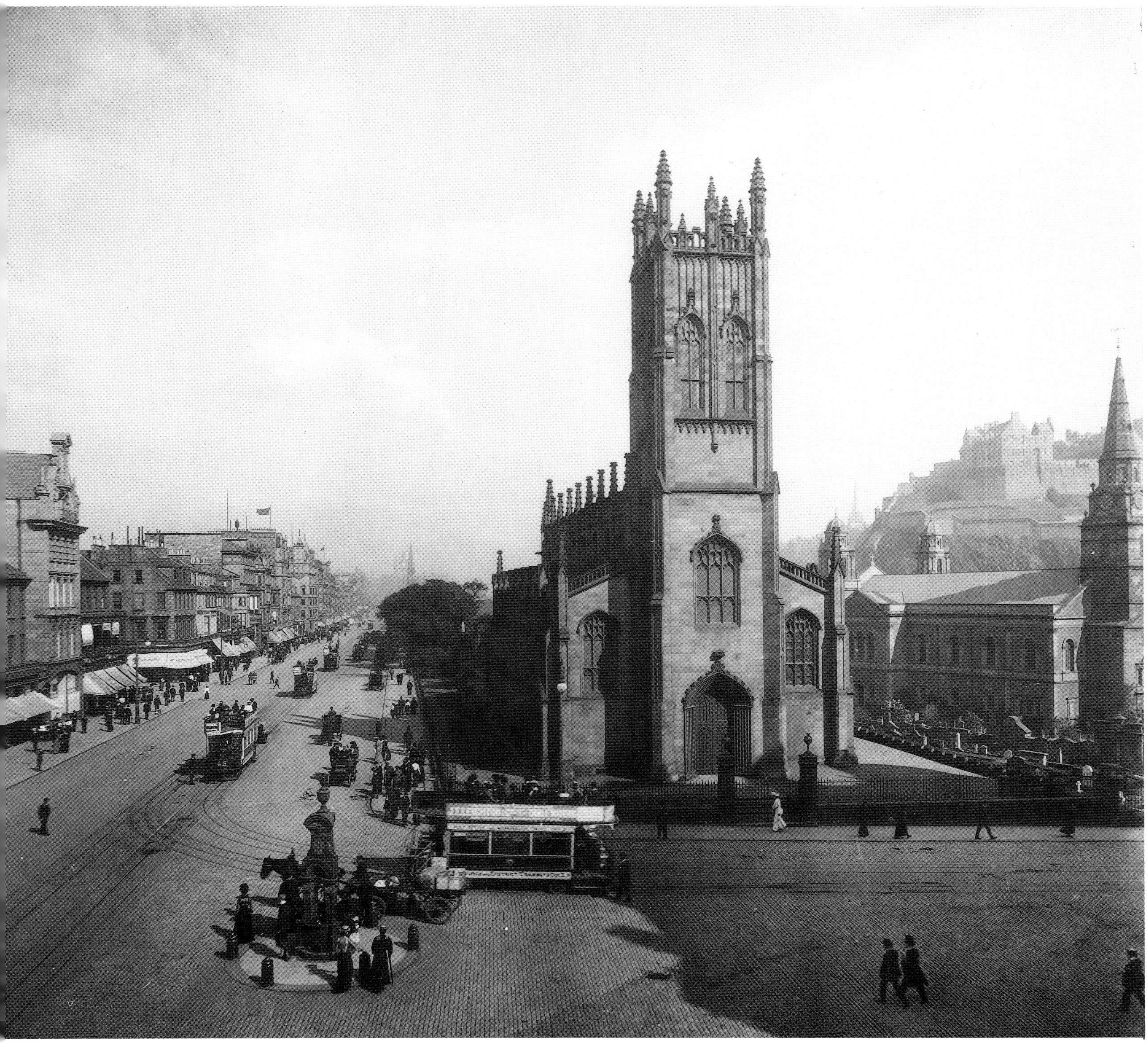

St Cuthbert's Parish Church Bell

An historic occasion captured at the raising of the tenor bell at St Cuthbert's Parish Church in 1902. The bell, cast at Loughborough, bears the inscription 'James MacGregor D.D., and A. Wallace Williamson D.D., Ministers of St. Cuthberts 1901'. The group includes, from left to right:

John MacDonald (Caretaker) — Mr Rankine (Beadle) — Mr Wood (Beadle)

Dr J. MacGregor — Dr Wallace Williamson

Archibald Ballantine (Artist) — Mrs Wallace Williamson — Hippolyte J. Blanc (Architect)

West End

The era of the motor car is beginning to make itself evident at the West End, although the traffic policeman still has time to include a pedestrian phase. The photograph is not dated, but the absence of the railings around St John's Episcopal Church places the photograph after 1940 but probably not after 1945. The newsboard on the corner reads 'Scots Double Tragedy'.

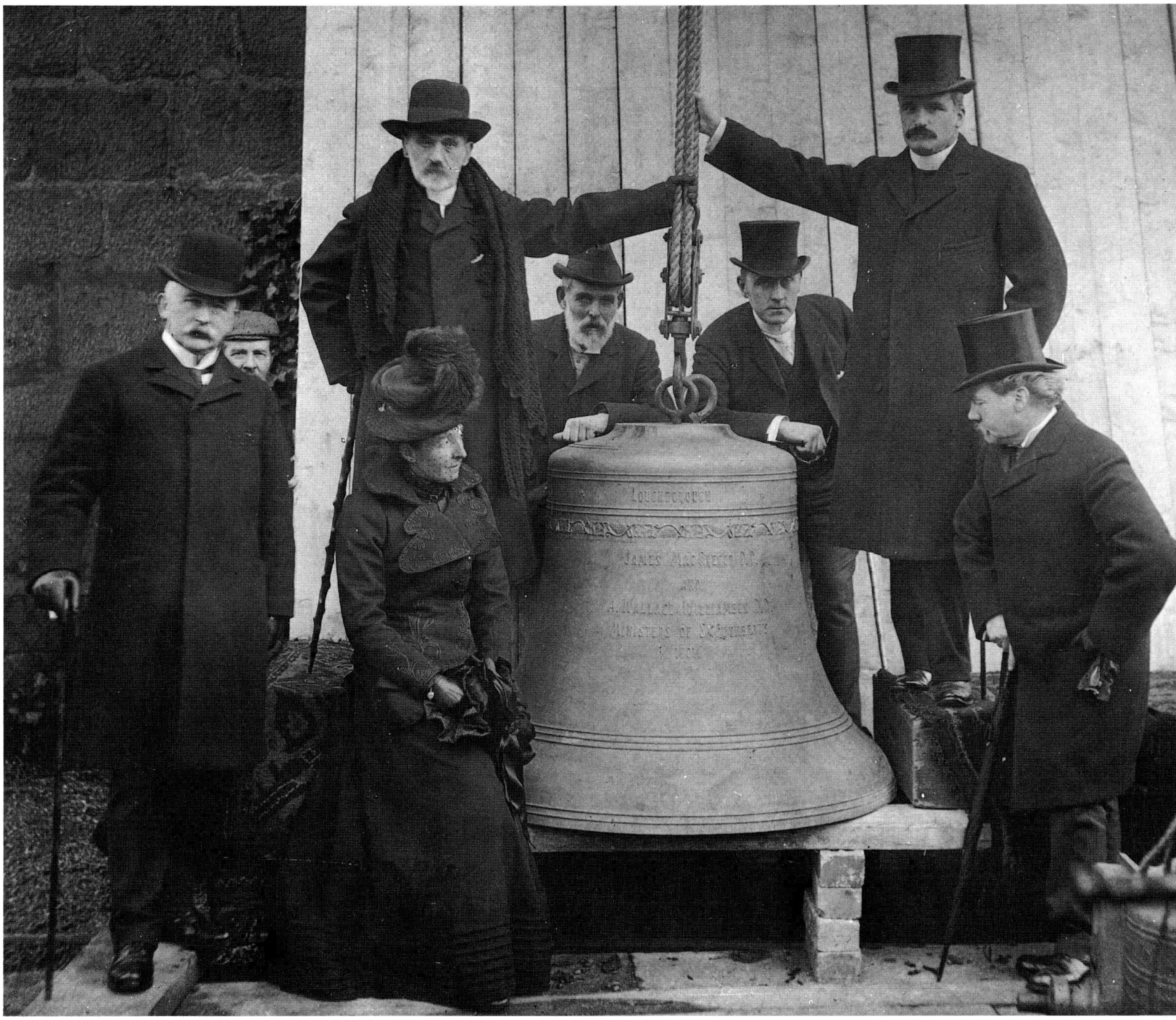

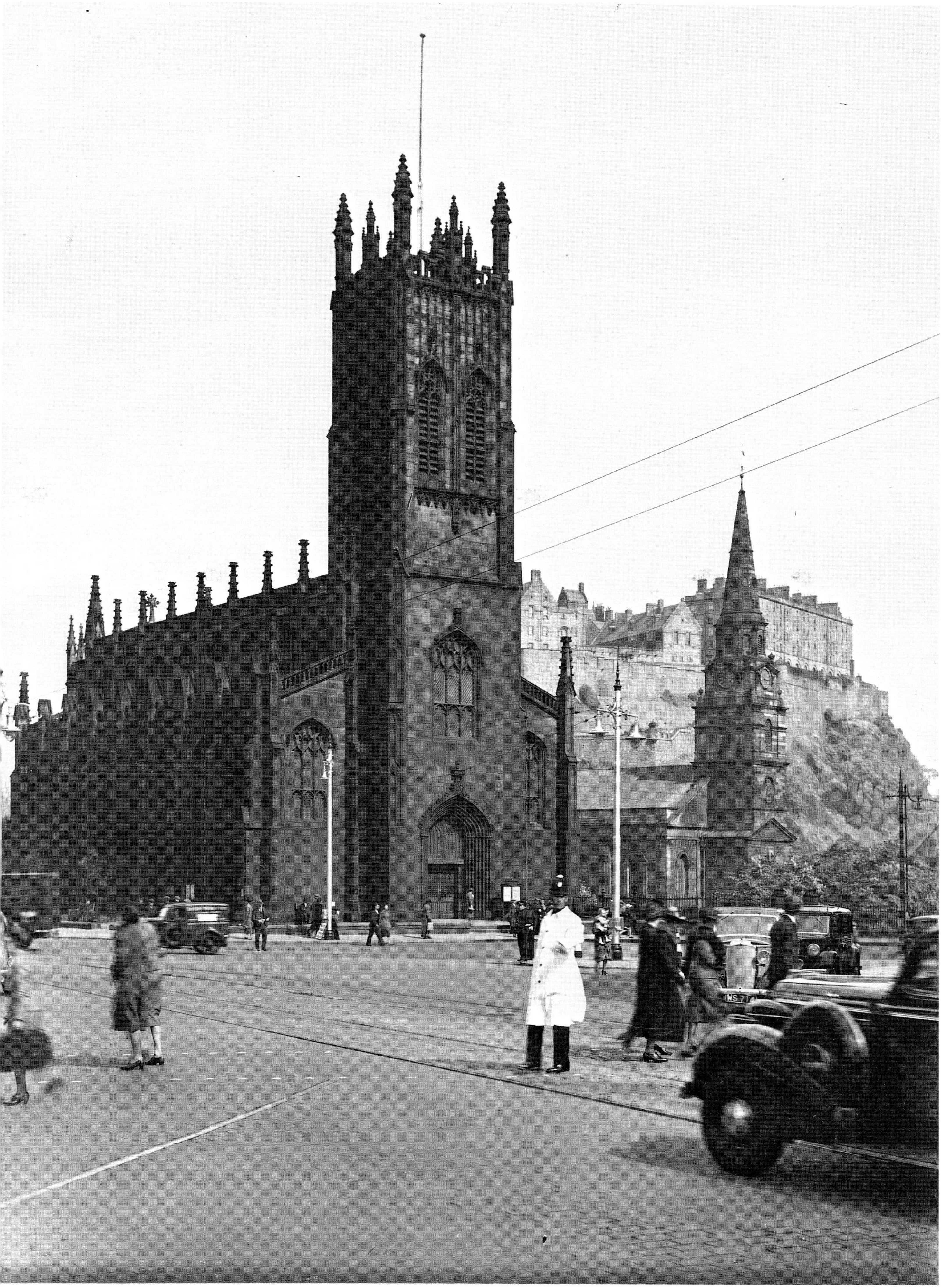

CHAPTER 4

George Watson's College

George Watson was born in 1654, the son of an Edinburgh merchant who died relatively young, leaving his family in a difficult financial position. When his mother remarried, George and his younger brother were looked after by an aunt. After visiting Holland to further his education, George returned to Edinburgh where he obtained an appointment with a prosperous merchant. During his lifetime he amassed a large fortune, and on his death, in 1723, he left £12,000 to found 'a hospital or charitable foundation school for the sons and grandsons of decayed merchants'. The first Hospital was opened in 1741, but the building was swallowed up by the new Edinburgh Royal Infirmary in Lauriston Place. In 1871 Watson's moved to the former Merchant Maiden Hospital at the foot of Archibald Place. The photograph shows this building *c.* 1911, retaining William Burn's original façade, but with the addition of new towers and wings added between 1883 and 1885. In 1932 the College moved from Archibald Place to Colinton Road, and amalgamated with George Watson's Ladies' College in 1974.

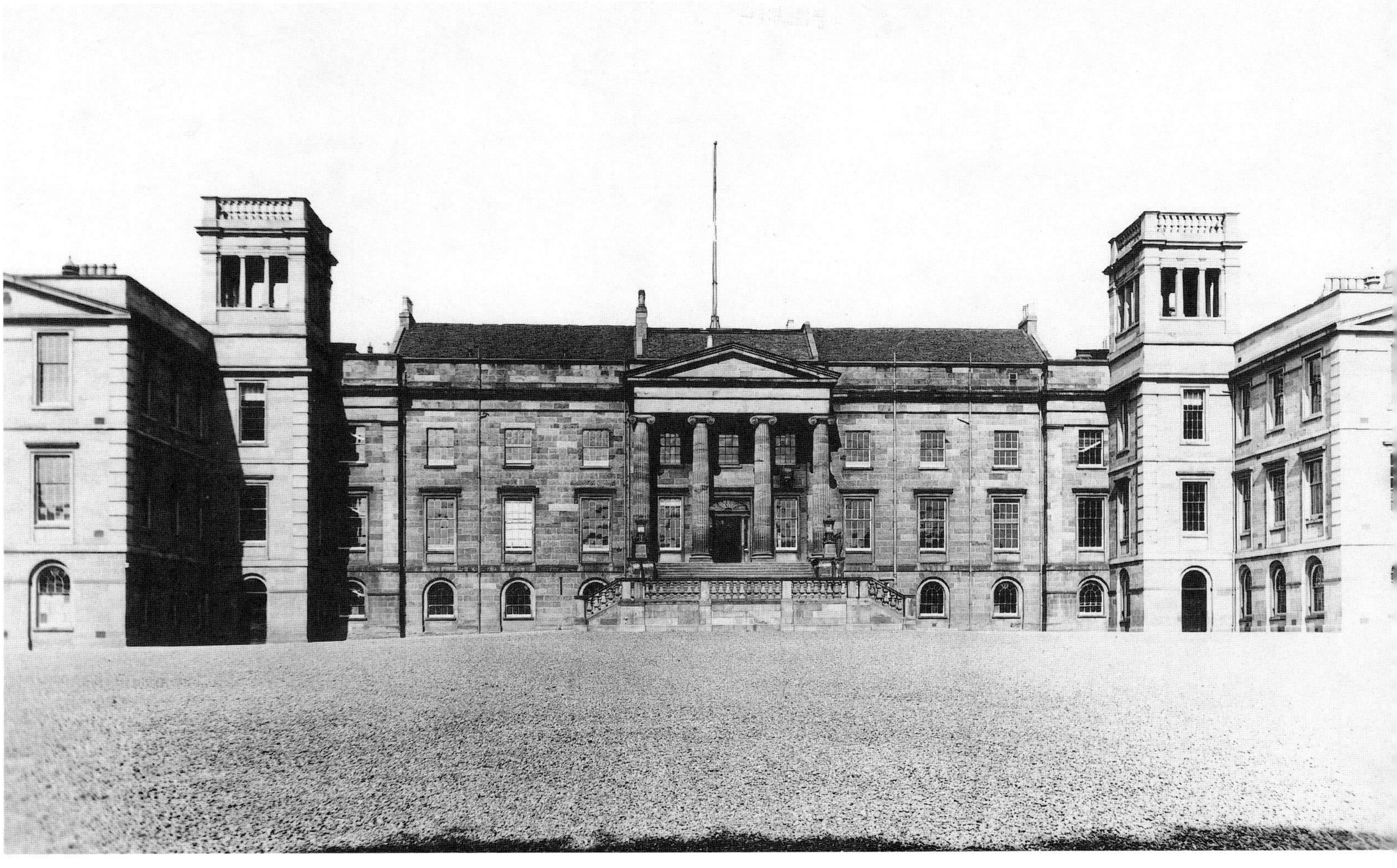

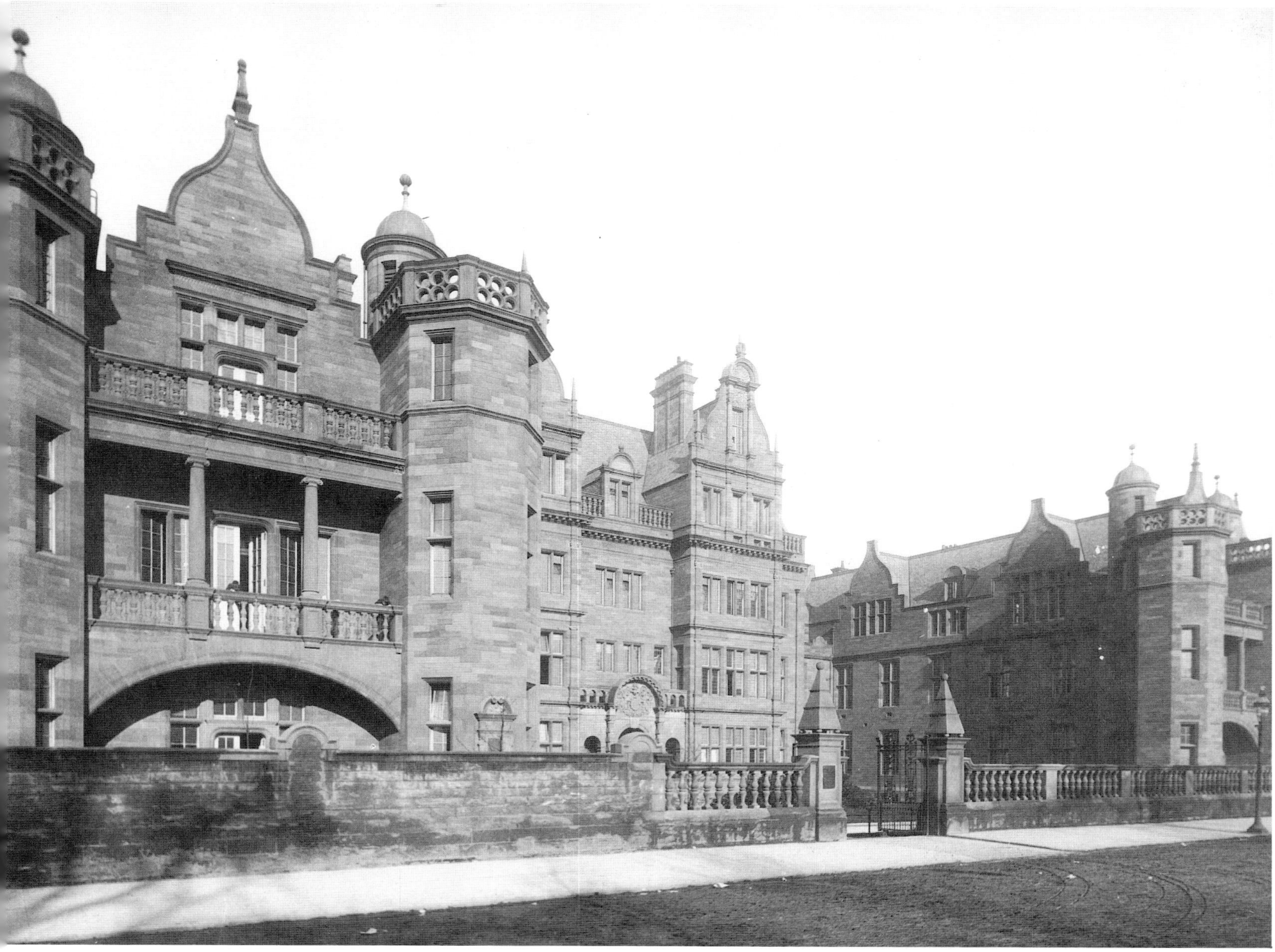

The Royal Edinburgh Hospital for Sick Children, Sciennes Road

The Royal Edinburgh Hospital for Sick Children owes its origins to a public meeting held in the Freemasons' Hall in George Street on 5th May 1859. The first hospital was opened at No. 7 Lauriston Lane on 15th February 1860, and was transferred to Meadowside House nearby on 18th May 1863. Royal Patronage was granted by Queen Victoria a few weeks prior to the 1863 opening. The third hospital (excluding the temporary move to Plewlands House at Morningside) was at Sciennes, built on the site of Rillbank House, previously used as the Trades Maiden Hospital. The Sciennes Road building, designed by George Washington Browne, was opened on 31st October 1895, with the assistance of a large donation from Lady Jane Dundas in memory of her sister Lady Caroline Charteris.

The Hospital has remained at the forefront of new development and teaching methods in the treatment of child ailments for more than a century.

The photograph, *c.* 1900, shows Browne's original south-facing façade with the open balconies (later enclosed) and the Lady Charteris Memorial stone (showing above the boundary wall) at the base of the right-hand tower of the west wing.

Hatton Place, The Grange

Hatton Place was built on the northern edge of the Grange Estate with large family houses instead of the flatted dwellings and shops envisaged by Robert Reid Raeburn's Feuing Plan of 1864. The north-west corner was reserved for Argyle Place United Presbyterian Church, designed in 1878 by Alexander McTavish and destroyed by fire in 1974.

The photograph shows the church officer's house and the church hall. Handsome street lighting *c.* 1900 is evident and the entrances to Lovers' Loan can be seen on each side of the road where the telephone pole stands.

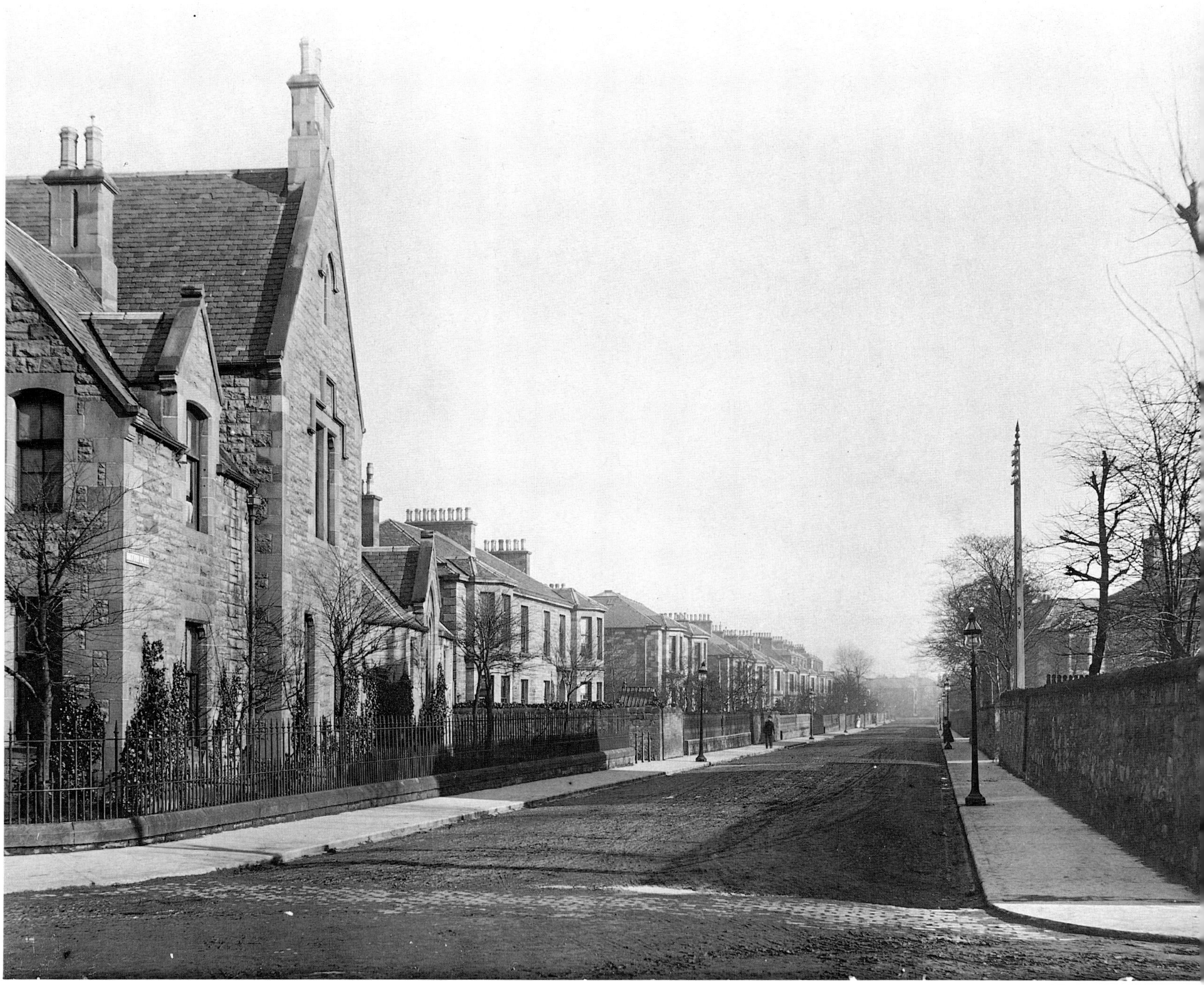

Grange Loan Toll House

This picture, probably more than any other from the early days of photography, shows the character of Grange Loan c. 1850. The toll stood at the east extremity of the Grange House policies, which were bounded by the high stone wall showing on the left of the picture. Immediately adjacent to it a small lane ran northwards to Dick Place. East of this lane, Lauder Road was in the process of construction with a few houses already planned, notably St Andrews Cottage which was completed in 1852.

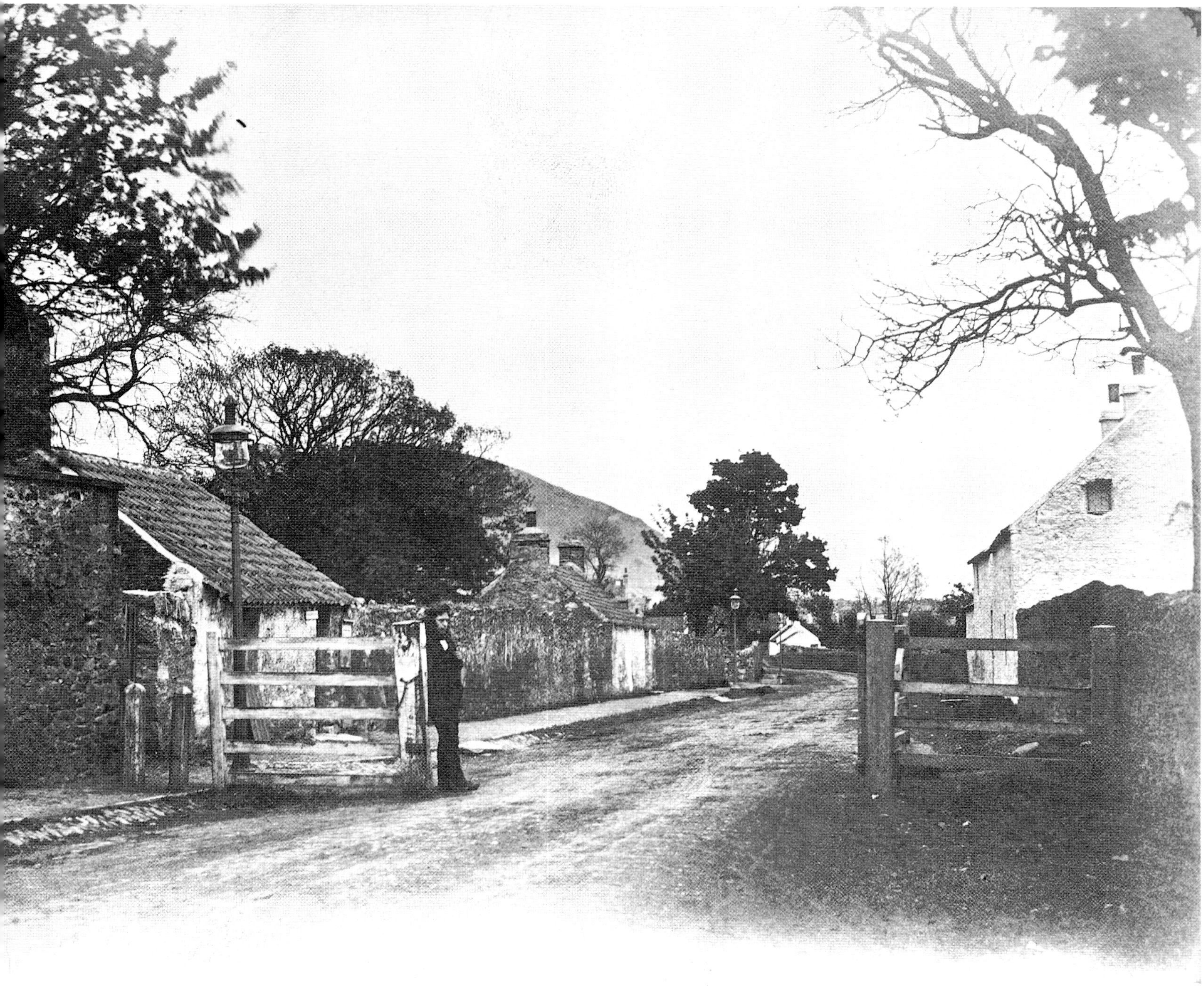

Grange Loan, at the Entrance to Grange House

The sixteenth-century Grange House was transformed into an elegant mansion around 1827 by W. H. Playfair for the owner, Sir Thomas Dick-Lauder. It was Sir Thomas who feued large parts of the estate for the construction of the Grange district. Grange House was demolished in 1936 along with the lodge-house seen on the right of the picture.

Looking west along Grange Loan, the entrance to Lovers' Loan can be seen on the right-hand pavement, opposite the lamp standard, and Carlton Cricket Club ground is behind the high stone wall. The left-hand pavement breaks for St Thomas Road which had plots of land still to feu when the photograph was taken in 1900. Beyond the 'To Feu' sign is the outline of the Artesian Well, and West Grange lodge-house protruding into the roadway.

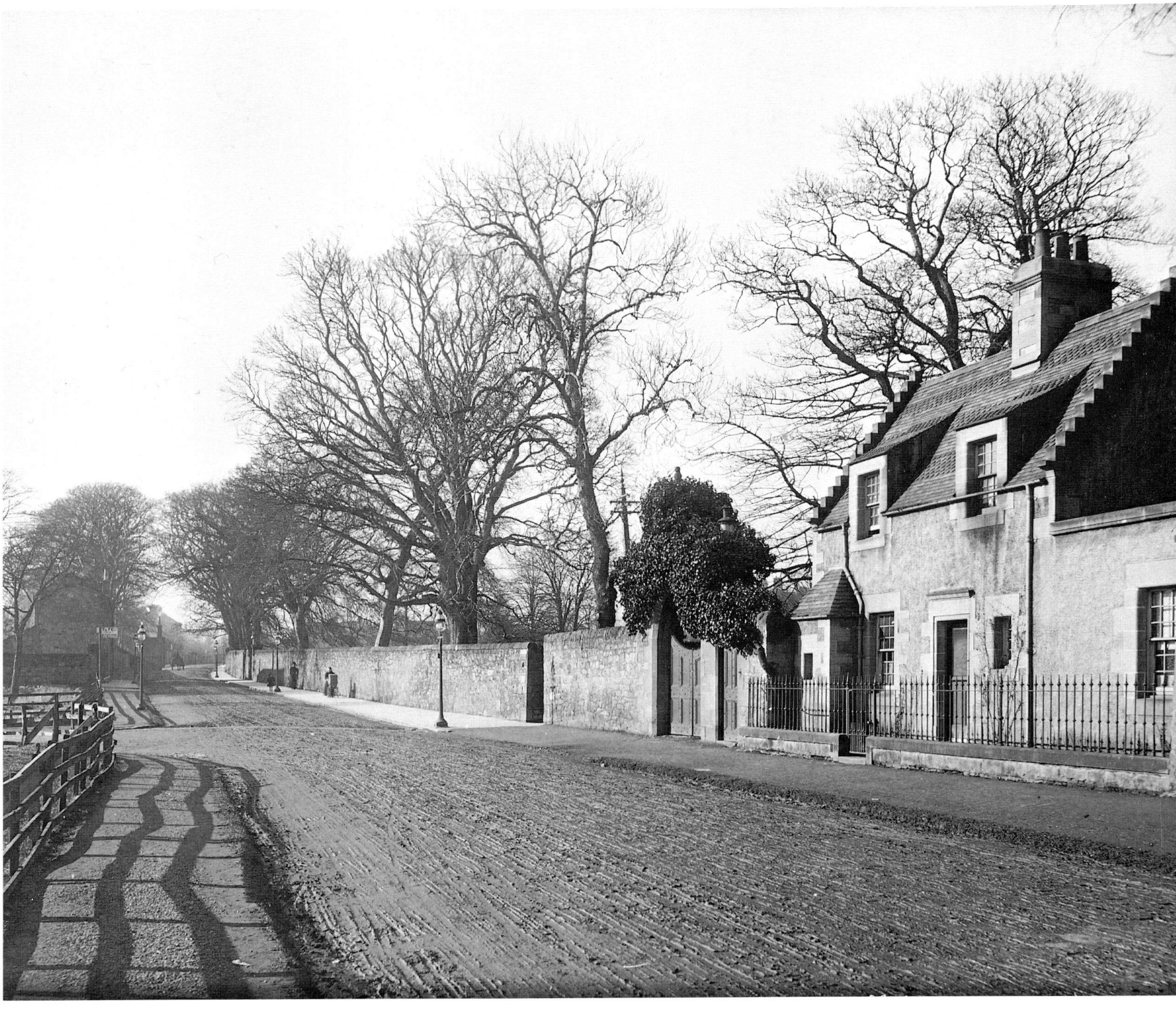

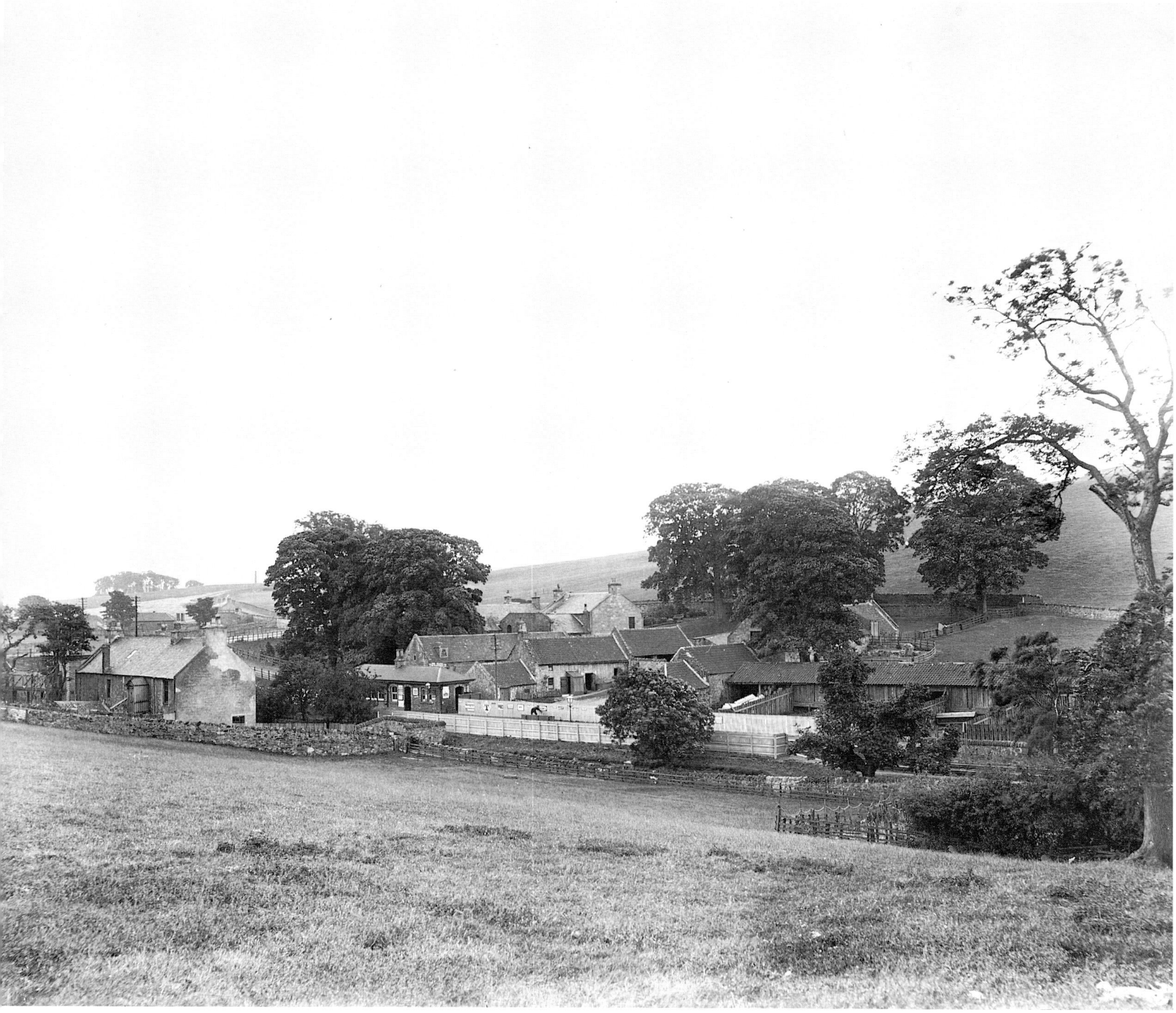

Blackford Hill Station

Blackford Station was opened as part of the suburban railway constructed in 1884 by Sir Thomas Bouch, who also designed the ill-fated Tay Bridge. The station and track separated Blackford Farmhouse from the steadings which lay at the junction of Charterhall Road and Blackford Avenue. The only surviving building is Blackford Farmhouse shown on the left of the picture, taken in 1900. The station building, platform, advertisements and a railway employee can be seen in the centre of the photograph.

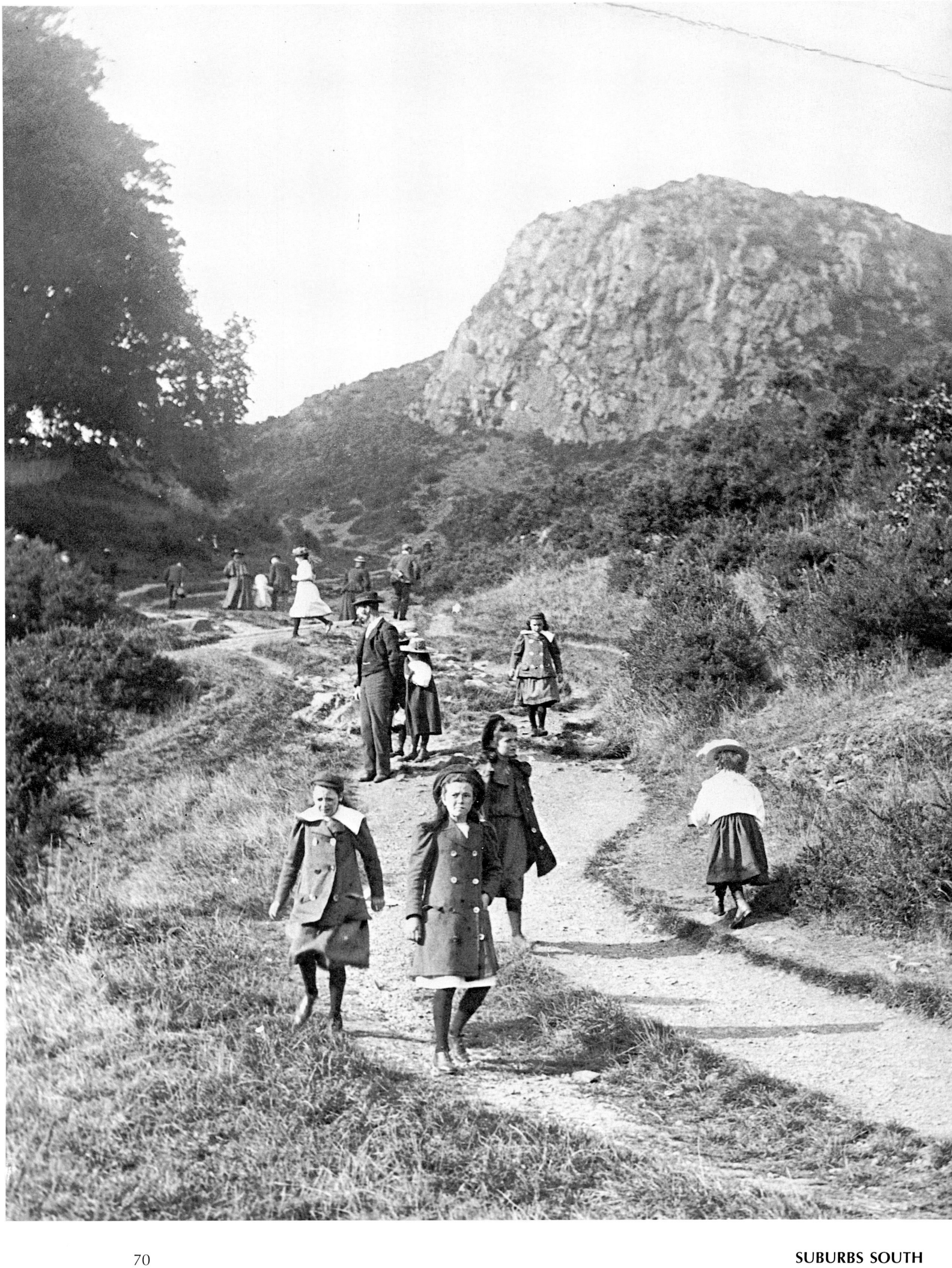

Blackford Hill

The hill path, between the east end of Hermitage of Braid and Corbie's Craig, attracted walkers of all ages in the 1880s. The photograph was probably taken shortly after Blackford Hill was opened to the citizens of Edinburgh in 1884. It was acquired by Edinburgh Town Council from the Trotters of Mortonhall for the sum of £8,000. An arch was erected on 12th September 1888 in Observatory Road to commemorate the event, and the work of Lord Provost Harrison in acquiring Blackford Hill for the public.

Photographers at Blackford Glen

A group of well-dressed photographers, c. 1900, relaxes at Blackford Glen, after logging up a few more hours carrying fairly bulky equipment. Unfortunately the identity of the photographers has not been established. The photograph appears to have been taken near Blackford Quarry, not far from the Agassiz Rock, an interesting geological feature, named after Louis Agassiz, the Swiss geologist.

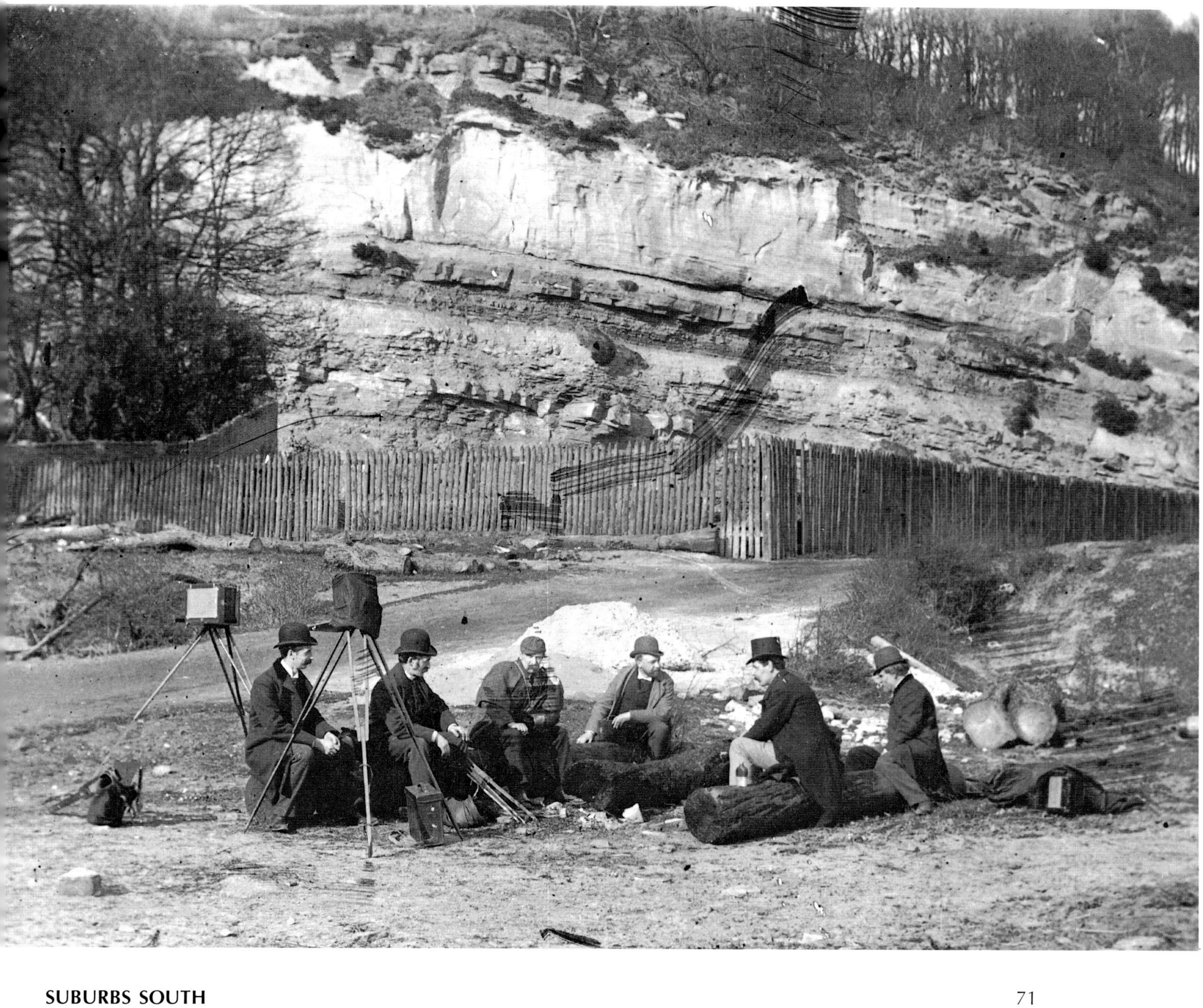

O'Hagan the Grocer

Despite the long-established look of the shop at No. 104 Morningside Road (previously No. 13 or 15 Marmion Terrace), Mr O'Hagan does not appear to have been the proprietor for very long, probably only for a few years in the early 1900s. The shop was taken over by Henry Blanche, the fruiterer, in 1906 and was still operating as Blanche's Fruit Bazaar in the late 1960s. There is evidence in the photograph that graffiti were as much a problem in 1900 as they are today.

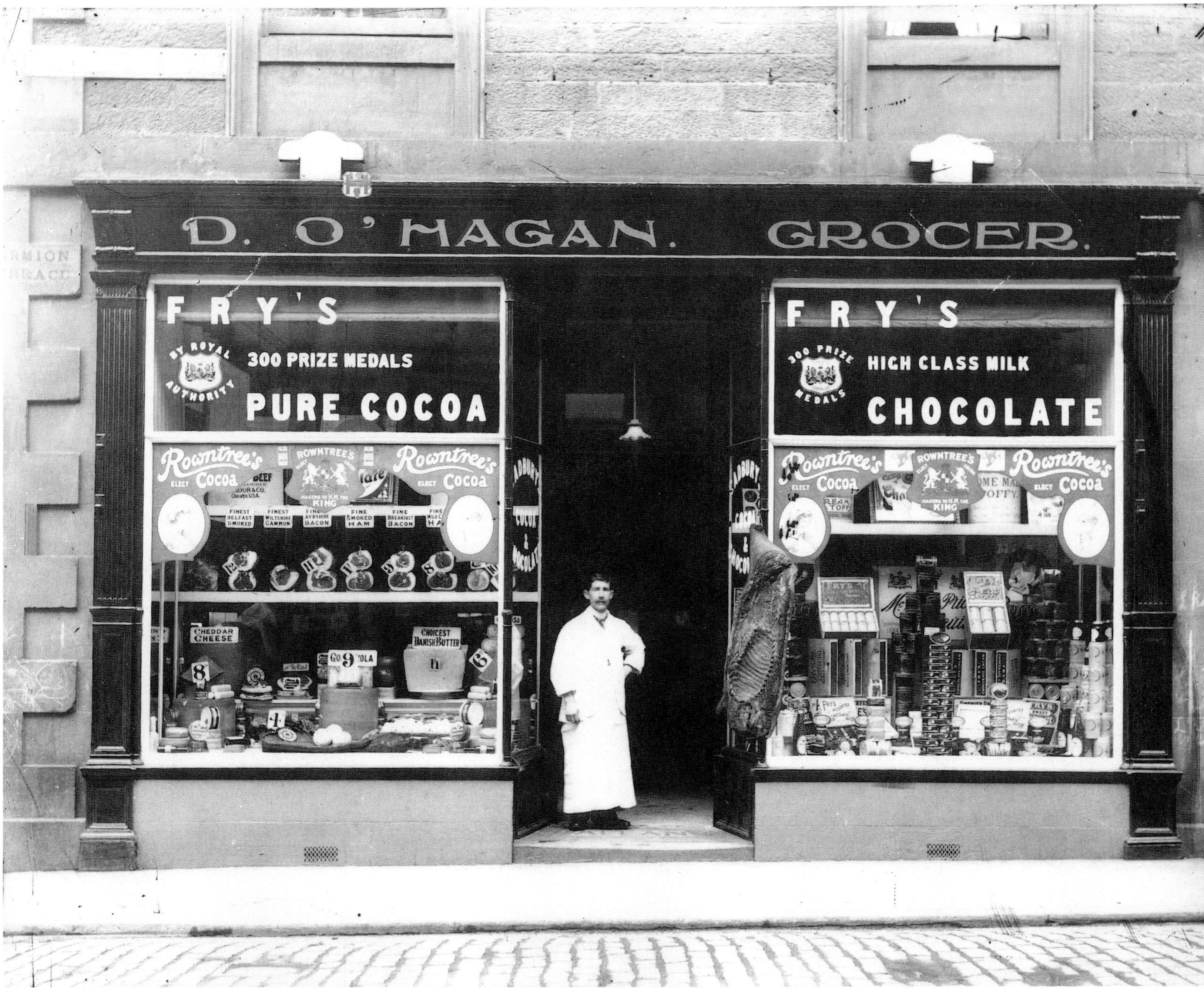

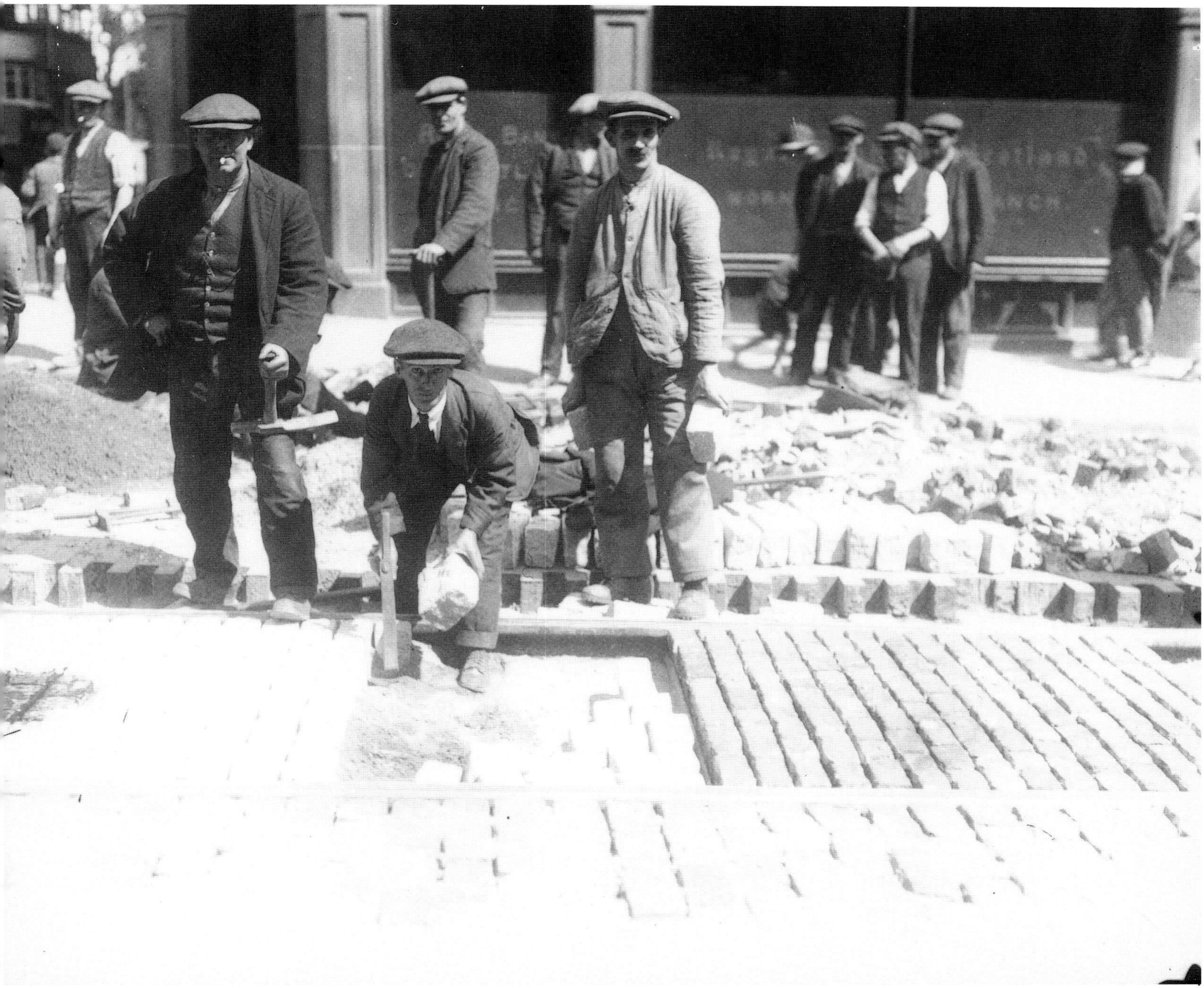

Navvies at Church Hill

Navvies at work laying granite setts between the tram rails in Morningside Road. When properly laid, the setts shed rainwater into the tram rails which acted like mini-gutters. The setts were not, however, popular with modern transport, especially when maintenance of the tram rails was at a low ebb in the early 1950s. The corner premises at Church Hill, shown in the photograph, are still occupied by the Royal Bank of Scotland.

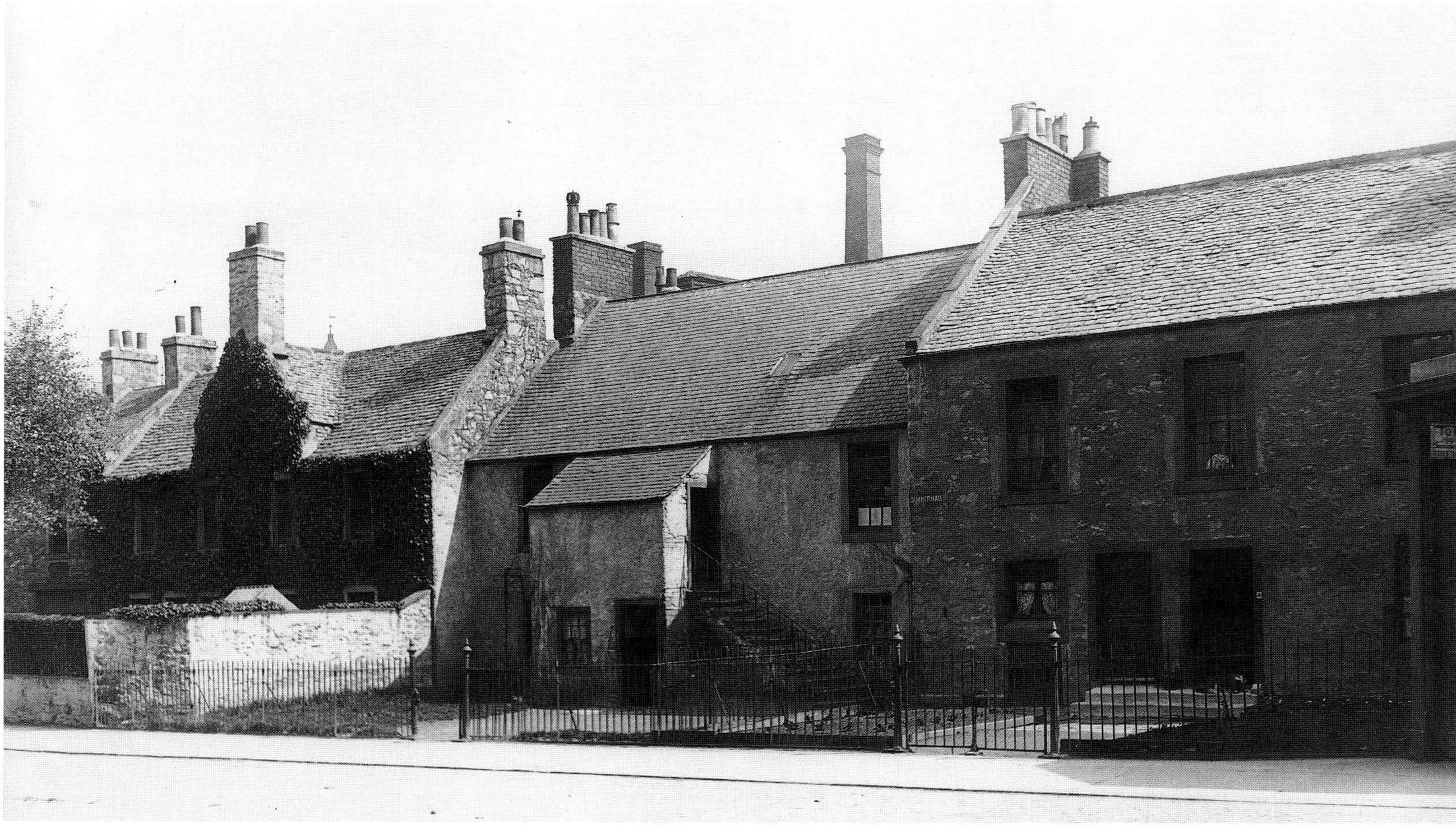

Summerhall

This short row of houses, c. 1900, stood at Summerhall at the east end of Melville Drive until around 1913, when the houses were demolished to make way for the construction of the Royal Dick Veterinary College. The doorway on the extreme right of the picture shows the name of the previous proprietor, J. Miller, Cabinetmaker, and a 'To Let' sign directs enquiries to Summer Hall Brewery. The entrance to the brewery, owned latterly by Edinburgh United Breweries Ltd., was off the picture to the left, but its high square brick chimney can be seen above the roofline of the centre cottage.

Causewayside at Sciennes Place

This short section of Causewayside at its junction with Sciennes Place was demolished many years ago and lay semi-derelict before being used by Bertrams and then developed in recent years for modern housing. The profusion of shop advertisements in this photograph, and in another glass negative made around the same time, gives some idea of the retail trade flourishing in Causewayside in 1900. The shop on the left of the picture, dealing in hay and straw, was run by Robert Stewart the corn merchant. James Hart's funeral office offered the use of a national telephone with local calls at one penny. Charles Carter, the electric light and power engineer, turned his hand to almost anything for bicycles: the New Departure Coaster Hub; Sturmey Archer 3-speed gears; cycles for hire; and all kinds of cycle accessories kept in stock.

Mr and Mrs Balmain and the Cycling Party

The house on the east corner of Salisbury Place and Upper Gray Street had a long connection with at least two of Edinburgh's early photographers. James G. Tunny was at South Clerk Street from c. 1850 and later moved to Princes Street and Maitland Street. From 1870 he also had a house/studio at No. 11 Salisbury Place (renumbered 19 in 1887). As early as 1888 J. C. H. Balmain is shown as a photographer with Tunny & Co., and about ten years later he was working from and residing at Nos. 19 and 21 Salisbury Place. The photograph, c. 1898, shows Mr and Mrs Balmain at No. 21 with an American party on a cycling trip. Mrs Balmain is third from the left and Mr Balmain is third from the right. The Longmore Hospital can be seen in the background.

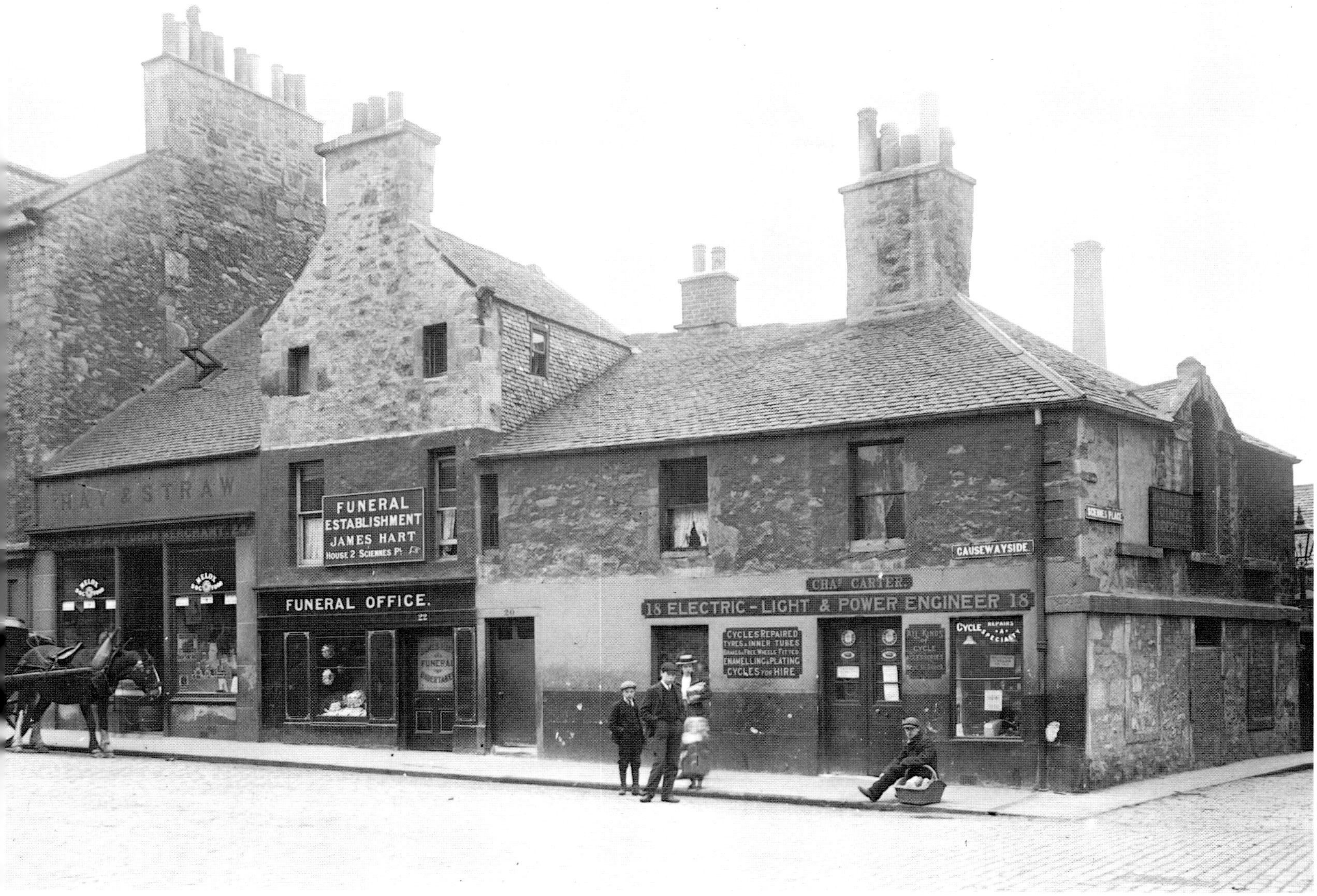
HAY & STRAW
FUNERAL
ESTABLISHMENT
JAMES HART
House 2 Sciennes Pl.
FUNERAL OFFICE.
CAUSEWAYSIDE
CHAs CARTER.
18 ELECTRIC - LIGHT & POWER ENGINEER 18
CYCLES REPAIRED
TYRES & INNER TUBES
ENAMELLING & PLATING
CYCLES FOR HIRE

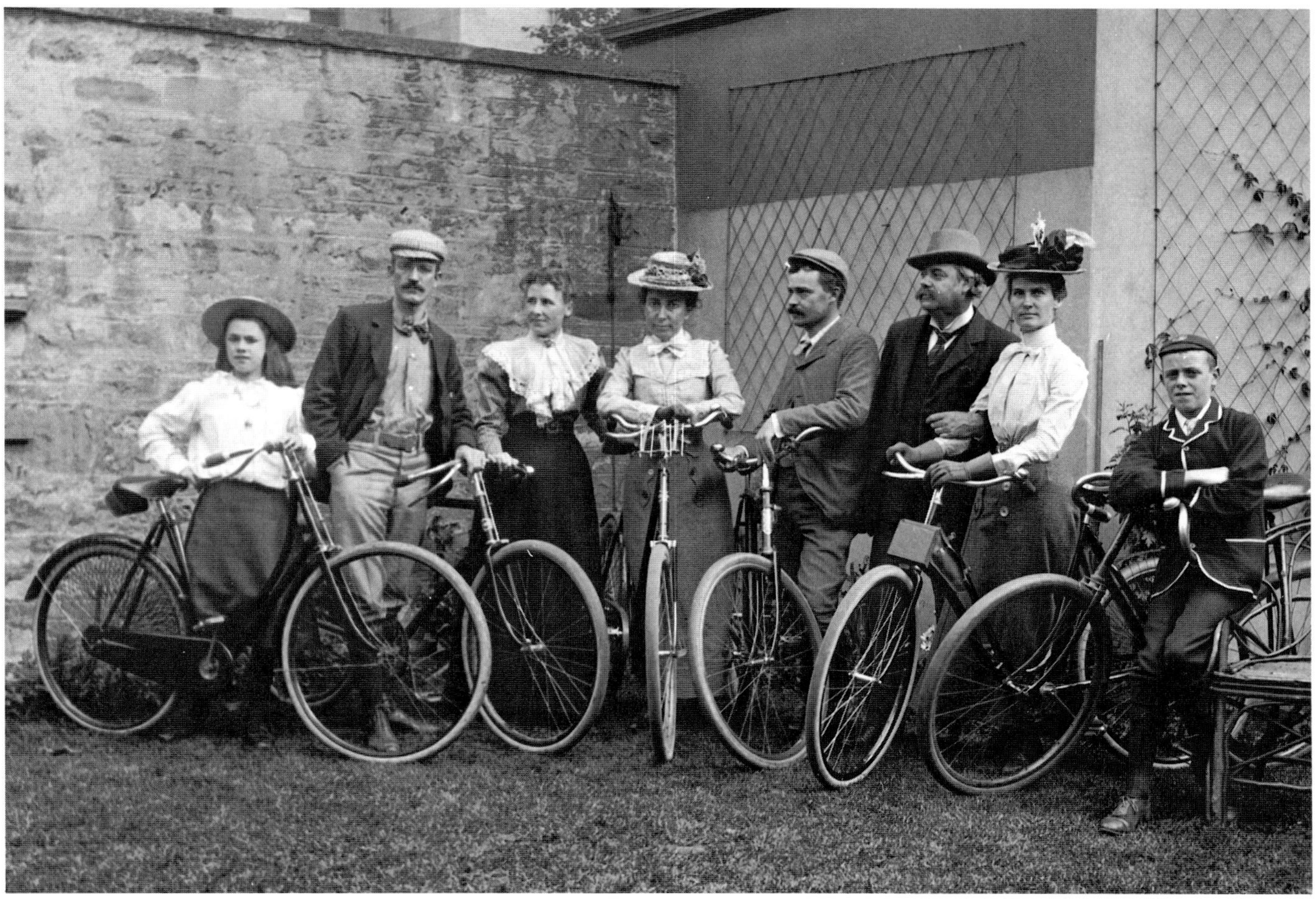

Longmore Hospital, Salisbury Place

In 1877 the Trustees of the late John Alexander Longmore of Deanshaugh made a gift of £10,000 to the Edinburgh Association for Incurables, provided the intended hospital 'should supply accommodation for incurable patients of all classes and at the same time commemorate Mr Longmore's munificent bequest for the relief of such sufferers'. The building was designed by Kinnear and Peddie and was opened on 10th December 1880 by Sir Thomas Jamieson Boyd, Lord Provost of Edinburgh. Over the years the hospital has been extended on numerous occasions and has enjoyed Royal Patronage since the visit of Queen Victoria on 5th November 1886. Following drastic reorganisation of hospital services in Lothian, Longmore has now closed. Currently the building is being renovated as the new headquarters of Historic Scotland.

The photograph shows the original frontage by Kinnear and Peddie, which has remained substantially unaltered to the present day. The street scene is bereft of motor transport, but the cable car rails are clearly visible in the cobbles, and the ornamental lamp standard carries one of the traditional 'Cars Stop' signs.

Causewayside, Nos. 200–208

The last outside stair in Causewayside was photographed in 1900, shortly before it was demolished. The building to the left-hand side of the lamp standard (No. 208) was occupied by Gibson, Mercer & Co., Contractors. The lane, with the name boards over the entrance, gave access to Horsburgh, the general smith and machine maker, and also to Thomas Sanderson, mineral water manufacturers. Opposite the barrow the shop with the shutters (No. 202) was for many years occupied by Mrs Ainslie's sweetie shop. No. 200, the house reached by the outside stair, looks derelict but for the two wee faces at the attic window.

The site was again redeveloped in 1990 as offices, and renamed Kittle Yards.

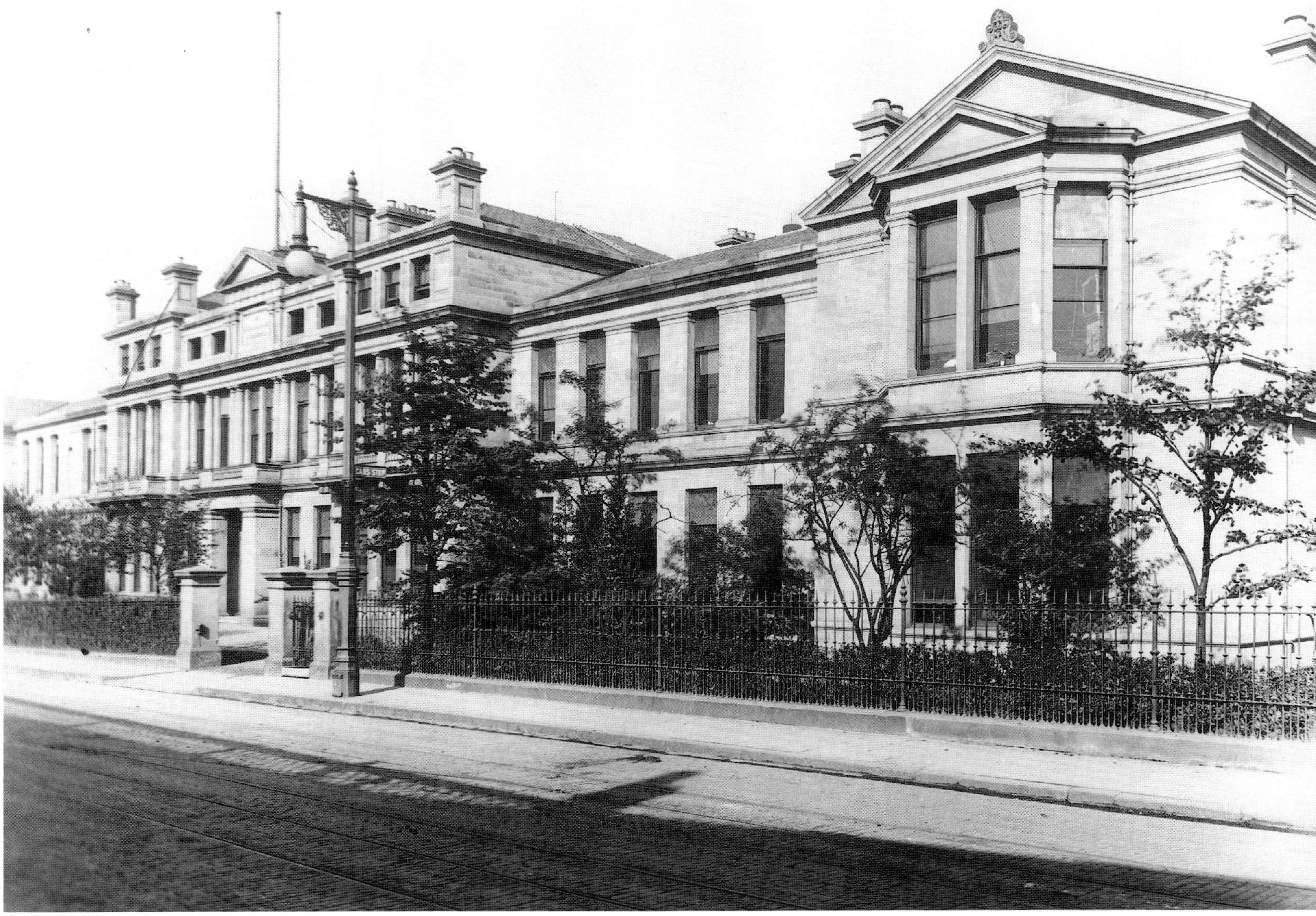

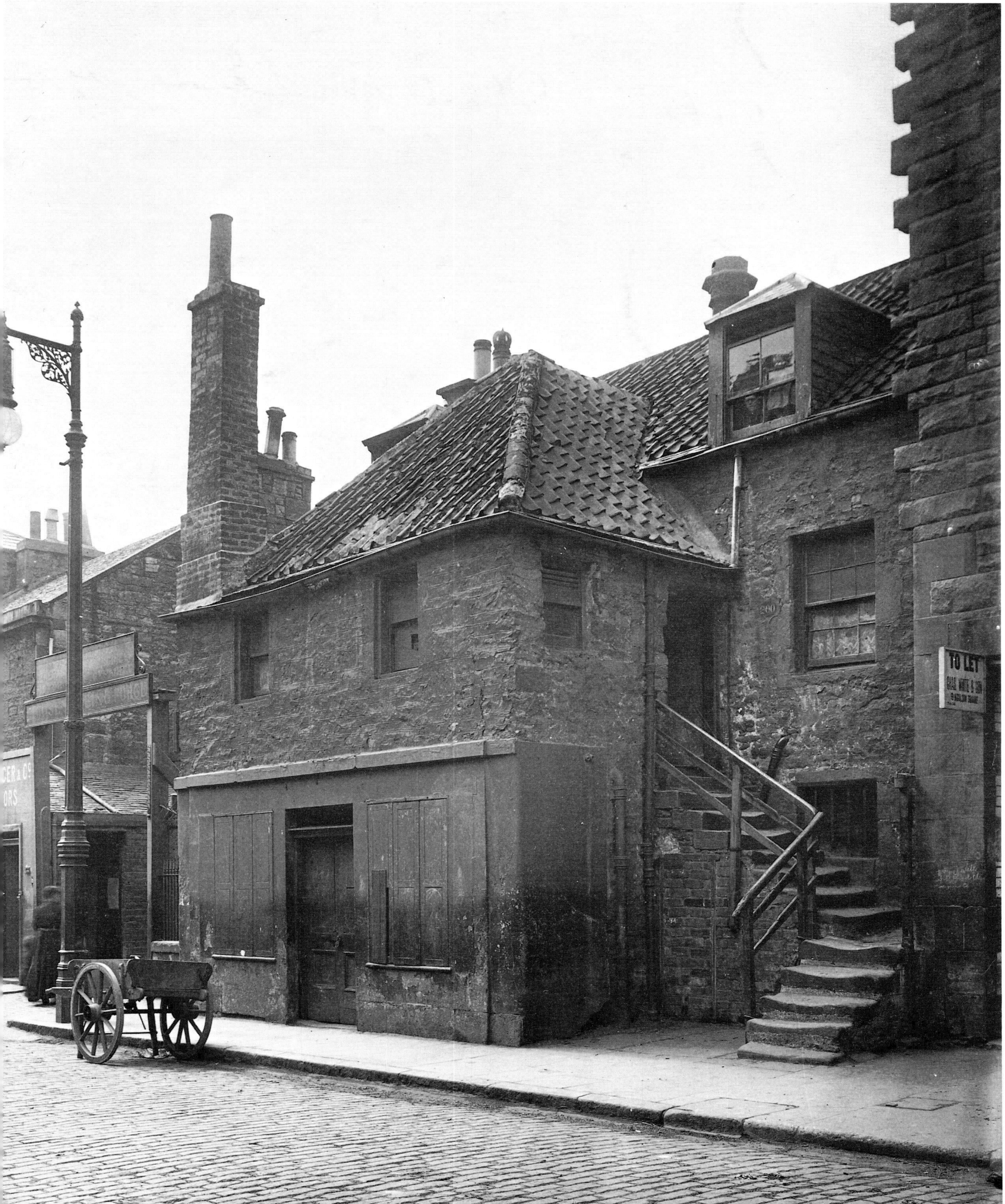
TO LET

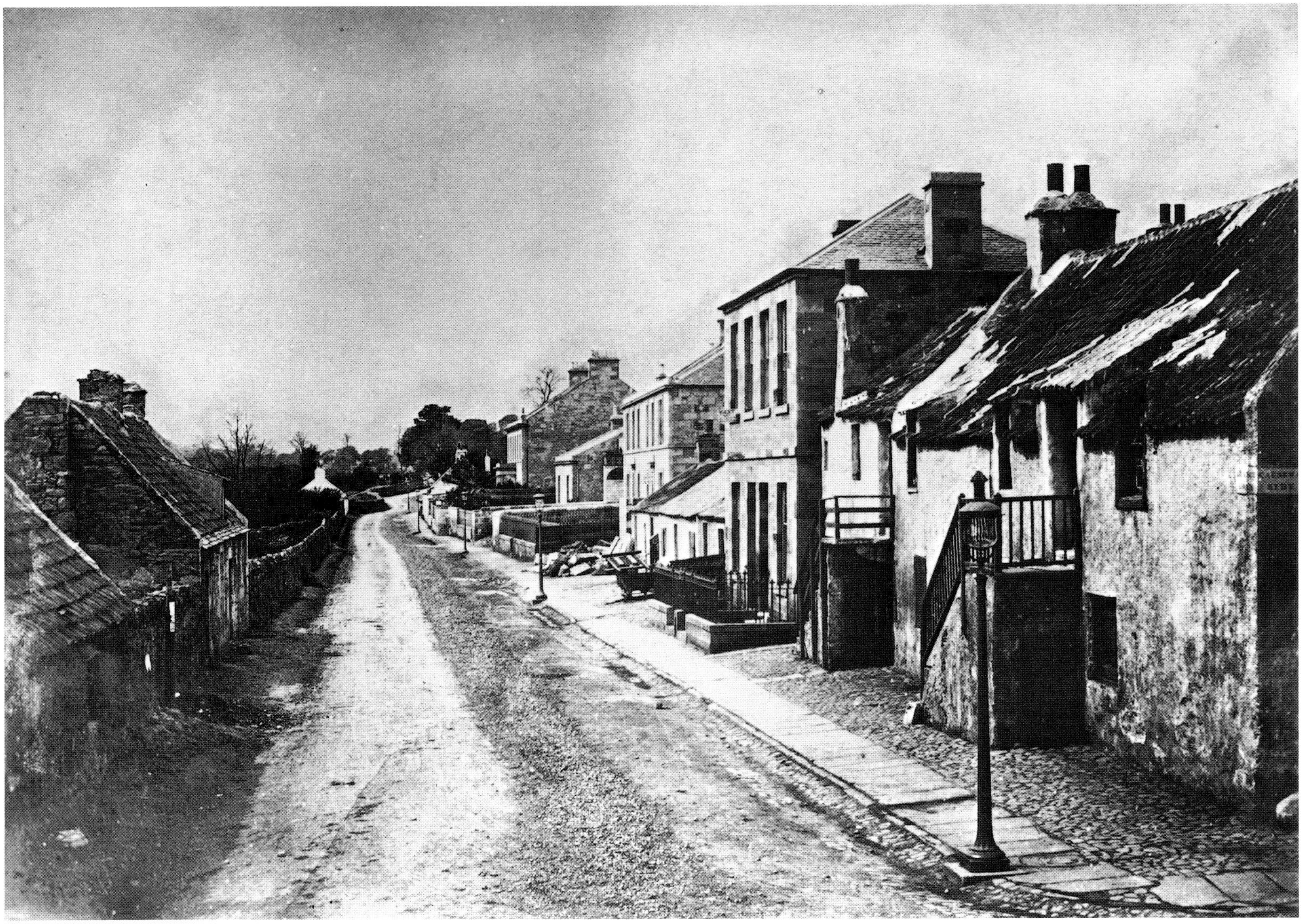

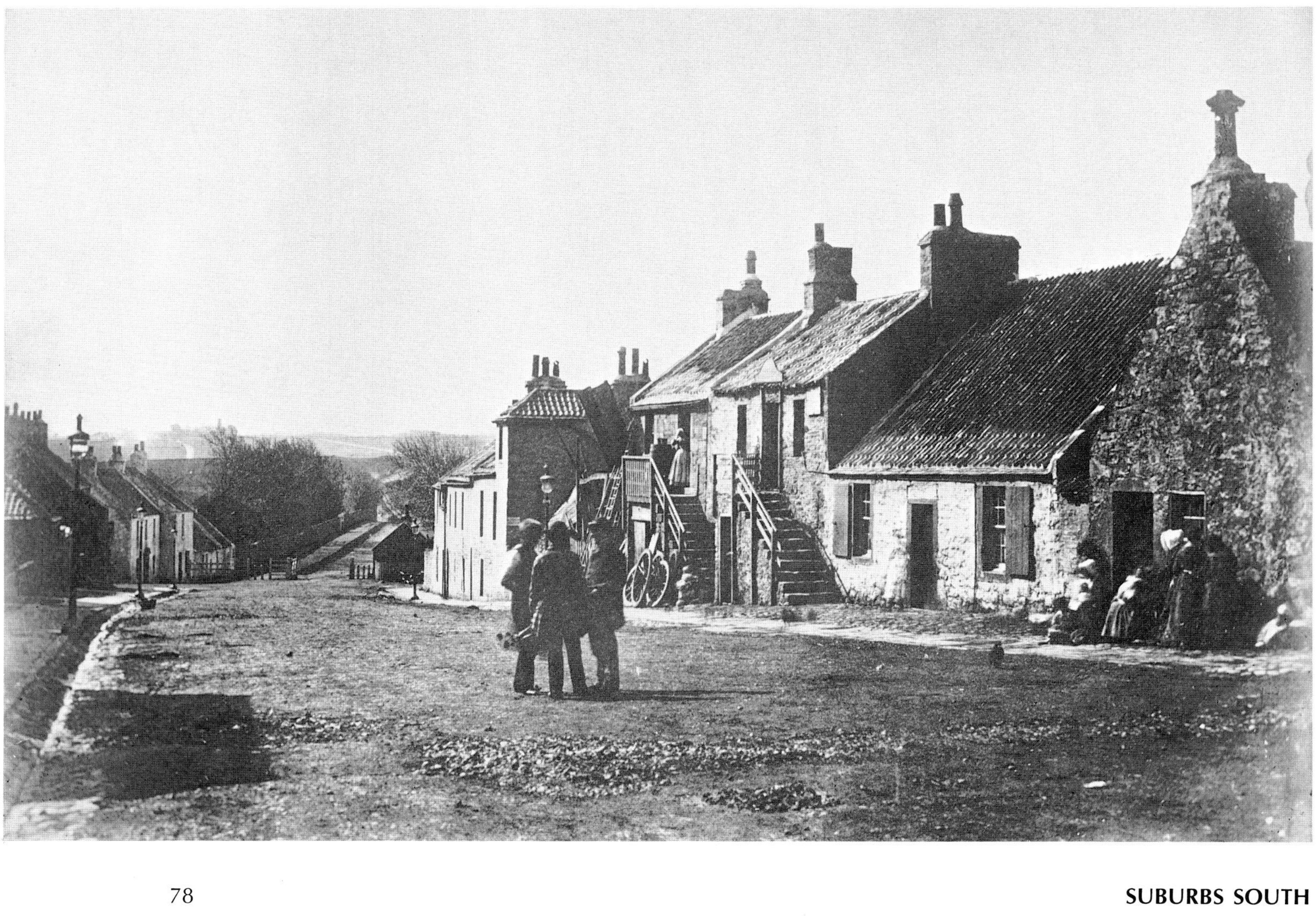

Grange Loan at Causewayside

This photograph shows Grange Loan looking west from its junction with Causewayside in 1850. All the land to the south was under cultivation with only occasional farm buildings. The north side shows a varied development with some substantial villas beside much humbler dwellings. The group of houses farthest into the picture was known as Hewit's Place, named after the Hewit family, tanners and leather merchants in Niddry Street, who lived in Grange Loan for several decades. The Penny Well appears on the right hand pavement where the garden wall curves outwards. Many of the houses were demolished at the end of the nineteenth century to make way for tenement flats.

Causewayside, 1850

This picture of Causewayside provides an excellent insight into the district as it was in the middle of the nineteenth century. It was one of the main roads out of Edinburgh to the toll barrier at the junction of Causewayside (later Ratcliffe Terrace), Grange Loan and West Mayfield.

The picture is taken looking south to the toll barrier beside the two white two-storey houses on the left. This site was later cleared for the construction of Mayfield Church. There are numerous houses with outside staircases, those on the right being a few yards south of the junction with Grange Loan.

The overall appearance of the houses is one of appalling poverty and deprivation, more especially when it is remembered that all were without electricity and most without running water or proper hygiene. James Goodfellow, the nineteenth-century Causewayside missionary, observed: 'Some of the people were very poor; in one case there was only one bed, such as it was — the children sleeping on bags of soot'. On the other hand, he also noted that 'a large supply of Christian literature was distributed in the districts and a substantial library of 340 volumes was provided at Causewayside'.

Tunny's Photographic Rooms

James G. Tunny was working in Edinburgh as a 'photographer calotypist and enammeller' from at least 1850, the year when this photograph was taken of a bridal couple as they arrived at Tunny's photographic rooms at No. 78 South Clerk Street. The studio gives the impression of having been grafted onto one of the old cottages which lined the east side of South Clerk Street before the tenements and shops were built. The studio site was later occupied by St Paul's Newington Church (now King's Hall). Salisbury Crags can be seen in the background of the photograph.

Tunny remained at South Clerk Street until c. 1860 when he moved to No. 93 Princes Street and later Maitland Street. In 1870 a branch studio was opened at No. 11 Salisbury Place (later renumbered 19). James C. H. Balmain is recorded as a photographer with James G. Tunny from c. 1888.

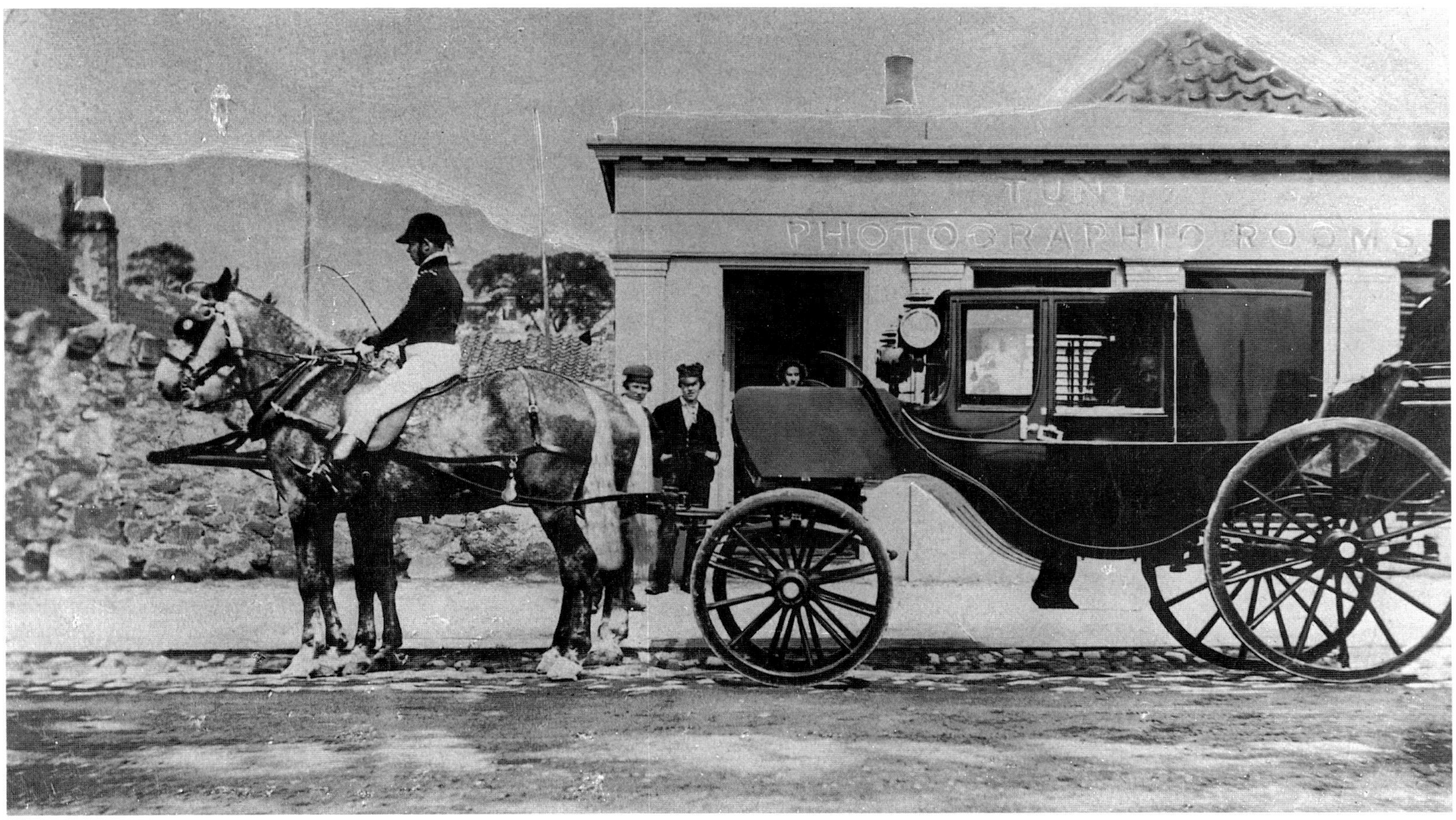

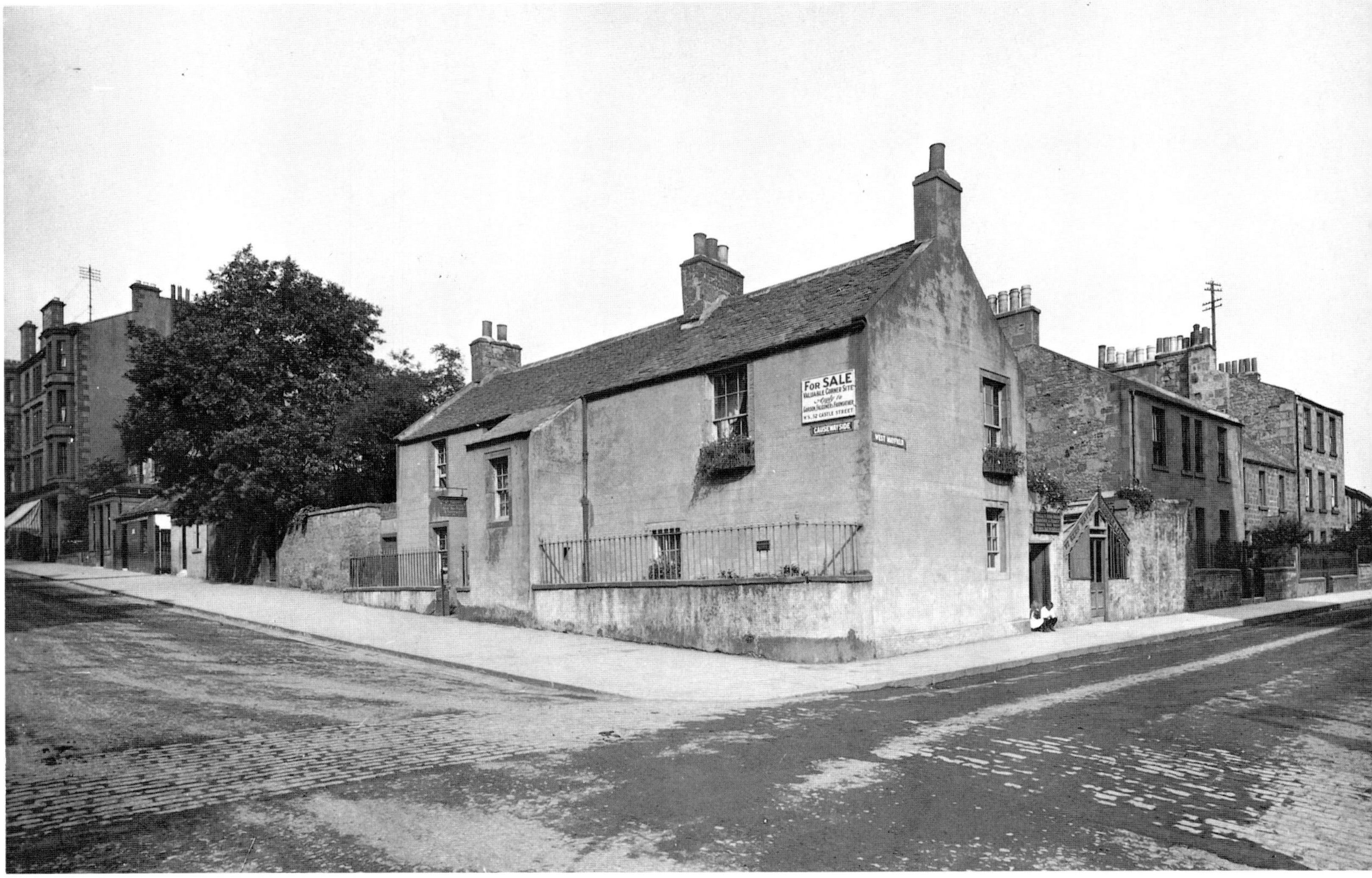
FOR SALE
VALUABLE CORNER SITE
Apply to
GORDON FALCONER & FAIRWEATHER
W.S. 52 CASTLE STREET
CAUSEWAYSIDE
WEST MAYFIELD

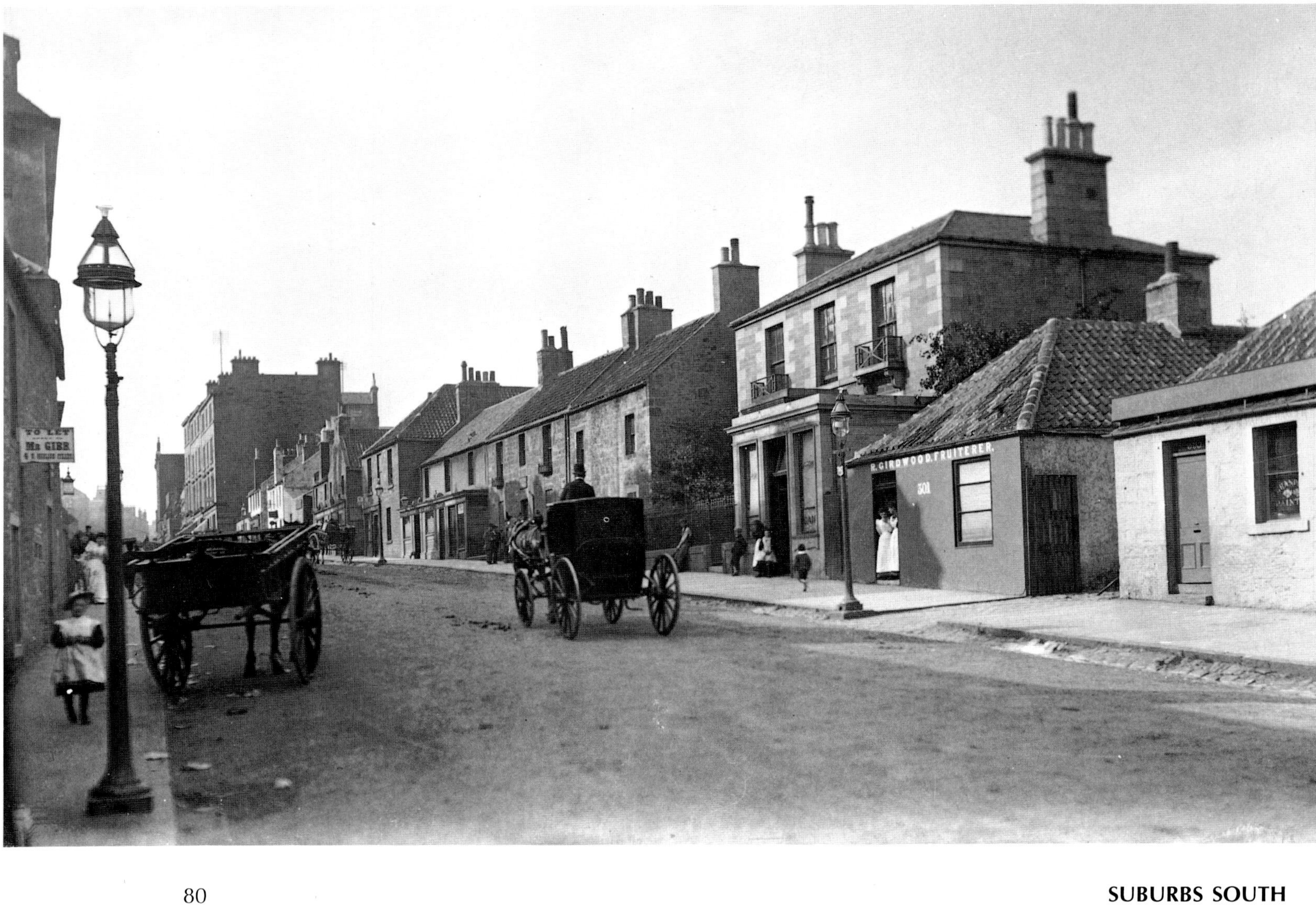
TO LET
Mr GIBB
GIRDWOOD, FRUITERER.
501

Causewayside, 1900

Fifty years on and Causewayside has improved immensely. The worst of the old buildings have been swept away, prosperous businesses are evident, and the children are well dressed. Even so, the street scene is greatly different to the present day.

The first picture shows the corner of Causewayside (Ratcliffe Terrace) and West Mayfield, later occupied by Wylie's car showroom. In 1900 the 'valuable corner site' was for sale. Round the corner in West Mayfield was William Kerr Watson, the florist, seen to the right of the children sitting on the doorstep. The second photograph continues the view of Causewayside northwards with the first small shop occupied by T. Grandison, Painter and Glazier, and then R. Girdwood, the fruiterer (with two female assistants at the door). On the opposite side of the road the 'To Let' sign directs enquiries to Mr Gibb, house agent, at No. 4 West Nicolson Street. The third picture is of the junction of Causewayside (Ratcliffe Terrace) and Fountainhall Road, the corner dominated by Ratcliffe's Family Laundry and James Cochrane, Coach Hirer: 'close and open carriages on hire: cabs had at any hour of the night'. The projecting sign reads 'Caledonian Railway Parcel Receiving Office'.

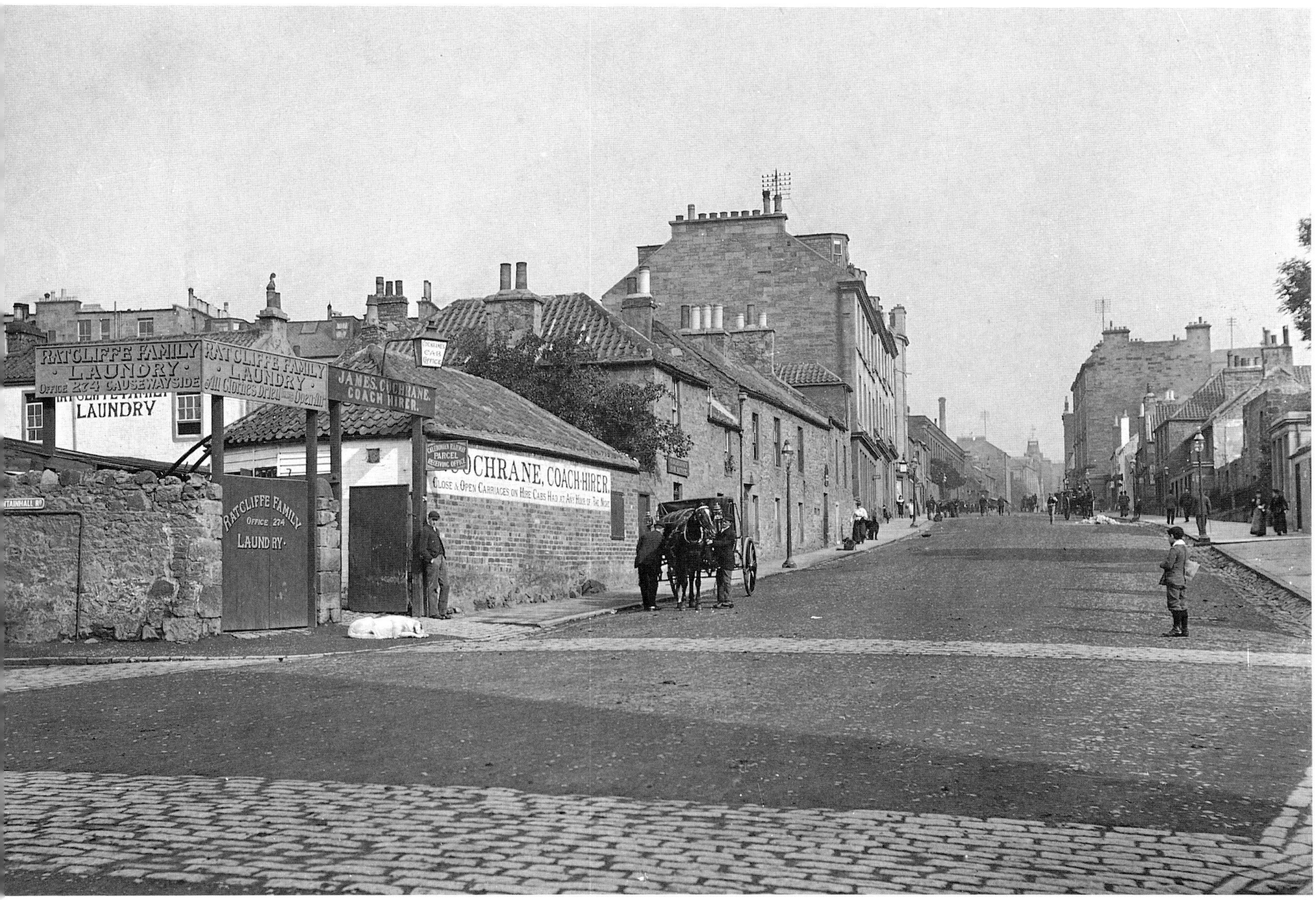

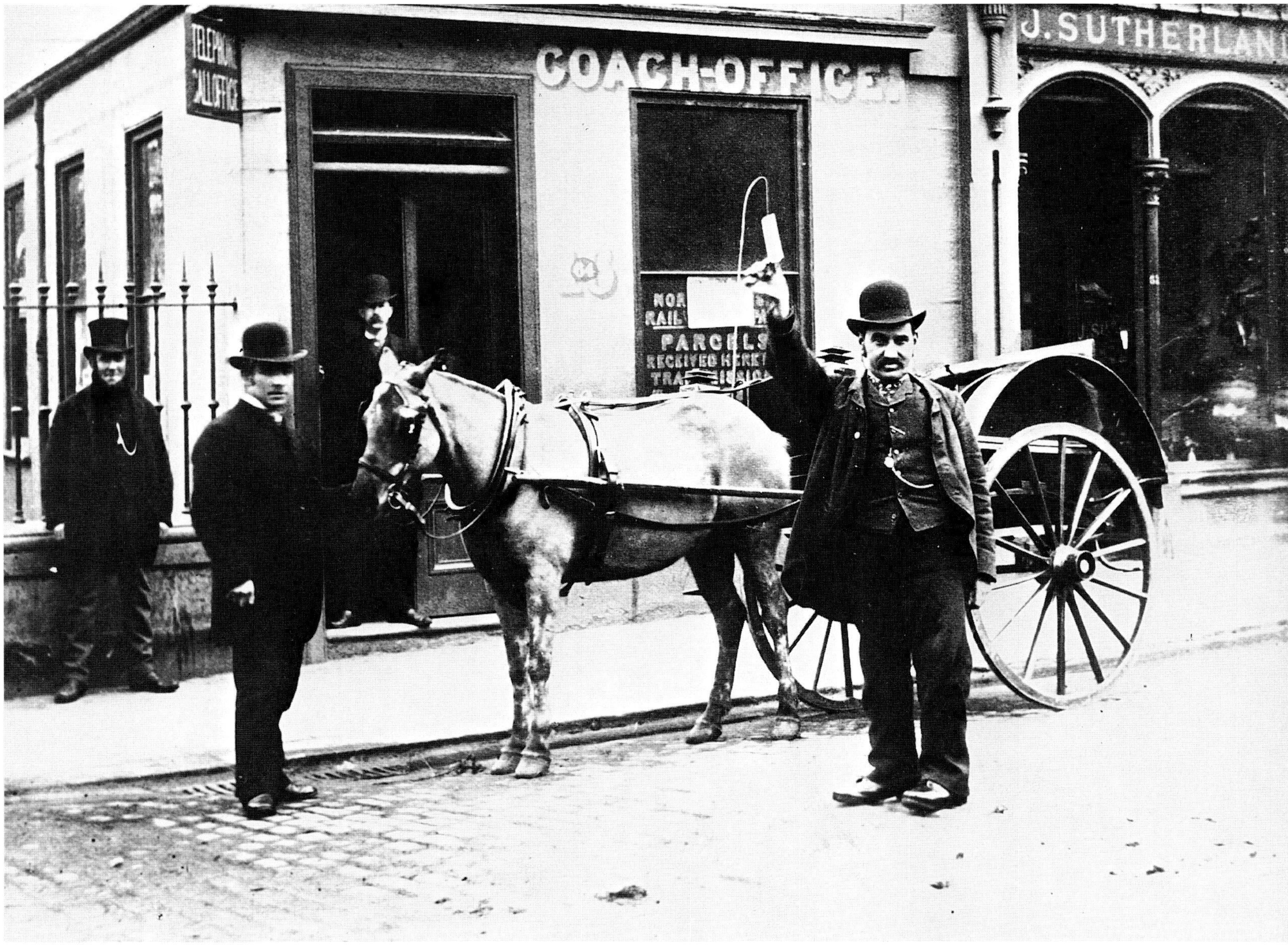

Coach Office

This photograph, taken in 1886, remains an enigma, in that no-one is really sure what the bowler-hatted man is doing. Identifying the exact location of the photograph was almost as difficult. David Adamson was operating as a coach hirer in Edinburgh prior to 1870. In 1880 he opened offices at No. 16 West Newington, which was renamed and renumbered 64 Newington Road in 1886. The change of number can be seen in the photograph between the door and the window. After Adamson left in 1889 the shop was acquired by Wood Bros., the butchers, and eventually demolished in 1900. A new tenement block was built on the site, on the corner of Newington Road and Salisbury Place, incorporating Wood Bros. and later Remnant Kings.

Newington Station

A typical scene, c. 1900, at Newington Station on the Edinburgh suburban line, opened in 1880. The numerous advertising boards include Melrose's Teas and Venus Soap. The photograph is taken looking east with Mentone Terrace on the left and some old glasshouses between it and the east-bound track. On the right is Craigmillar Park Parish Church, opened in 1879 as Mayfield, later Mayfield South. The small building with the turret roof, to the left of the church, is the lodge-house to the Royal Blind Asylum designed in 1874 by Charles Leadbetter.

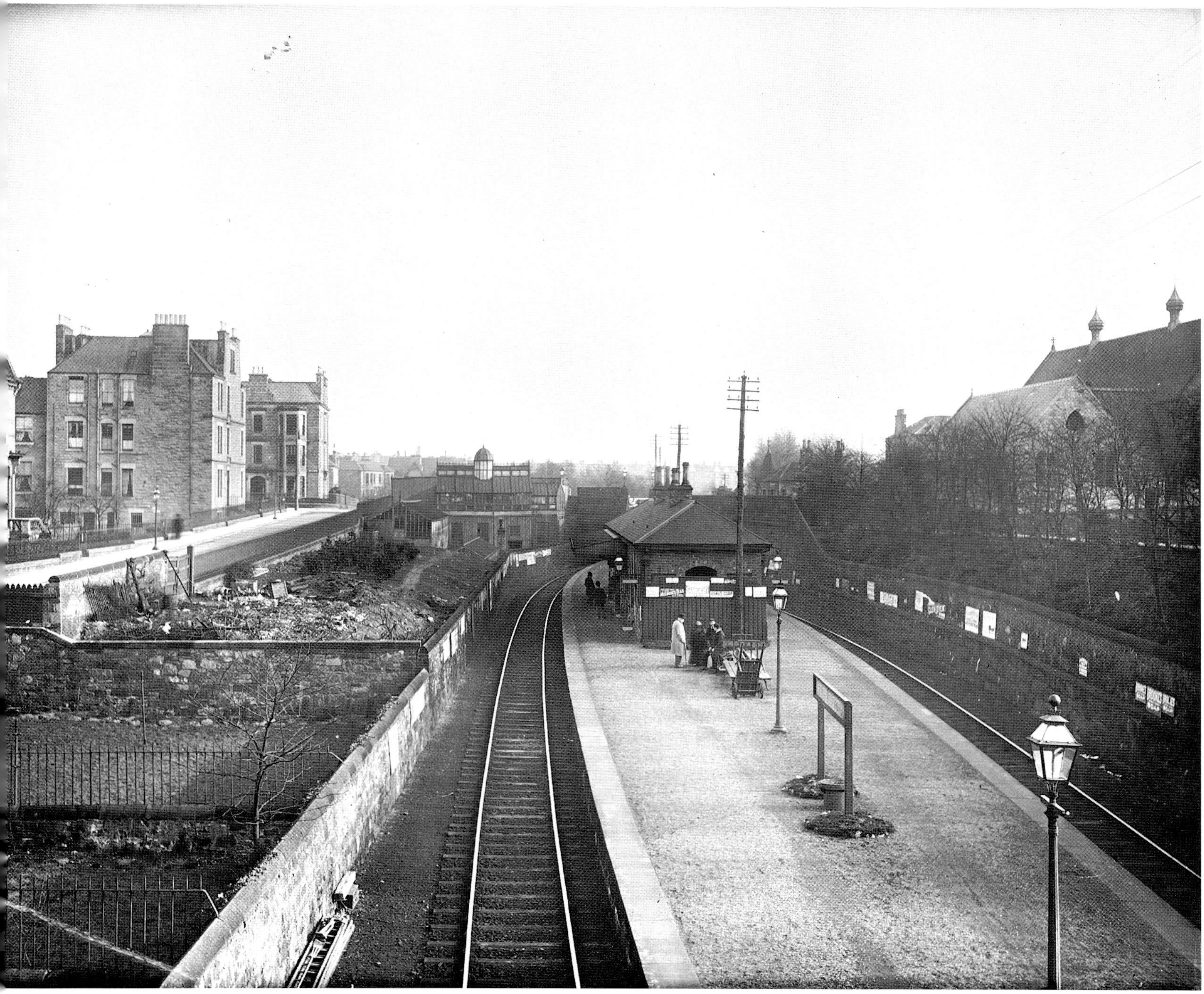

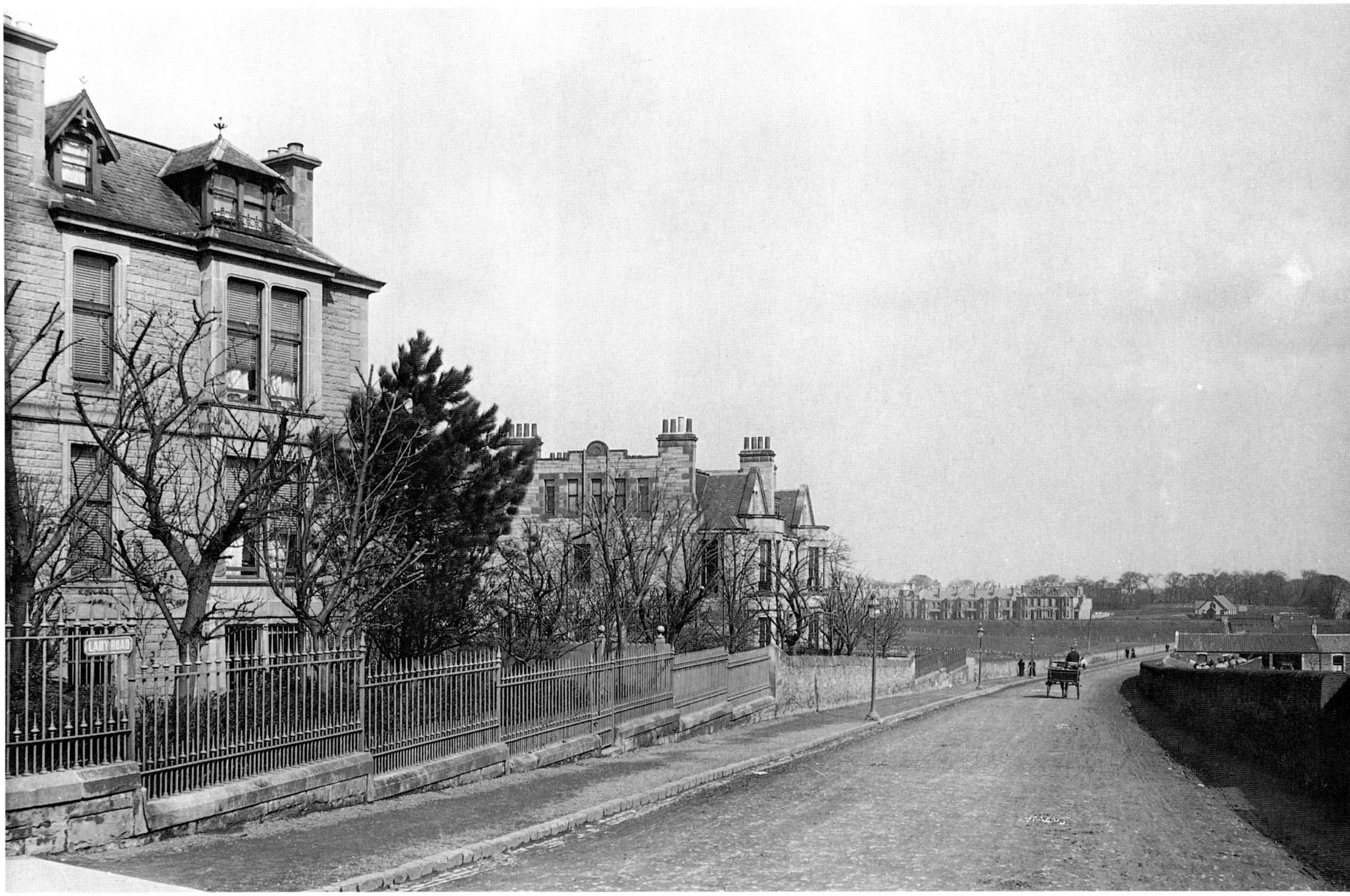

Lady Road

Lady Road in 1900 has changed almost out of recognition, although most of that change has occurred in the last decade, after the opening of Cameron Toll Shopping Centre. The entrance to the modern shopping centre is near to the position of the cottages on the right of the picture. After Lady Road curves slightly to the right it goes under the railway bridge at Cameron Toll. In the distance the terraced houses on Dalkeith Road can be seen, and to their right is the hall of Prestonfield Church. In recent years the line of Lady Road has been greatly altered.

Liberton Dams

Liberton Dams is shown on *Laidlaw's Map* of 1766 although Liberton Brae and Craigmillar Park were not constructed until 1815.

The photograph was taken in Mayfield Road in 1890 looking south-east to the tower of Liberton Kirk. The Braid Burn crosses under the roadway beside the white buildings on the left, where the sluice-gate mechanism can be seen to the right of the doorway. Latterly these buildings were occupied as Laidlaw's Dairy.

Today all the corner buildings have been demolished, the junction is controlled by traffic lights, and houses have been built on most of the fields.

Crossroads at the Top of Liberton Brae

When this photograph was taken in 1890 the handsome square tower and pinnacles of Liberton Kirk dominated the crossroads at the top of Liberton Brae. The church was built in 1815 to designs by James Gillespie Graham, exactly on the site of an earlier church dating from at least a century earlier. Opposite the church, in Kirkgate, the centre building is the Anderson Church Hall erected in 1888.

The junction now has houses and commercial buildings on all four corners, and the horse and carriage would have difficulty competing with the speed of commuter traffic.

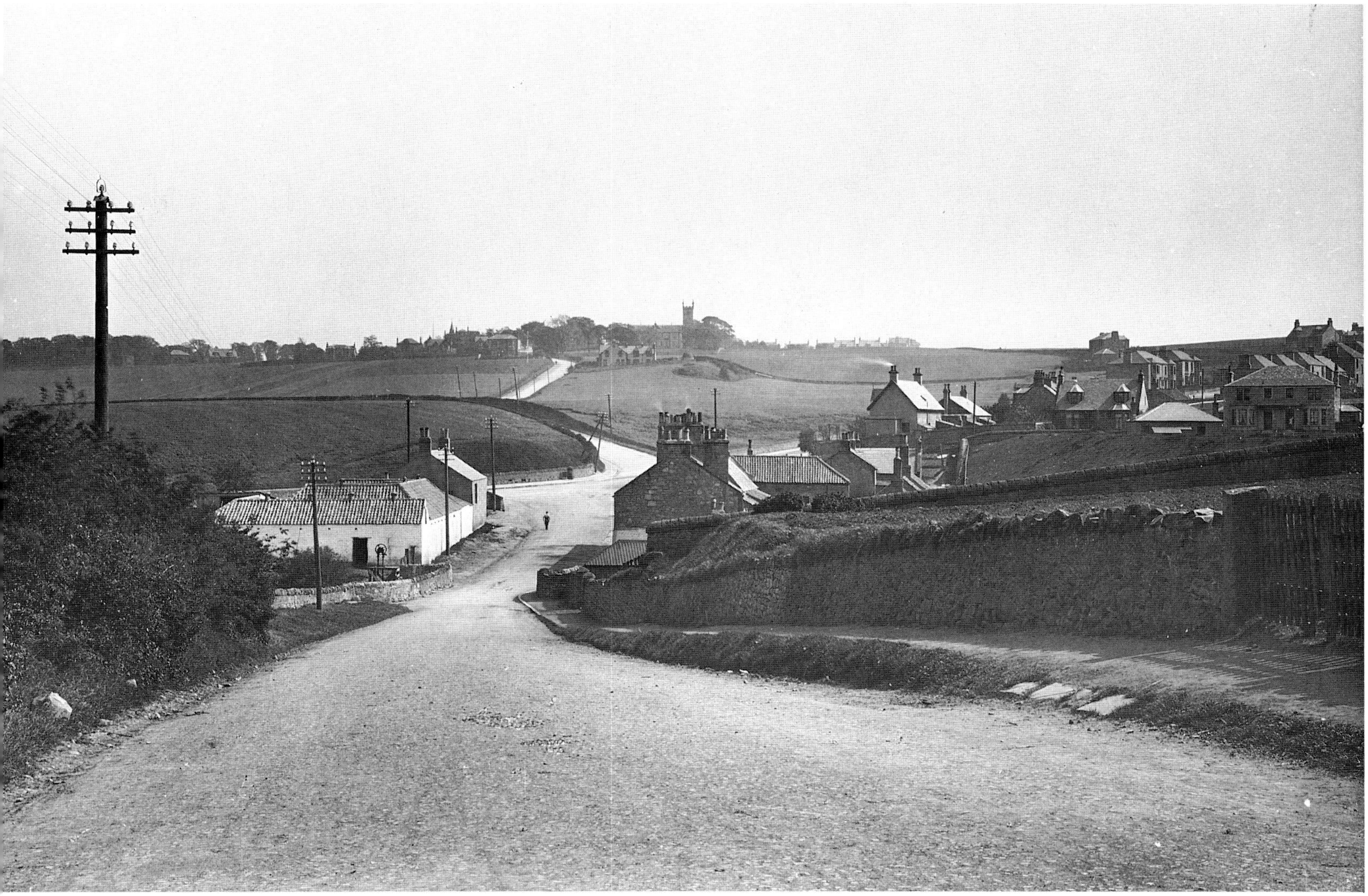

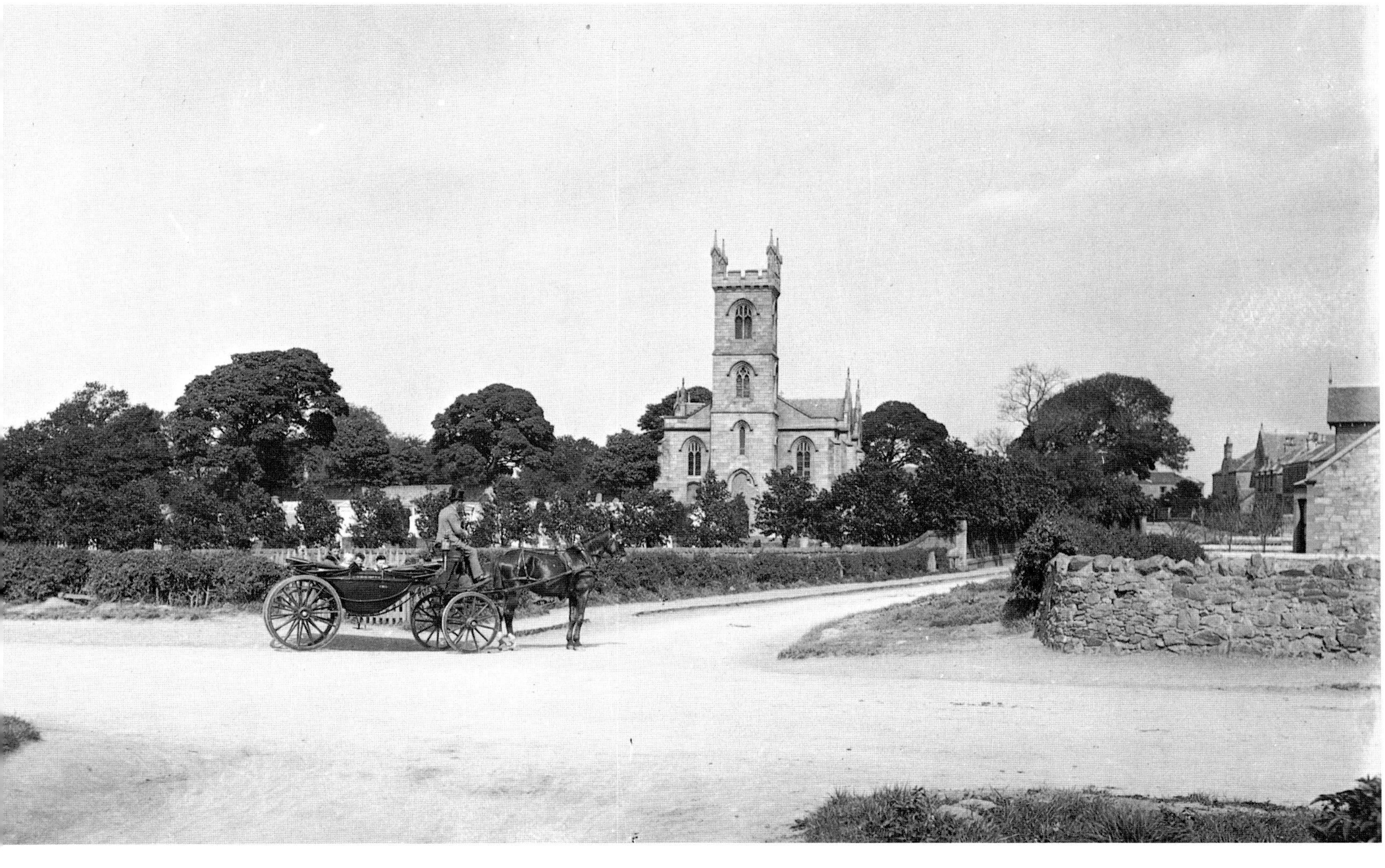

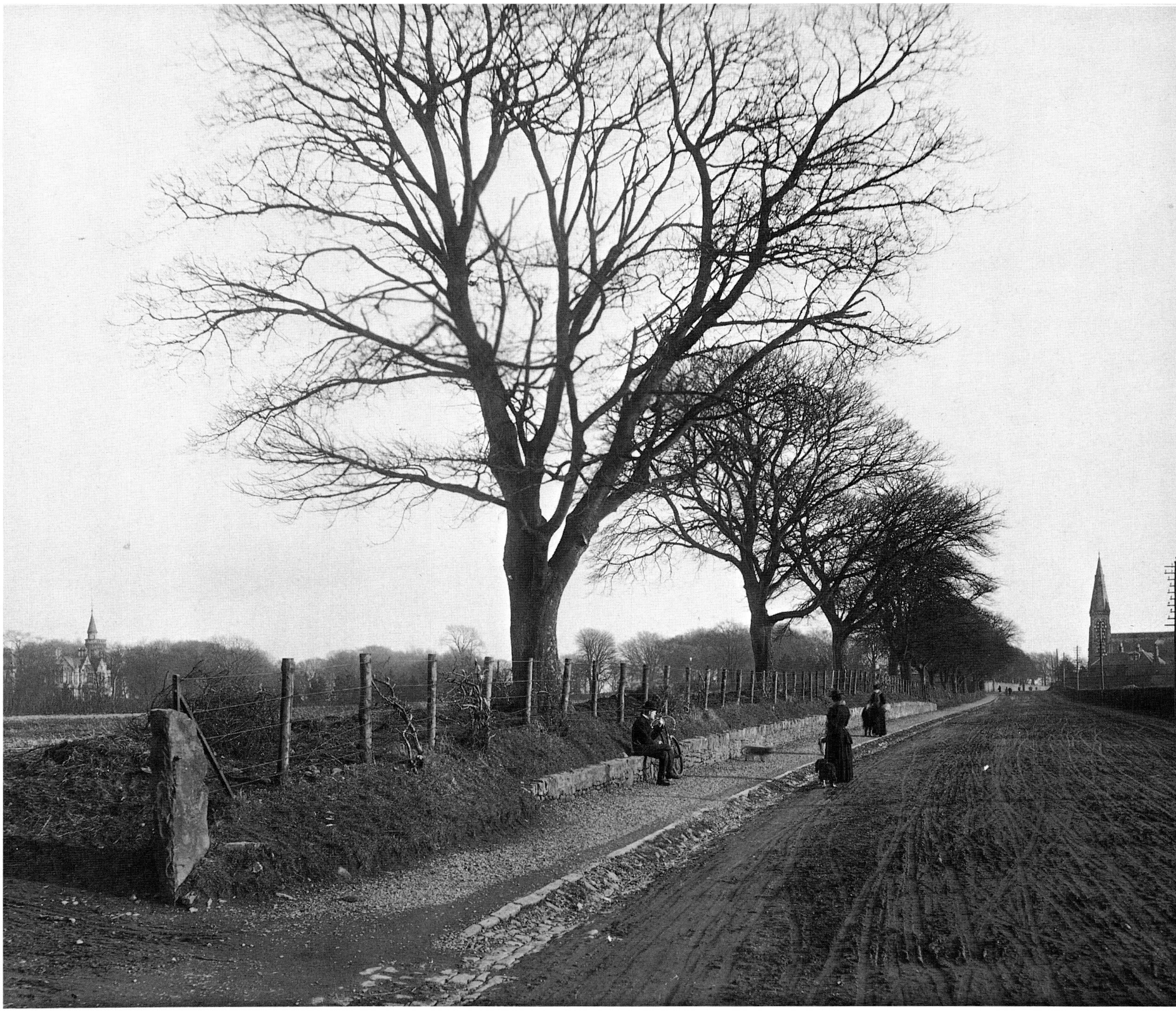

Gilmerton Road, near Kingston Avenue

This winter scene was taken in 1900 looking south-east on Gilmerton Road near the junction with Kingston Avenue and Mount Vernon Road. The absence of foliage on the trees allows a view of Craigend Park (later Kingston Clinic) on the extreme left, built for William Christie, the tailor, between 1867 and 1869. It is considered to be one of F. T. Pilkington's most grandiose designs. On the right is Liberton Northfield Parish Church, designed by J. W. Smith in 1869.

Craigend Dairy, Old Dalkeith Road

Craigend Dairy was on Old Dalkeith Road immediately opposite the junction with Kingston Avenue. It was run for many years by Gideon Paris whose son, James Paris, the Edinburgh athlete, continued the family business, supplying milk to many shops in Edinburgh. The photograph, c. 1900, shows the house with the byre on the left and a small bothy for the workers on the right. The cattle grazed on land now used as Liberton Golf Course, but nothing remains of the dairy buildings.

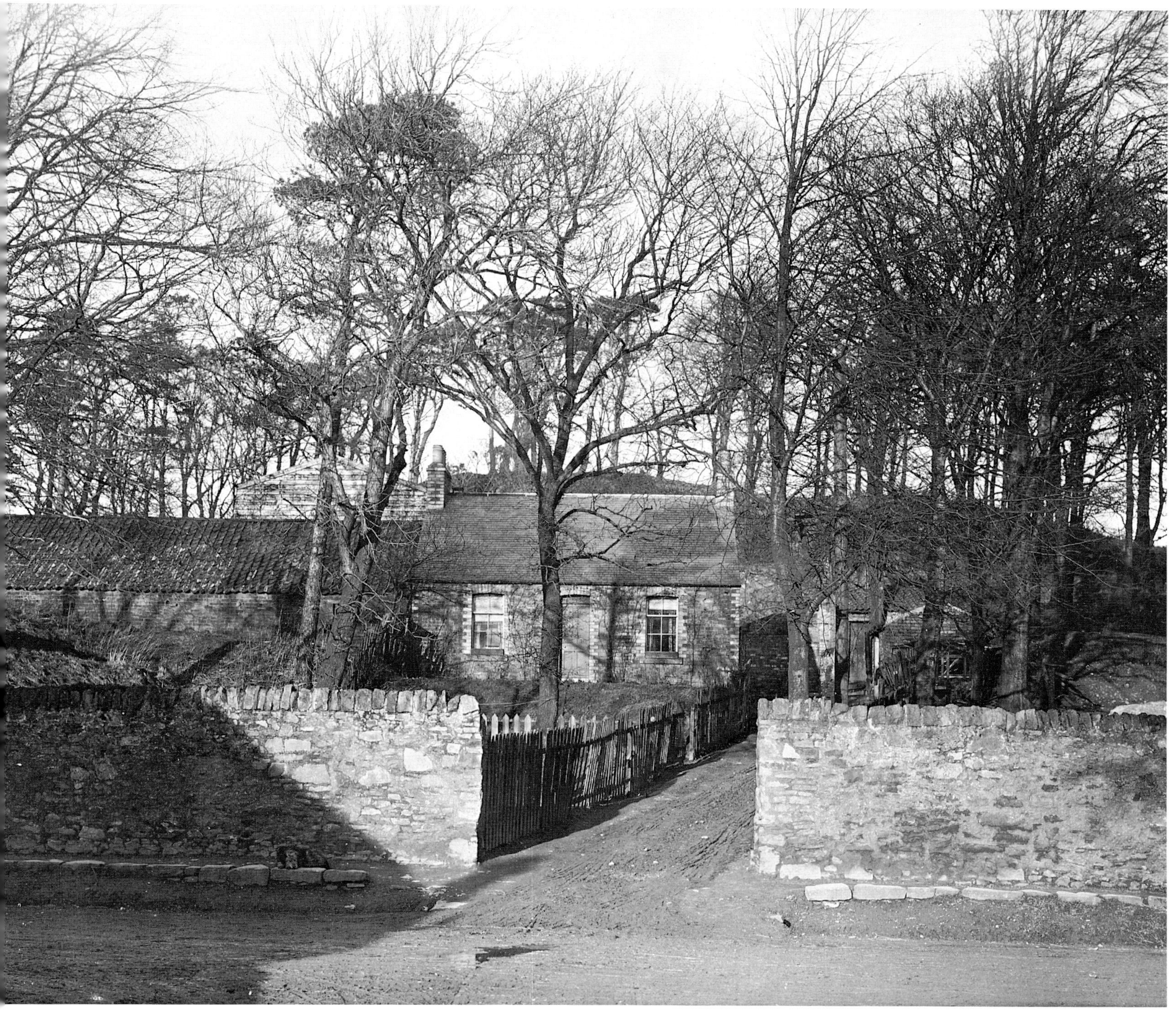

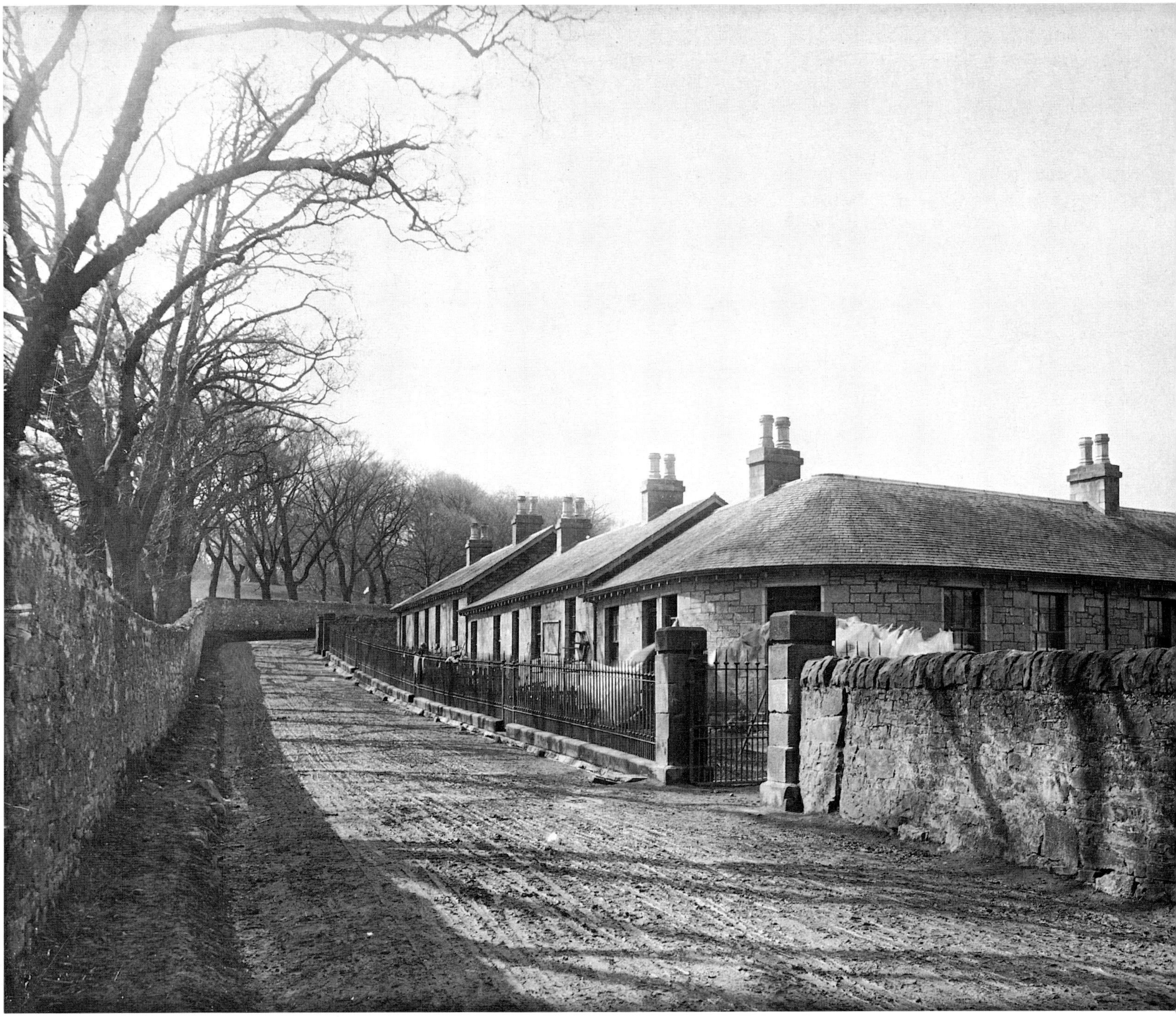

Lower Craigend Cottages

Upper Craigend and Lower Craigend lay at the north end of Kingston Avenue. This photograph, taken in 1900 near the junction with Old Dalkeith Road, shows Lower Craigend Cottages on the right with the distinctive curved roof-line. The cottages have recently been renovated and the external stonework has been repaired. The ornamental railings have been replaced with a more modern design, and the left-hand square pillar has been removed, as has the stone wall on the right. Otherwise, the scene has not greatly changed except for the road surface and the presence of motor vehicles.

Craigmillar Castle

Craigmillar Castle owes its existence to the Preston family, who acquired the barony in 1374. It was used by the Crown from the late fifteenth century to the early seventeenth century but was captured at the time of the Hertford invasion in 1544. In 1660 the property was bought by Sir John Gilmour, whose descendants lived there until the late eighteenth century when they moved to the Inch. The oldest part of the castle is the late fifteenth-century L-shaped tower house. A range of buildings on the west side was added in the seventeenth century, and the entire castle is surrounded by a high curtain wall. Internally the most important features are the Great Hall and Queen Mary's room, where she is reputed to have recuperated after the murder of Rizzio. The photograph, taken in 1900, looks west to the castle with farm buildings behind the trees on the left, and the custodian's house, with the crowstepped gable, on the right.

At the present day the castle is cared for by Historic Scotland and is open to the public all the year round.

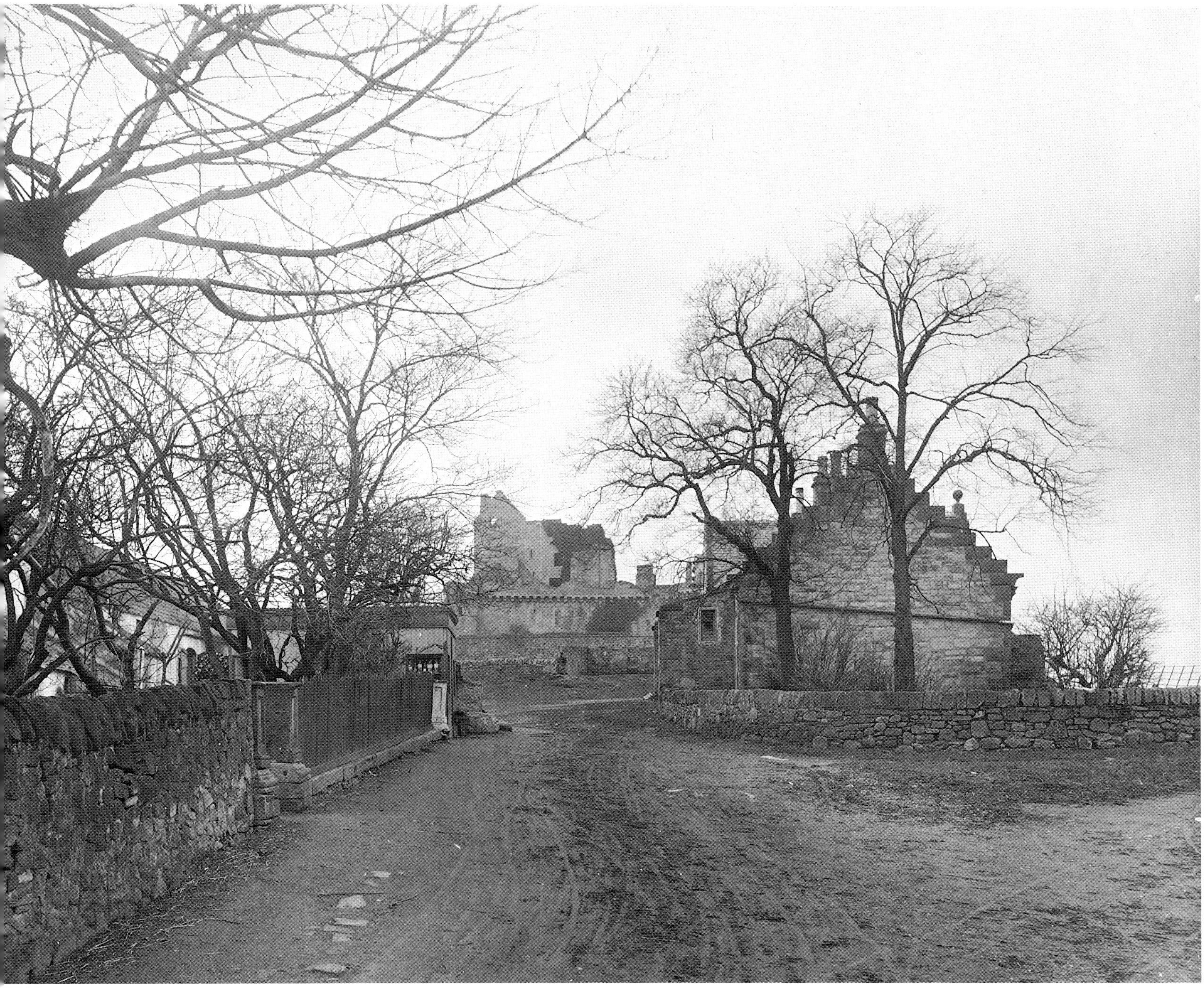

Queen Mary's Tree on Old Dalkeith Road

Within a mile of Craigmillar Castle, this ancient sycamore, photographed at Little France in 1900, is said to have been planted by Mary Queen of Scots. Tom Speedy, writing in 1892, stated that about 1880 the tree was showing signs of decay and had its branches cut back to reduce resistance to the west wind. Several saplings were grown from its seeds, one of which was planted at Linlithgow Palace on 24th September 1886. In recent decades Queen Mary's tree lost much of its vigour, and was eventually destroyed when vandals set fire to it.

The traditional cottage in the middle ground of the picture is still there, and the steadings on the left have recently been redeveloped as private housing at Little France Mills.

Dalkeith Road

The view looking north up Dalkeith Road, *c.* 1900, has not changed significantly, except for the absence of motorised transport. The villas on the left-hand side of the road remain substantially unaltered, as do the lodge house and gate pillars at the east end of Mayfield Terrace. On the right-hand side the tenement buildings were constructed at the end of the nineteenth century beside Rosehall Church (now Priestfield). Its pedimented façade can just be seen beyond the line of the tenements. The church and the tenements were built on the site of the hamlet of Rosehall, whose entire population was described in *The Print of His Shoe* as 'eighteen families, mostly simple in their habits, refined in manners, and some of them with literary and scientific tastes'.

Cameron Toll

An elegant lamp standard, with an indecipherable inscription, and a water trough protected by three bollards, stood at Cameron Toll at the foot of Dalkeith Road in 1900. The entrance to Lady Road is off to the left, obscured by the horse and cart. On the right is the hall of Prestonfield Church, used until the stone church was built in 1902. The row of terraced houses on the left with the shop at the far end was demolished many years ago and the whole junction was redesigned into a one-way system to negotiate the Braid Burn and two railway bridges.

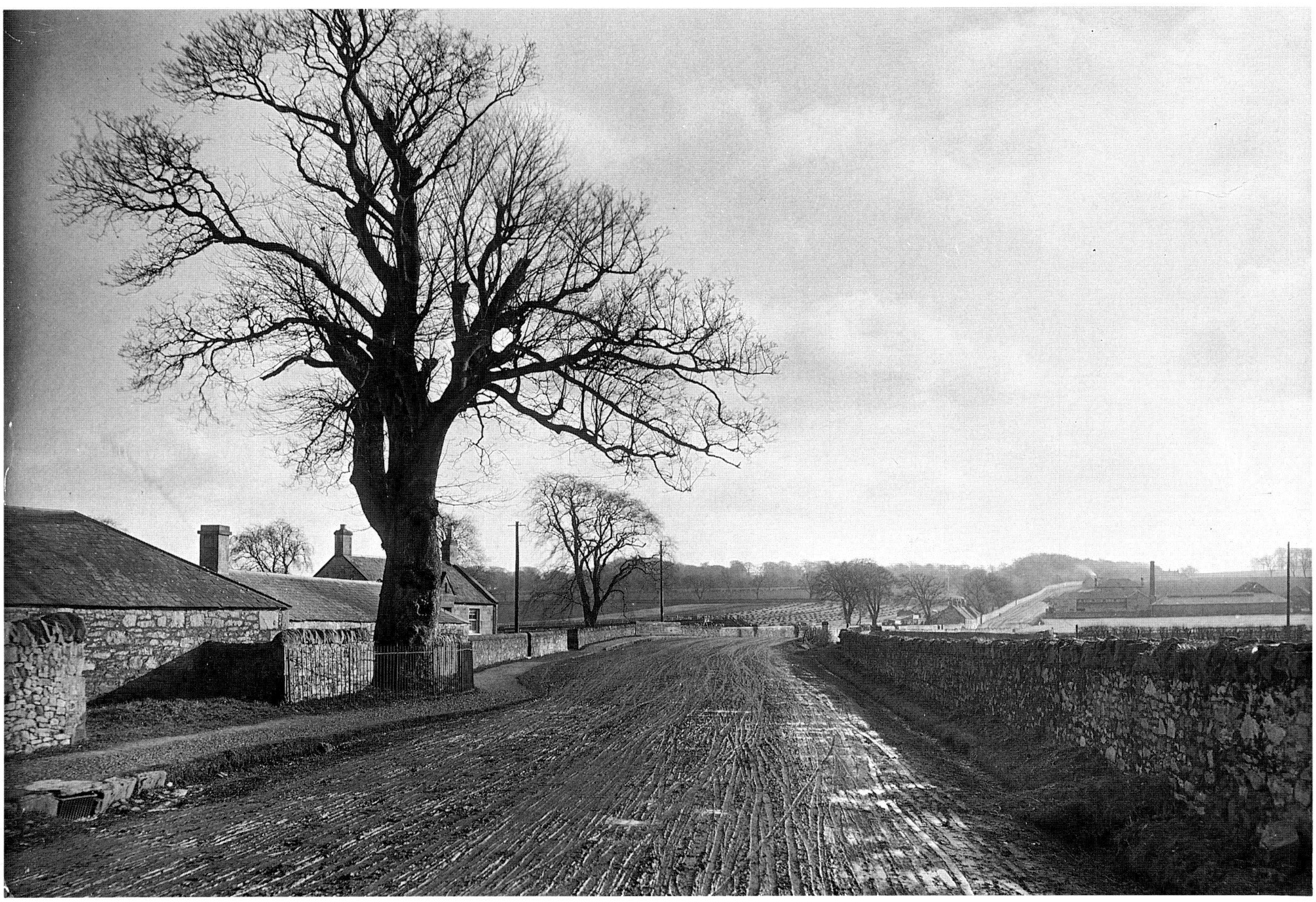

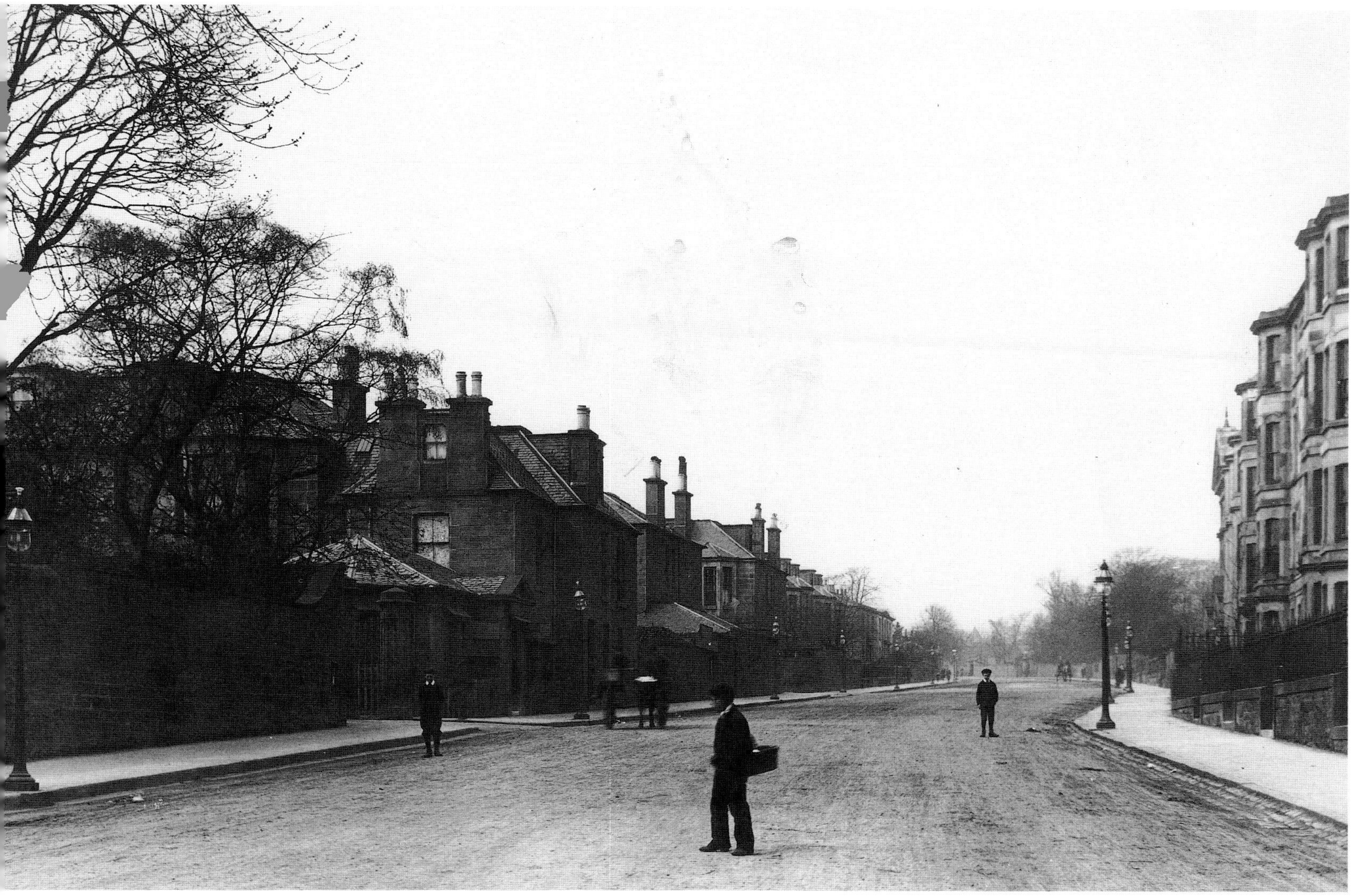

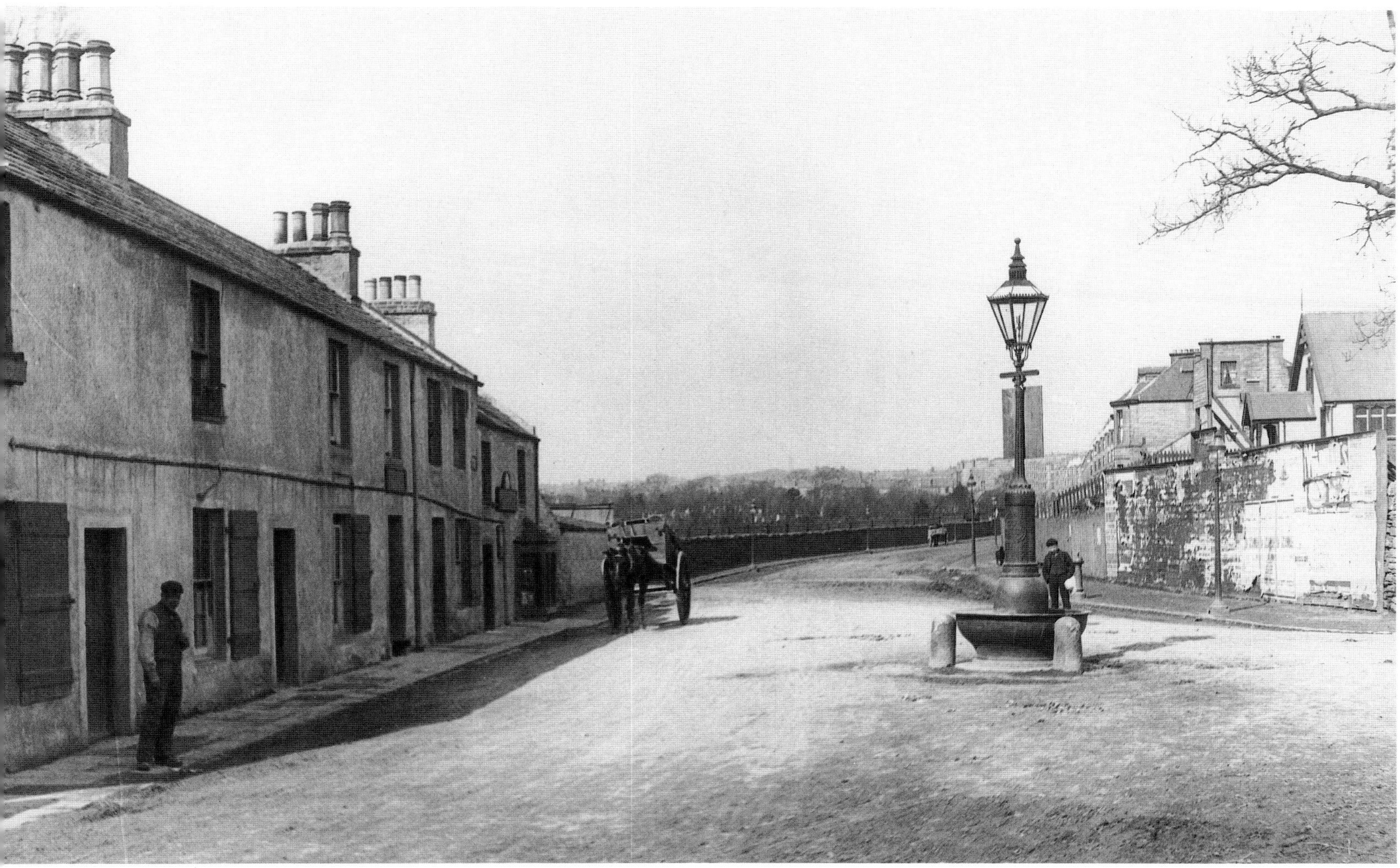

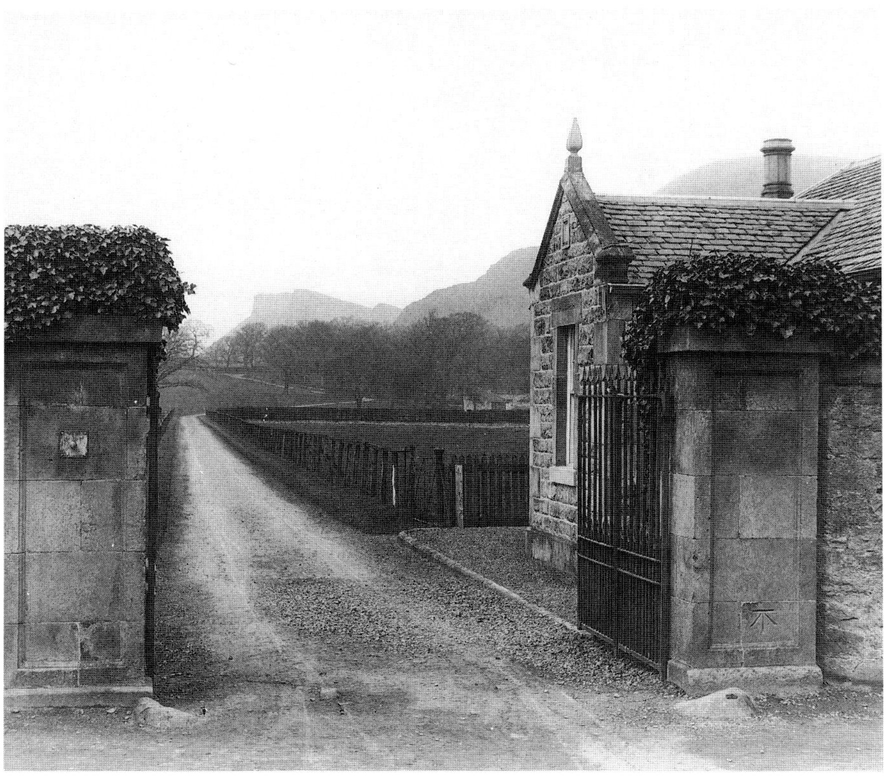

Clearburn Lodge

Clearburn Lodge, at the junction of Prestonfield Avenue and Peffermill Road, marked the south entrance to Clearburn House, which lay a few hundred yards south of Prestonfield House. The long curving driveway seen in the photograph ran from Clearburn Lodge to Dalkeith Road. Clearburn House, demolished around 1890, was inhabited for several generations by farmers and brewers. Its most famous resident, born there in 1708, was the Rev. Thomas Gillespie, founder of the Synod of Relief.

Clearburn Lodge still exists although it is not inhabited and faces an uncertain future as the ground around it is developed.

Peffermill Road at Peffermill House

At this point Peffermill Road is facing directly to Rosehall Church in Dalkeith Road, its twin towers just visible on the skyline. To the right, Arthur's Seat creates a backcloth to the grounds of Peffermill House, reached through the heavy stone gate pillars. The white gable-ended cottage, demolished several years ago, marks the position of the Braid Burn, which passes under Peffermill Road midway between the two horse-drawn carts in the photograph.

Peffermill House dates from 1656 and was restored in the early 1980s by the architects Nicholas Groves-Raines, for their own use.

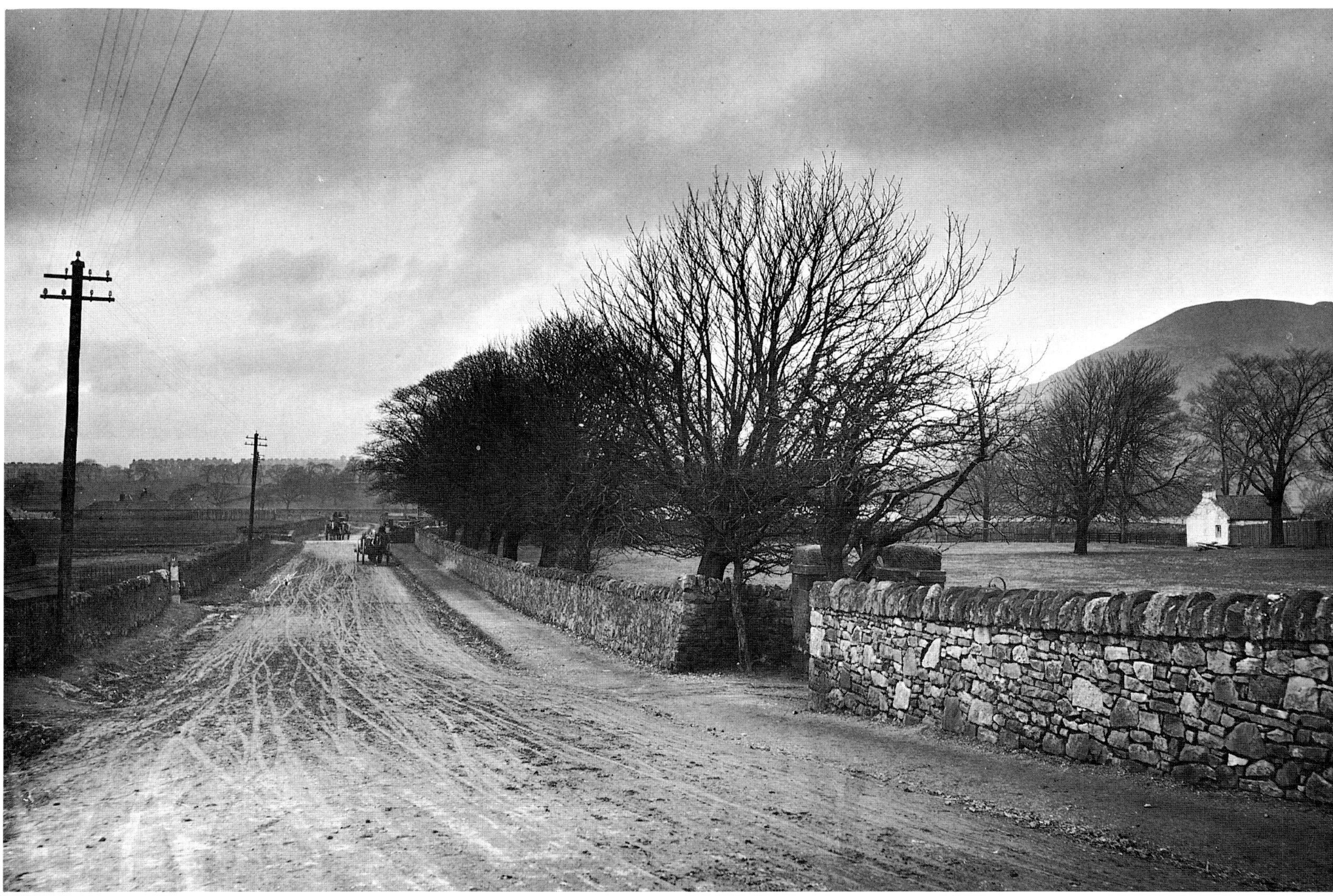

CHAPTER 5

OTHER SUBURBS AND LOCATIONS

Horse Bus at Levenhall

The North British Railway Company ran a horse bus service between Musselburgh Station and Levenhall from 1847 to 1904. The photograph, c. 1886, shows a fully laden bus at Adam Flockhart's hostelry at Levenhall (now the Levenhall Arms). No-one was left in any doubt about the scale of charges prominently displayed on the side of the bus: through fares to Edinburgh, 1st Class Rail and Inside Coach 10d; 2nd Class Rail and Inside Coach 8d; 3rd Class Rail and Outside Coach 5d; other Passengers charged 2d inside and 1d outside for the Coach journey. This photograph at one time wrongly described the building as 'Mrs Forman's Pub at Levenhall' but an examination of the stonework of both buildings (which are very similar to one another) suggests that it is Flockhart's and not Forman's.

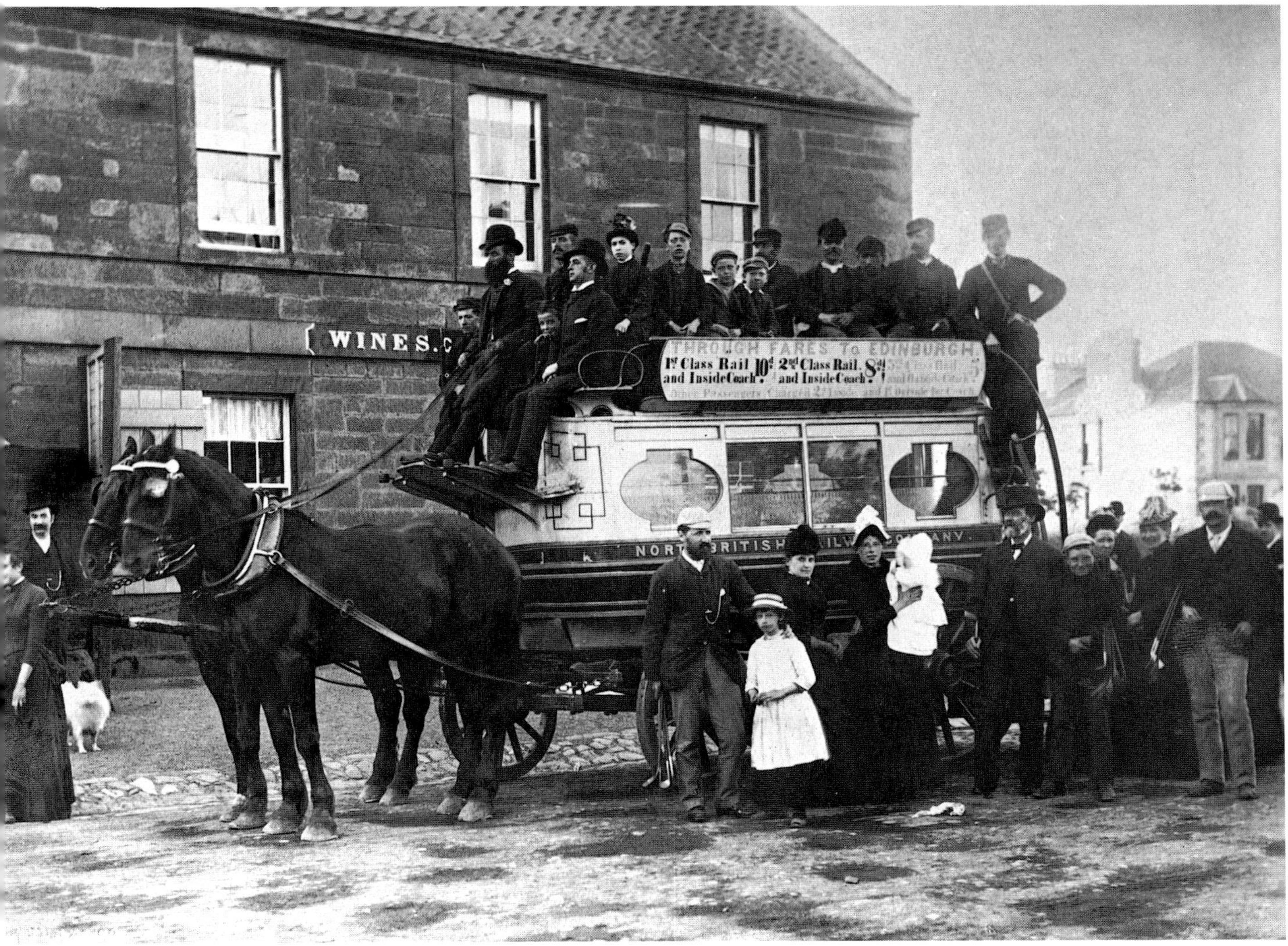

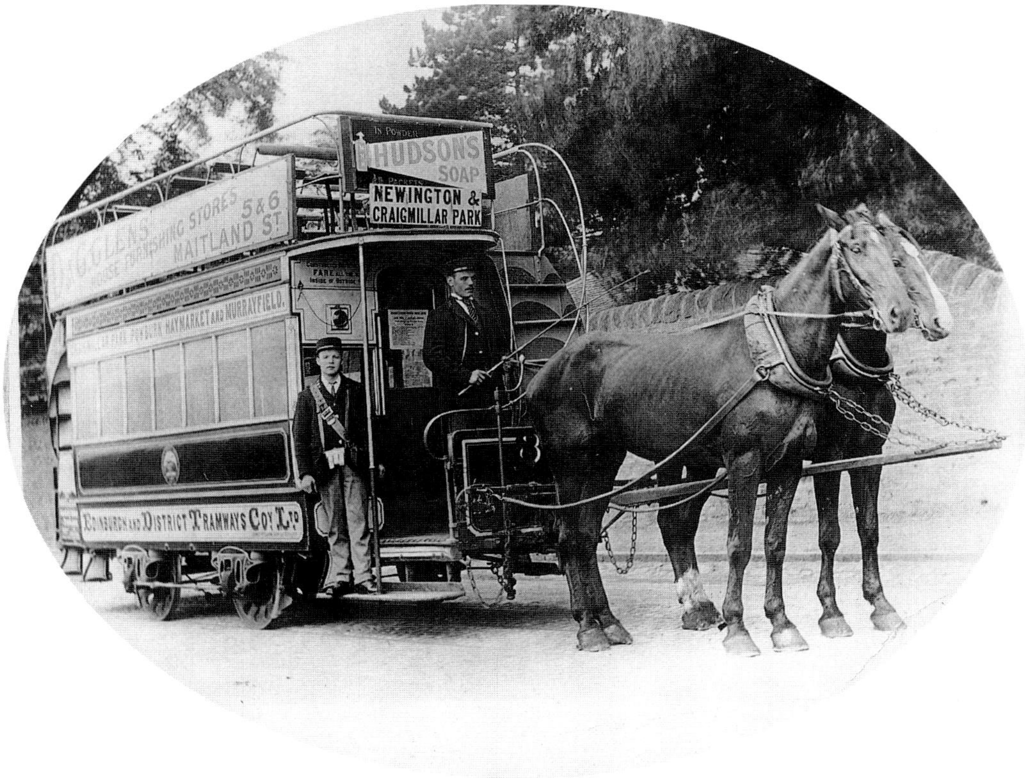
HUDSON'S
SOAP
NEWINGTON &
CRAIGMILLAR PARK
5&6
MAITLAND ST.
HAYMARKET AND MURRAYFIELD.
EDINBURGH AND DISTRICT TRAMWAYS COY LTD

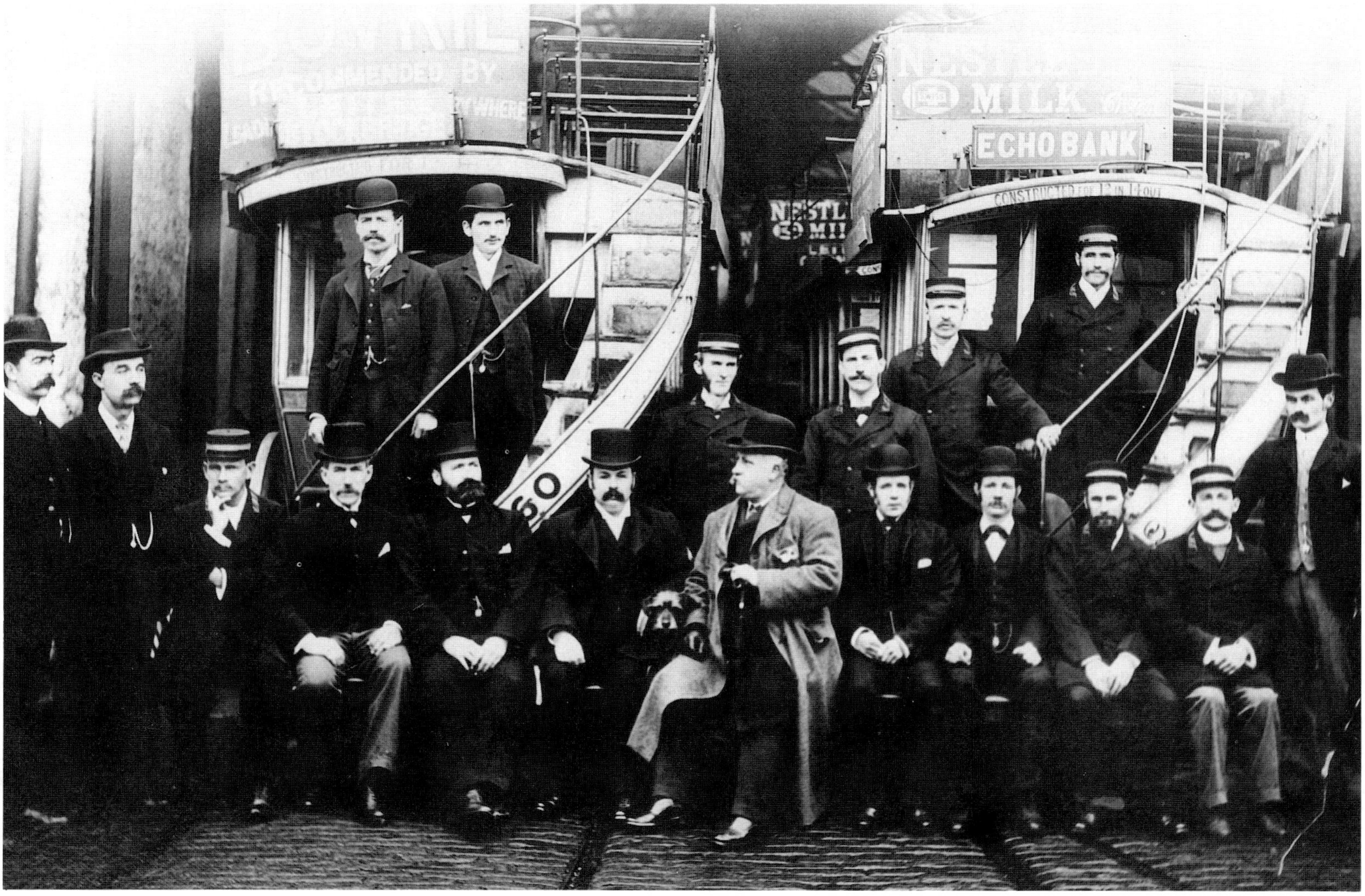
RECOMMENDED BY
MILK
ECHO BANK

Horse-drawn Tram at Murrayfield Terminus

Horse-drawn tram No. 88 was built at Shrubhill by Edinburgh and District Tramways Co. and entered service on 1st January 1896. It is seen here at the Murrayfield terminus (Saughtonhall Drive) sometime after 18th December 1897 and before 28th May 1899 when the car was renumbered from 88. The route was from Murrayfield to Nether Liberton via Haymarket, the General Post Office and Craigmillar Park. The advertisements are Hudson's Soap and D. & G. Glen's House Furnishing Stores Nos. 5 & 6 Maitland Street.

Transport Officials and Staff

A wide variety of head gear is evident in this photograph of officials and staff taken either at Shrubhill depot or perhaps at the Edinburgh Street Tramways Co.'s new premises at Morton Street. The occasion could be the transfer of ownership of much of the Edinburgh Street Tramways Co. to the Edinburgh and District Tramways Co. Ltd. in June 1894. In the background are two horse-buses 'constructed for 12 in, 14 out', the left-hand one with a destination board for Leith and Stockbridge, and the right-hand one for Echo Bank, at the foot of Dalkeith Road.

Wilkie & Paul

Wilkie & Paul, brassfounders and tin plate manufacturers, were at Montgomery Street in 1861, moving to Grove Works in Brandfield Street (off Grove Street) in 1864. By 1877 the nature of their business had expanded to 'tin plate and sheet metal workers, manufacturers of tin boxes and canisters of all descriptions for home and export use'. After the First World War the firm moved to Slateford Road, modernising and developing new processes and products. In the mid-1970s they were 'manufacturers of plastic sheet and decorated pressure-formed and vacuum formed plastic containers'. The photograph was taken at the Grove Works. The vehicle in the works entrance is a model T Ford, dated between 1918 and 1920, and the larger vehicle, S9807, is an Albion A10 32 horse power 4 cylinder dating from 1919–20. Almost 6,000 were made for military use during the 1914–18 War and many were reconditioned for commercial use at the end of hostilities.

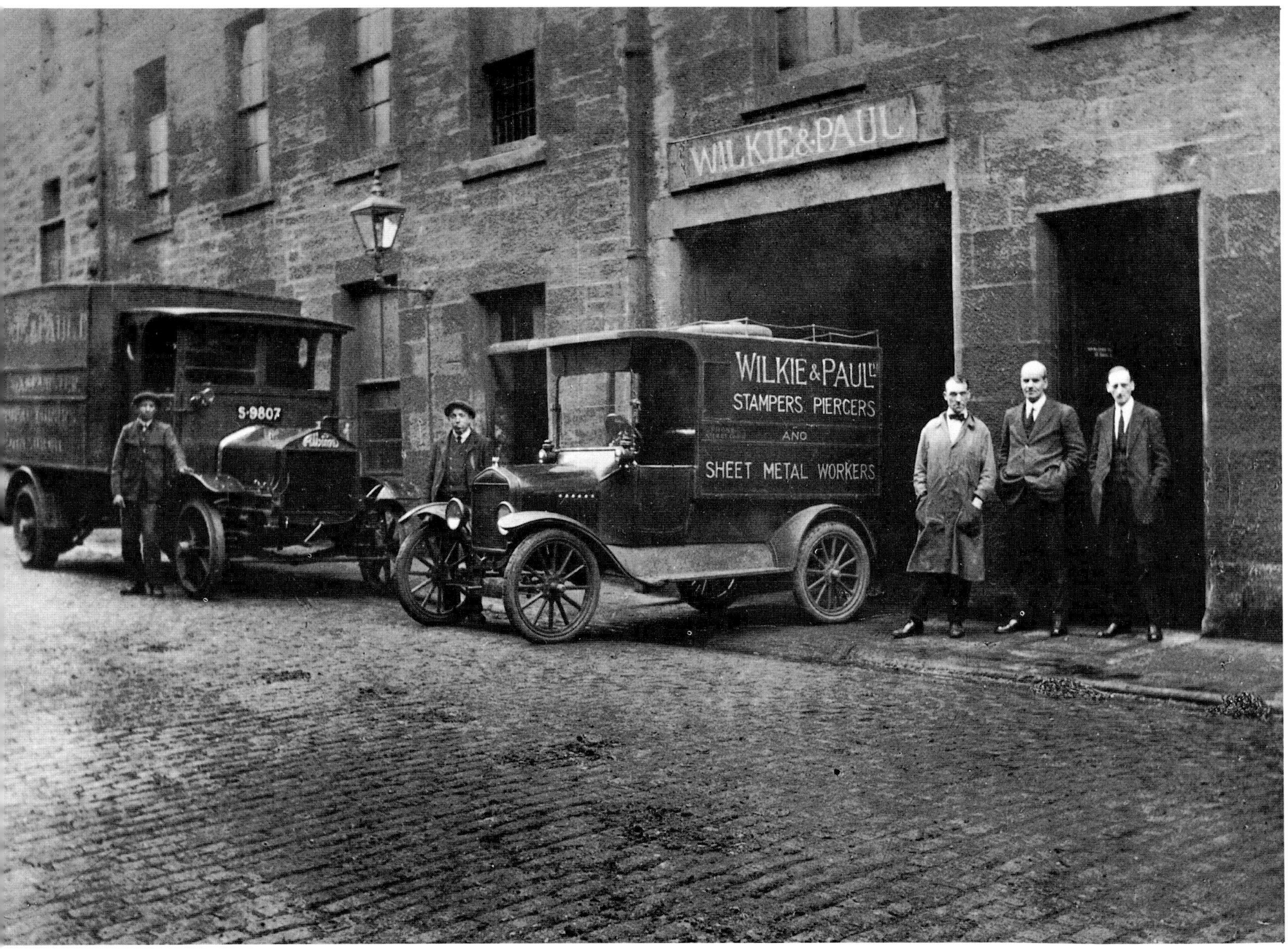

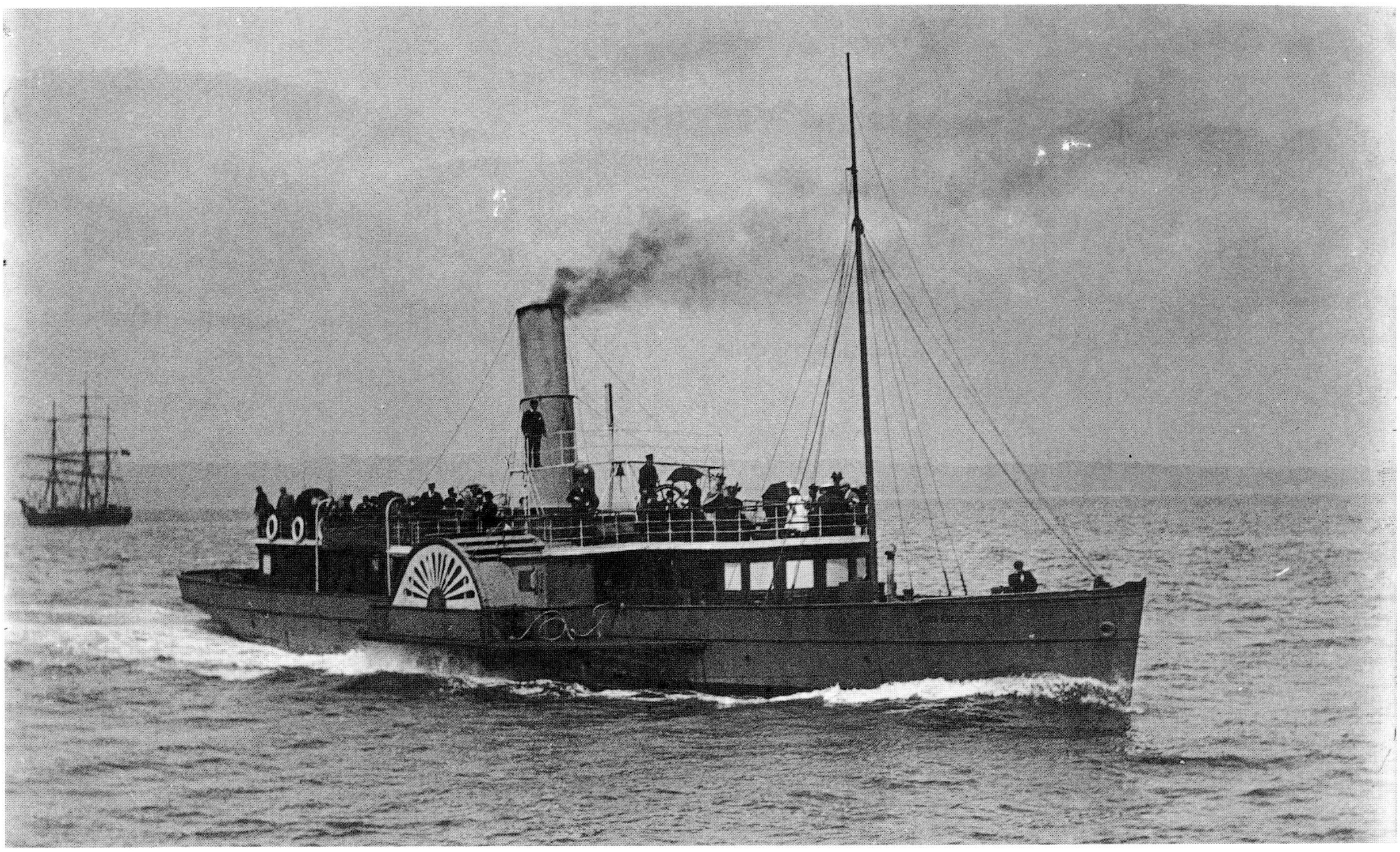

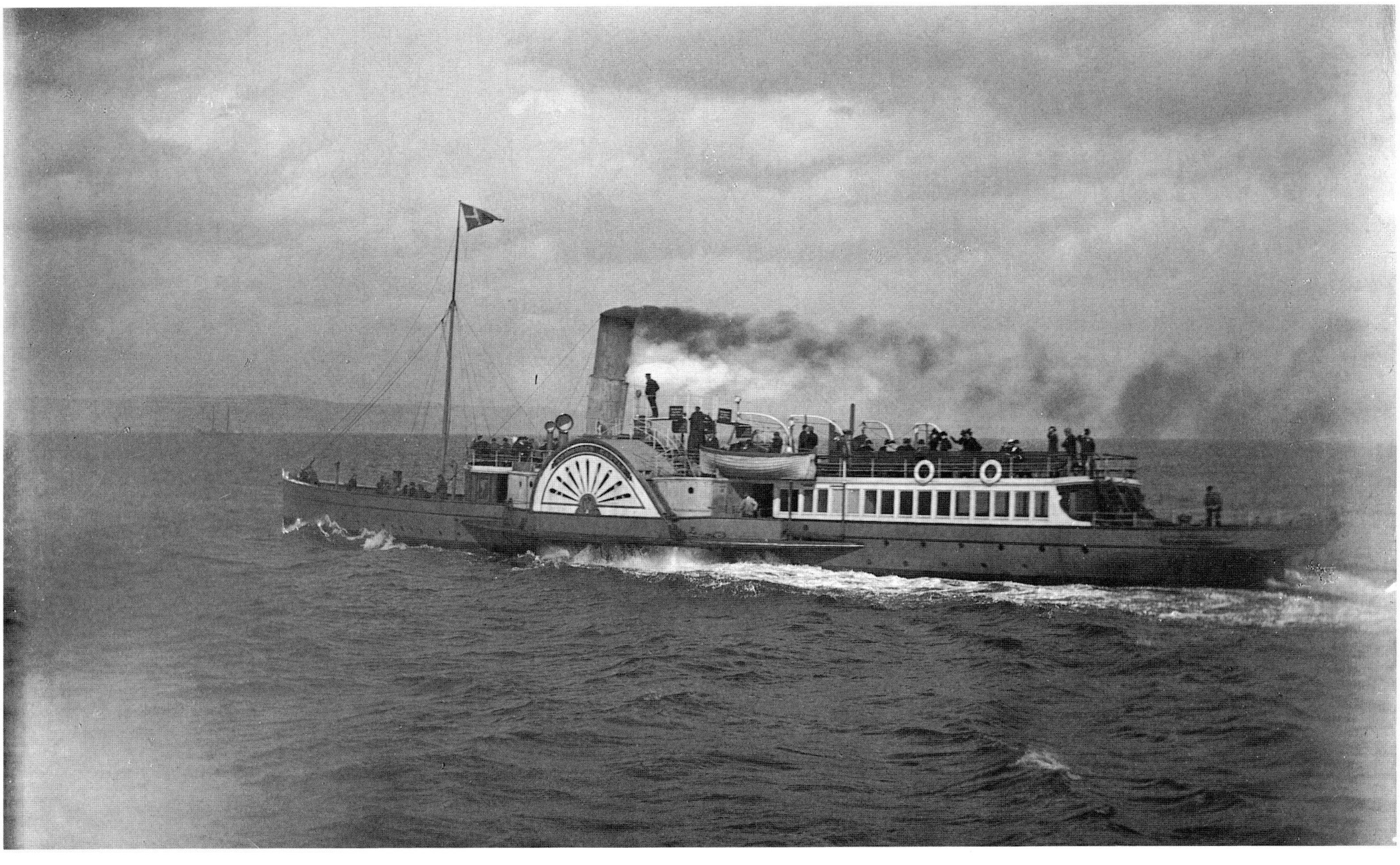

The *Lord Aberdour*

The iron paddle steamer, *Lord Aberdour,* was built in 1866 by Aitken and Mansel of Glasgow, owned by The Galloway Saloon Steam Packet Co., and registered at Leith. Its twin-cylinder oscillating engine was built by J. Aitken & Co. of Glasgow. Note the telescopic funnel to enable it to negotiate low bridges, and the absence of protection around the wheel. The photograph was taken in the Forth, c. 1897.

The *Edinburgh Castle*

The *Edinburgh Castle* — on a clear day within sight of its namesake — is far from its place of origin, having been built in 1879 by R. Duncan & Co. of Port Glasgow. The engine was also built in the west by Rankin and Blackmore of Greenock and The Lochgoil and Lochlong Steamboat Co. Ltd. was the original owner.

The Fleet at Port Edgar

The fleet of paddle steamers belonging to Galloway's of Leith was laid up for the winter at Port Edgar, South Queensferry. The Port takes its name from Edgar Atheling, who arrived there in 1066 with his sister Margaret, later Queen of Scotland, to take refuge at the Scottish court. In the early nineteenth century the harbour walls (with those at North and South Queensferry) were greatly improved at a cost of £35,825 from designs by Rennie, the civil engineer. George IV embarked from the improved harbour after his famous visit to Edinburgh in 1822. Today Port Edgar is a centre for water sports and all manner of pleasure craft.

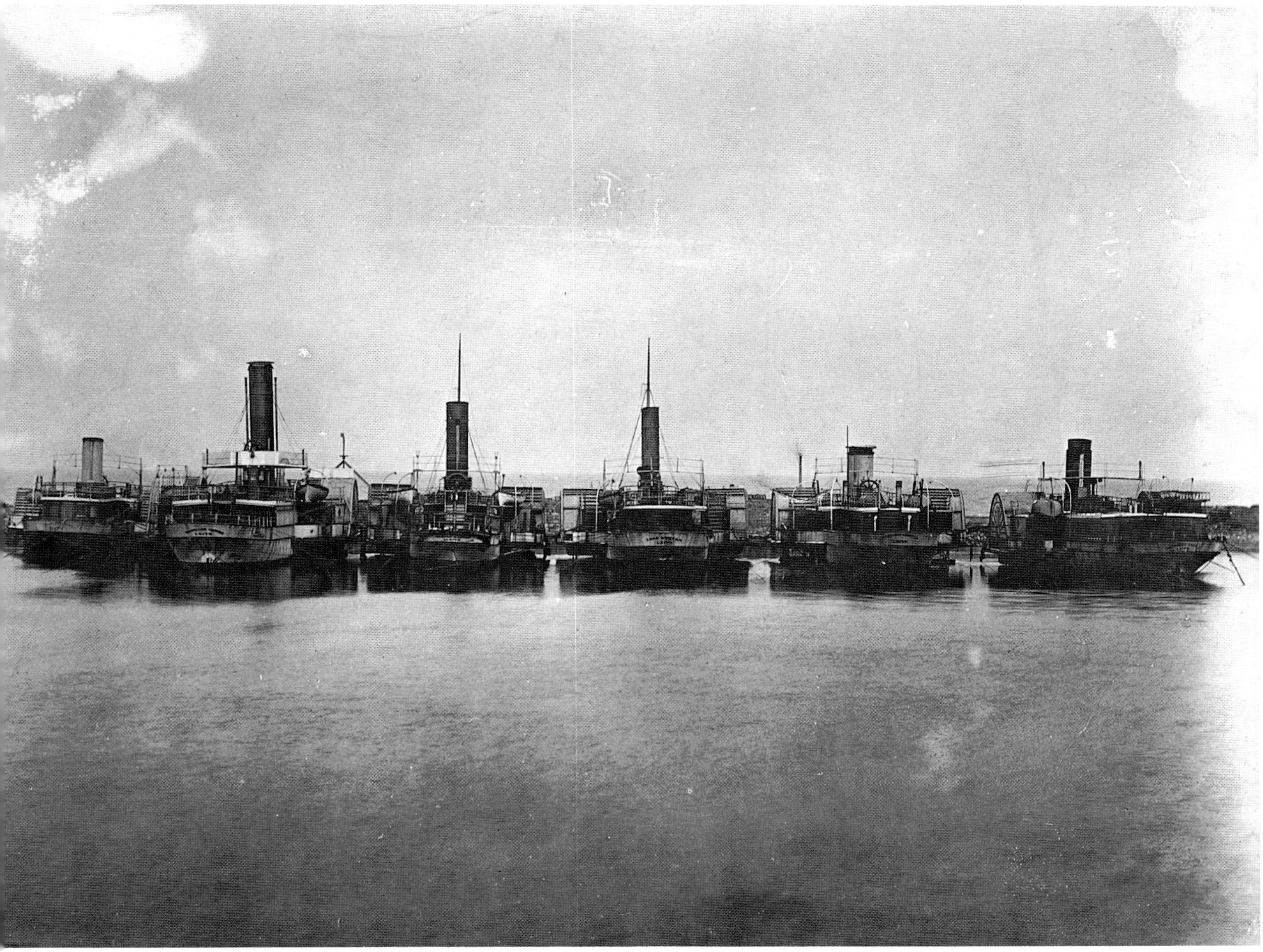

South Queensferry

There has been a ferry crossing at South Queensferry almost from time immemorial: Malcolm IV (1153–1165) 'made the monks of Dunfermline a grant of the right of ferry at the place'. In 1821 a ferry steamboat, the *Queen Margaret,* operated on the same route, but the available traffic was greatly reduced when the Granton to Burntisland ferry was opened. The photograph shows a later *Queen Margaret* at the quayside shortly before the opening of the Forth Road Bridge in 1964. In 1991 the *Spirit of Fife,* a high speed catamaran capable of carrying 250 passengers, reopened the Burntisland to Granton ferry in response to the long delays being experienced on the Forth Road Bridge.

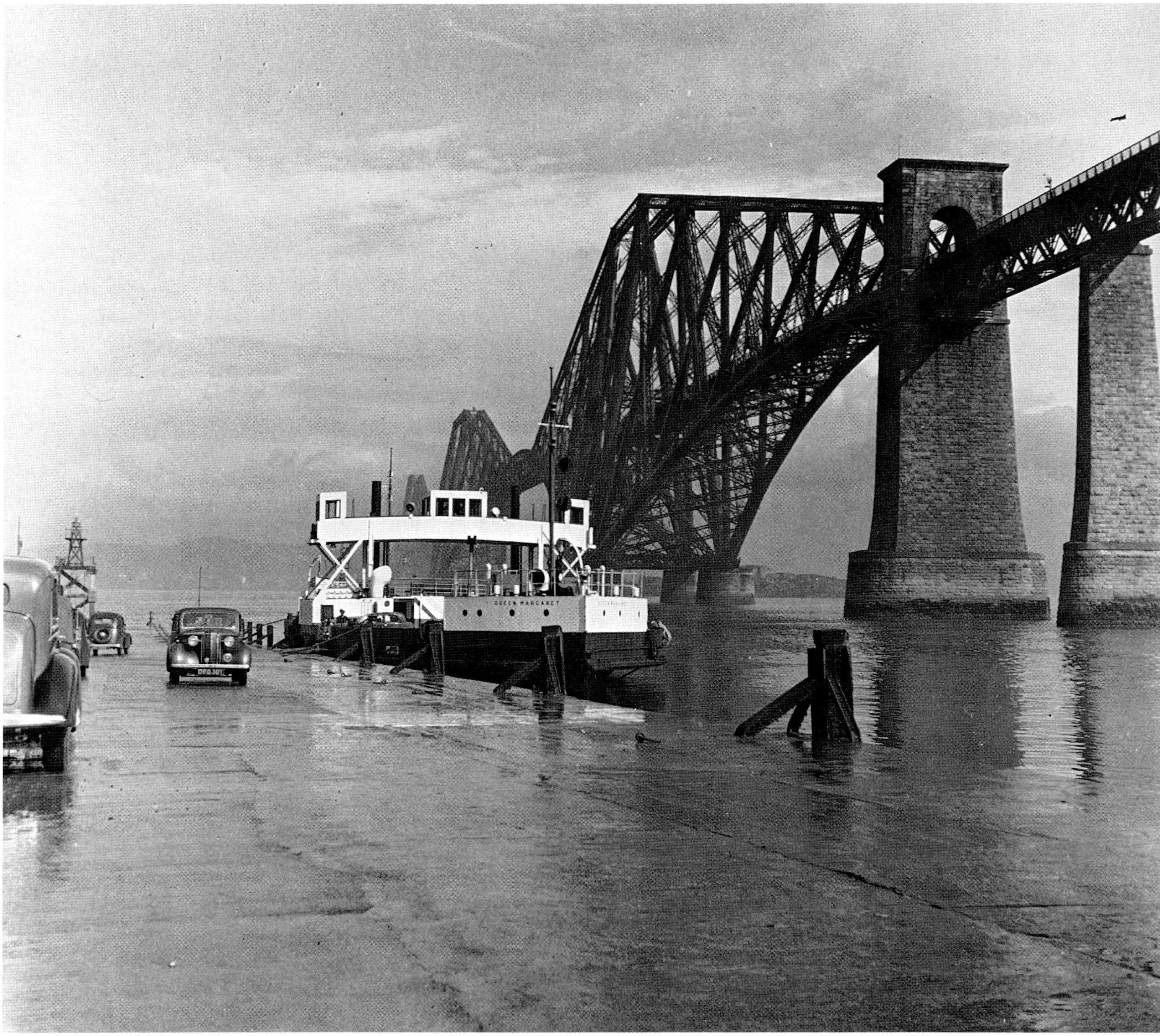

Sailing Ships at Cramond

At Cramond the River Almond was navigable for small boats up to at least Cockle Mill on the east bank. The photograph, *c.* 1850, is taken from the west bank on land belonging to Lord Rosebery and shows the old houses on the foreshore of Cramond village. Around 1700 at least five grain mills relied upon water power from the Almond at various locations up to Cramond Brig. This rural industry was later displaced by the iron industry in the latter part of the eighteenth century when nails, spades, hoes and anchors were made. Cramond never smelted its own iron but imported bar iron through Leith from Russia, Sweden and Holland.

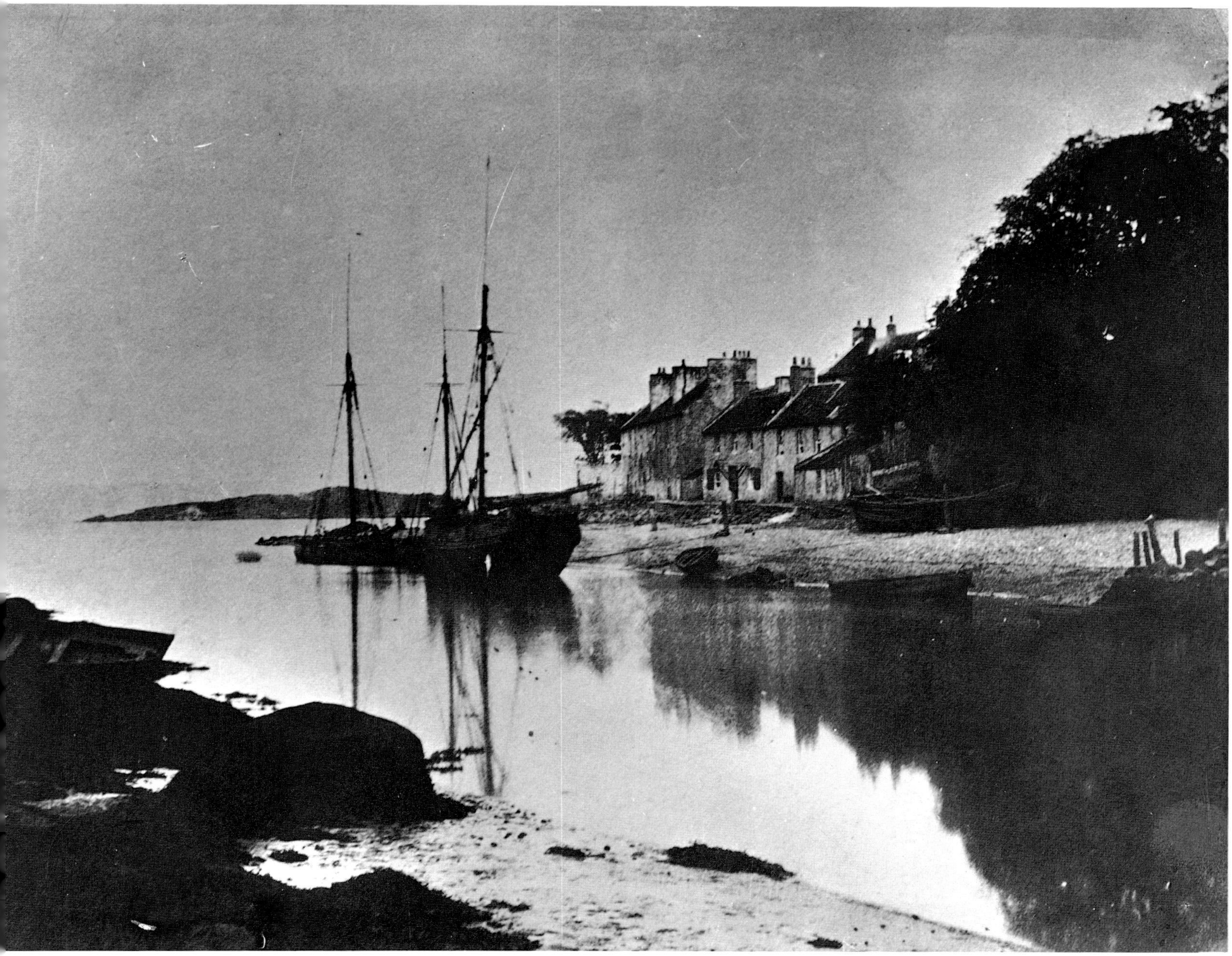

Cockle Mill on the River Almond

By 1900 Cramond was a popular day-outing from Edinburgh, although still maintaining its distinct character as a separate village. The riverside walk, seen on the left of the picture, was a popular venue for Sunday strollers of all ages — particularly with bowler hats. The building in the centre is Cockle Mill which took its name from the cockle weed which grows with corn crops. The mill was first recorded in 1178 as a possession of the Abbot of Inchcolm. In the middle of the eighteenth century it was converted from corn to iron slitting by the Smith and Wright Work Company of Leith. The cutting in the bank near the white tent was where the boats berthed carrying the coal to heat the iron. The shaping and cutting machines were powered by water from the Almond.

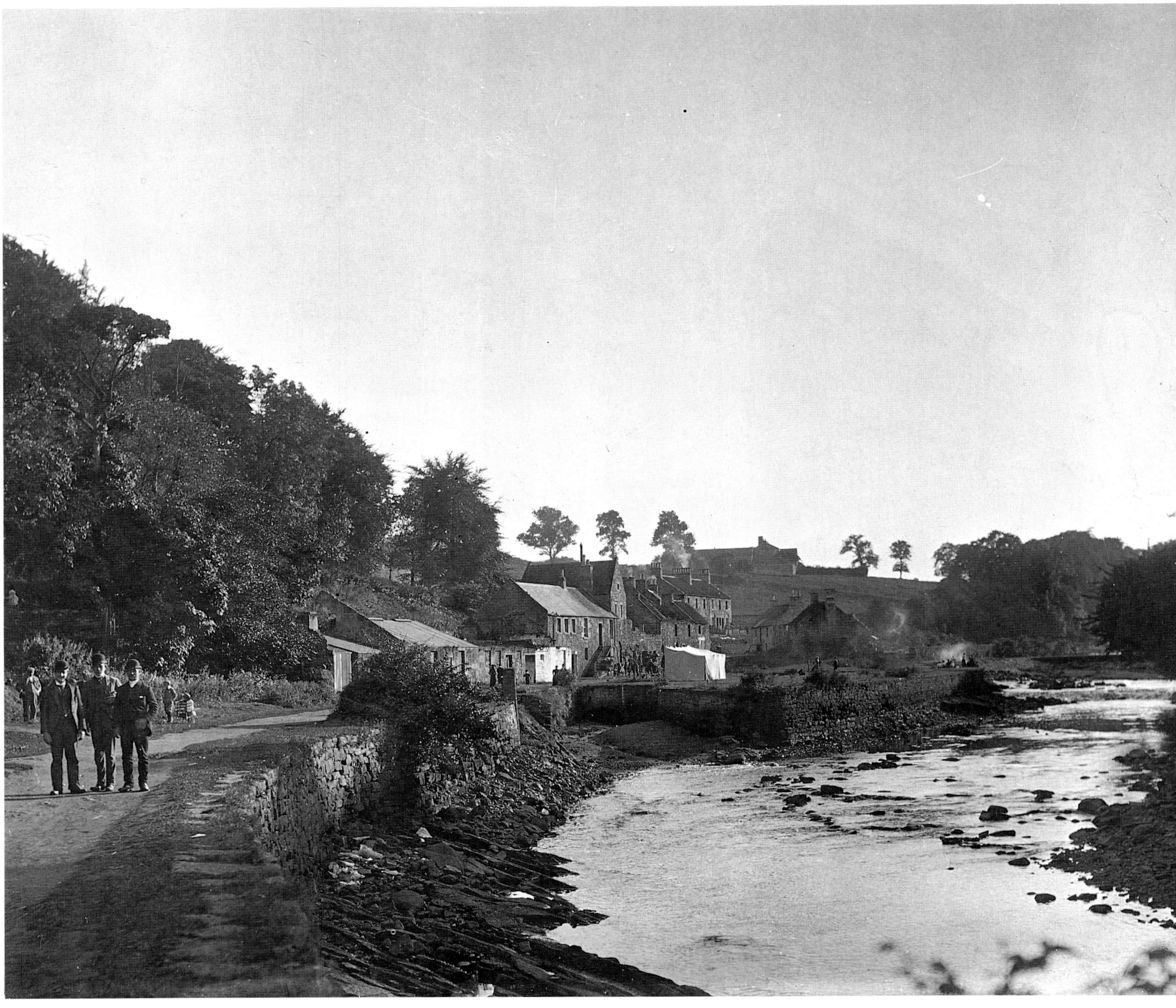

Cramond Foreshore

Cramond foreshore, in 1900, was popular with families — and hens — long before the promenade was built. On the far bank the ferryman has just collected passengers from Lord Rosebery's estate. A carriage or pony and trap was available for hire at Barnton Station to take visitors down to the sea. At the present day, the Old Maltings, on the left of the picture, is occupied as the Interpretation Centre for the Cramond Heritage Park, where exhibitions are mounted in the summer months by the Cramond Heritage Trust.

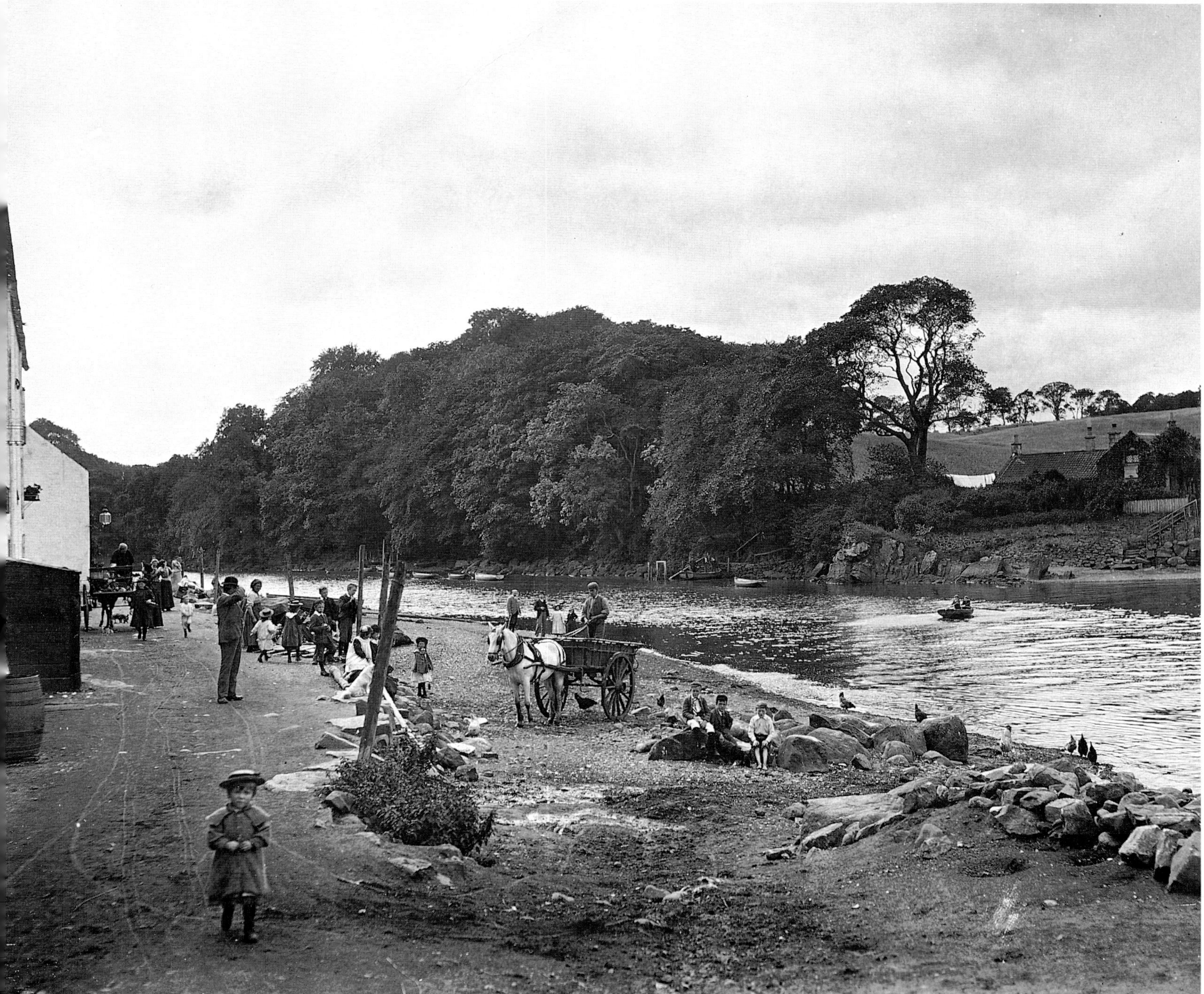

Peacock Inn, Newhaven

The Peacock Inn is a hostelry of great antiquity which for many years has been a centre of local activity at Newhaven, as well as attracting visitors from much further afield to sample its gastronomic delights. Originally the Peacock consisted of a few one-storey cottages facing the sea, but later a more substantial building was erected in Peacock's Court with bar accommodation on the ground floor and the dining room and bedrooms on the upper floor. The photograph shows Main Street *c.* 1850 looking west, with the Peacock Inn on the right and fishermen's cottages on the left.

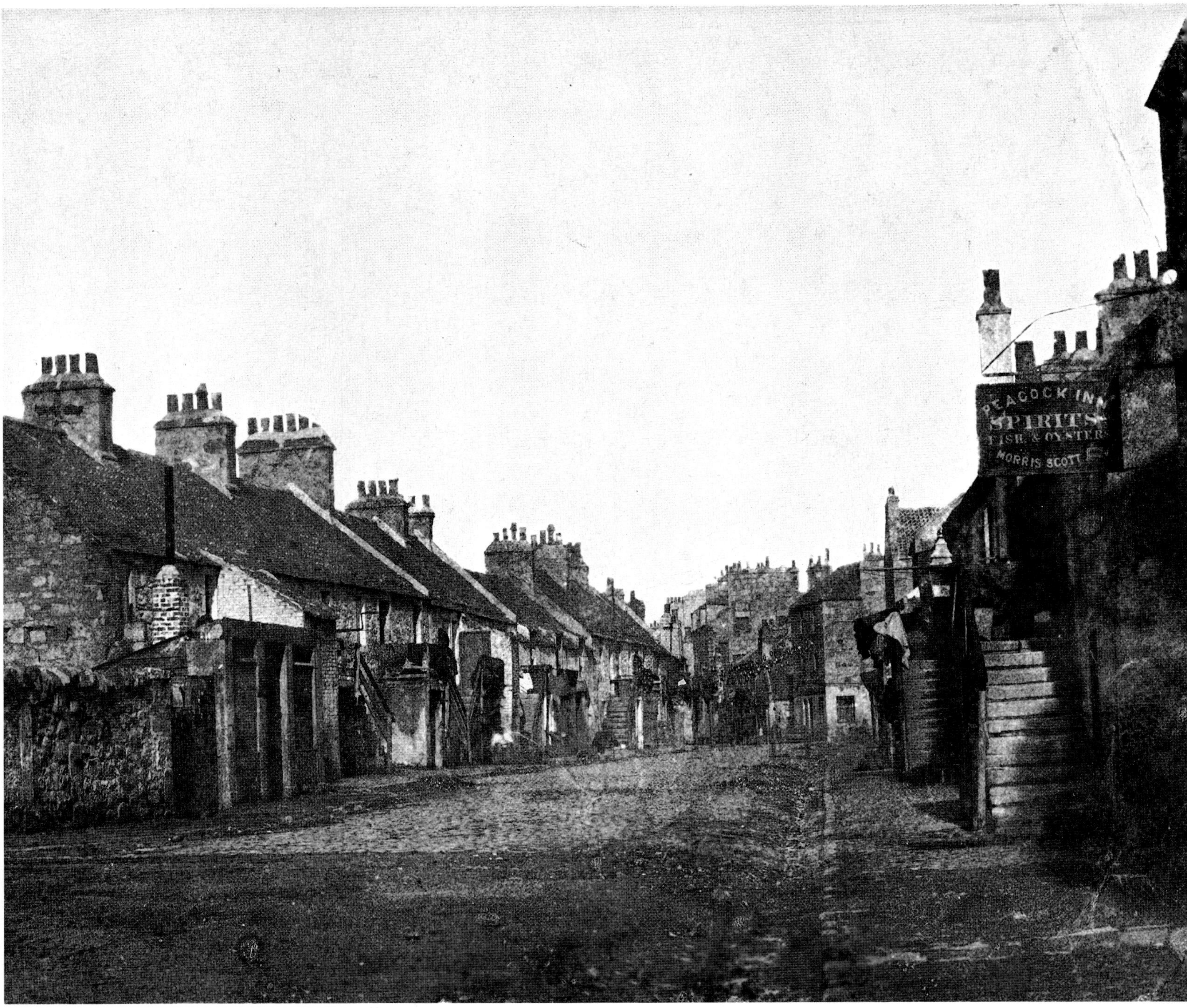

Fishwives at Newhaven

The 'New Haven' came to prominence in the early sixteenth century in opposition to the 'Old Haven' of Blackness on the Forth. It was for generations a very close-knit community in which young men and women were discouraged from marrying outside the village. The fishing industry was centred on the harbour which, in its heyday, launched the *Great Michael* in 1511. Whilst the fathers and sons went to sea the mothers and daughters repaired the nets and carried their creels of fish, for sale, to almost every district of Edinburgh. The group seen in the photograph are at the harbour with the outline of St Andrew's Free Church, built in 1852, in the background.

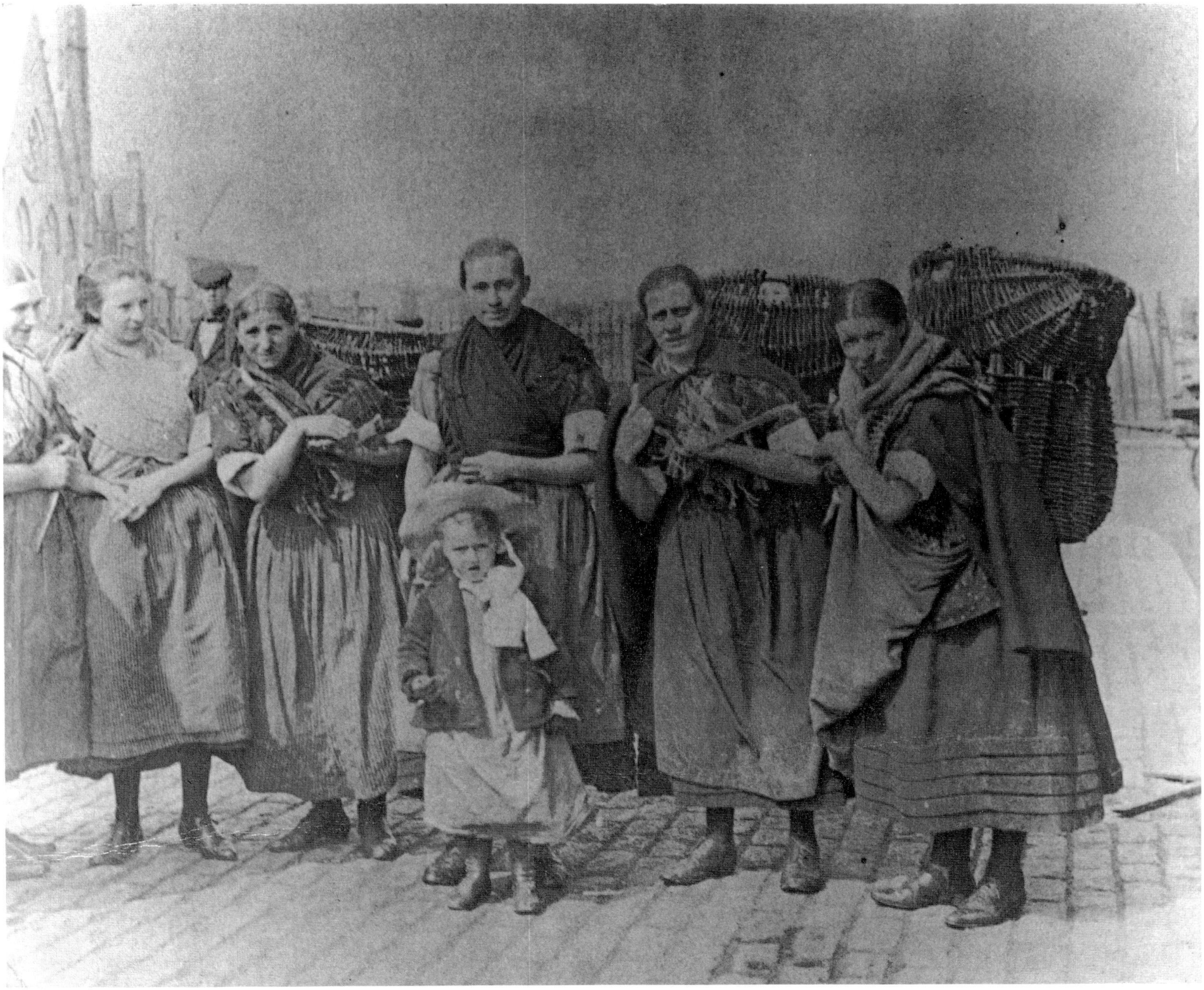

Portobello Pier

High fashion does not appear to stand in the way of a day on the pleasure boats at Portobello in 1880: the men even retain their bowler hats. In the background the famous Portobello pier extends 1,250 feet into the Firth of Forth. It was constructed of iron in 1871 at a cost of £7,000, near the foot of Bath Street. From the shore a broad flight of steps led to the 20-foot wide pier, which opened out at the head into a wide arena with an observatory and a restaurant, where a band provided entertainment in the summer months. It was also a port of call for several excursion steamers to various ports on the Forth and beyond.

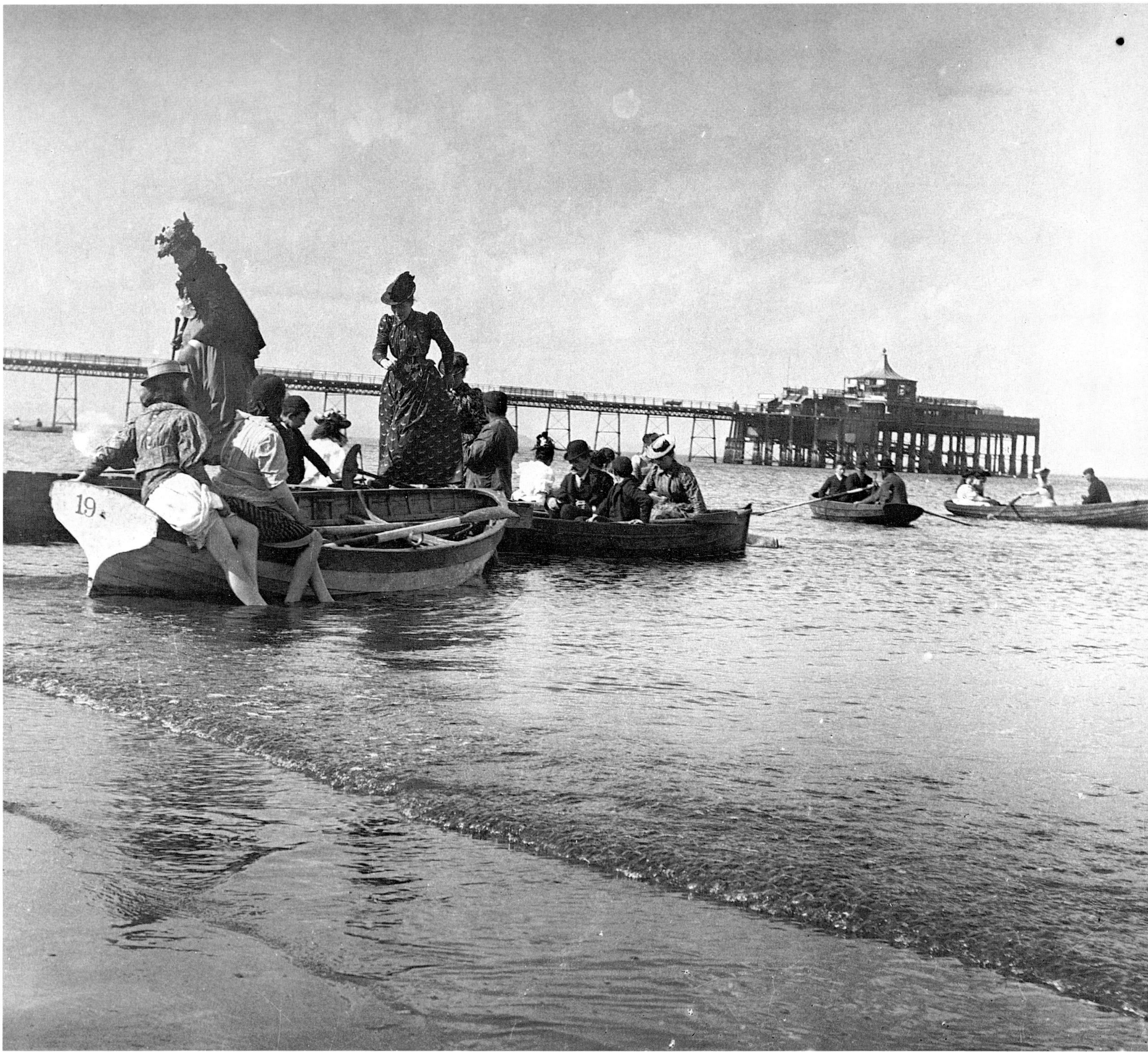

Amusement Arcade at Portobello

Follow the crowd and join in the fun — at the Tower Amusements at the foot of Tower Street, Portobello, owned in the 1950s by Erin A. Deane, amusement caterer. Candy floss and a camera man compete for custom close to the canvas canopies. In the background, in sharp contrast, is the castellated architecture of Portobello Tower built in 1785 for the lawyer, John Cunningham.

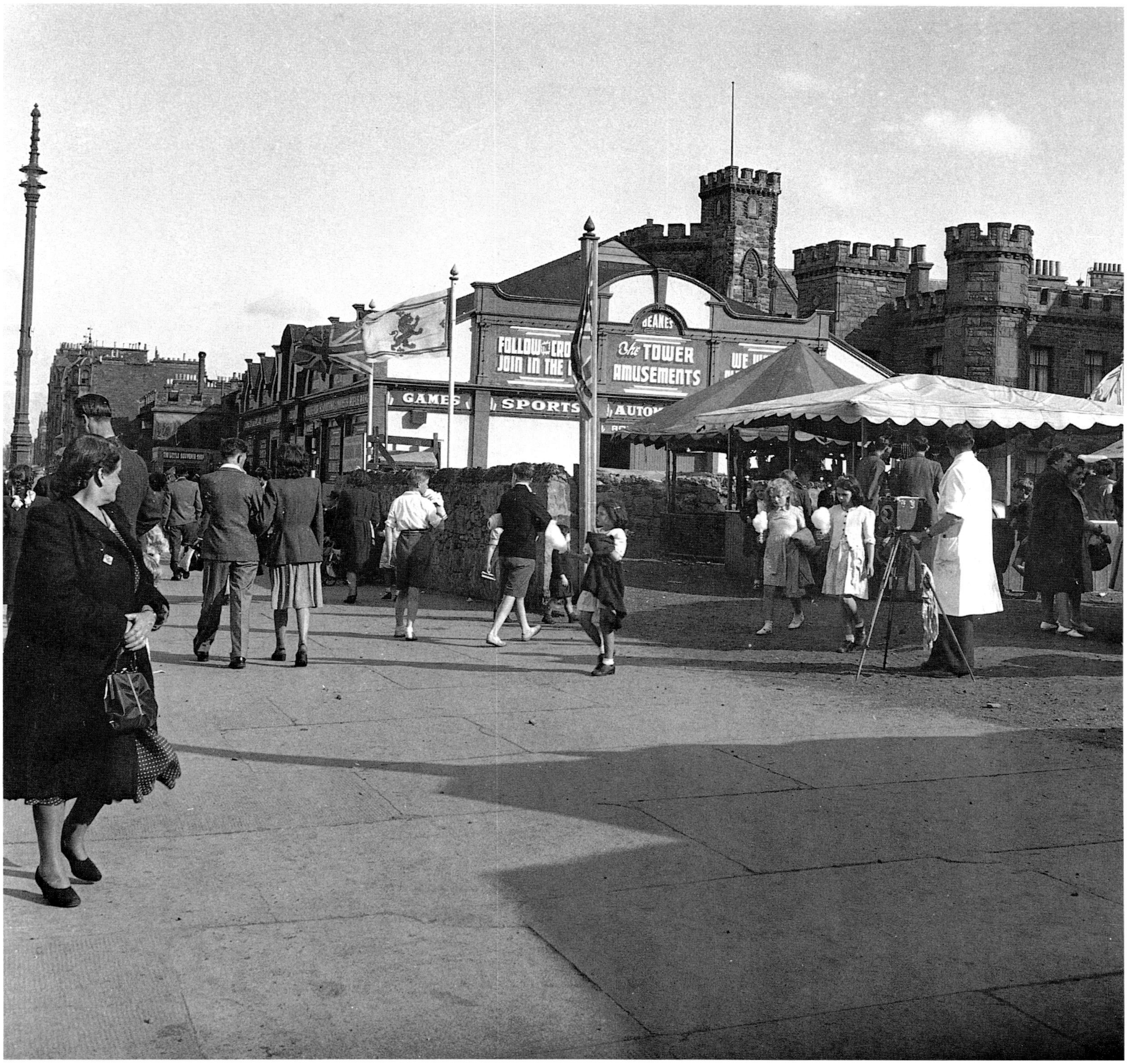

Portobello Fairground

This gentle merry-go-round, designed for the younger children, fails to hold the attention of the older boys when there is a chance to face the camera. On the right, the boy with the towel under his arm has probably been to Portobello Open Air Pool nearby. Left of centre the best dressed scout has socks with school colours, stocking tabs, and black Gibson shoes — but his friends are less fortunate.

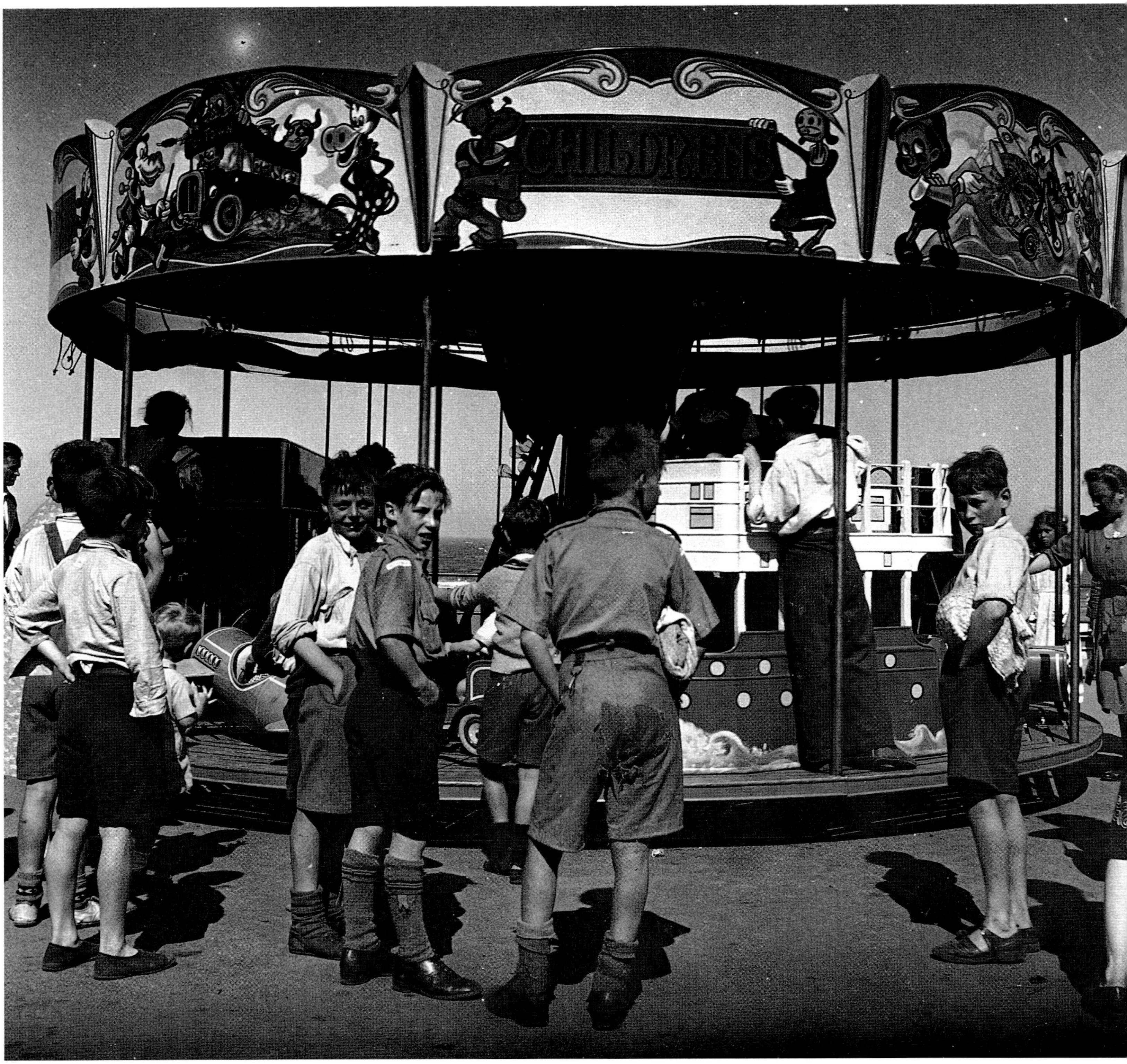

Portobello Open Air Pool

Portobello Open Air Pool was designed in cream and green painted concrete by the City Engineer, W. A. Macartney, and constructed between 1934 and 1936. It measured 100 metres by 50 yards and was equipped with a five-level high dive, flanked by two spring boards on each side. The normal outdoor temperature of the salt water was raised a few degrees by having come through the cooling plant of Portobello Power Station nearby.

The pool, opened in May 1936, also had a system of artificial waves, actuated for ten minutes every hour by machinery at the deep end of the pool, regulated so that the waves broke at the shallow end like a natural tide. Spectators were charged 3d. and bathers 6d. without time restriction. The pool was patrolled by lifeguards dressed in white trousers and jerseys, at least one of whom — Sean Connery — went on to greater things.

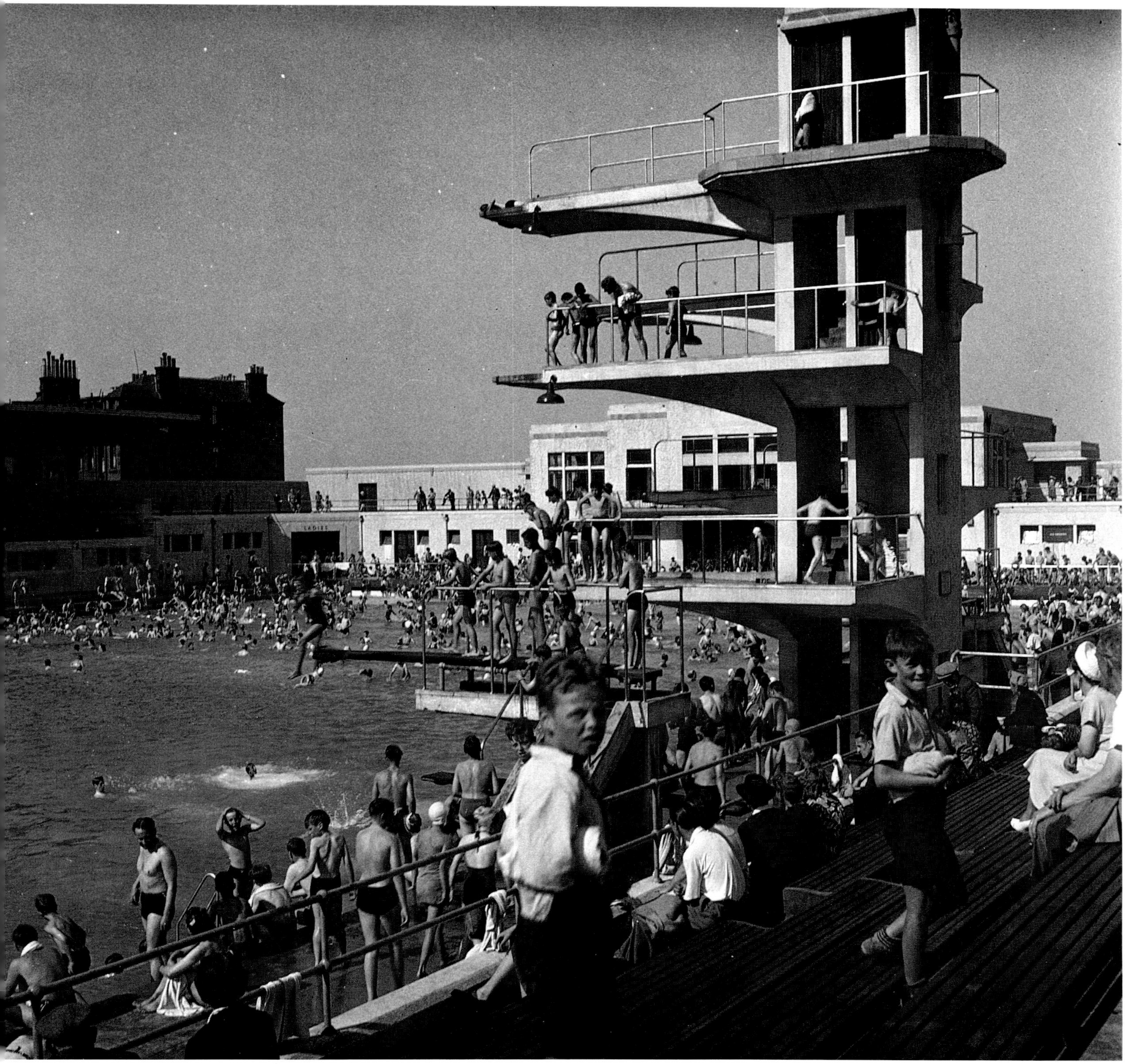

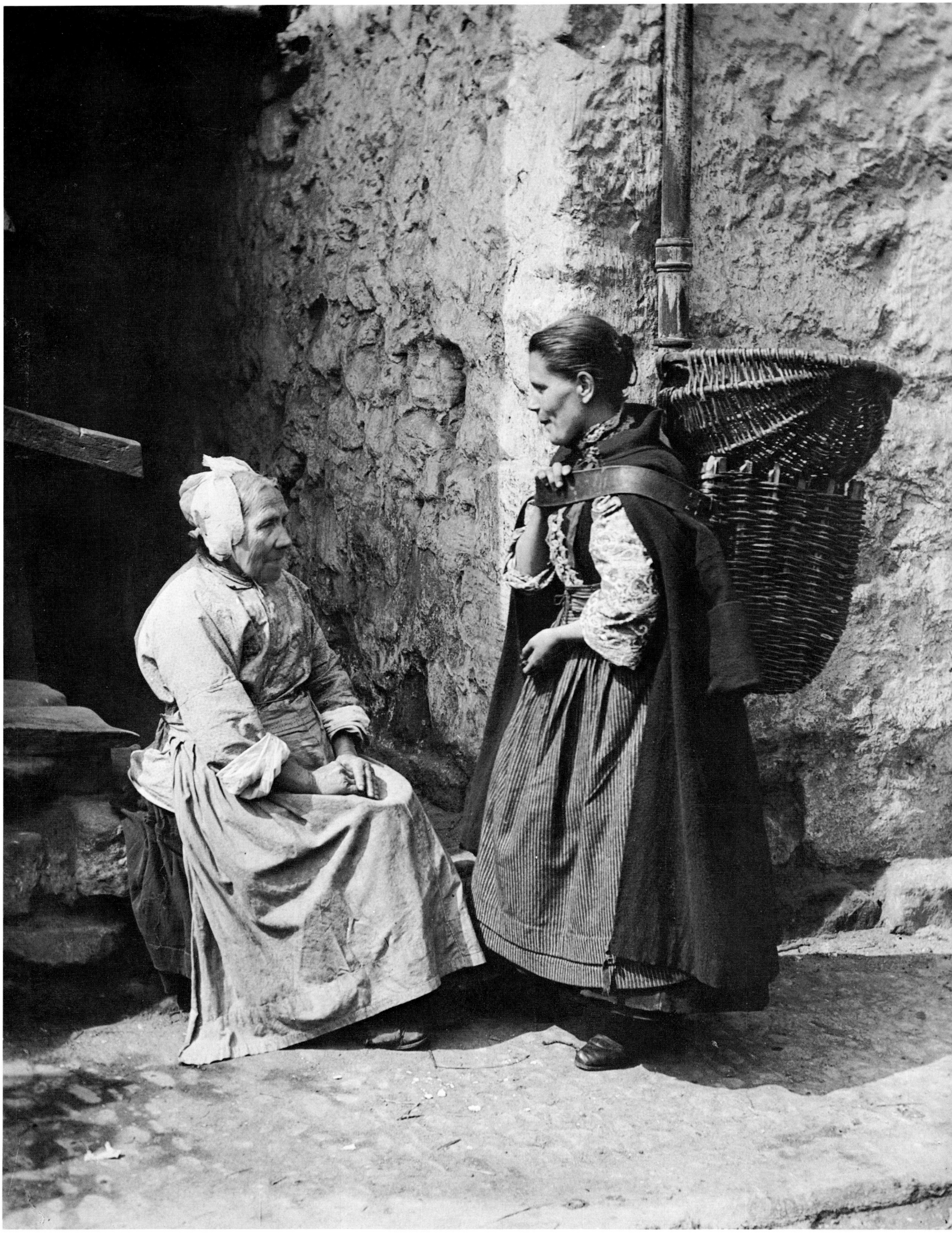

Fishwives at Fisherrow

Fish have been landed at Fisherrow almost from time immemorial. *The Statistical Account of Scotland* described in 1795 the arduous task of distribution, when a group of three fishwives would take it in turn to carry a heavy creel of fish five miles 'to reach Edinburgh before dinner'. Between the two World Wars several fishwives were operating from Fisherrow, but they attended the early morning fish auctions at Newhaven before setting out to Edinburgh, Fife and the Borders. The young lady in the photograph, *c.* 1880, is carrying a creel and scull. The scull is the top shallow basket used for white fish, and the creel, or deep basket, was normally used for dry fish such as kippers.

Baiting the Line

After a lifetime carrying the creel, the older generation took on the tasks of repairing the nets, washing the bait, and baiting the lines. In the early days, one boat might cast five or six lines, each line 'belonging' to a different family. The photograph, believed to be at Fisherrow, shows an elderly lady baiting the line with mussels. To her right, the baited line is being laid in a rough bed of cut grass, which prevented the line from becoming tangled and also helped to keep the bait fresh. In the background the old man is probably washing the mussels before they are put on the line.

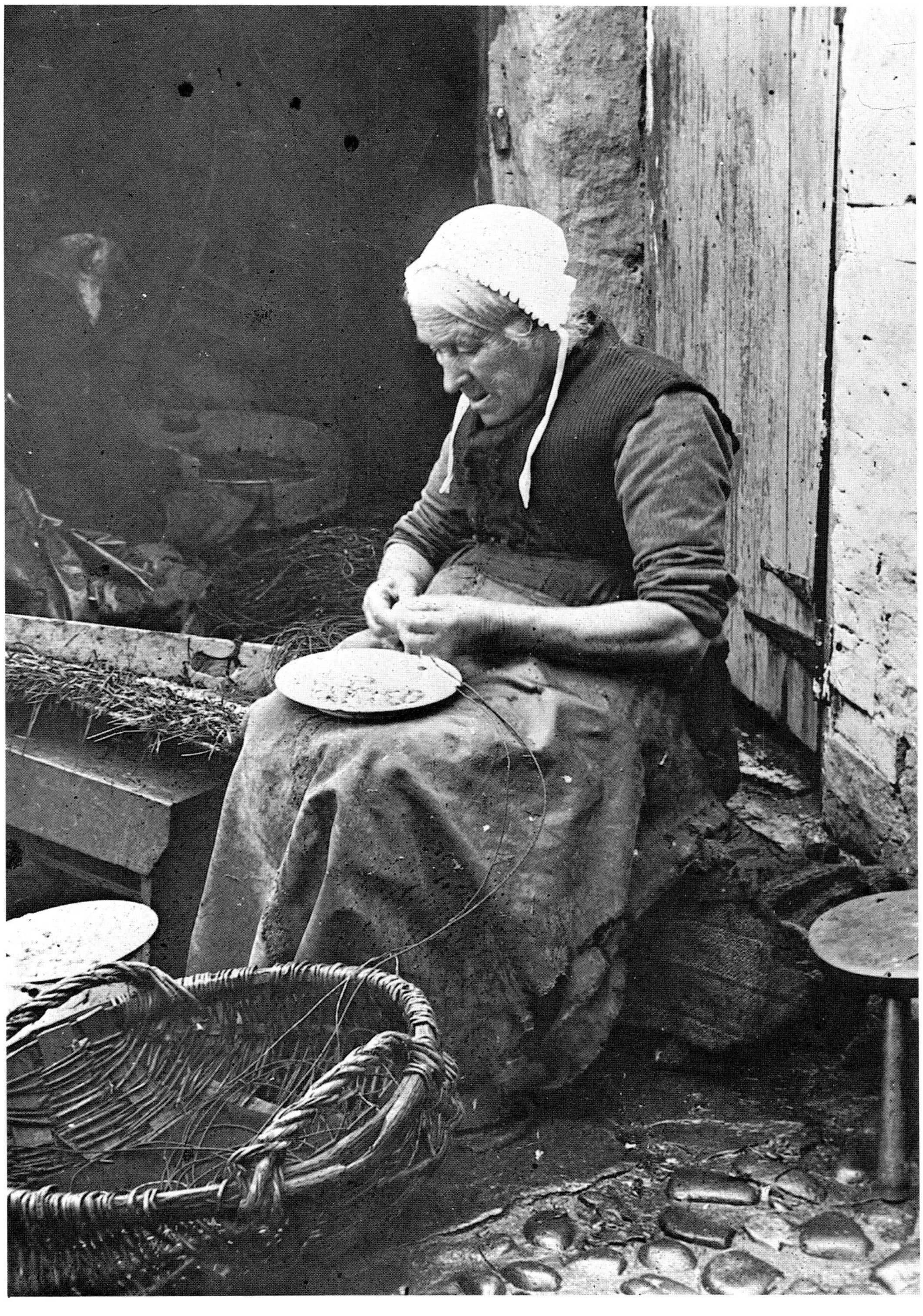

Street Scene in Fishing Community

This busy, somewhat theatrical street scene has not been clearly identified as there are two conflicting claims. The older residents of Fisherrow say that the house with the outside stairway still exists at New Street, Fisherrow, and that a copy of this picture hangs in the Old Fishermen's Club nearby. Equally interesting is the evidence that the scene is at the east end of North Street, St Andrews, and that a copy of the Yerbury picture hangs in the Scottish Fisheries Museum in Anstruther. Unfortunately, known photographs of the North Street house do not confirm certain details of construction, i.e., in the North Street house the door is too high and the roof does not show dormer windows, which the Yerbury house is known to have had. The most compelling evidence, which is clearly in favour of the St Andrews' argument (although probably not at North Street) comes from quite another source. The lady in the centre of the picture, carrying a shallow basket in her right hand, is Mary Duff, identified by relatives and from other photographs as a lifelong resident of St Andrews who had no known connection with Fisherrow.

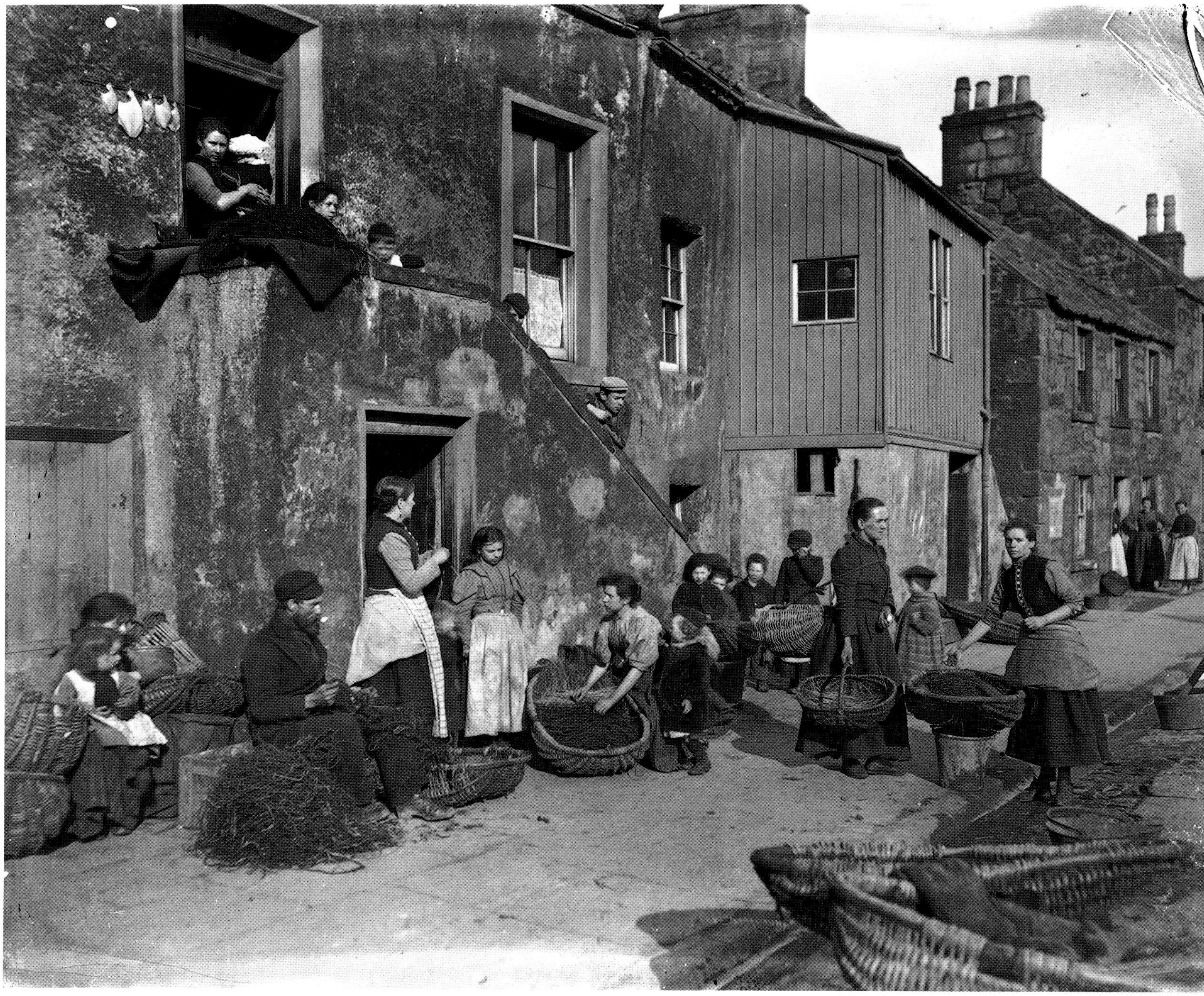

The Original Rosslyn Inn

The Original Rosslyn Inn is said to have been established in 1827 but no written record of it can be traced before 1857. The photograph was probably taken c. 1864 when David Neil became the proprietor. His name appears above the entrance on the left, and on the gable end: DAVID NEIL LATE OUGHTON. Mrs Oughton, whose family were farmers at Moat, Roslin, was the proprietor from 1857 to 1864. It is still a thriving hotel in Roslin, although many of the original features have been lost. The stables to the right of the picture were demolished many years ago and the site is now occupied by an extension to the hotel. The extension bears a date stone, 1892, and the initials M.P. for Margaret Pringle.

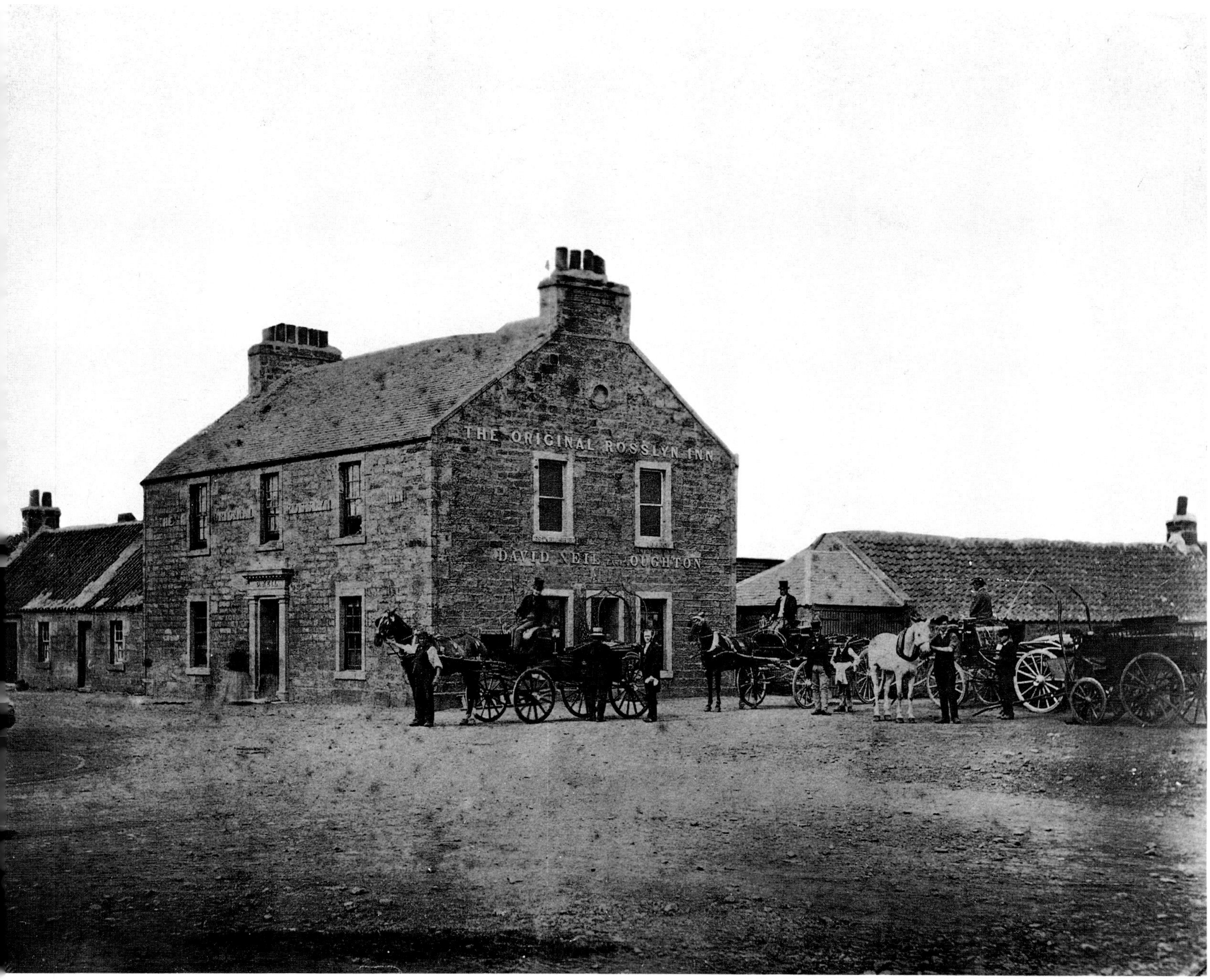

Seaside at North Berwick

At North Berwick in 1890 the attractions of the seaside appear timeless. In the twentieth century North Berwick became a popular seaside resort frequented by people from Edinburgh and throughout Scotland. Its history, however, dates from at least the fourteenth century when it became a royal burgh during the reign of Robert III. The Bass Rock, seen in the background of the picture, rises to 320 feet, and is a famous breeding ground for gannets and other seabirds. It belonged for centuries to the Lauder family and has housed a hermitage, a chapel and a prison at various times in its history.

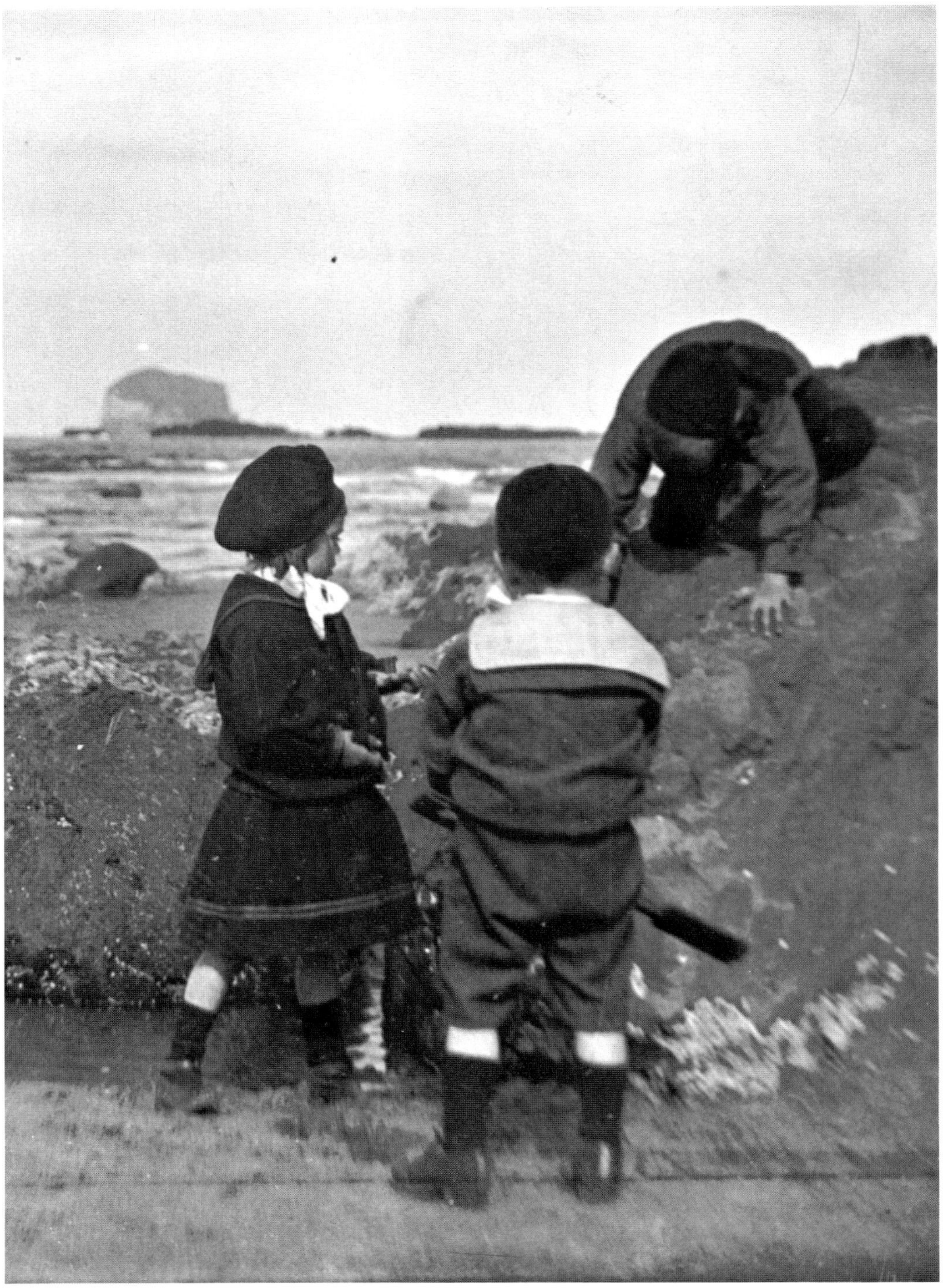

Seaside Boarding Party at North Berwick

All aboard for Treasure Island! There is no shortage of children keen to set sail from this very rudimentary boarding plank at North Berwick c. 1890. Each child is a study in itself. The would-be sailor in the centre of the picture has brought along his hoop and stick in case interest should begin to flag. Has the boy with the very short trousers had a lovers' tiff or has he spied something more attractive in the water?

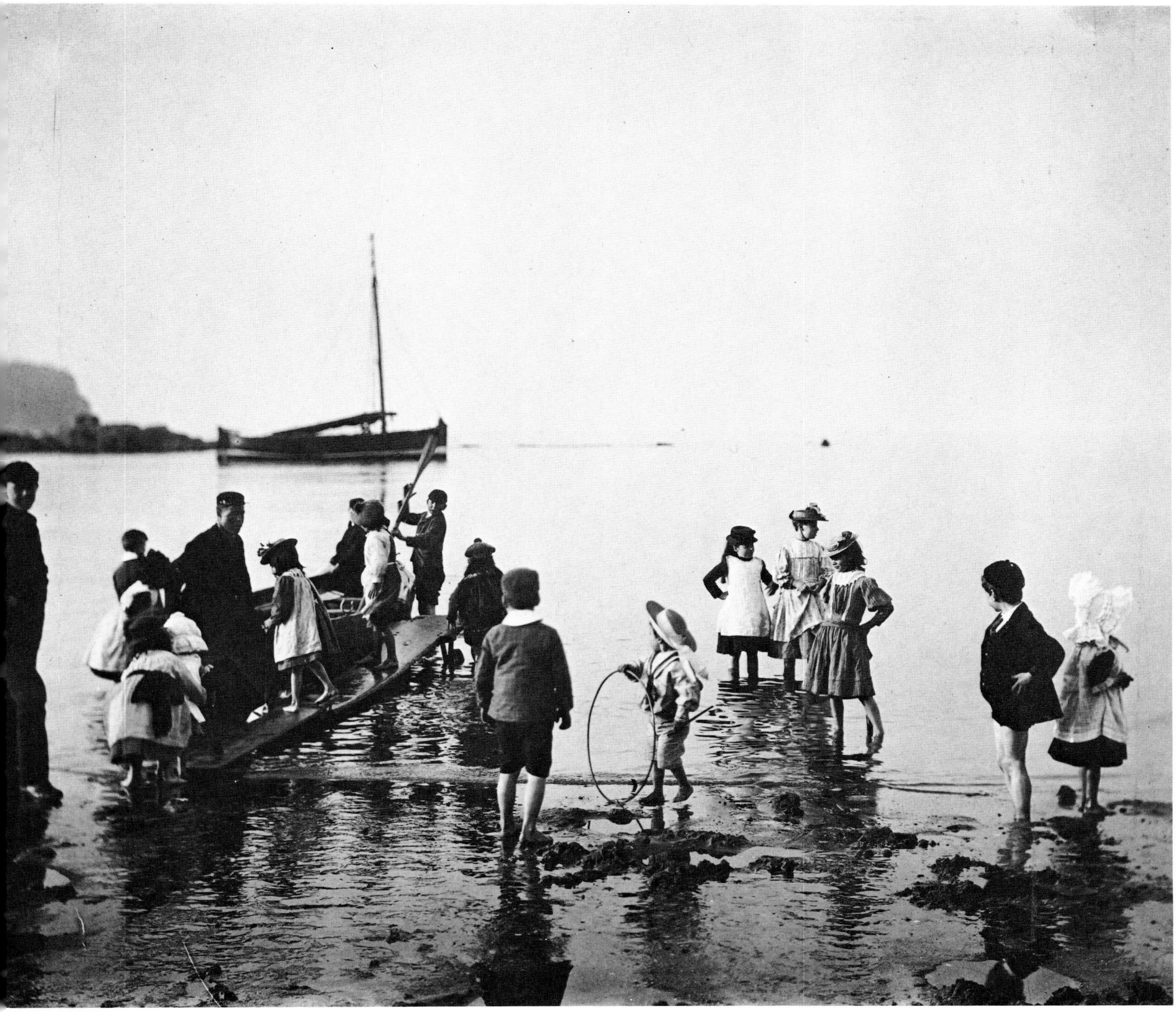

CHAPTER 6

Arrival in Edinburgh of King Edward VII and Queen Alexandra

Edward VII came to the throne on 22nd January 1901 on the death of his mother, Queen Victoria, who had reigned since 1837. His coronation was at Westminster Abbey on 9th August 1902. In May 1903 King Edward and Queen Alexandra visited Edinburgh, arriving at Waverley Station, where they were met by the Lord Provost, Town Clerk, City Chamberlain and members of Edinburgh Corporation. Forming the main part of the Guard of Honour were one hundred men of the Royal Navy from HMS *Anson,* dressed in straw hats, blue uniforms and brown gaiters. On arrival the Lord Provost presented to the King the keys of the city.

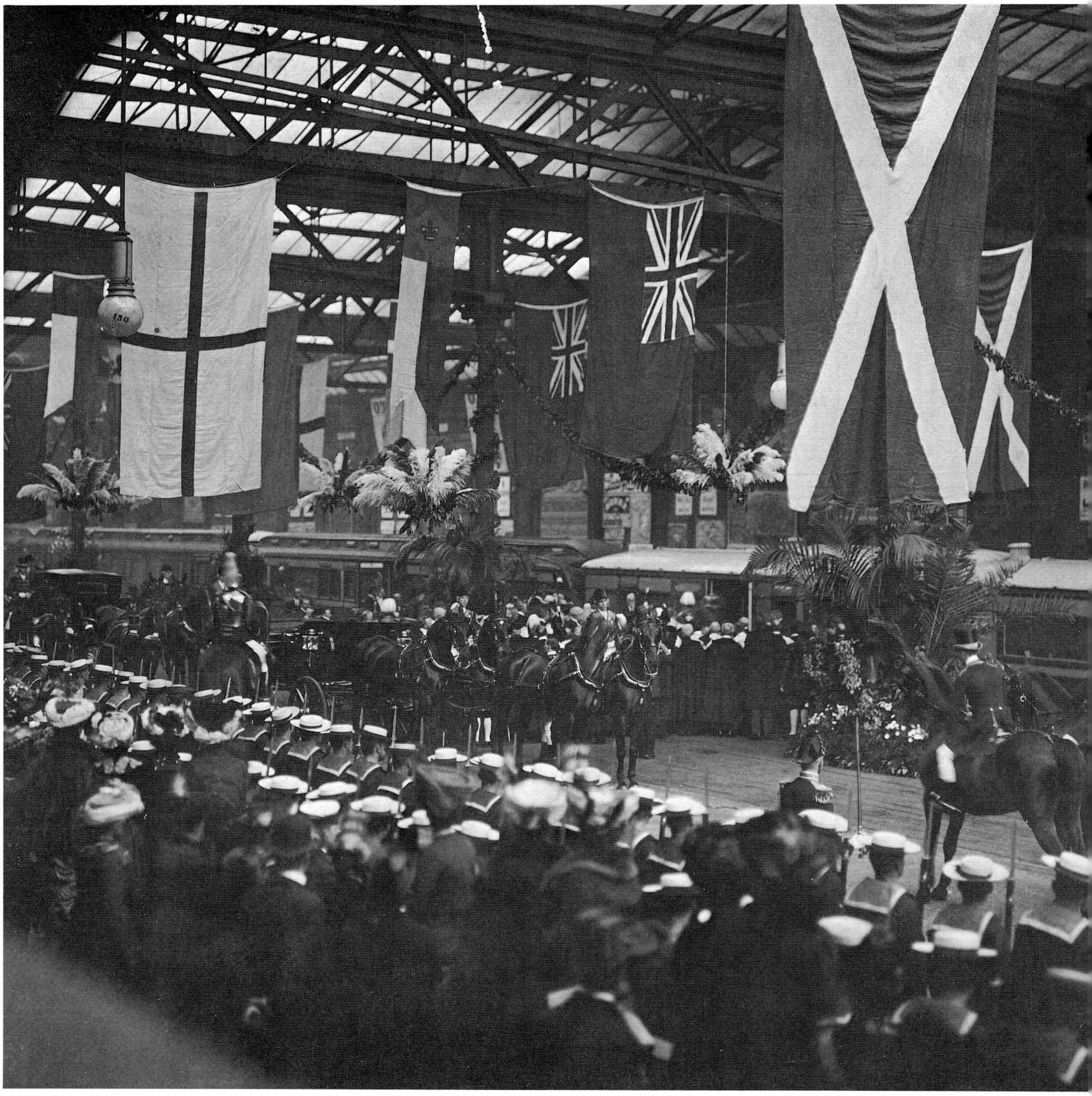

Maule's Corner

Maule's spared no expense in 1903 in decking out their corner premises at the west end of Princes Street with LONG LIVE THEIR MAJESTIES on the top floor, insignia and photographs of King Edward and Queen Alexandra on the middle floors, and the serious business of THE SALE OF SUMMER SALES at street level, proclaiming 'Substantial Reductions', 'Each Floor a Market', and 'Elegance with Economy'. To the right of Maule's, above the white sun-blind, are Barclay Bros., the photographers. Round into Hope Street is a Luncheon Bar with Wines and Spirits, and the Post Office beyond.

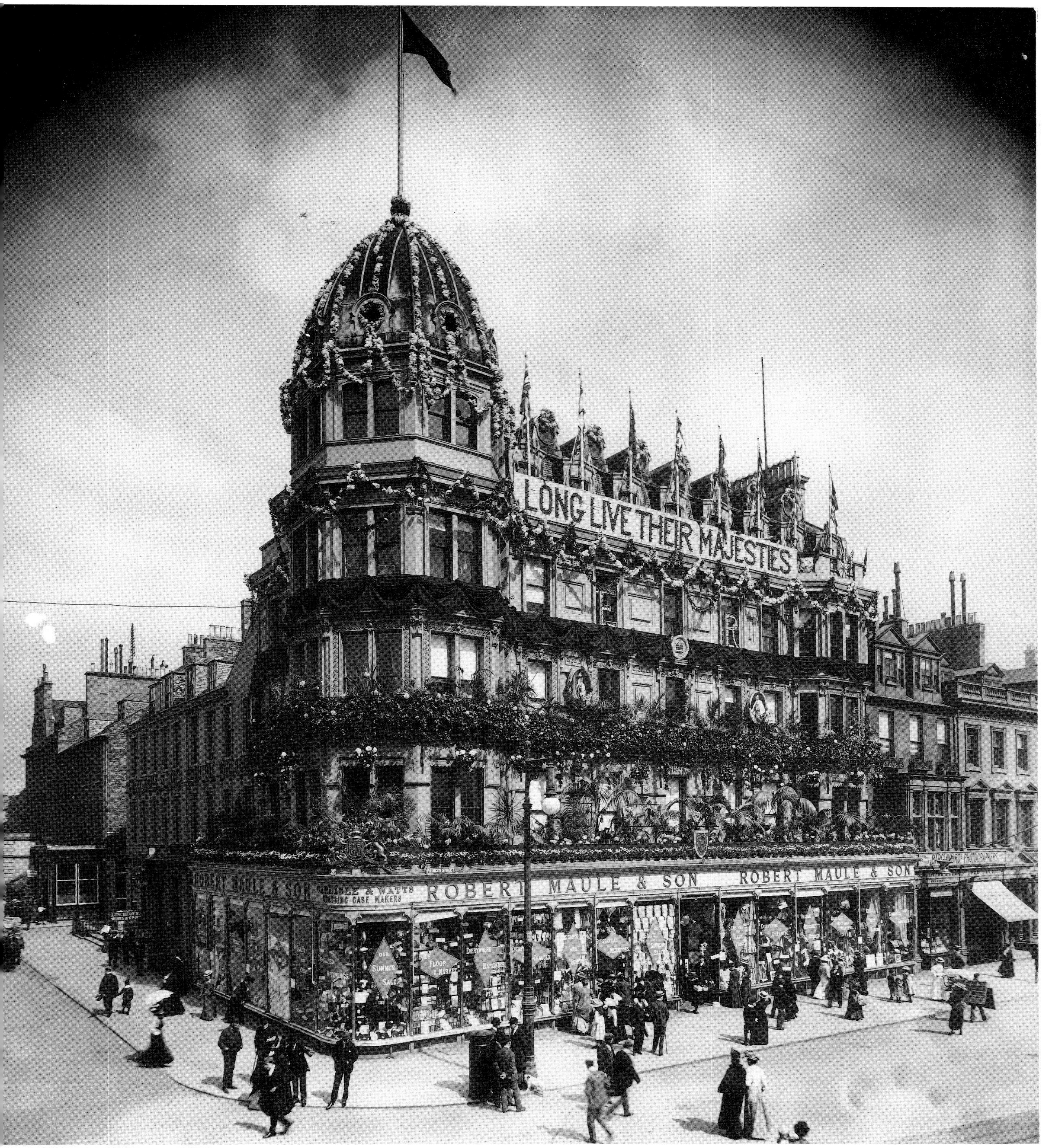

West End Arch

During their visit to Edinburgh in 1903 King Edward, Queen Alexandra and Princess Victoria stayed at Dalkeith Palace, vacated for the occasion by the Duke and Duchess of Buccleuch. Their Majesties' route to various engagements was decorated by several triumphal arches, similar to this one at the west end of Princes Street. To the left of the arch the shop with the white canopy is Wilson and Sharp, the jeweller: between it and the pillars is Duncan, Flockhart & Co., the chemists, with a mortar and pestle above the doorway.

Triumphal Arch at Lothian Road

A twin square-tower archway was erected at the foot of Lothian Road near the junction with King's Stables Road, with the message: LONG LIVE YOUR MAJESTIES. Several of the arches were in place many months before the royal visit in May 1903.

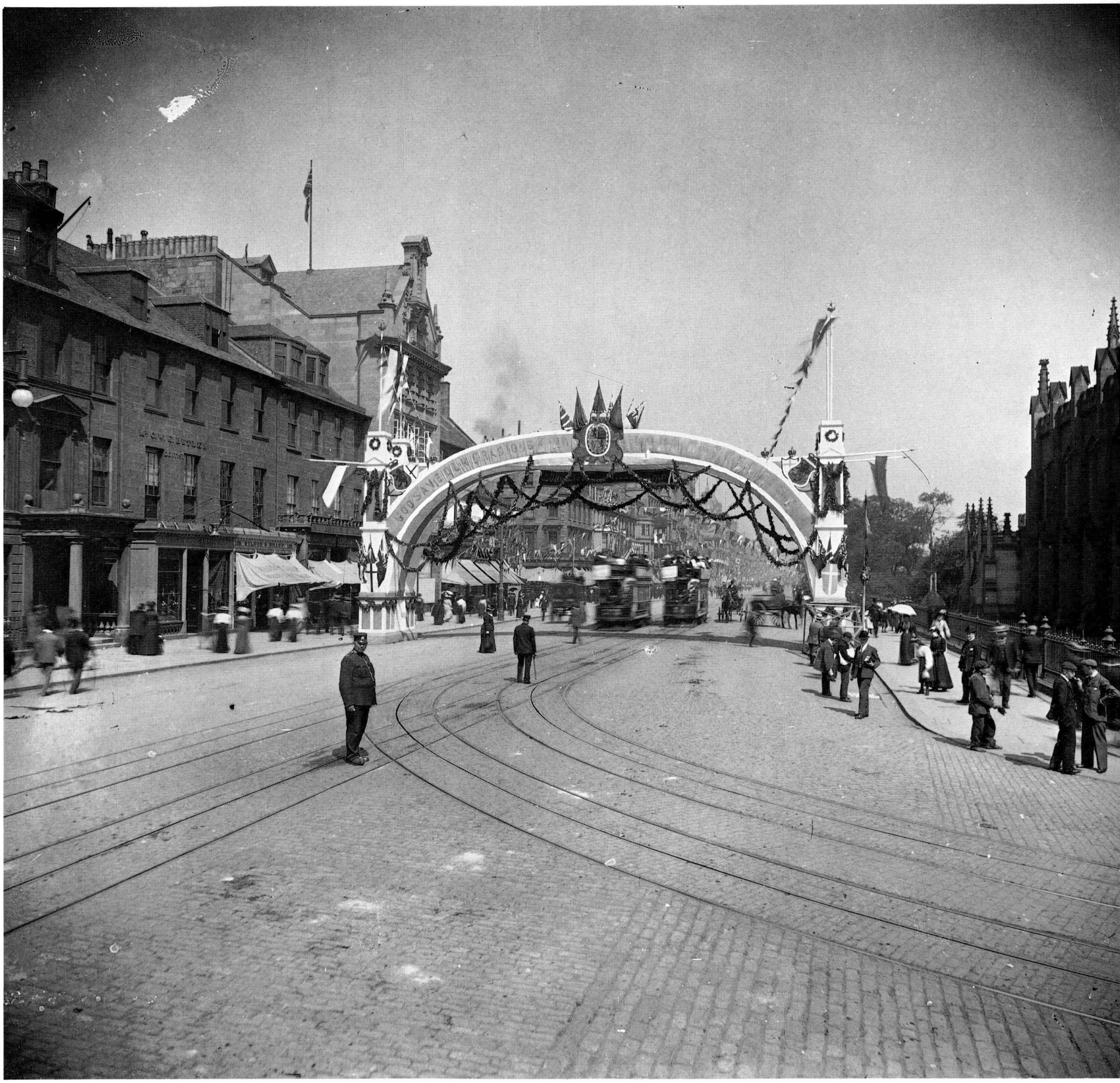

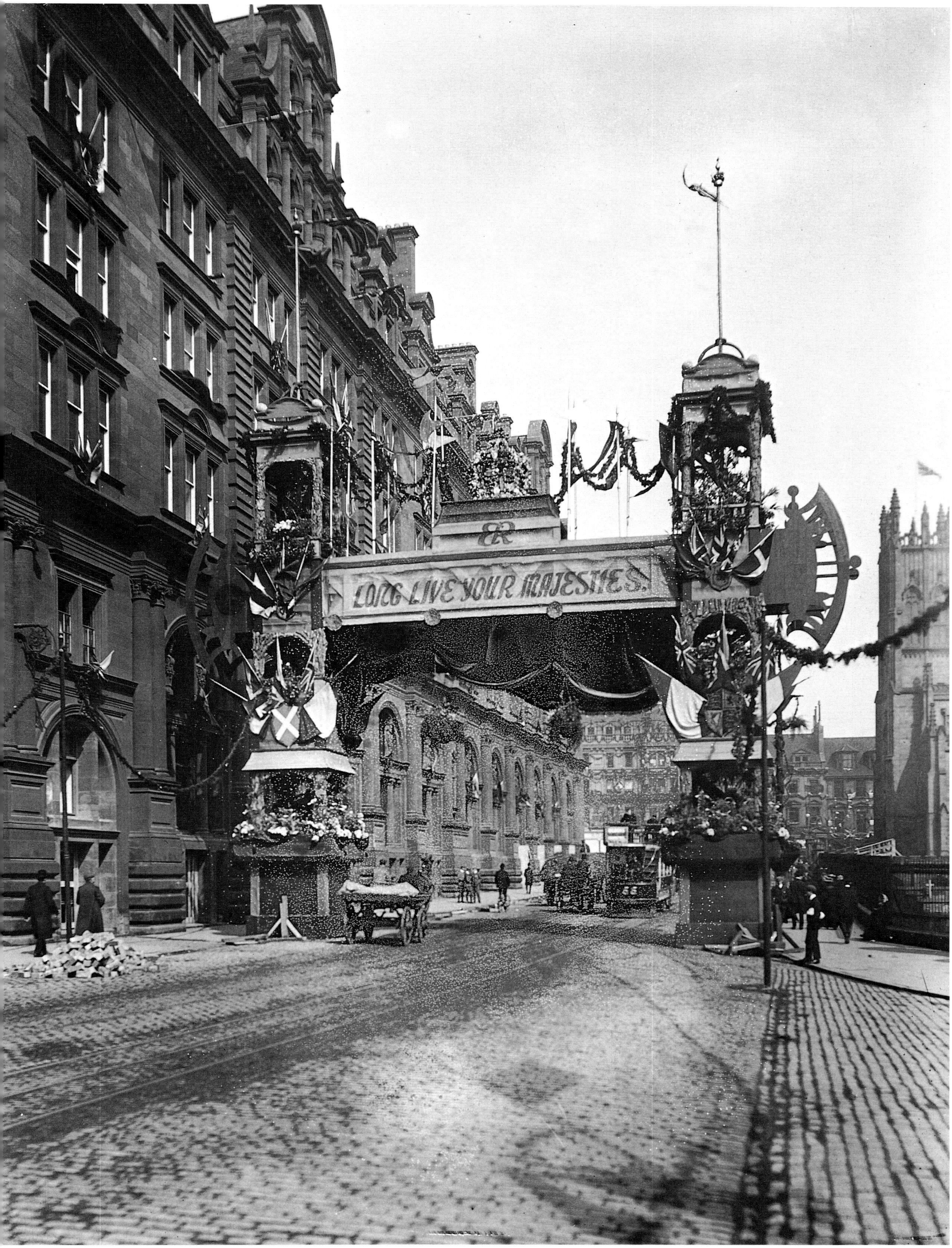
ER
LONG LIVE YOUR MAJESTIES.

Triumphal Arch at Hanover Street

The junction of Hanover Street and Princes Street was decorated in 1902 by this imposing archway formed by twin columns and supporting the message: LONG LIVE THE KING. Several interesting shops can be seen in Hanover Street: Thornton & Co., India Rubber Manufacturers; Macara & Co., stationers; and James Goldie, hat and cap manufacturers. On the top right-hand corner of the photograph is the sign, E. R. Yerbury, the photographers, whose premises were at No. 3 Hanover Street.

Cranston and Elliot Salute His Majesty

Cranston and Elliot, house furnishers at No. 36 Princes Street (formerly at North Bridge) decorated the entire building in keeping with its prominent position on the royal route. The building was demolished many years ago and the site is now occupied by C. & A. Modes. The founder of Cranston and Elliot, Robert Cranston, was Lord Provost of Edinburgh from 1903 to 1906 and was knighted by King Edward VII during the royal visit. The balconies along the processional routes assumed an importance well beyond their use at other times. Although there was little dispute about who owned the balconies in Princes Street, those above the shops on the processional routes at Bruntsfield and Morningside were the subject of serious disputes between the shopkeepers and the occupiers of the tenement flats above.

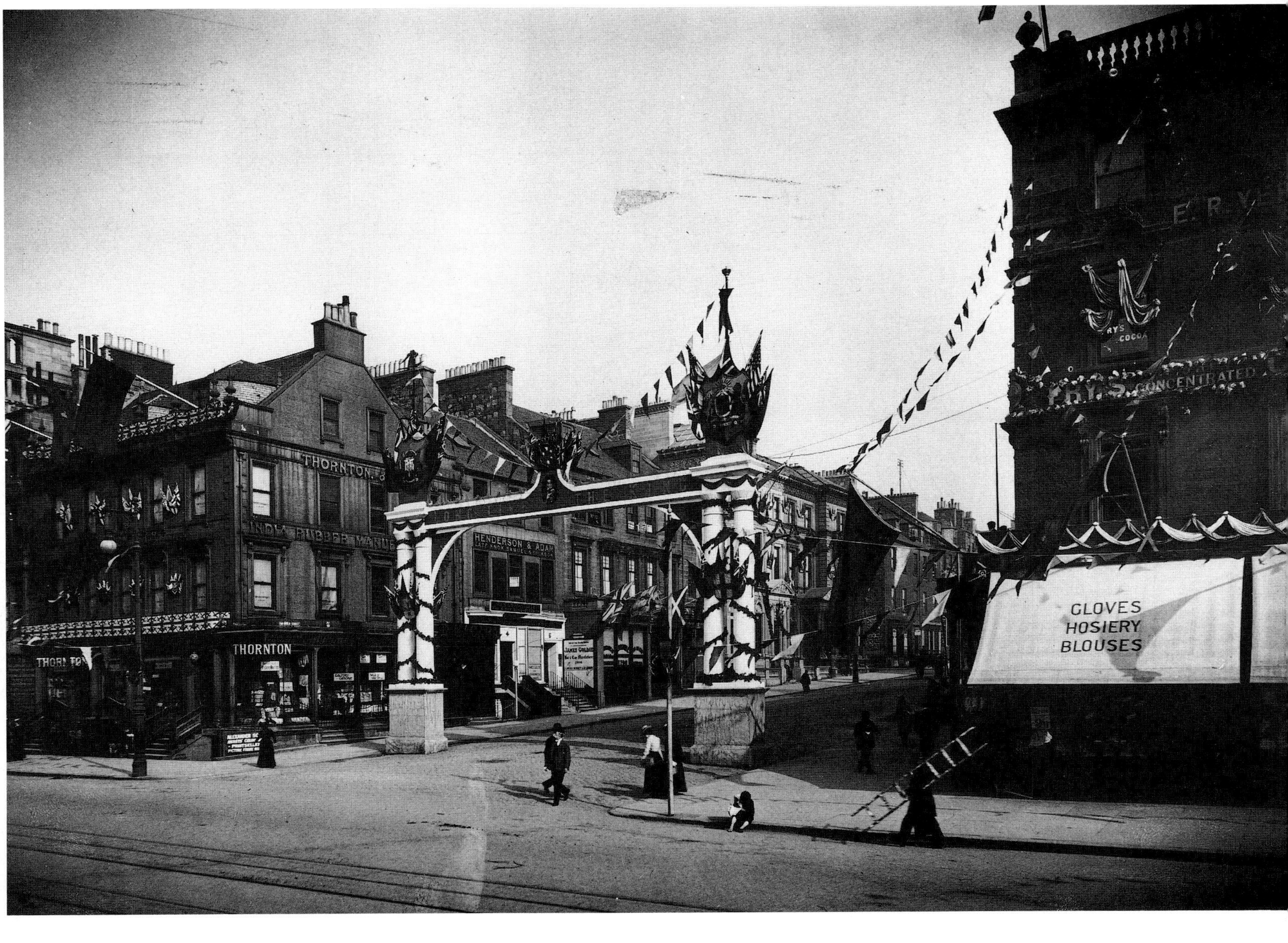

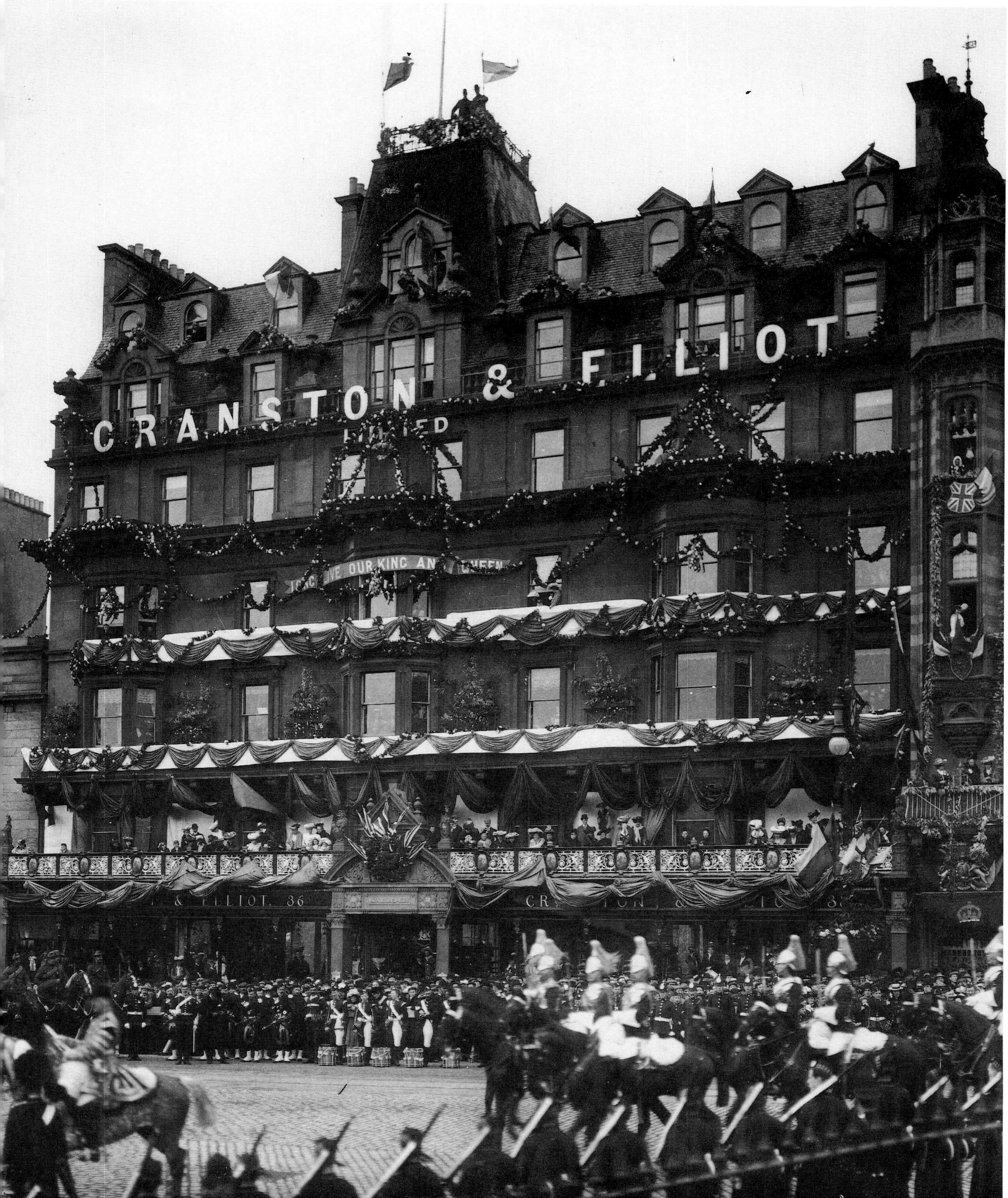
CRANSTON & ELLIOT
LONG LIVE OUR KING AND QUEEN

The Royal Panorama

During the week-long visit, the King and Queen attended several public engagements, including the laying of two foundation stones at the Usher Hall on 19th July 1911. This magnificent panoramic picture shows the full splendour of Edinburgh's public buildings, and Princes Street thronged with crowds of people who had gathered to watch the royal procession. Crowd control was a matter of particular concern to the Edinburgh police, who had been unable to obtain assistance from the Glasgow police on account of their own problems with the seamen's strike. A special Order had also been signed by one of the Principal Secretaries of State, Winston S. Churchill, prohibiting 'the navigation of aircraft of every description over the city of Edinburgh, or over any place within four miles of the said city'. The Order was definitely temporary and was lifted on 21st July 1911.

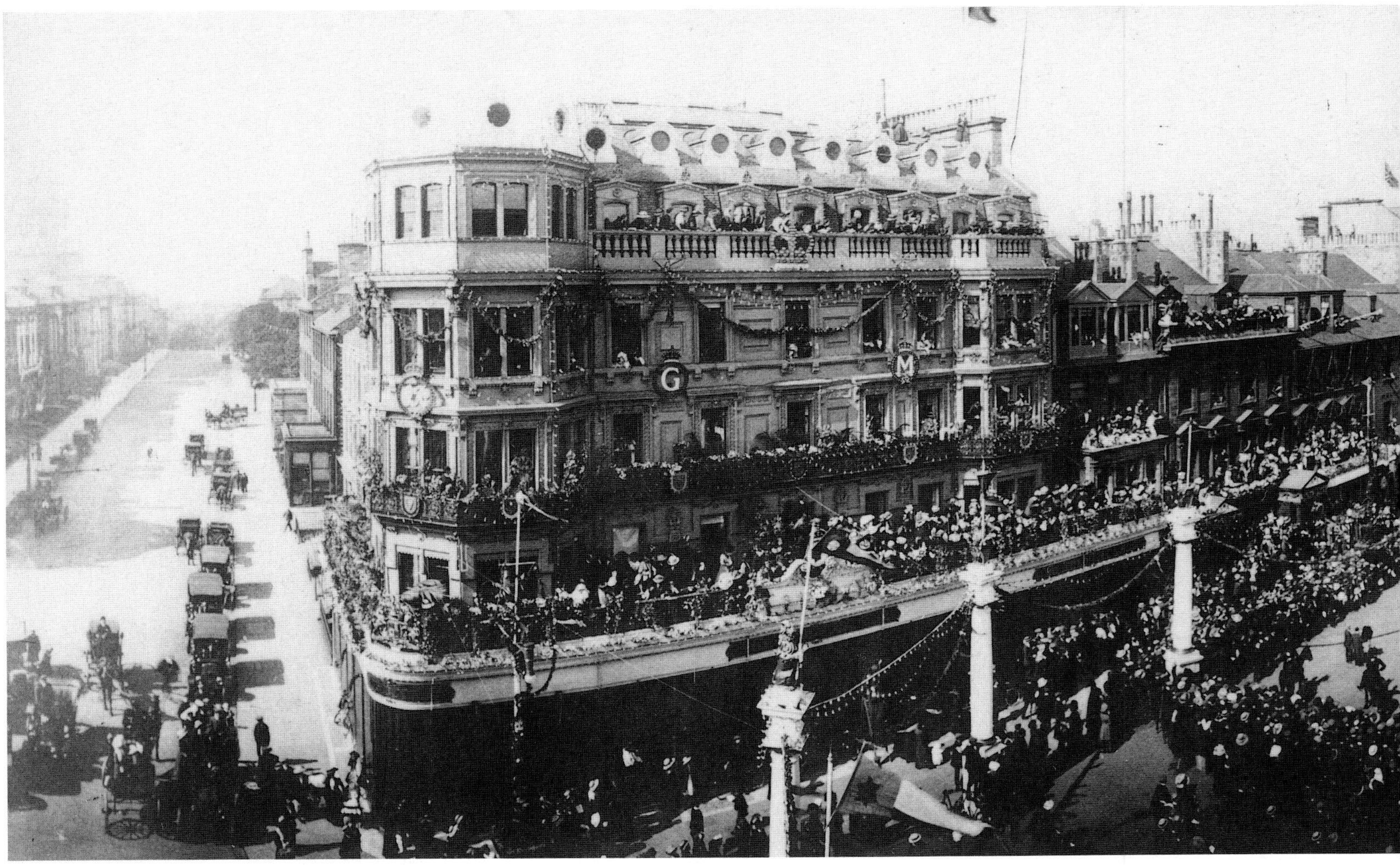

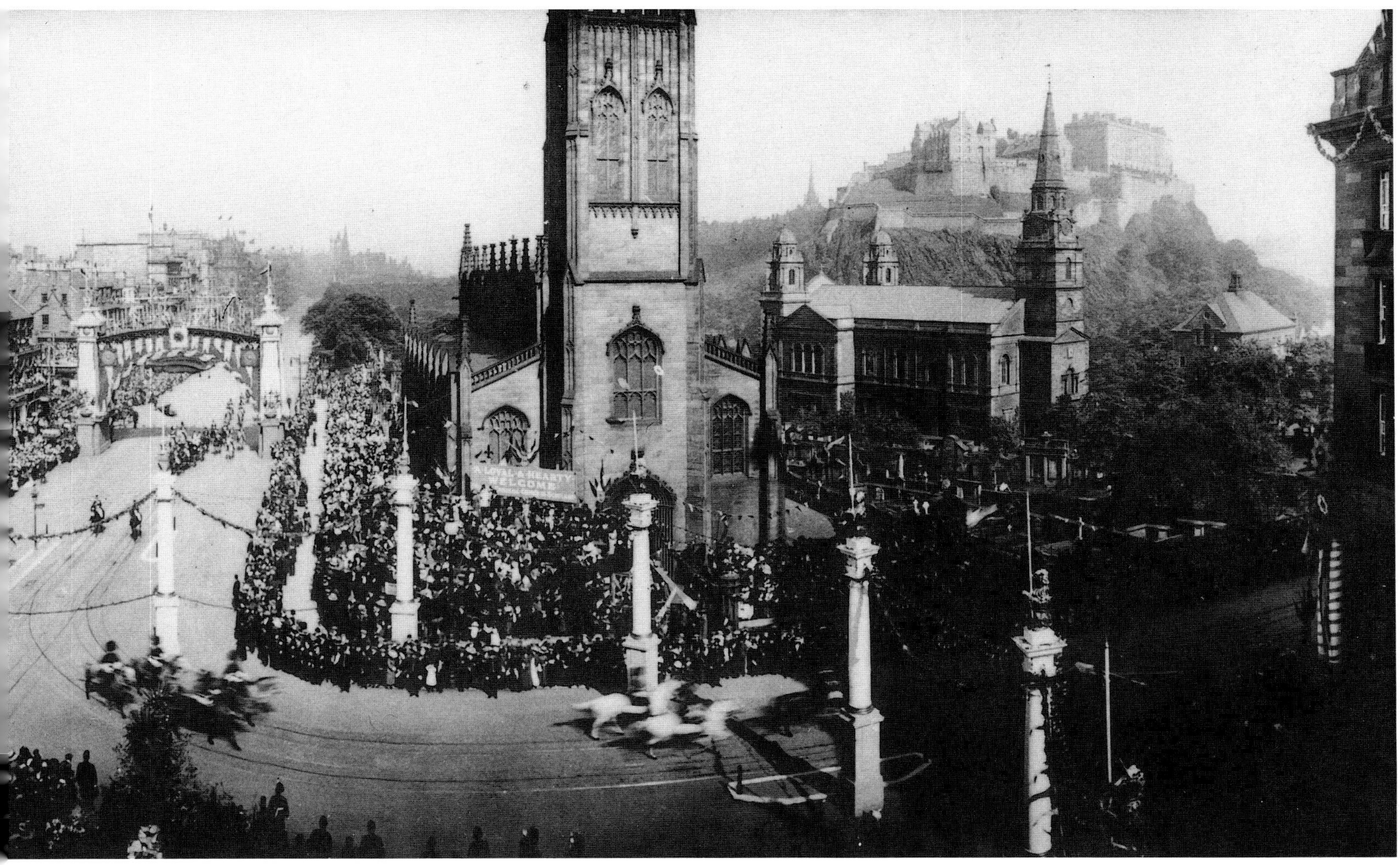
A LOYAL & HEARTY
WELCOME

Royal Entourage at the East End of Princes Street

Every window, balcony and vantage point, however precarious, was taken up at the Royal British Hotel as the royal entourage passed along the east end of Princes Street. Although most of the five-day visit in May 1903 was taken up by engagements in the capital, the Edinburgh press were ever mindful that an important part of Scotland lay to the west of Edinburgh: 'That the King would visit Edinburgh has been pretty well known for some time though the exact date was doubtful. Nothing had been said about Glasgow, and it has come as a pleasant surprise to the Lord Provost, Magistrates and Councillors of the commercial metropolis of the West that His Majesty is to spend one day in their midst'.

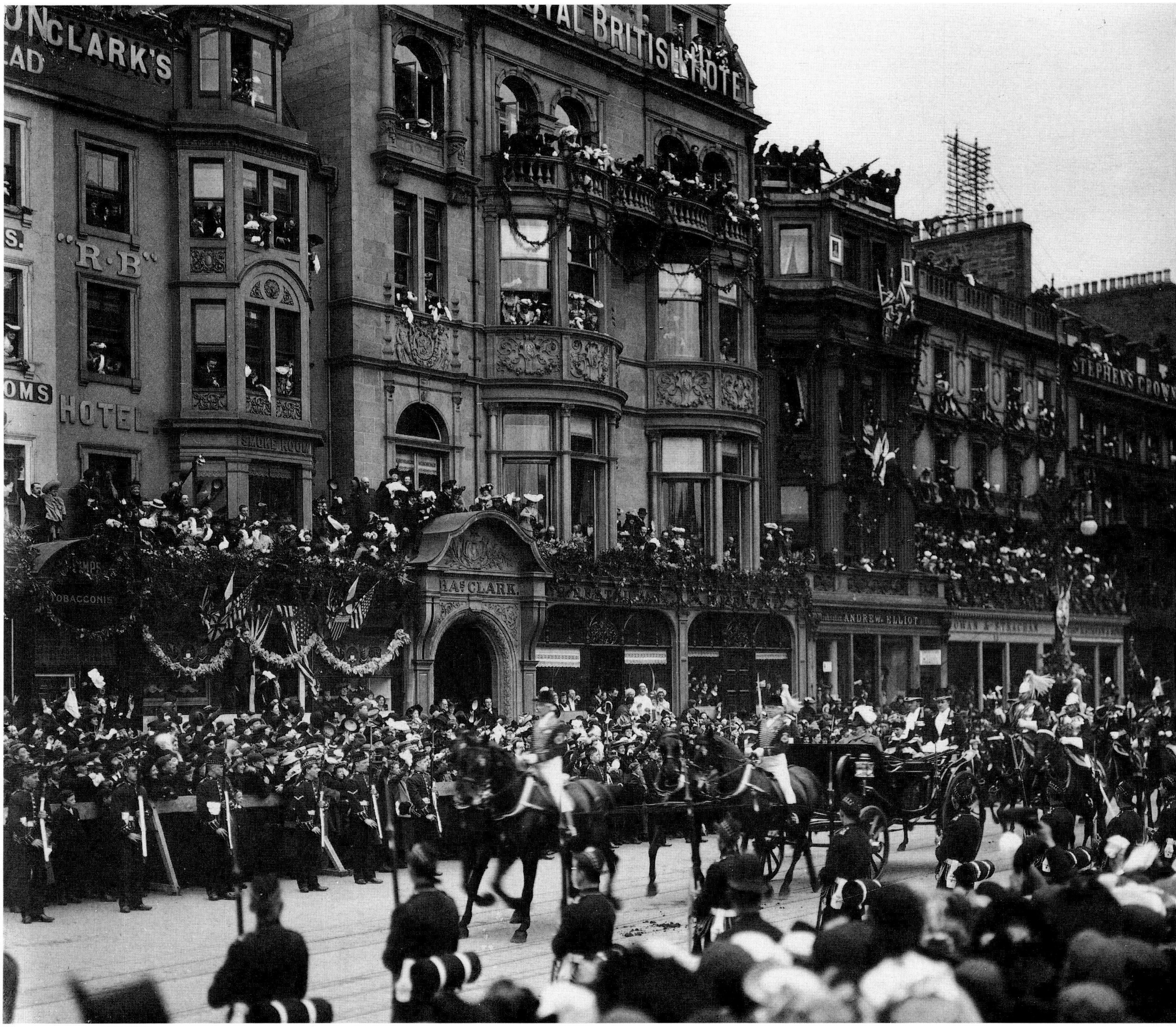

Triumphal Arch at the East End of Princes Street

The Empire arch at the east end of Princes Street shows no sign of crumbling in 1903: NEW GUINEA, NEWFOUNDLAND, AUSTRALIA, CEYLON, CAPE COLONY, NEW ZEALAND, TASMANIA. Underneath the arches, with bucket and stiff brush, there is much to be done to return Princes Street to its former grandeur after the excitement of the royal procession had subsided.

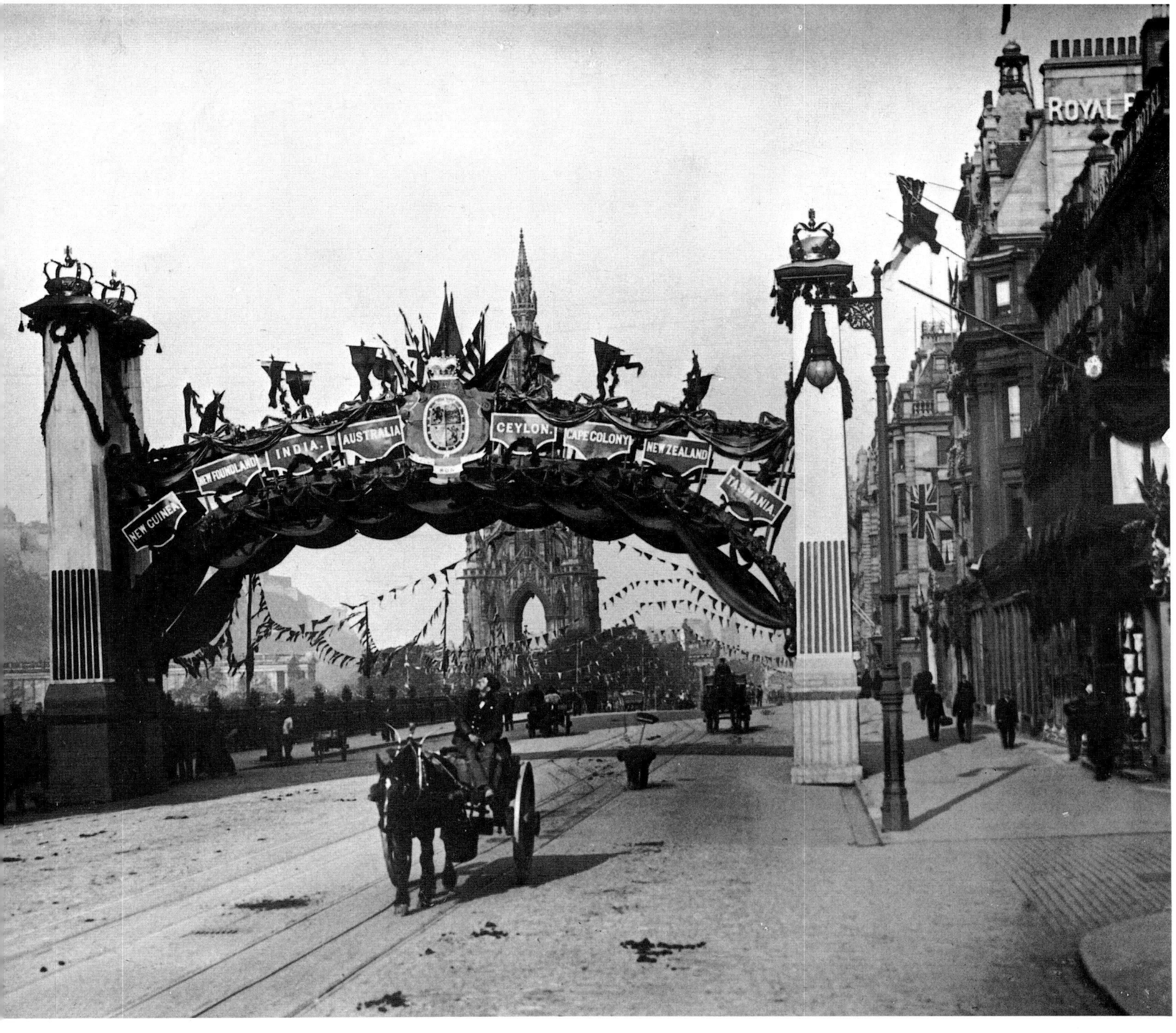

Triumphal Arch in Waterloo Place

This elaborate arch was erected in 1902 in Waterloo Place and was profusely decorated with shields, flags and flowers. More flowers have arrived by horse and cart, at the right hand side of the picture, to be placed in position with the help of the fire tender ladders on the opposite side of the street. The decorative arch was positioned at right angles to the stone arches of Regent Bridge, designed in 1816 by Archibald Elliot to carry Waterloo Place across Calton Road.

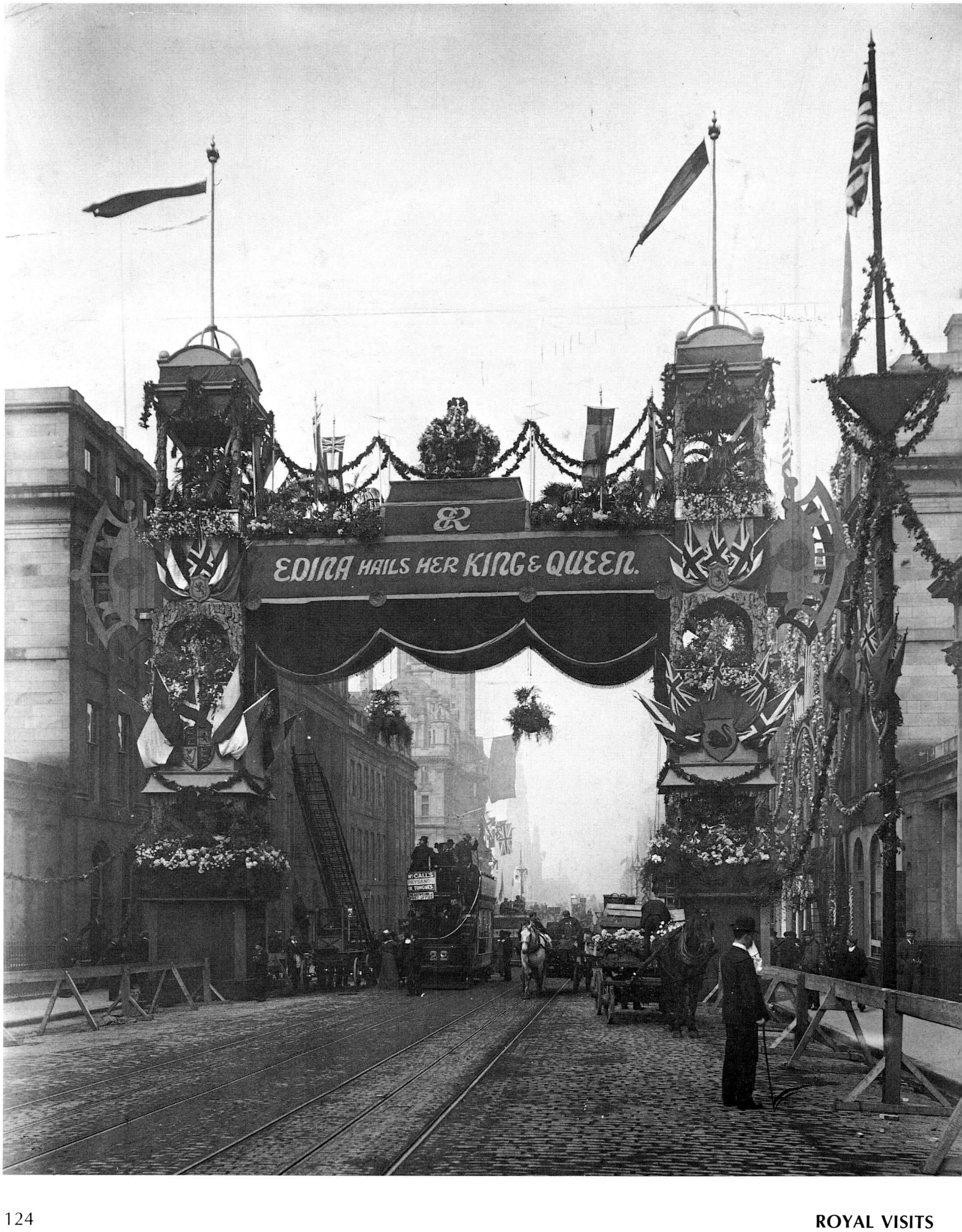

Triumphal Arch in Minto Street

When Edward VII and Queen Alexandra arrived at Waverley Station on 11th May 1903 their route to Dalkeith Palace was by North Bridge, East Preston Street, Dalkeith Road, Cameron Toll and Bridgend. This grand square arch, WELCOME TO YOUR ANCIENT CITY, at the north end of Minto Street, would be visible *only* on their return journey. The photograph was taken in 1903 looking north to Salisbury with the entrance to Salisbury Place on the left. The decorated tenement building, framed in the archway, is that occupied by Wood Bros., butchers, and is referred to in the photograph in Chapter 4 under the heading 'Coach Office'.

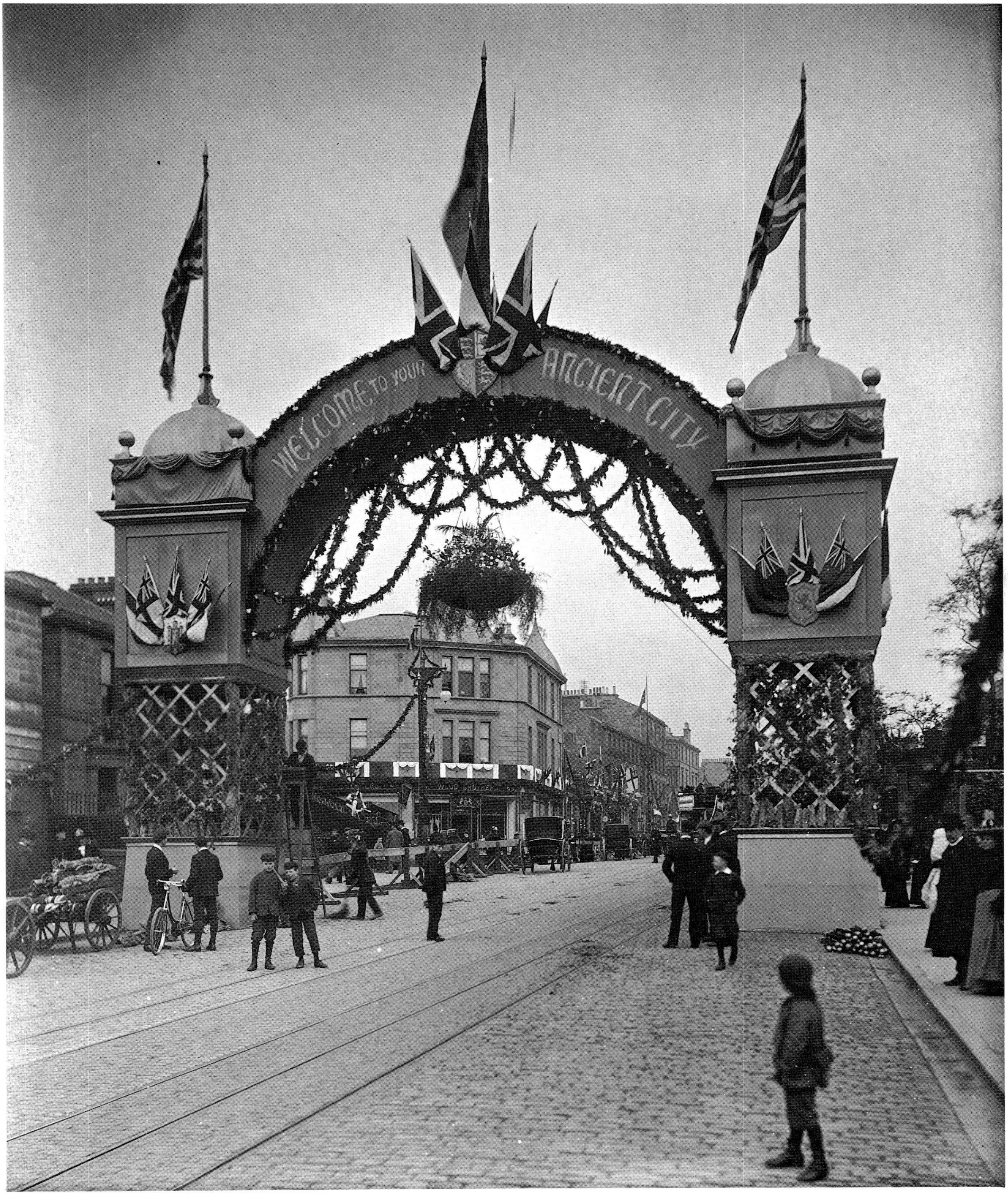

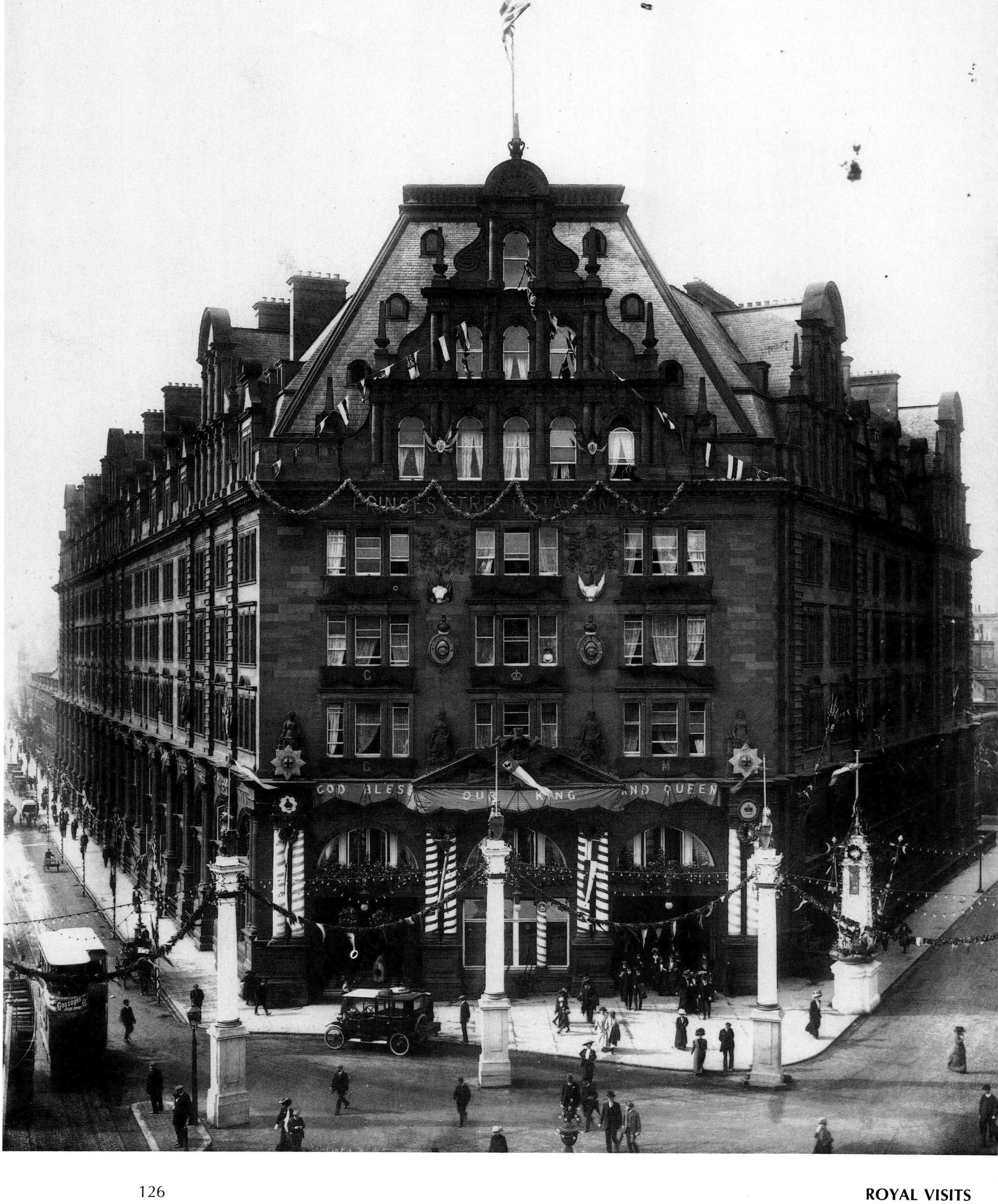
GOD BLESS OUR KING AND QUEEN

Visit of George V and Queen Mary

George V came to the throne on the death of his father Edward VII on 6th May 1910, and was crowned at Westminster Abbey on 22nd June 1911. He visited Edinburgh with Queen Mary, the Prince of Wales and Princess Mary from 17th to 21st July 1911, taking up residence at Holyrood Palace. The photograph shows Caledonian Station and Hotel, where the King and Queen arrived and were presented, in customary style, with the keys of the city by Lord Provost Sir William Slater Brown. The somewhat restrained decoration of the hotel frontage probably belied the amount of effort which went into cleaning up the station, prior to the arrival of the royal visitors.

Maule's by Night

In 1911, as a tribute to King George V and Queen Mary, Maule's, on the corner of Princes Street and Hope Street, decorated their building by night with a tasteful arrangement of lights which transformed the corner dome into a huge crown. Smaller crowns and the letters G.R. and G and M were also features of the display.

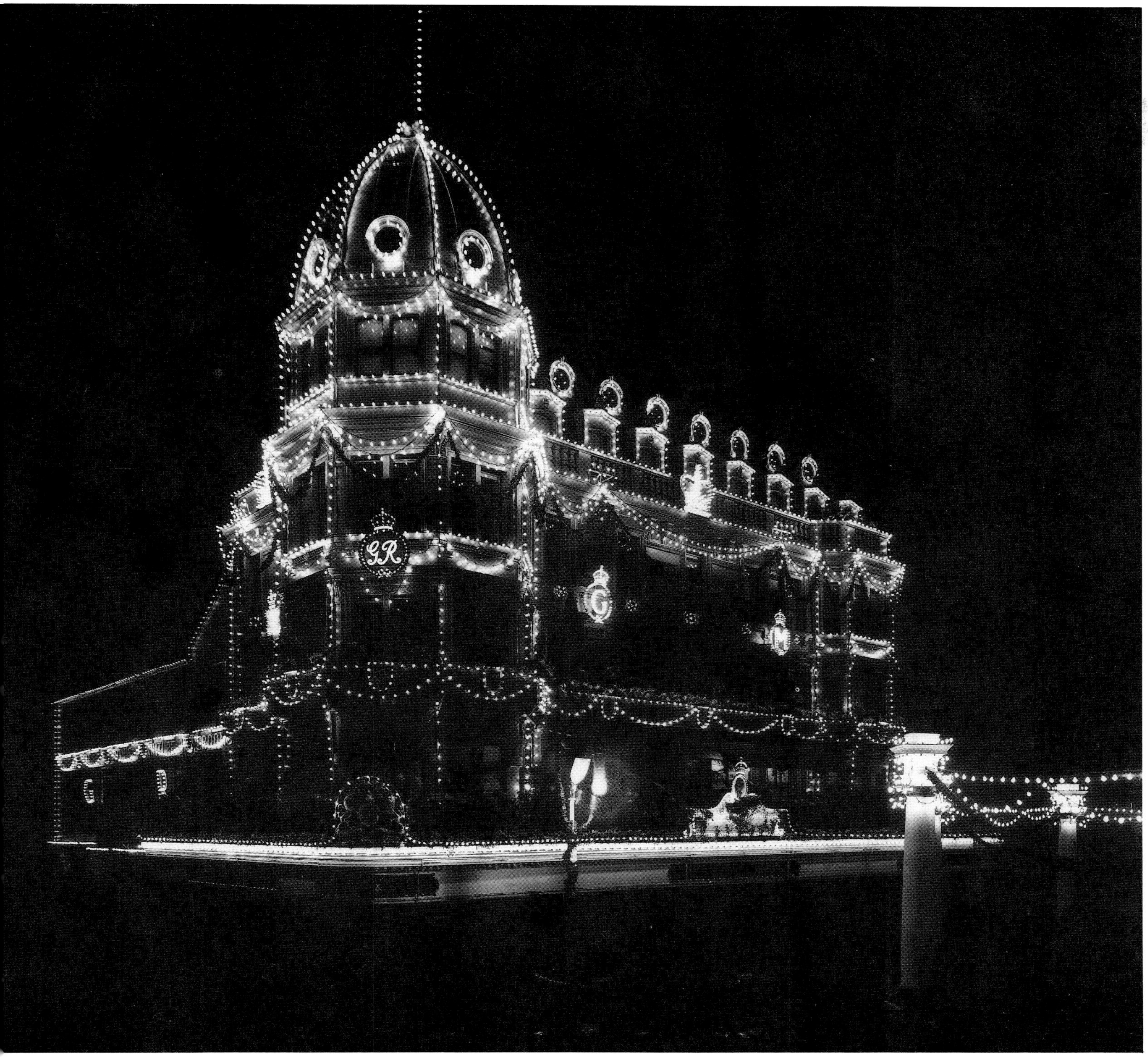

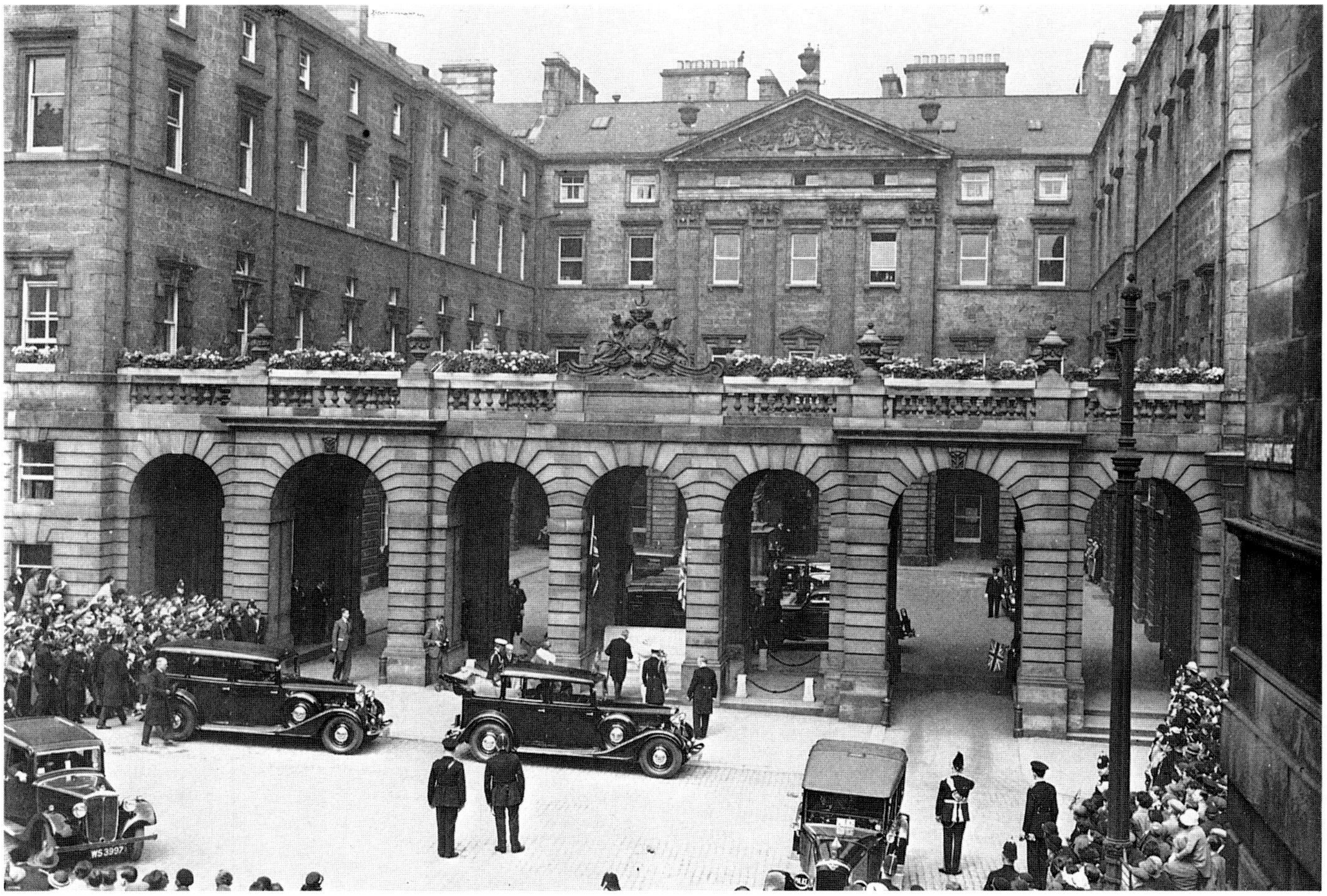

Silver Jubilee Visit

These two royal occasions, obviously drawing capacity crowds, have not been clearly established, although it is likely that they were photographed in either 1935 or 1937. Unfortunately the royal visitors are not identifiable, either at the front of the City Chambers in the High Street or in the motorcade as it makes its way along Princes Street. The year 1935 was the Silver Jubilee of George V's accession to the throne on 6th May 1910. He died on 20th January 1936. After the abdication of Edward VIII in December 1936 his brother, George, acceded to the throne and was crowned George VI at Westminster Abbey on 12th May 1937.

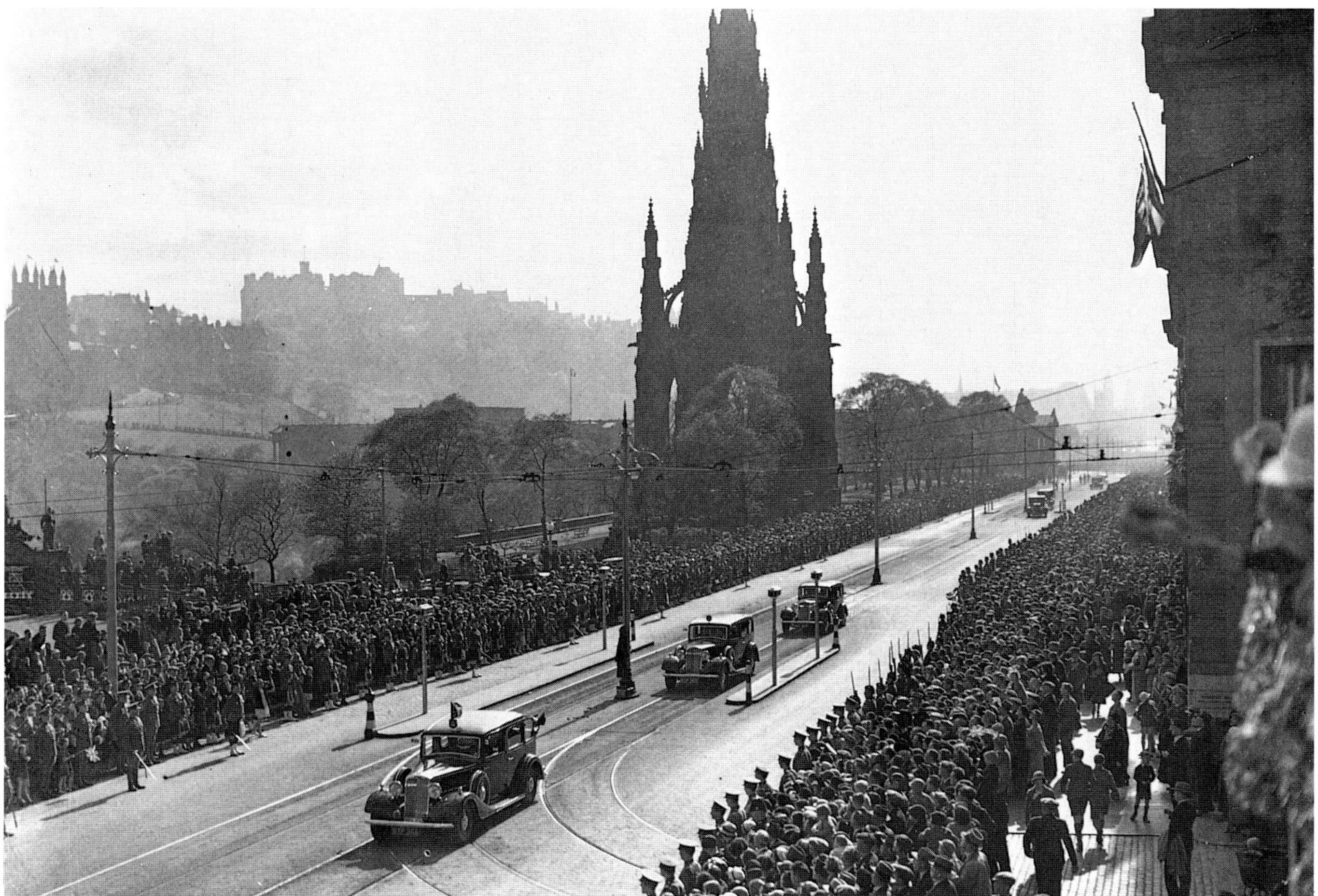

CHAPTER 7

SPORT AND LEISURE

Carlton Cricket Club

The Carlton Cricket Club was formed during the winter of 1862–63 by members of the Young Men's Christian Association who had been expelled from the Literary and Debating Society for staging 'a dramatic performance in which some of the members appeared in costumes appropriate to the characters represented'. Their first cricket matches were played on the Meadows, but in 1866 the committee obtained permission to use a field in Grange Loan which they shared with the Edinburgh Caledonian Cricket Club. It was not until 1905 that the Club secured its present ground on the north side of Grange Loan, near Lovers' Loan. The group at the stumps was photographed *c.* 1889.

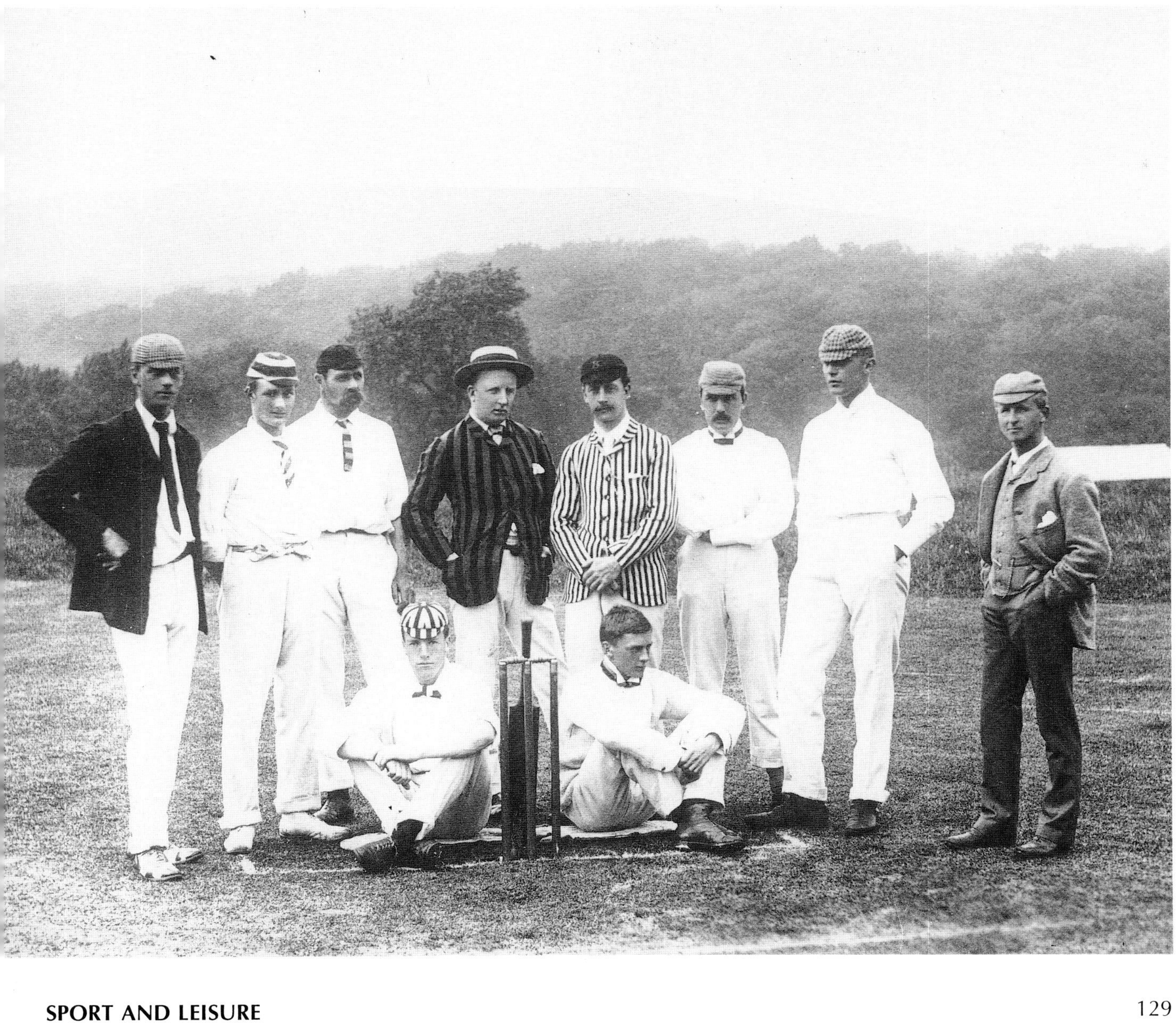

Cupar Cricket Club

Cupar Cricket Club XI played in the match against Forfarshire at the opening of Bonvil Park by Provost Hain on 16th May 1885. D. Martin Stenhouse, father-in-law of Edward Reuben Yerbury, is at the front with the pads and arms folded.

Vardon and Braid

The photograph shows Harry Vardon on the left and James Braid on the right. Harry Vardon learned to play golf on his native island of Jersey on a course laid out in 1878 on Grouville Common. At an early age he left Jersey to be a greenkeeper at Harrogate, and became Pro at the Bury Club a year later. He won his first Open in 1896 at Muirfield and repeated that achievement in 1898, 1899, 1903, 1911 and 1914. James Braid was born and bred in Earlsferry in Fife only a few miles from the home of golf at St Andrews. Like Vardon he won his first Open at Muirfield in 1901 and took the Championship again in 1905, 1906, 1908 and 1910.

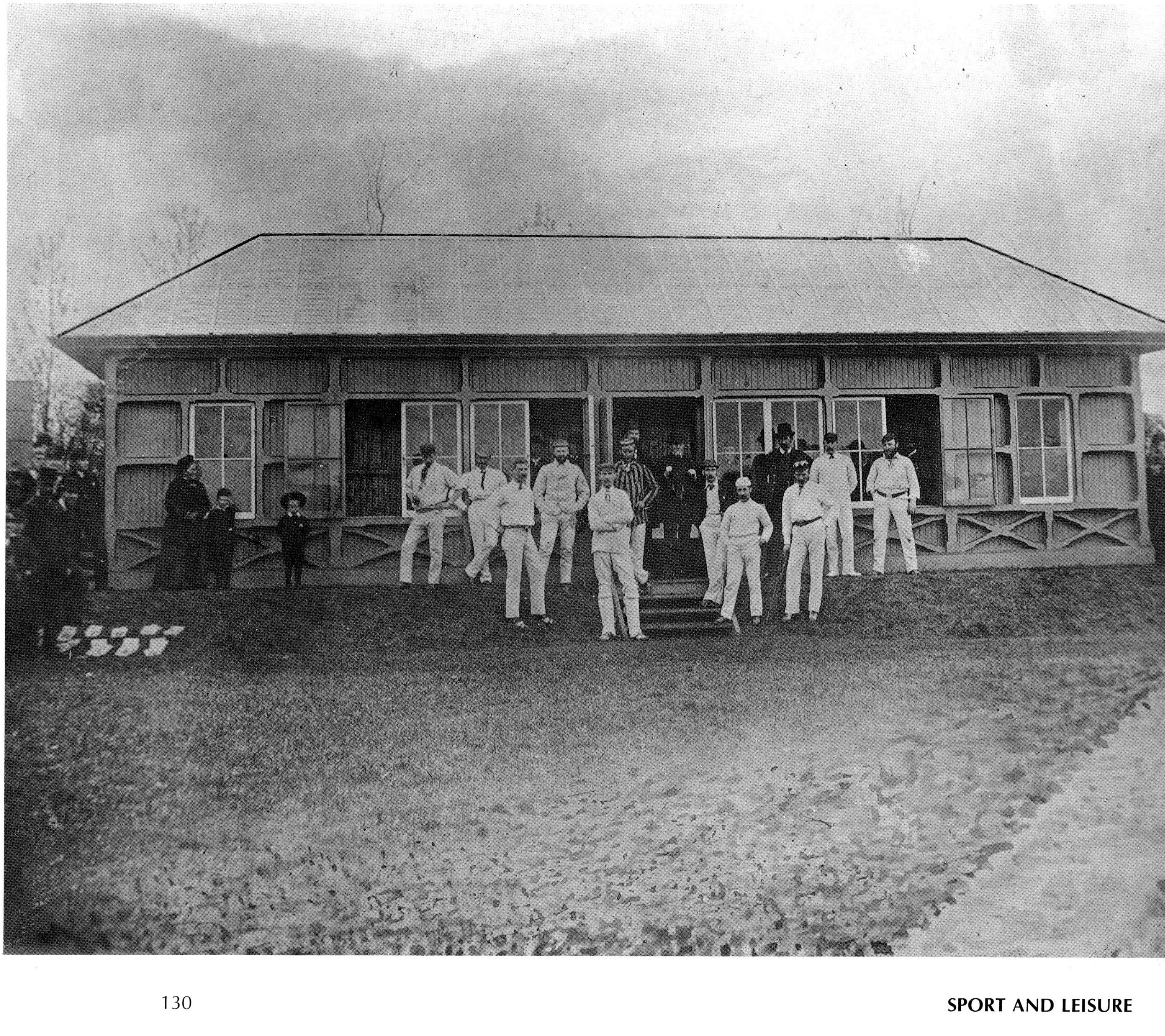

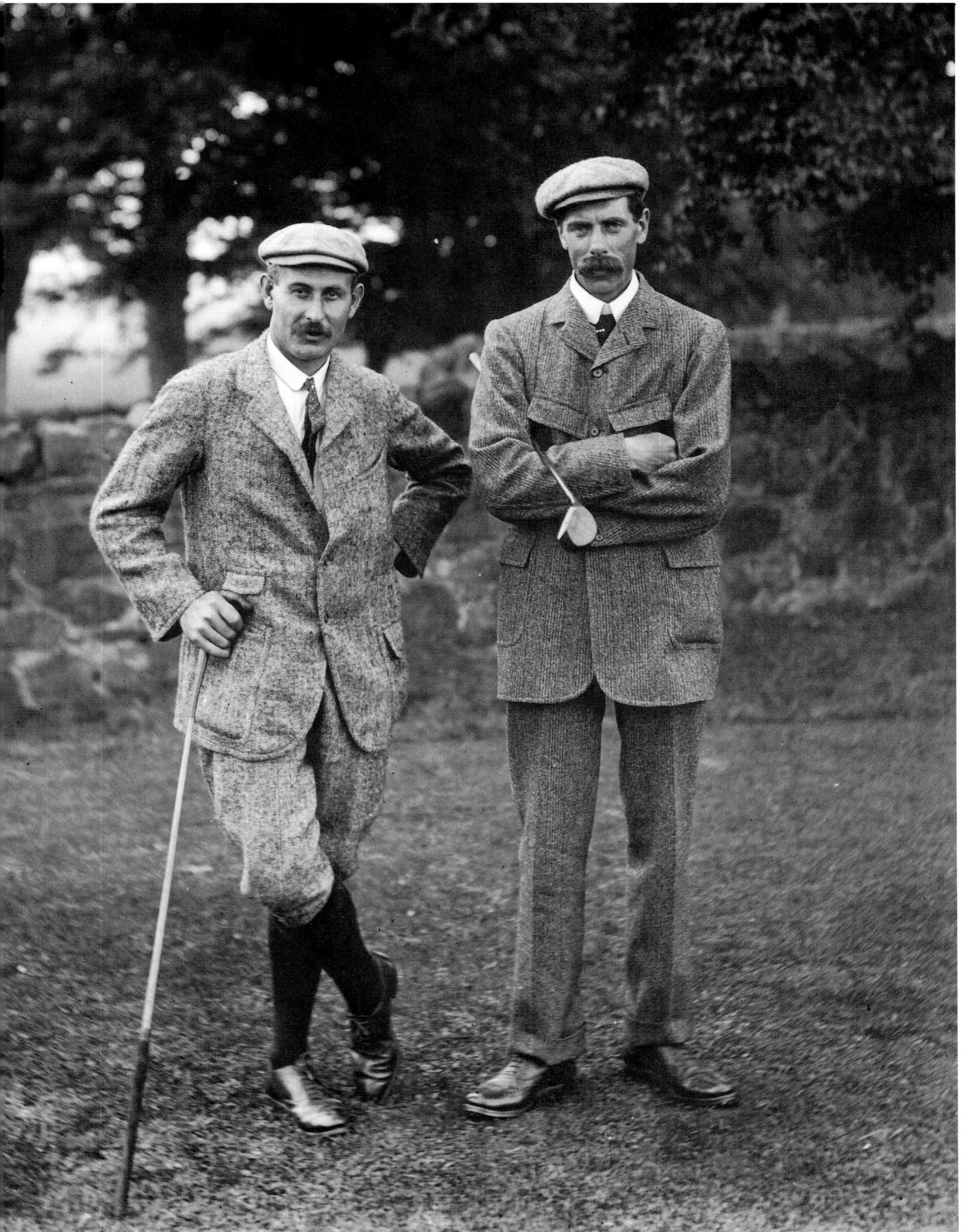

Murrayfield Golf Club

Dressed for the occasion and watched by an enthusiastic crowd, a competitor drives off from the first tee at Murrayfield Golf Club during a match in 1904 when both Vardon and Braid were playing. Murrayfield Golf Club was established by a group of Edinburgh business men in 1896, who first occupied a 12-hole course to the east of Murrayfield Road. On the extreme left of the photograph a short section of Ravelston Dykes can be seen, to the right of which was the old 12-hole course. The original clubhouse can be seen through the trees to the right of the player.

Fiery, the Musselburgh Caddy

Johnny Carey, or 'Fiery' as he was affectionately known on account of his ruddy complexion, was a caddie at Musselburgh for upwards of forty years. He caddied for Willie Park Jnr., winner of the Open in 1887 and 1889, and for William C. Maughan, author of *Picturesque Musselburgh and its Golf Links* published in 1906. Maughan was an amateur player whose limited ability at the game probably tested Fiery's legendary patience and discretion to the full. In Maughan's own words: 'No smiles [sic] illumes his imperturbable visage as with wild sweep the club passes innocuously over the ball calmly reposing on the tee'.

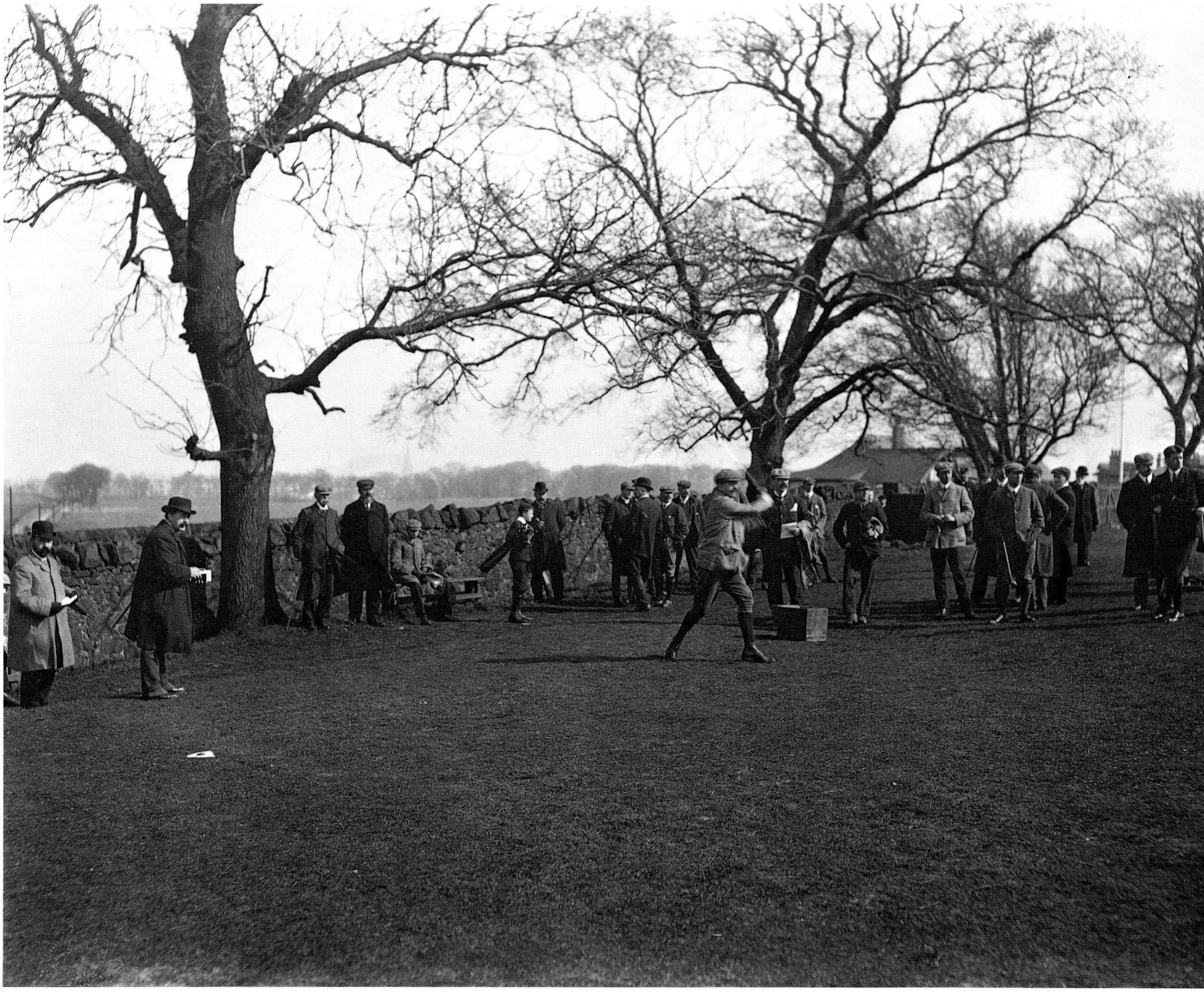

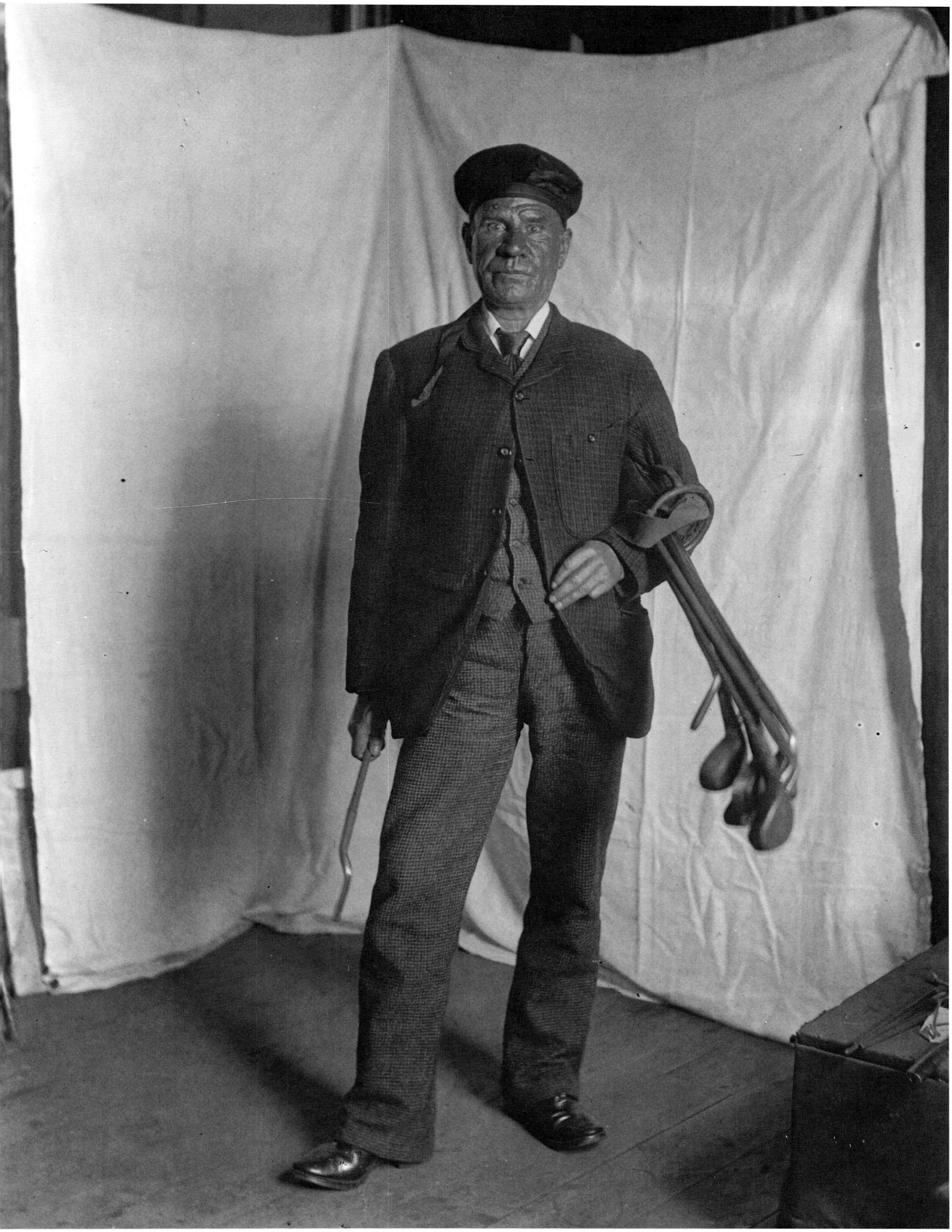

Gowffing in the Fifties

The reference to 'gowffing in the fifties' refers, of course, to the 1850s when this photograph was taken of several members of the Bruntsfield Links Golfing Society at Bruntsfield Links. The picture is believed to be at the 5th or 6th hole, with the buildings of Wrychtishousis in the background. The original caption for the photograph stated that the following well-known Edinburgh gentlemen are included: Aitken Taylor, William Cotton, Anthony Shiels, James Ritchie, Thomas Usher, Robert Chambers, Thomas Hall, James Bryson and James Ballantyne. Unfortunately the caption does not identify their position in the group but it is known that Thomas Usher was captain in 1875. The earliest records confirm that the Bruntsfield Golfing Society was established by 1761 on the links at Bruntsfield.

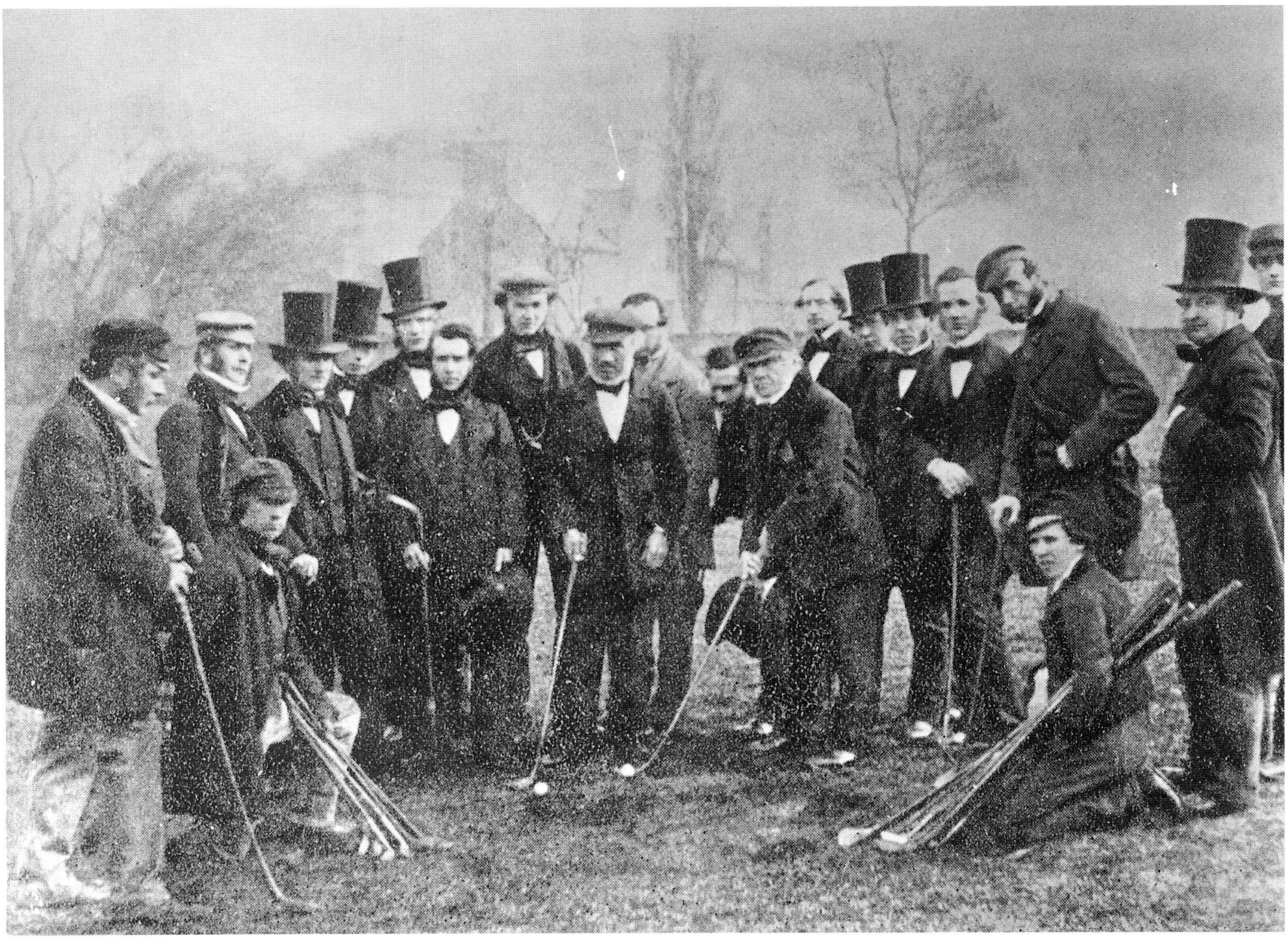

Golfers at North Berwick

The unmistakable shape of Berwick Law looms large over the old town of North Berwick. The action, however, is near the end of the game on the green at the seventeenth hole, Point Garry (in), at the North Berwick Golf Club in 1900. The club was formed in 1832 and the course has not been greatly altered since the photograph was taken. The bearded gentleman with the dark cap on the extreme right of the group is the late Sir Francis James Grant, KCVO, Lord Lyon King of Arms in Scotland. He held the appointment of Lord Lyon and Secretary of the Thistle from 10th May 1929 to 30th June 1945.

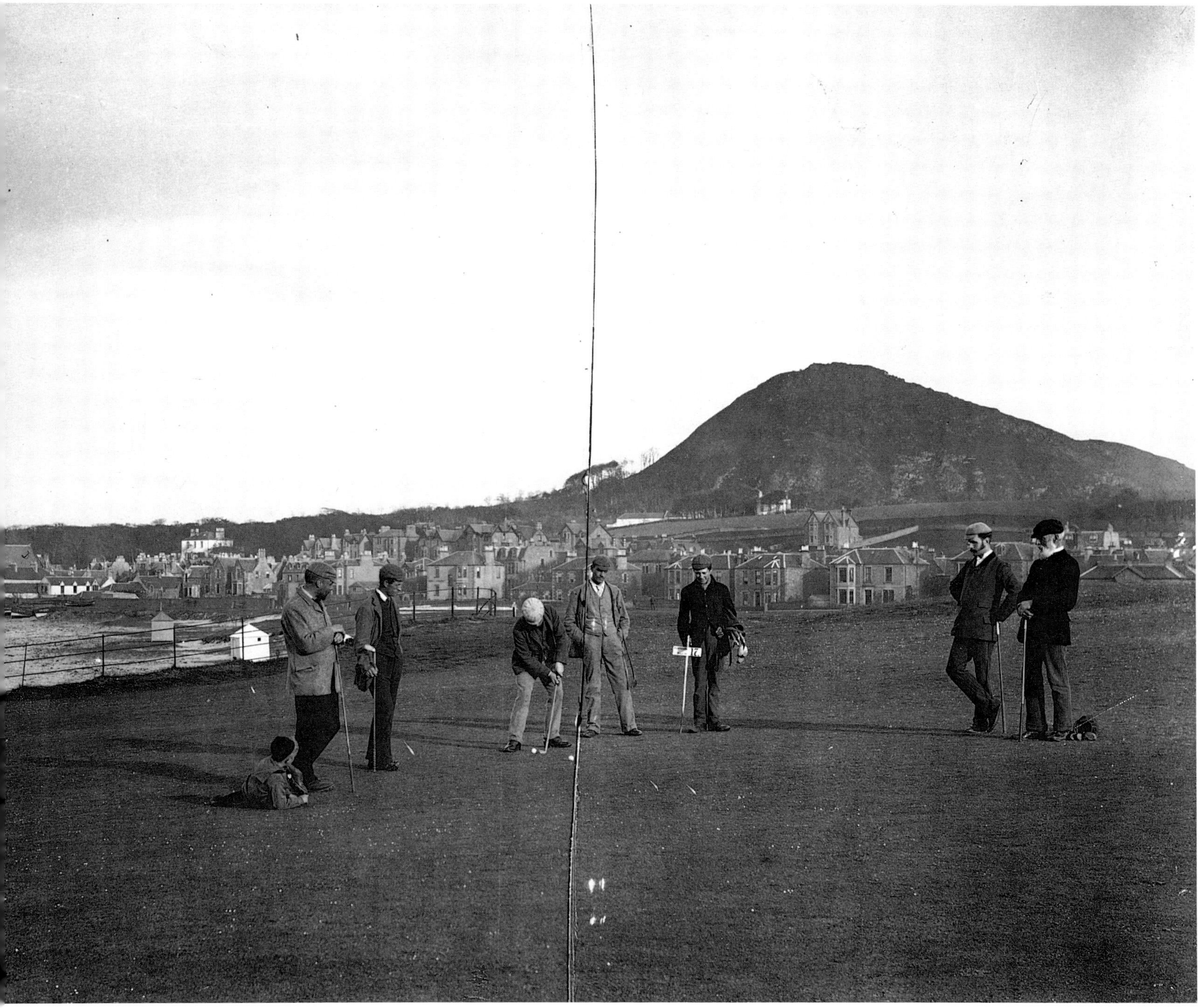

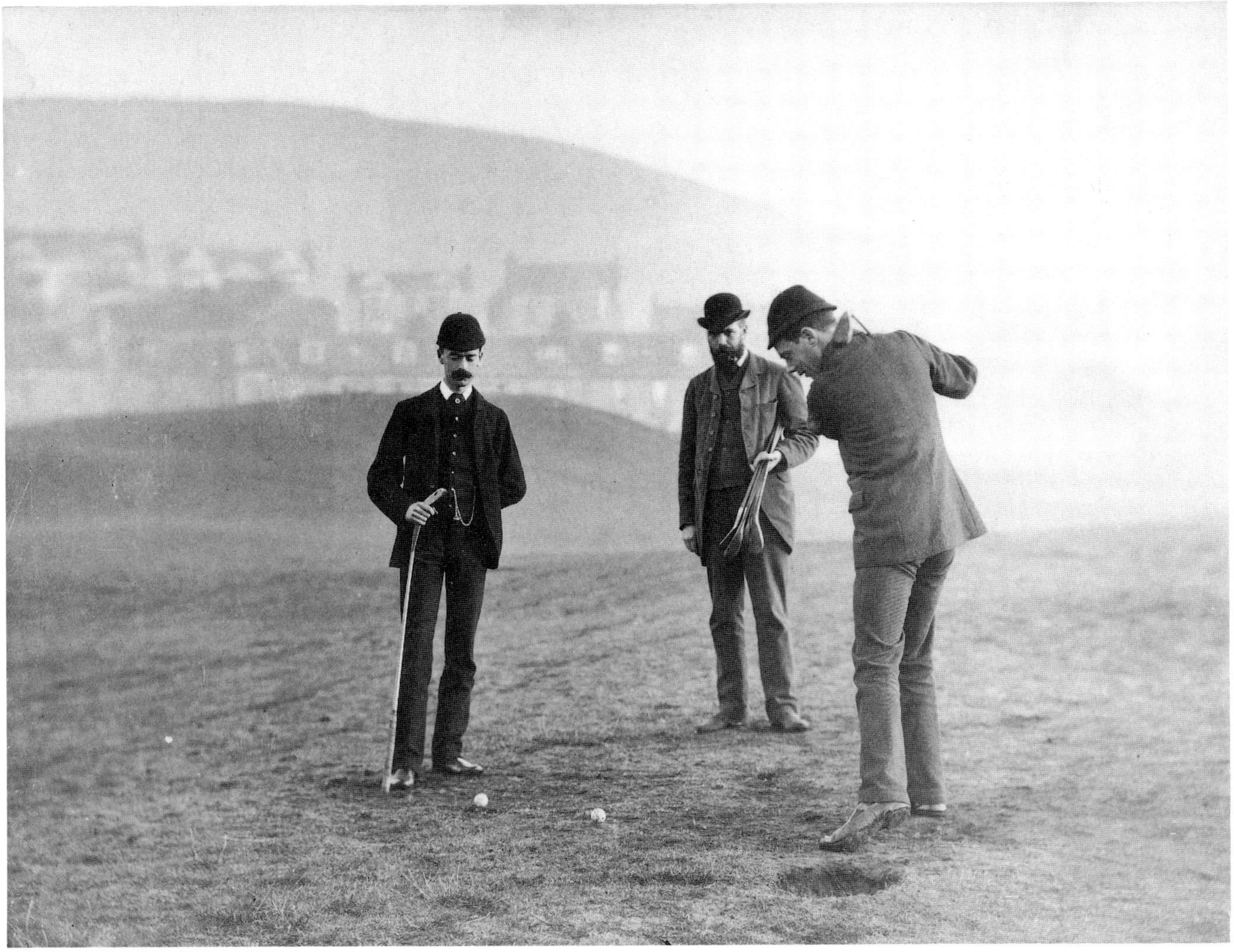

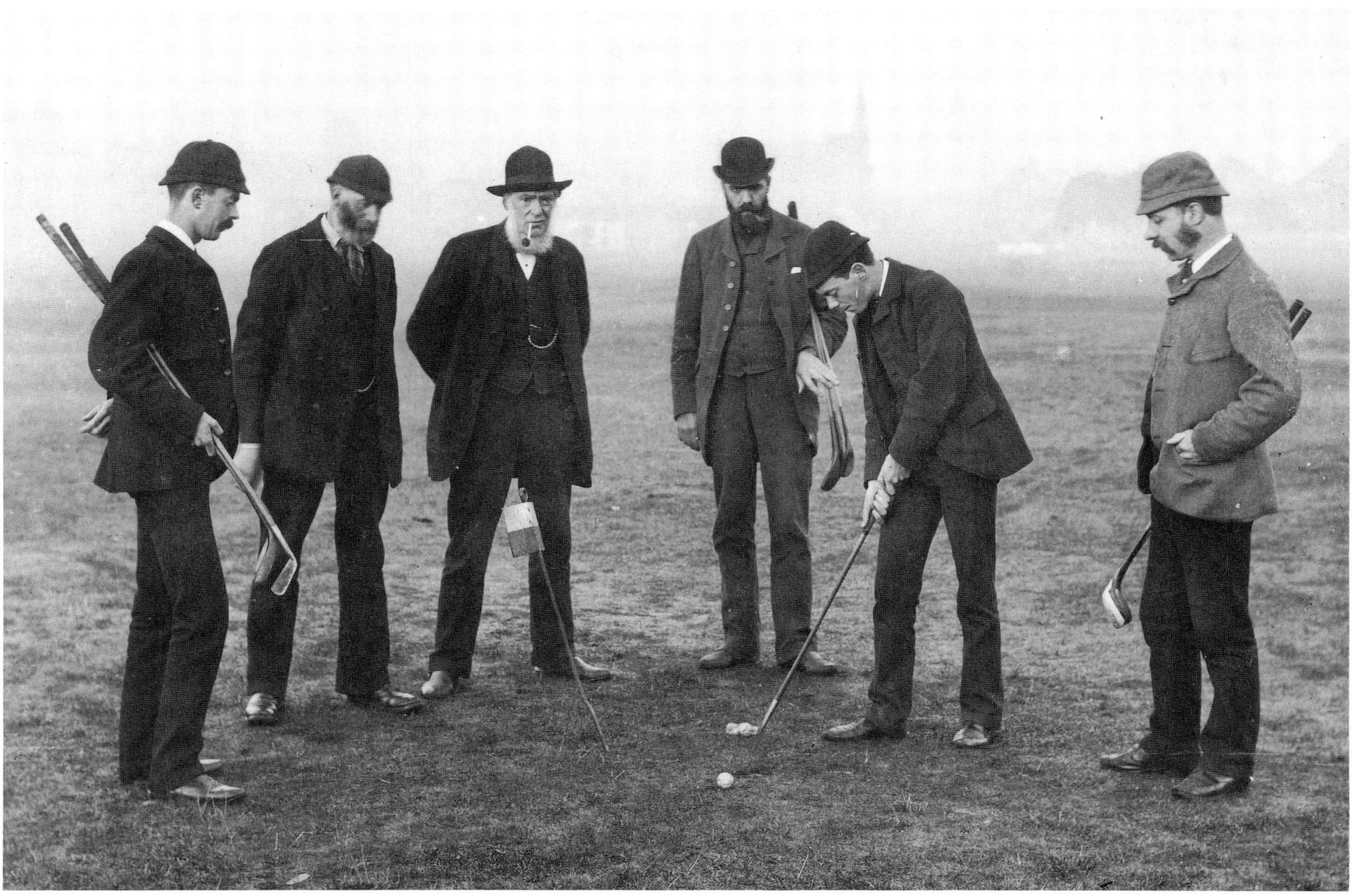

Golfing on the Links

These two golfing scenes with the same caddie and two of the players have always been recorded by Yerbury as at Bruntsfield Links c. 1870. The records of the Bruntsfield Links Golfing Society show that the Society was established at Bruntsfield Links by 1761, but moved to Musselburgh in 1876, and returned to Davidson's Mains in 1898. Unfortunately the topography shown does not suggest any of these locations.

Centre Court

This sheltered idyllic setting of unknown date and locality was centre court for mixed doubles, watched by a less than capacity crowd. The pith helmet, buttoned-up jackets, long flowing dresses and elegant headgear may have contributed in some way to the number of tennis balls which lie dangerously abandoned around the court.

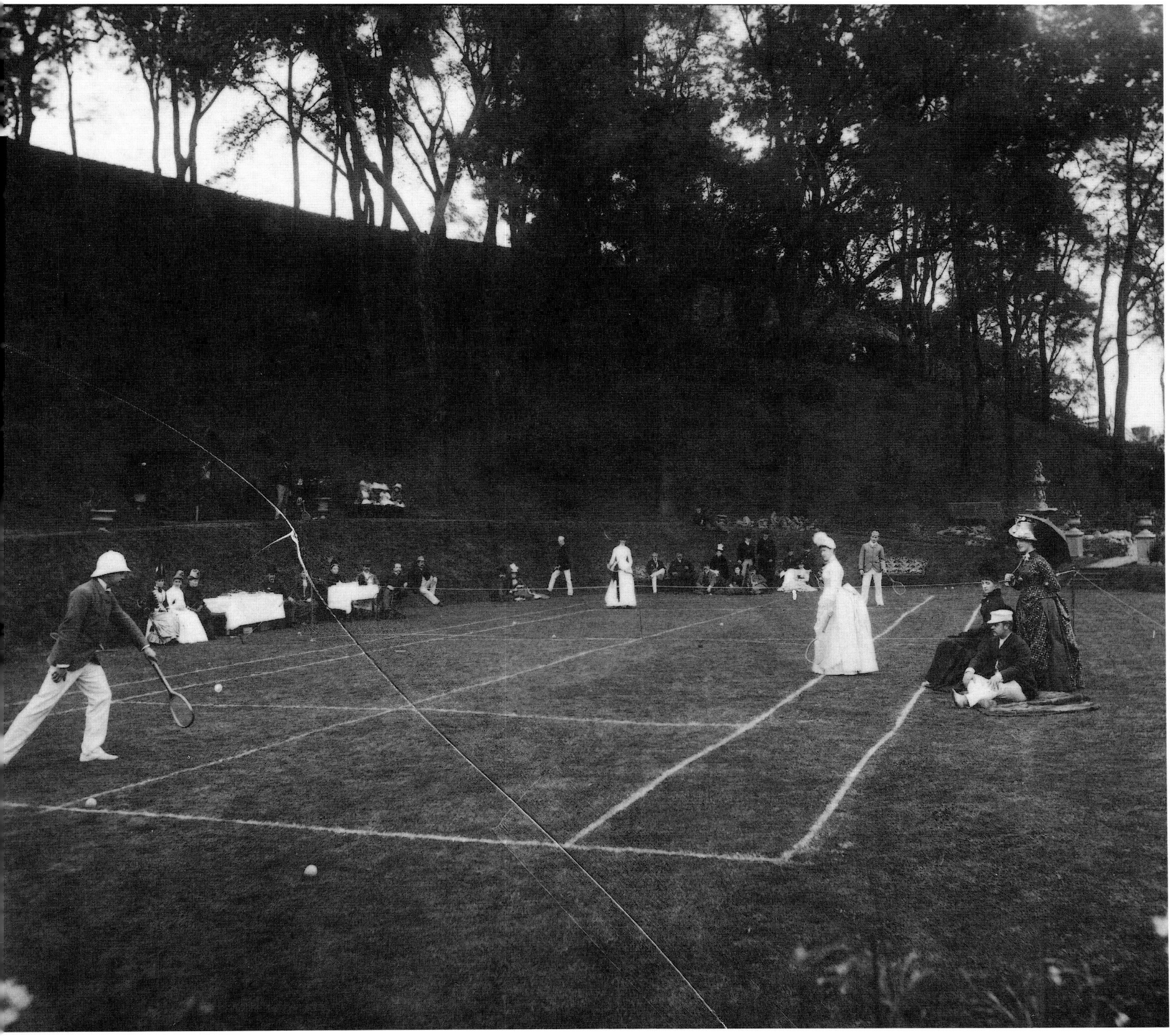

Car Rally

A 16 HP two-cylinder Albion being driven confidently in Holyrood Park with Salisbury Crags in the background, *c.* 1946.

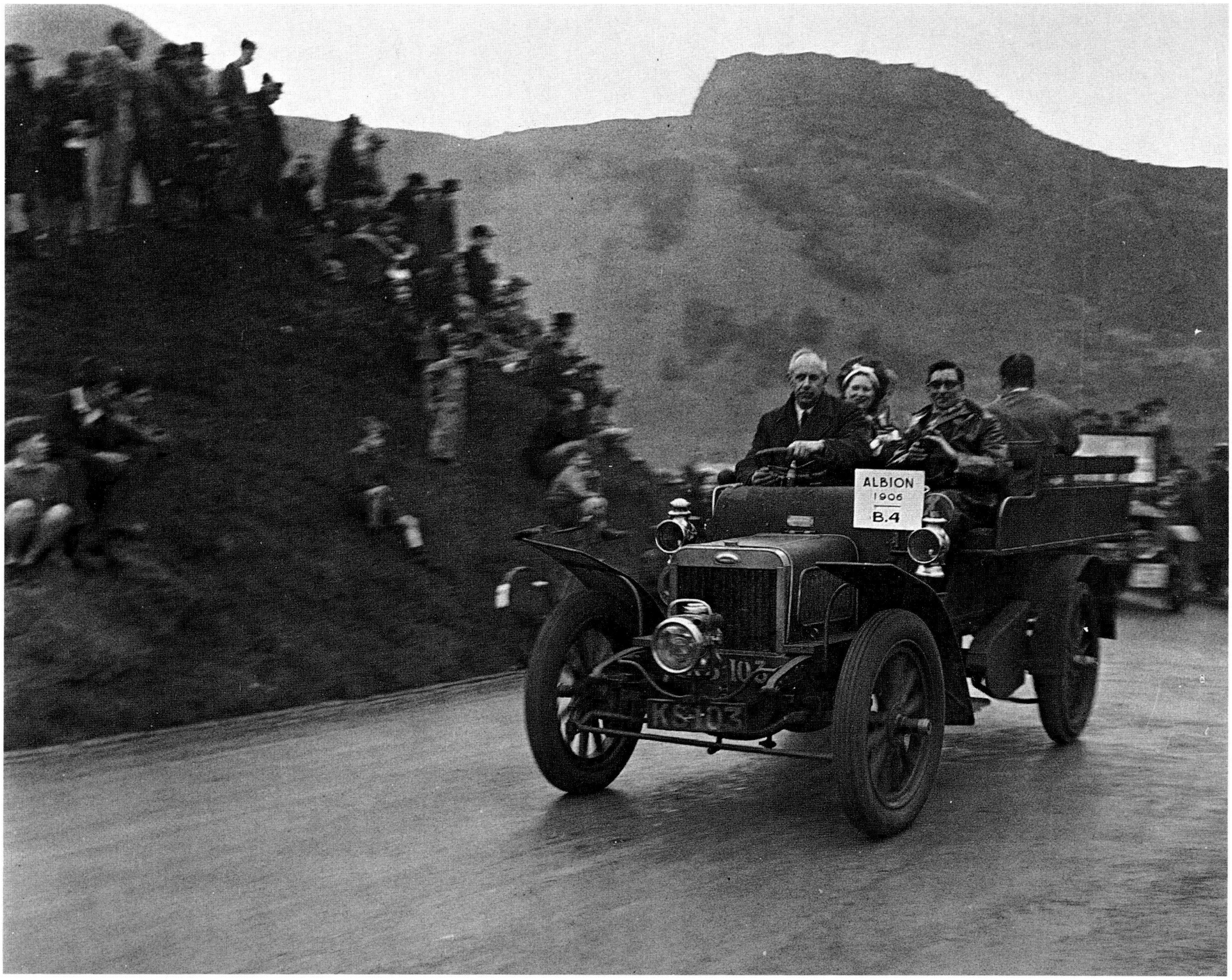

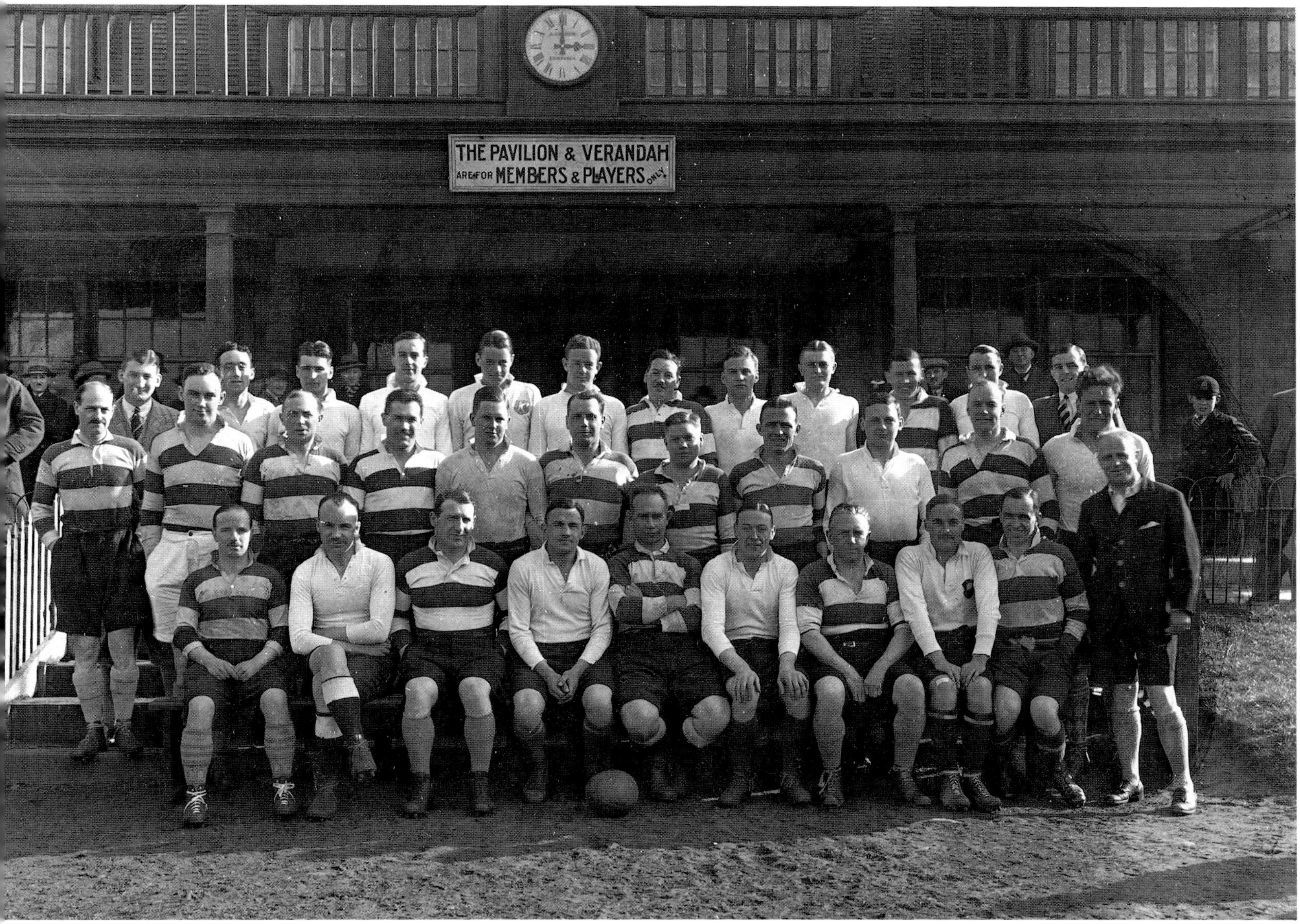

Watsonians v Crocks

The Watsonian Football Club was formed in 1876 by a small group of boys who had not long left school. In the early days there was neither referee nor whistle, the game being conducted by two umpires, one from each team. When the umpires disagreed the matter was referred to the two captains, but the complete absence of any neutral adjudication frequently brought the game to a complete standstill. The Club's jubilee was celebrated, somewhat belatedly, on 29th March 1930 by a game at Myreside between Watsonians and the Crocks, won by Watsonians, eleven points to four. The team was (Watsonians in white jerseys):

Back Row: W. C. Morrison, J. L. Blair, E. W. Thomas, T. D. Hay, W. Arthur, J. R. Thom, J. Aitken, W. C. Allan, D. S. Wilson, R. H. Horne, T. S. Roxburgh, T. C. Garden

Middle Row: D. K. Duff, A. C. Gillies, G. G. Marshall, F. J. C. Moffat, A. J. Bain, G. J. Alexander, W. D. Bertram, J. A. R. Selby, A. Montgomery, Rev. A. N. Gordon Boxer, J. M. Johnstone

Front Row: D. M. Morison, R. Allan, A. W. Angus, D. P. Henshaw, J. C. MacCallum, R. F. Kelly, A. F. Wilson, J. H. Purves, J. H. Carmichael, W. D. Macniven (referee)

Heart of Midlothian F.C.—Scottish Cup Winners

21ST APRIL 1956

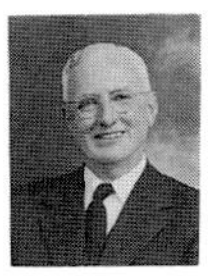

A. W. STRACHAN

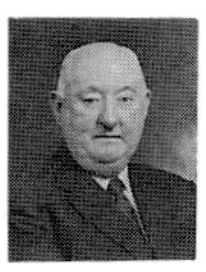

A. IRVINE

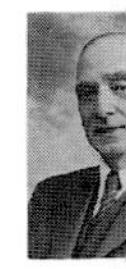

R. S. K. G

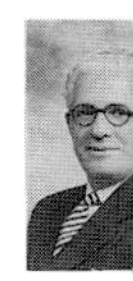

R. T

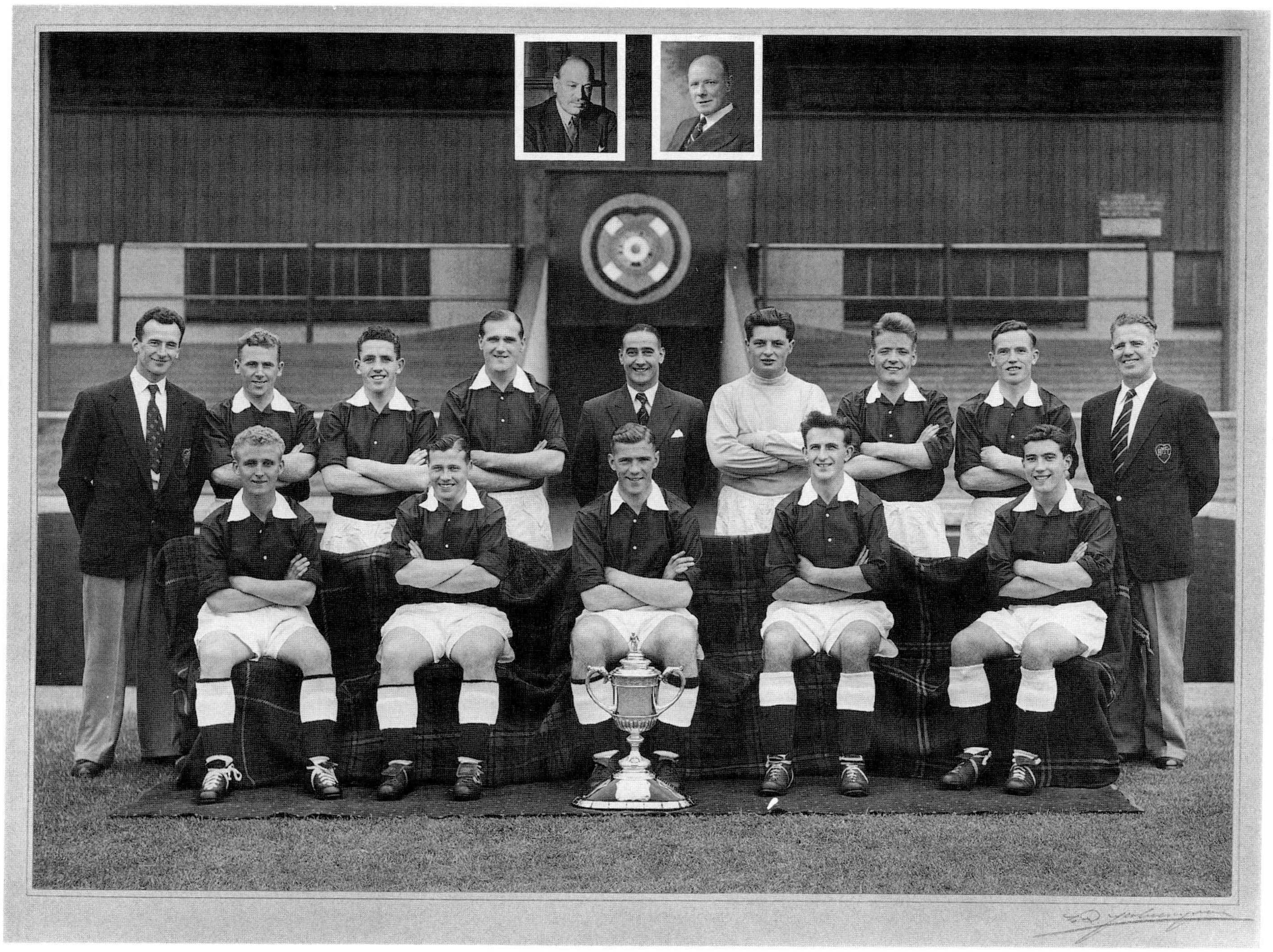

D. Macleod *Assistant Trainer* R. Kirk D. Mackay T. Mackenzie T. Walker *Manager* W. Duff W. Bauld J. Cumming J. Harvey *Trainer*

A. Young A. Conn F. Glidden *Captain* J. Wardhaugh J. Crawford

N. G. KILGOUR *Chairman*

THE RT. HON. THE EARL OF ROSEBERY, K.T. *Honorary President*

First Scottish XV v England

The first-ever rugby international was the Scotland v England match played at Raeburn Place, Edinburgh, on 27th March 1871 when Scotland won by one goal and one try to one try. Scotland's other early internationals included: Ireland, at Ormeau, Belfast on 19th February 1877; Wales at Raeburn Place, Edinburgh on 8th January 1883; and France at Inverleith, Edinburgh on 22nd January 1910.

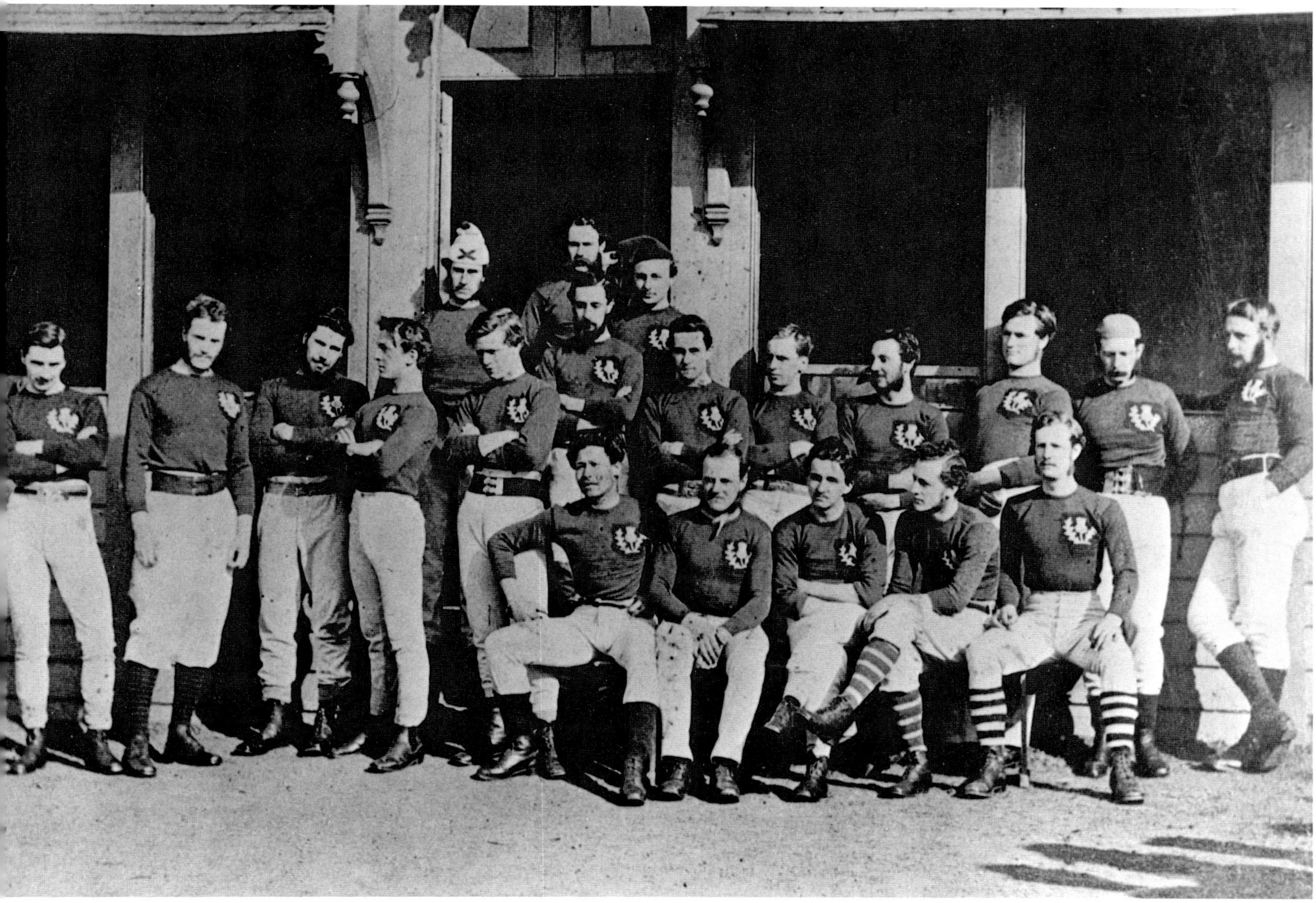

Holyrood Curling Club

Eighteen stalwart gentlemen from Holyrood Curling Club have brushes at the ready for the roarin' game, c. 1886. The photograph is believed to have been taken at Duddingston Loch, but there is insufficient detail in the background to be certain. There were several shallow rinks on the south side of the Loch, also used by Duddingston Curling Club. Holyrood Curling Club was established in 1849, was admitted to the Royal Caledonian Curling Club in 1854, and still exists in Edinburgh almost 150 years later.

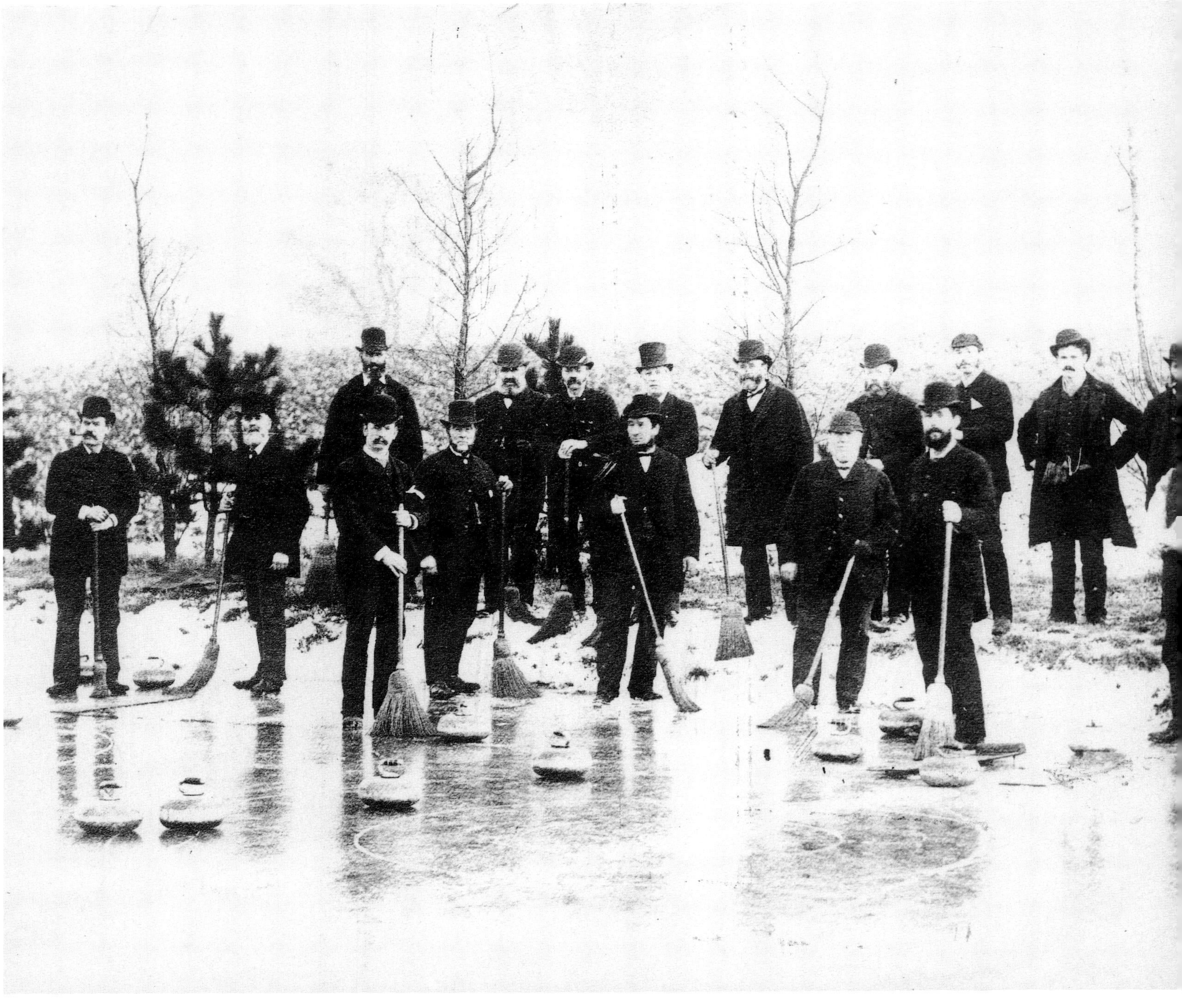

Skaters on Duddingston Loch

Young and old alike appear to be enjoying the advantages of a sustained period of sub-zero temperatures at Duddingston Loch *c.* 1894. Some appear to stroll, some sweep, whilst others sit at the side and spectate. On the skyline is Duddingston Kirk, built originally in the twelfth century by the Monks of Kelso on land gifted by David I to the Abbot of Kelso. Almost in the centre of the picture, on the far side of the loch, is the tall stone tower, the upper storey of which was used as a studio by the artist minister of Duddingston, the Rev. John Thomson.

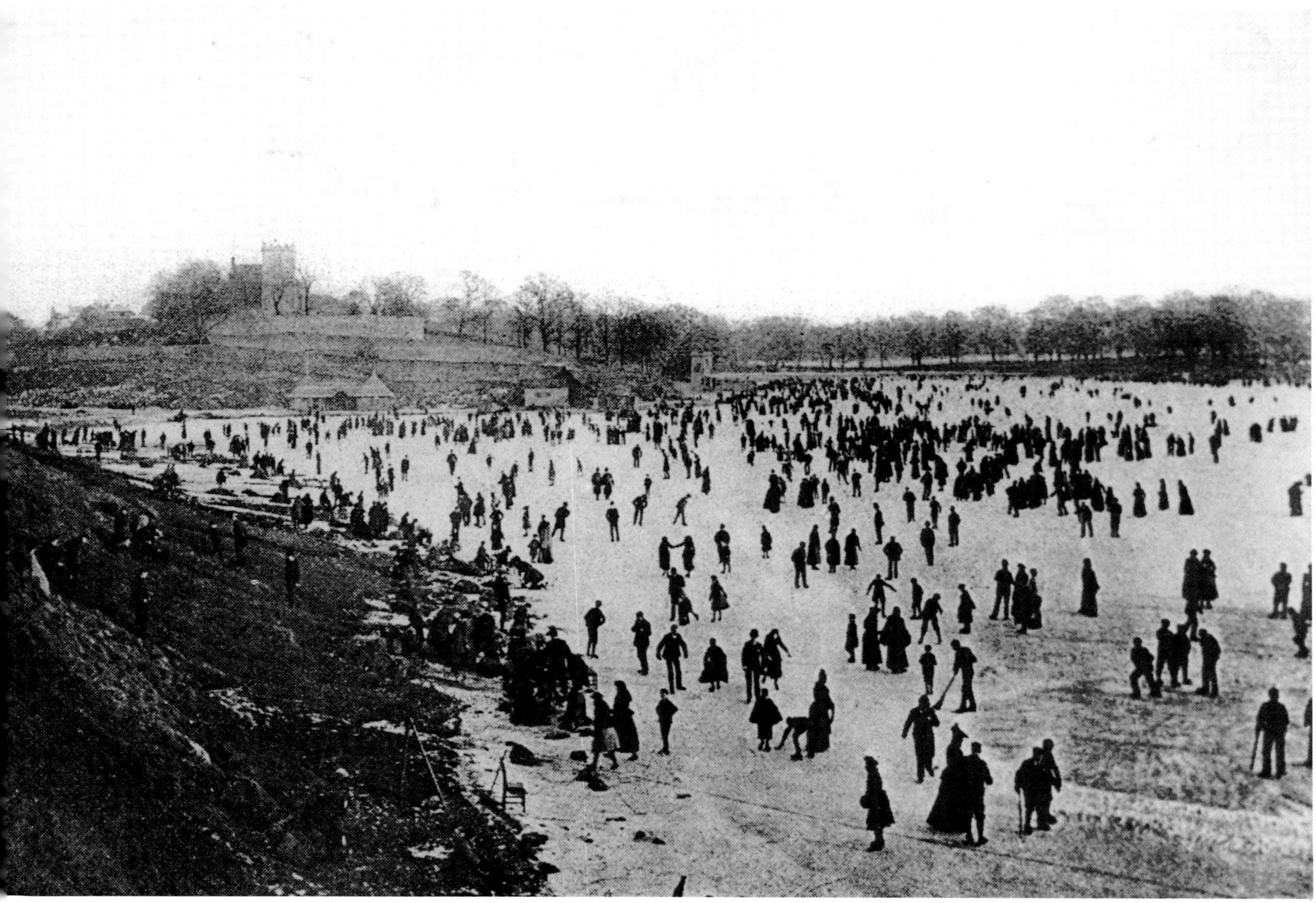

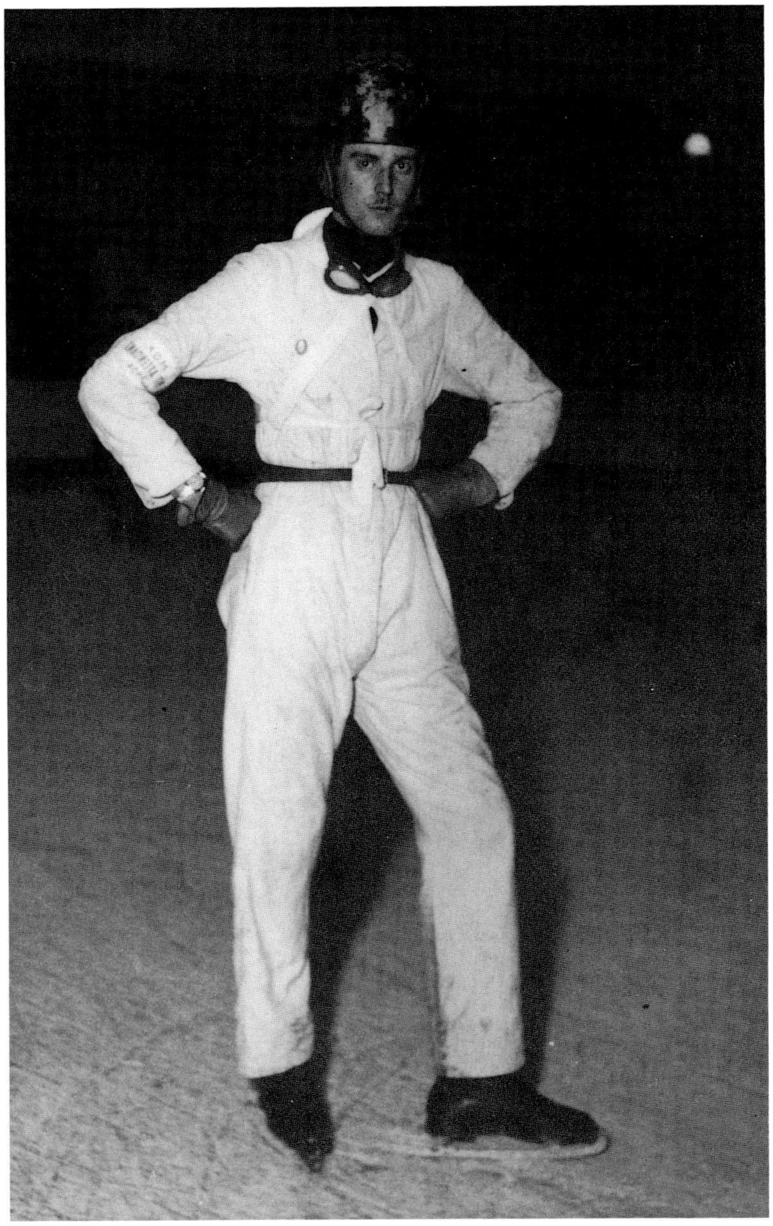

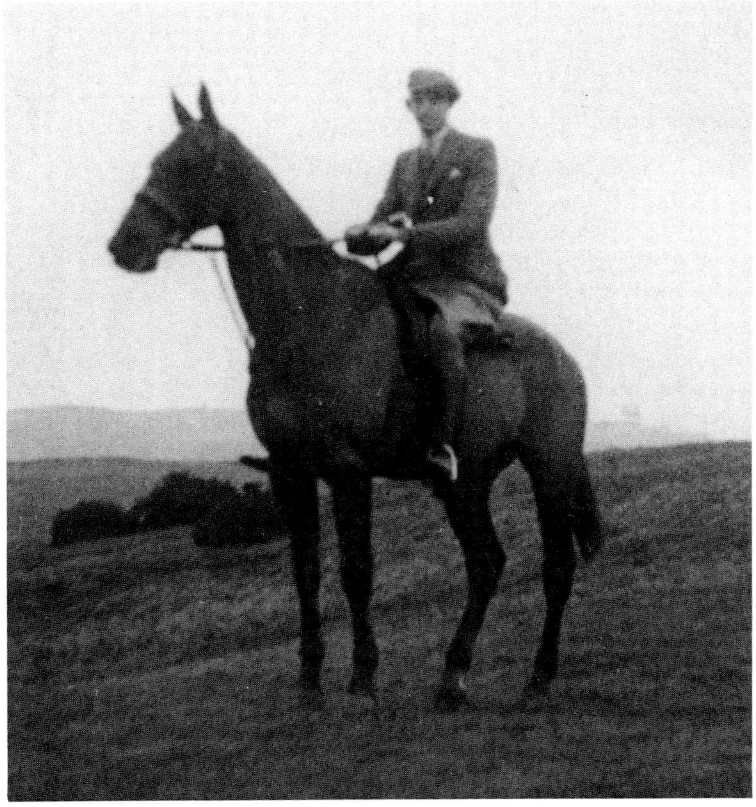

Horse-riding: The Braid Hills, January 1935.

Skating: Ice Carnival, January 1935

Edward Roper Yerbury

Edward Roper Yerbury, elder son of E. R. Yerbury, went to Rhodesia in 1937, but died tragically at the age of twenty-five on 1st June 1940, as a result of a motor cycle accident a few days earlier. His youthful exuberance and keen interest in sport and the outdoor life are amply illustrated in these three pictures taken in the first flush of youth.

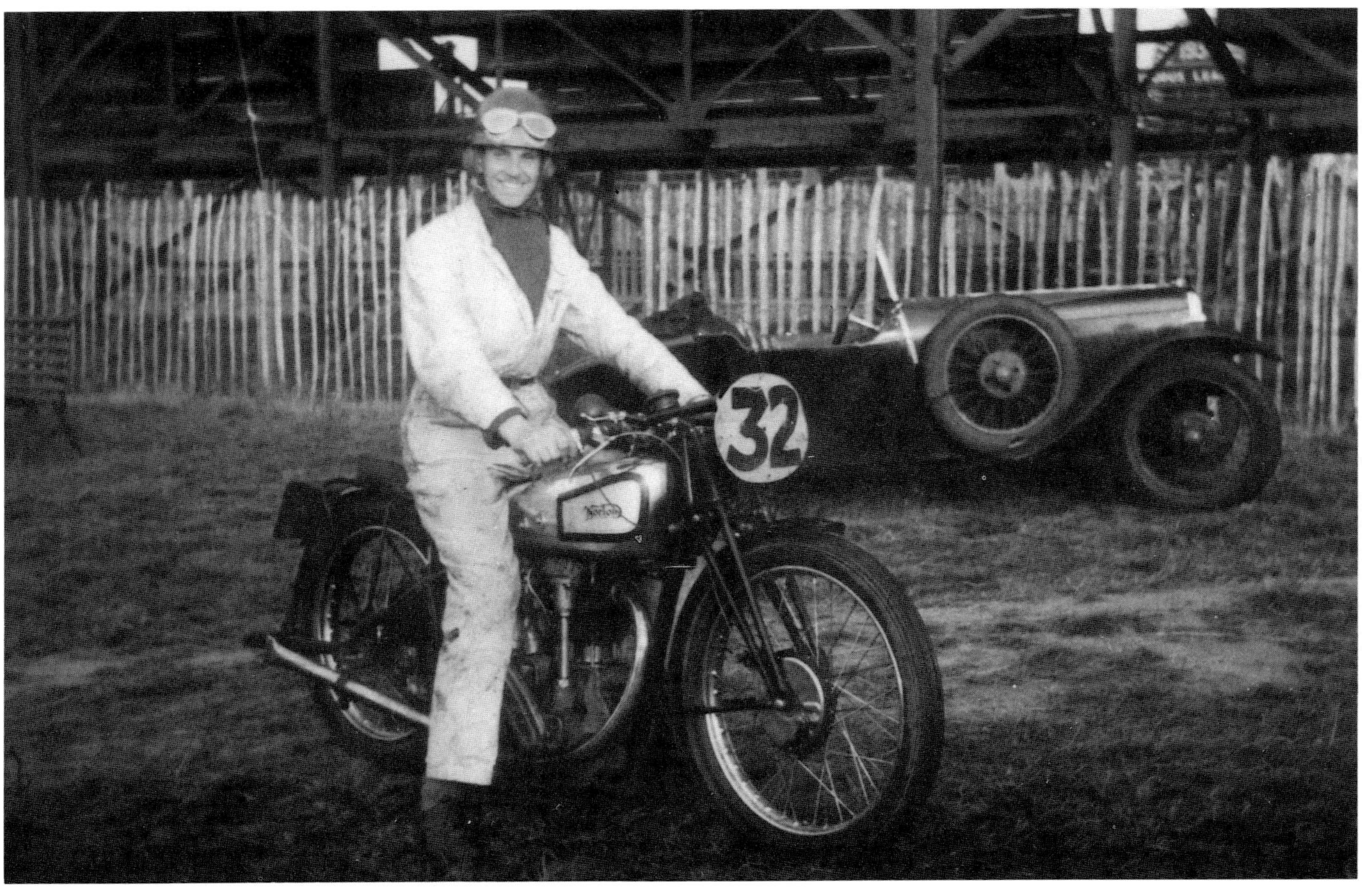

Motor-cycling: Manx Grand Prix, September 1934

Edward Roper Yerbury

Edward Roper Yerbury on his Norton Special motor-cycle, flanked by another two youthful motor-cyclists — complete with motor-cycle boots, waterproof clothing and goggles — but, as yet, no crash helmets.

St George Motor Club

A wide variety of riders and bikes (some with sidecars) assemble for the start of the St George Motor Club Trial from Corstorphine on 5th May 1934. The position of Edward Roper Yerbury, towards the right of the picture, is marked by a small cross.

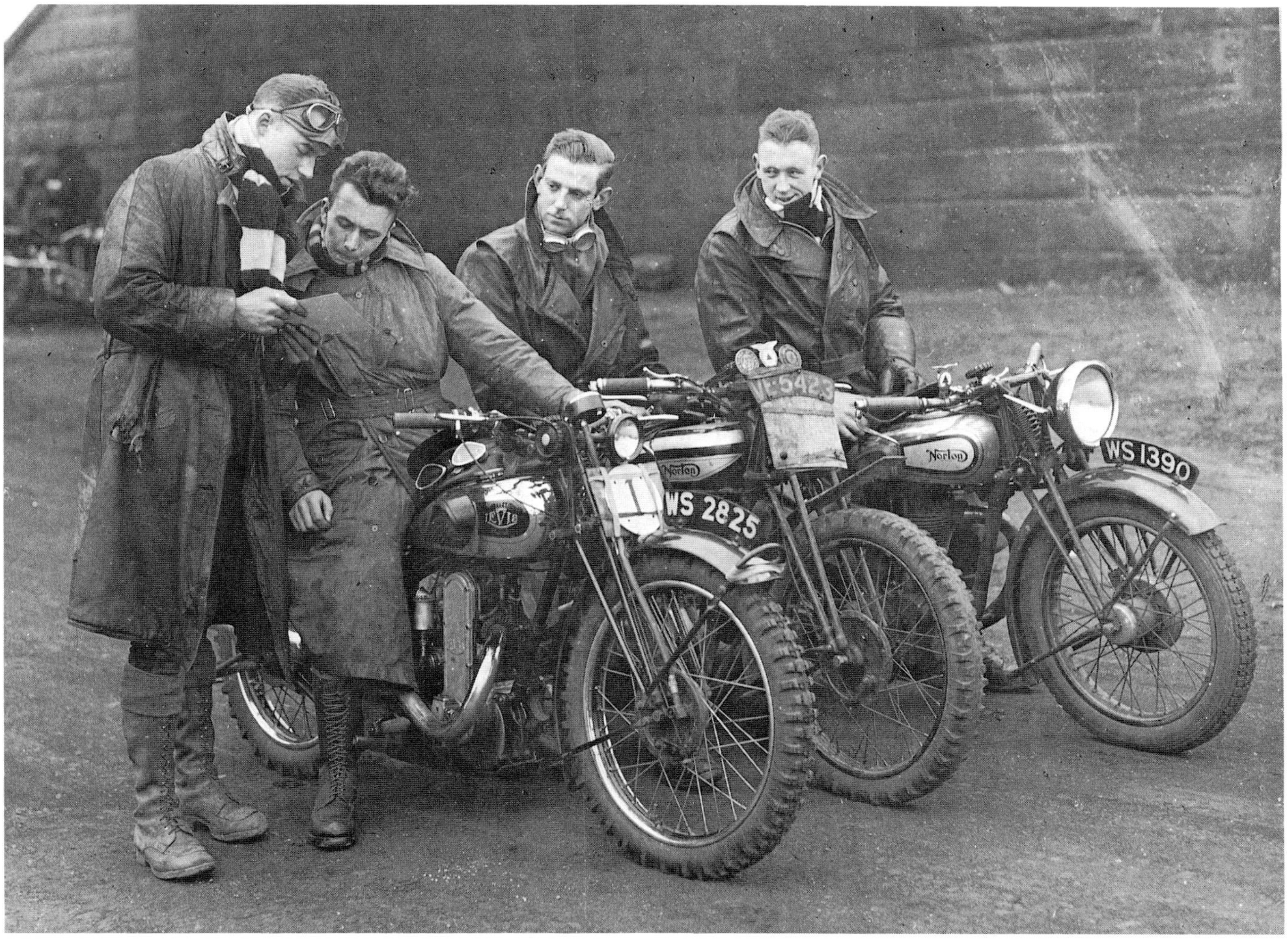

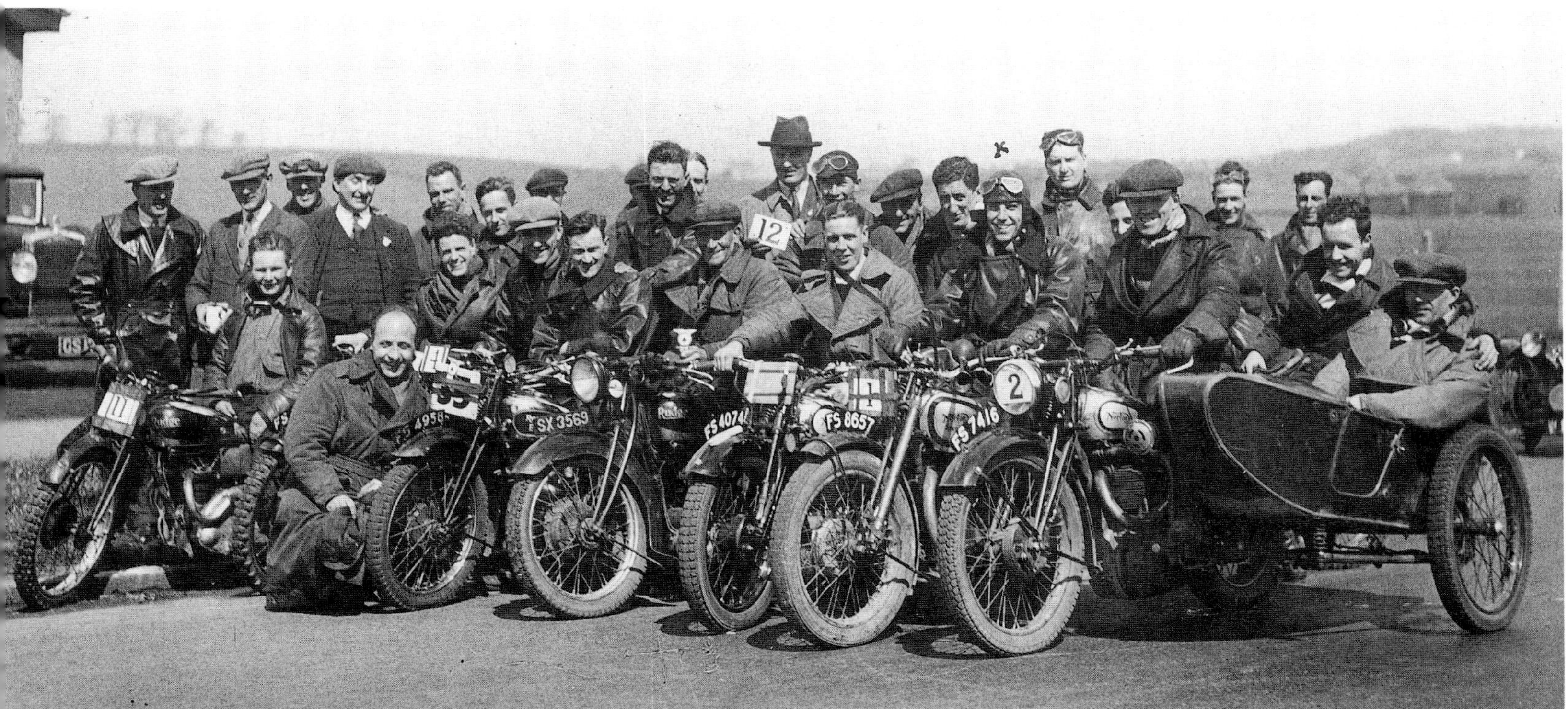

Photographic Outing to Aberdour

Courtesy of Wilson's of Aberdour, this group of photographers takes a short break by the roadside, near Aberdour in Fife 1900, whilst the driver and his young assistant maintain a formal pose. The gentleman with the straw hat is William Hume, a well known camera maker in Edinburgh in the nineteenth century.

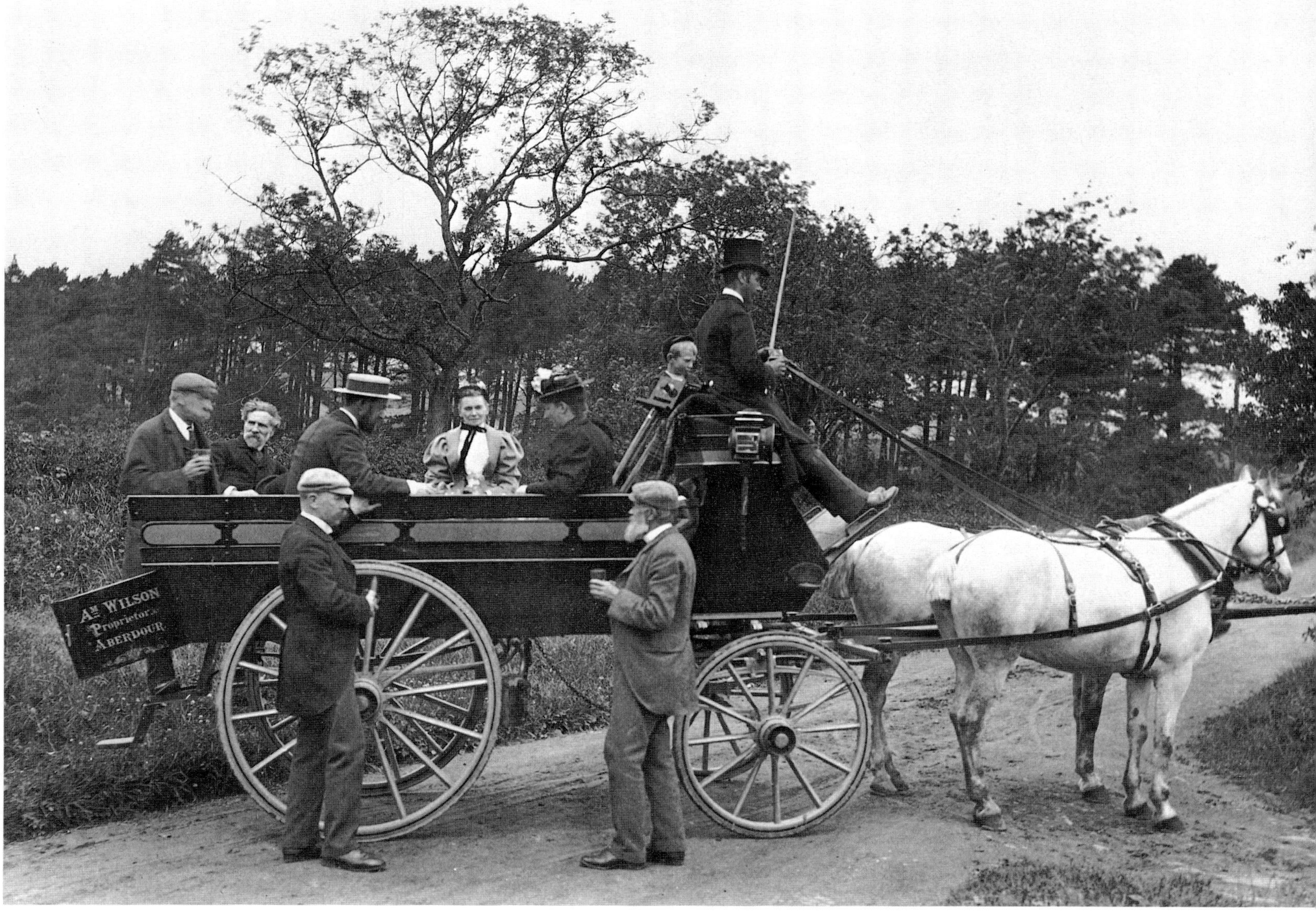

CHAPTER 8

General de Gaulle, 1890–1970, by E. R. Yerbury.

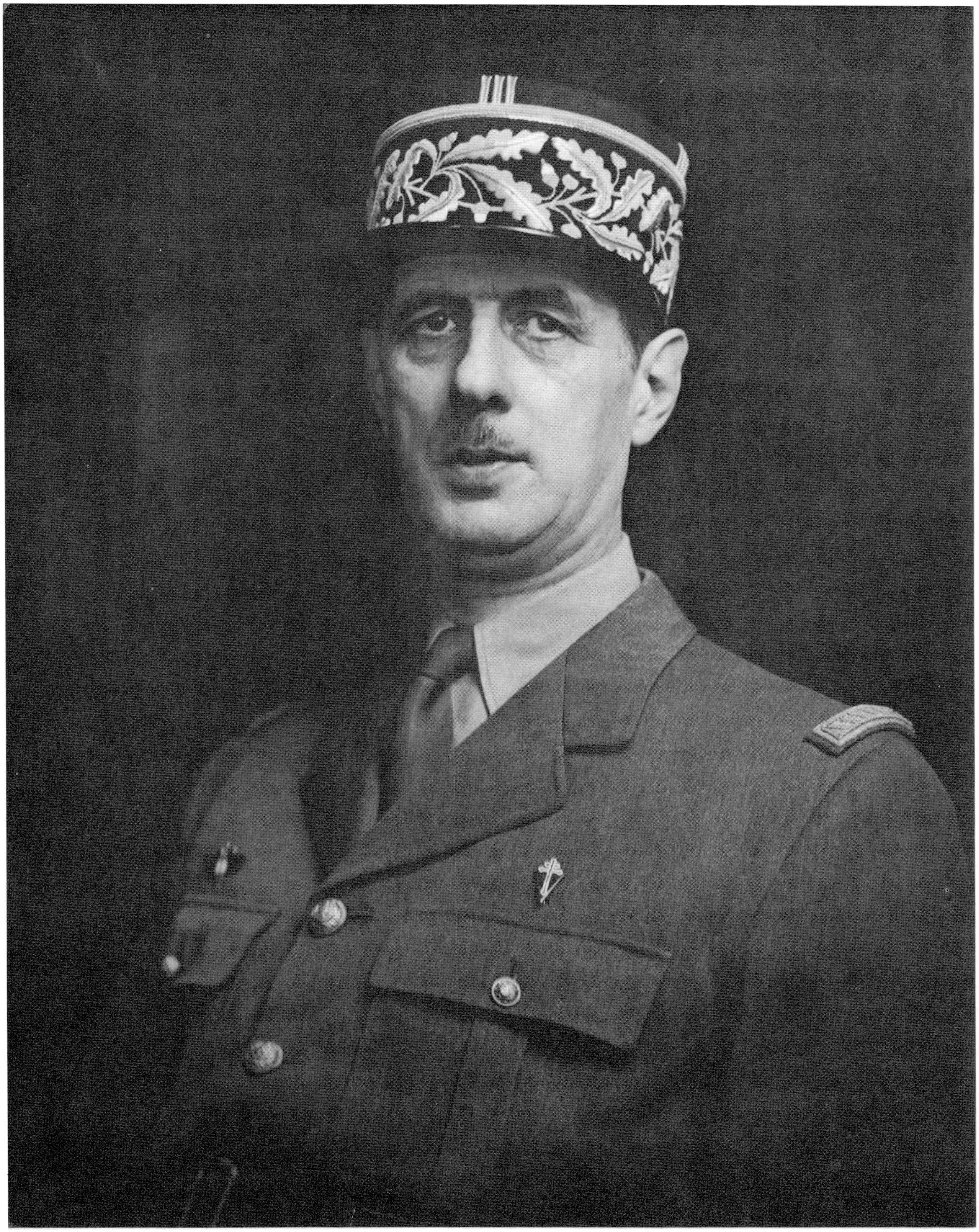

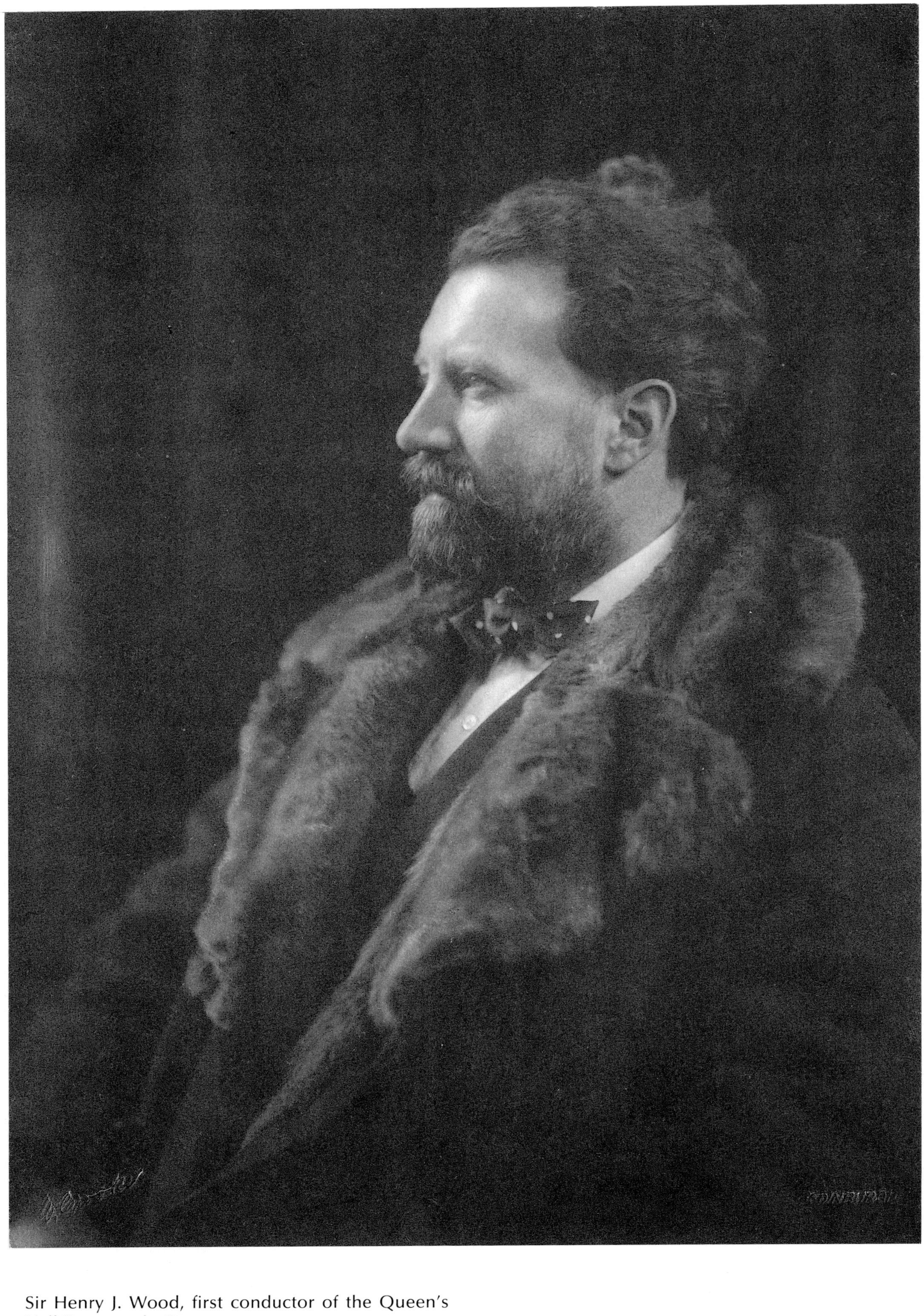

Sir Henry J. Wood, first conductor of the Queen's Hall Promenade Concerts.

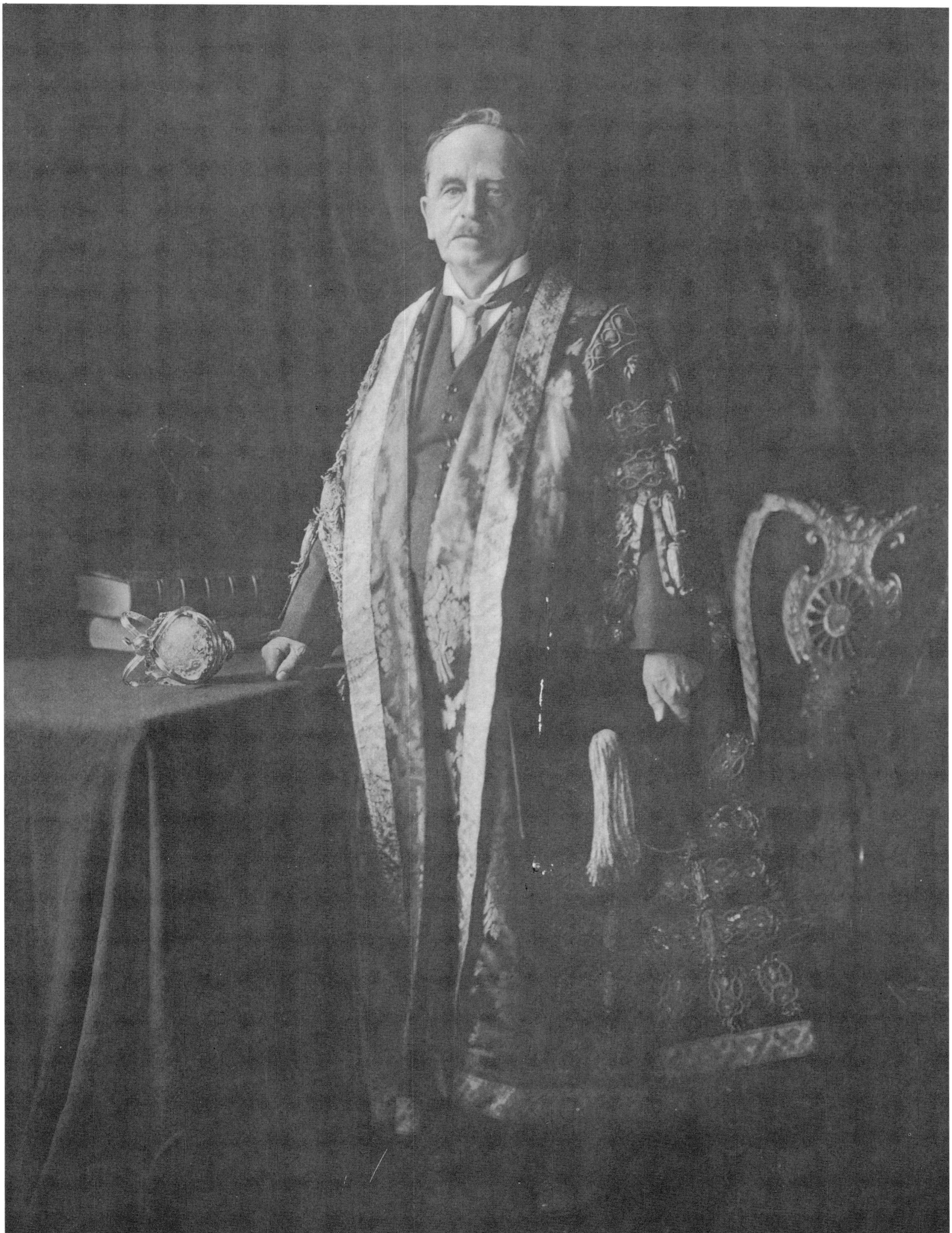

Sir James M. Barrie, Bart., OM, LL.D, Chancellor of Edinburgh University, 25th October 1930, by E. R. Yerbury & Son.

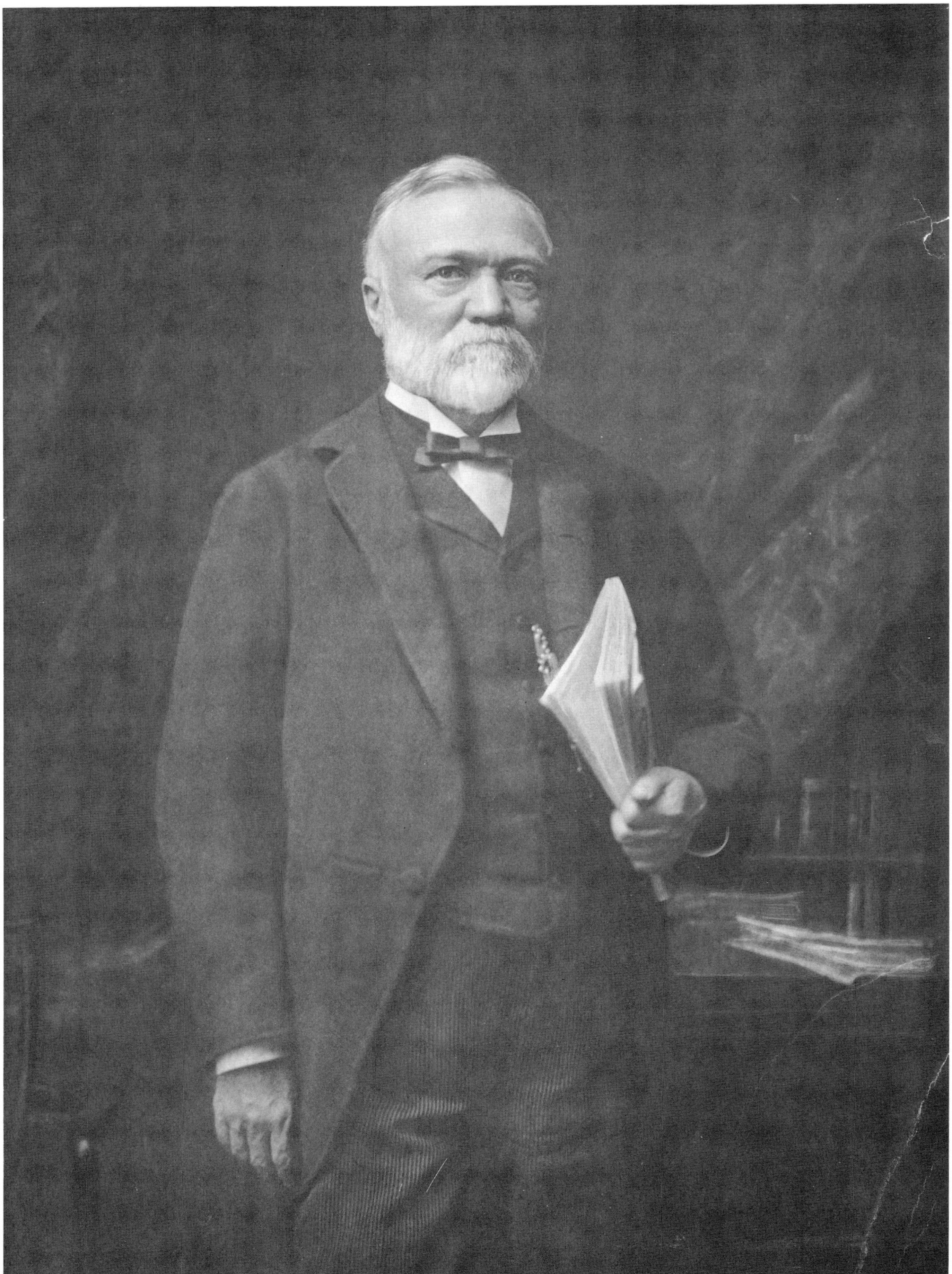

Andrew Carnegie, by W. Crooke.

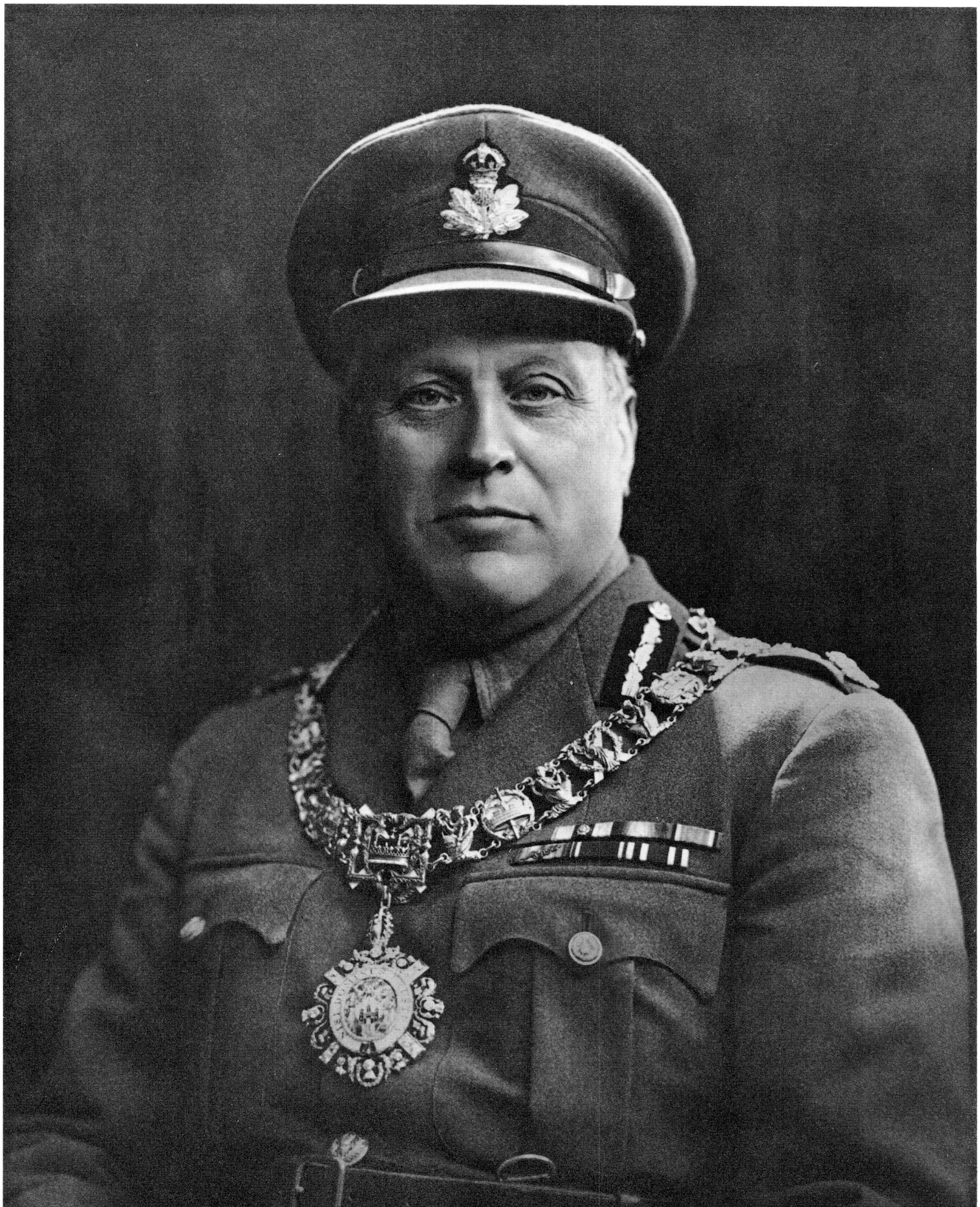

Sir William Young Darling, Lord Provost of Edinburgh 1941–44 by Edward R. Yerbury.

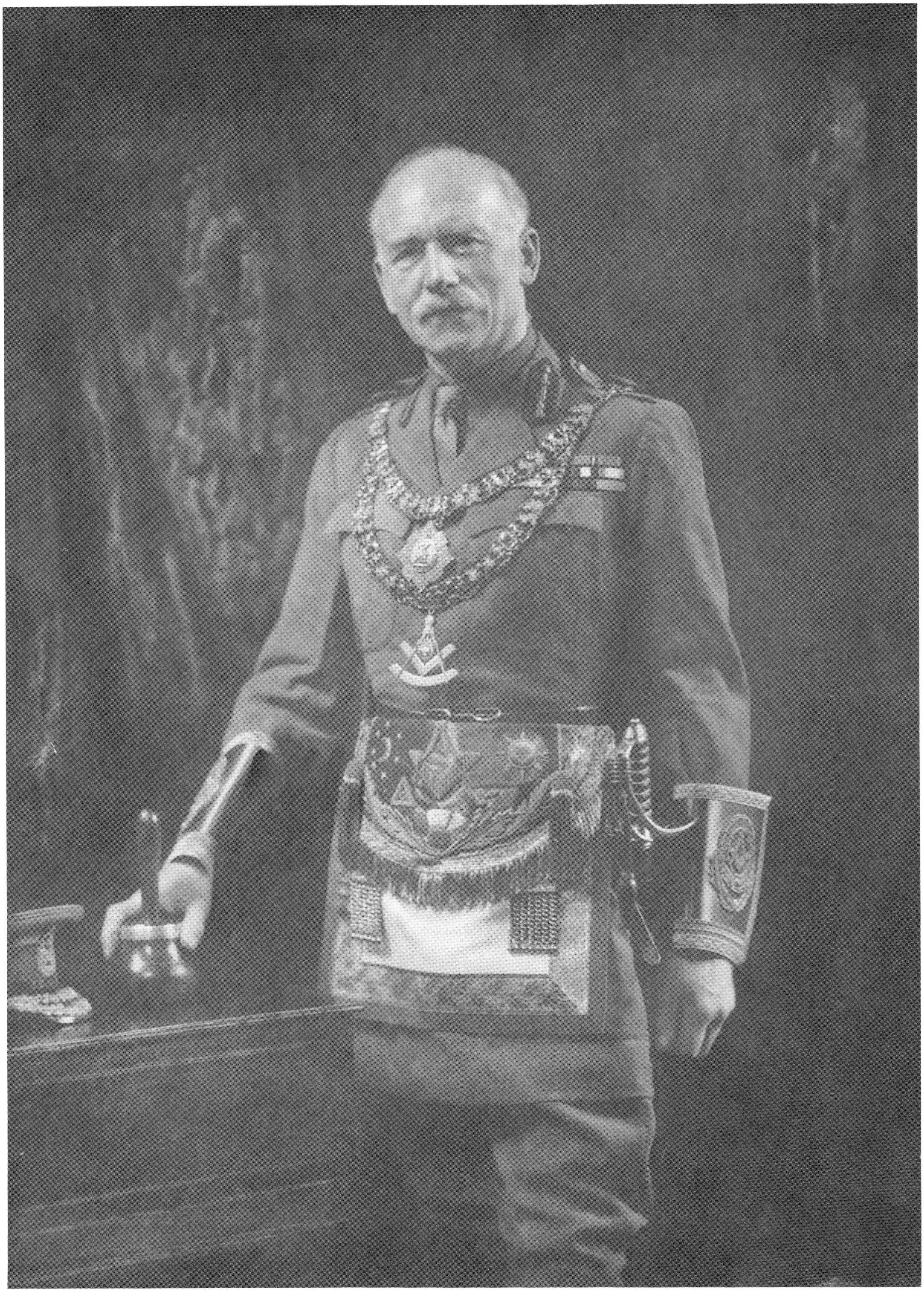

Brigadier-General Robert Gordon Gilmour, CB, CVO, DSO, JP, DL, by W. Crooke.

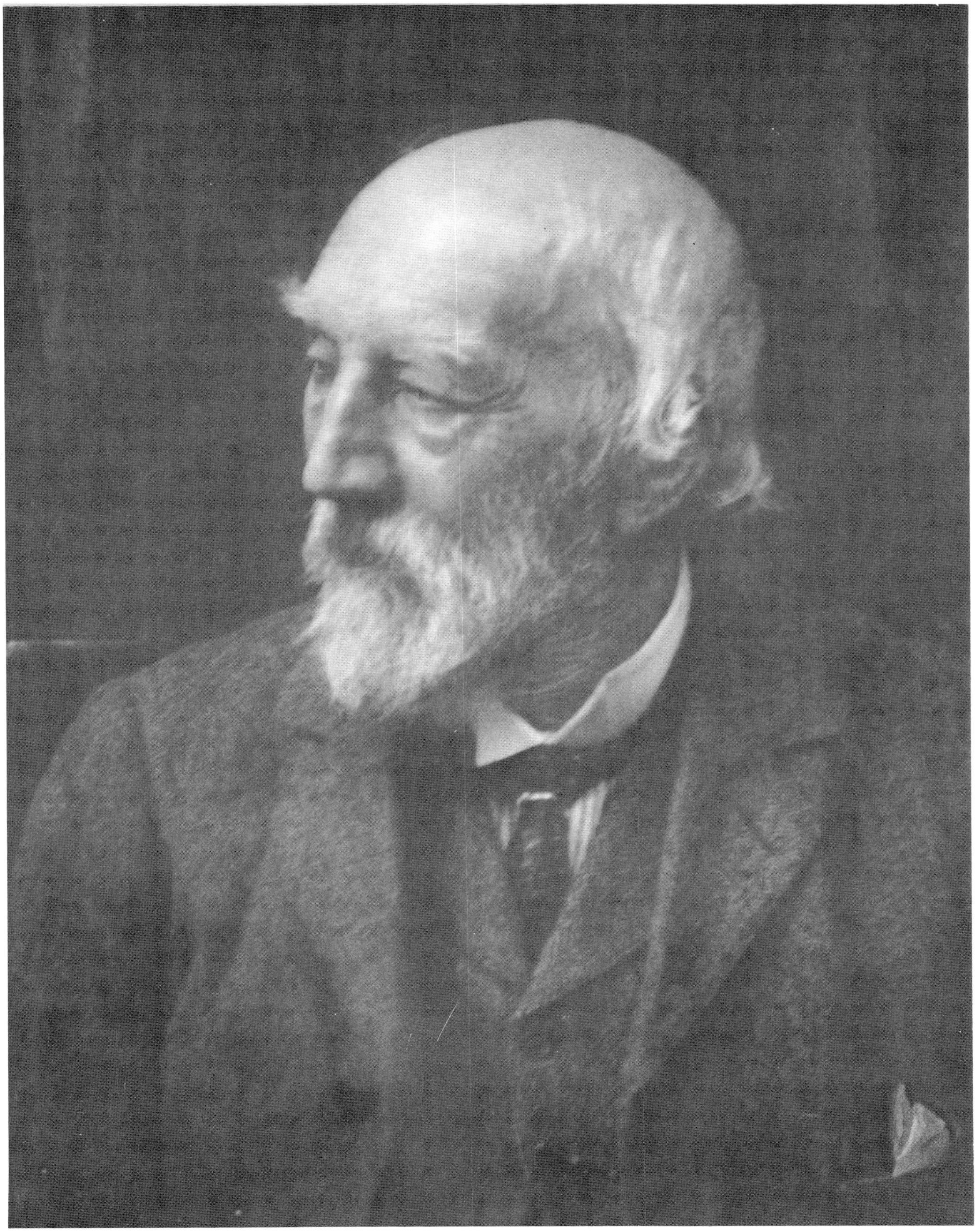

Sir James Ramsay of Banff, by W. Crooke.

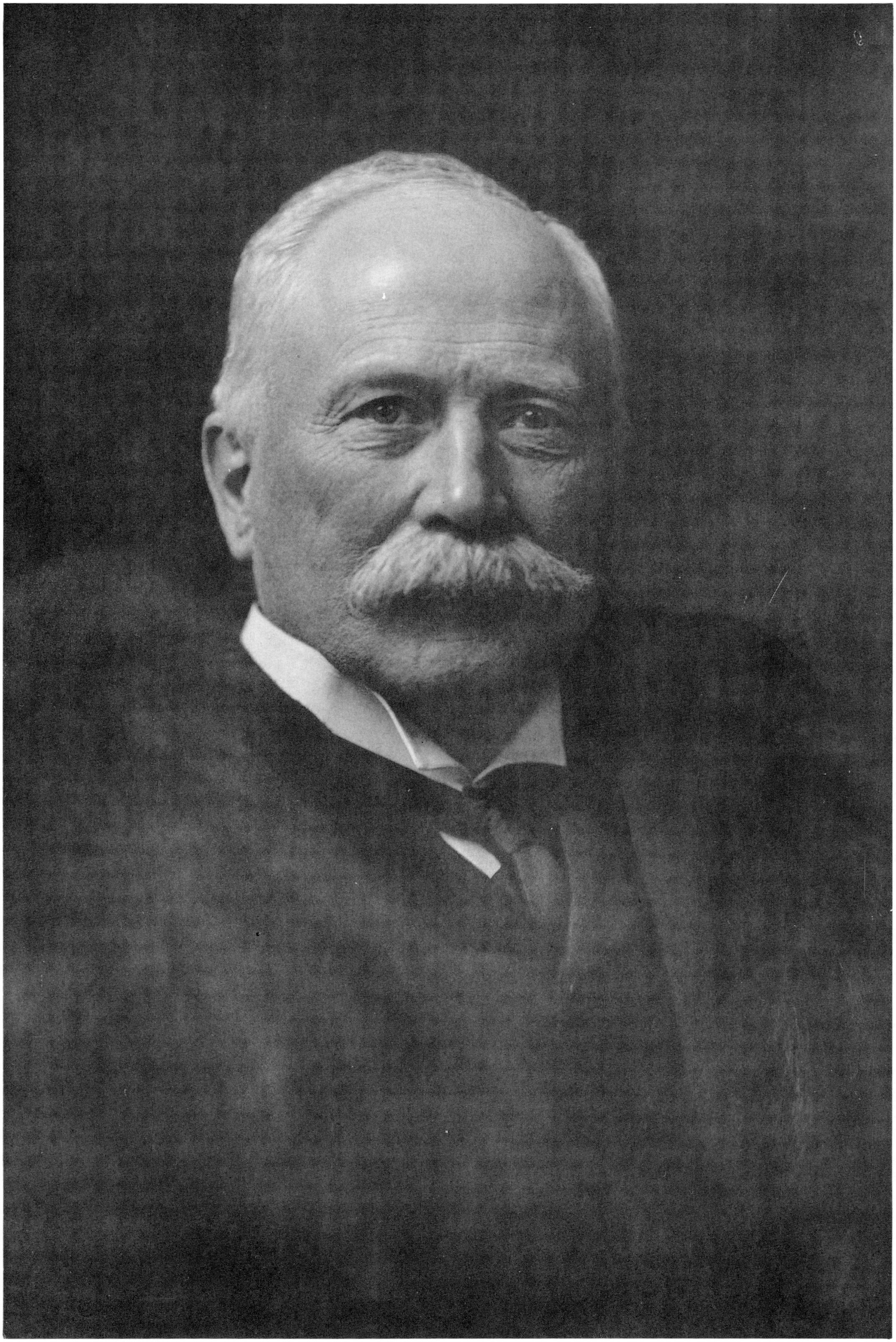

Sir R. Rowand Anderson, Architect, by W. Crooke.

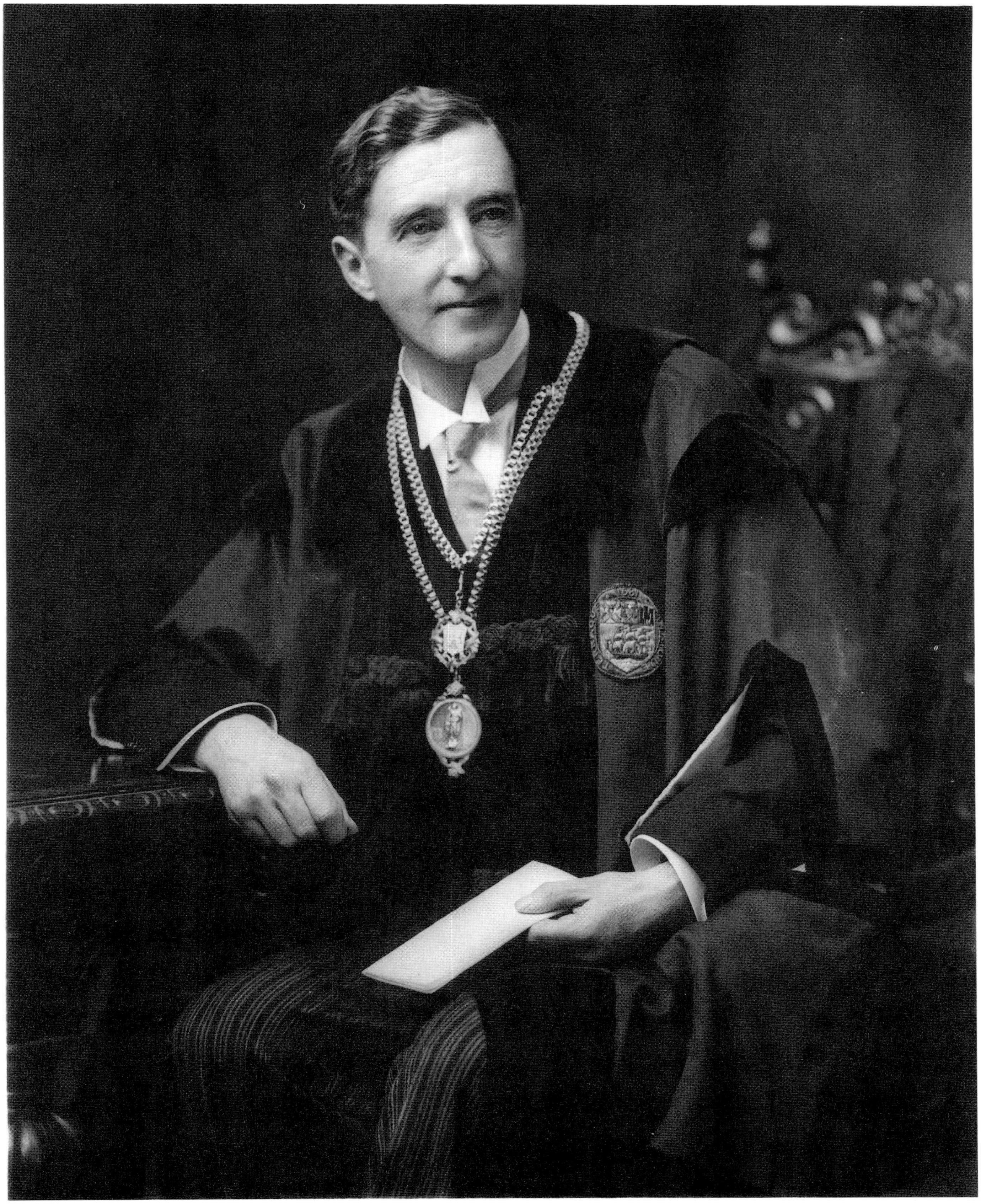

Iver R. R. Salvesen, TD, Master of the Edinburgh Merchant Company 1949–51, by E. R. Yerbury.

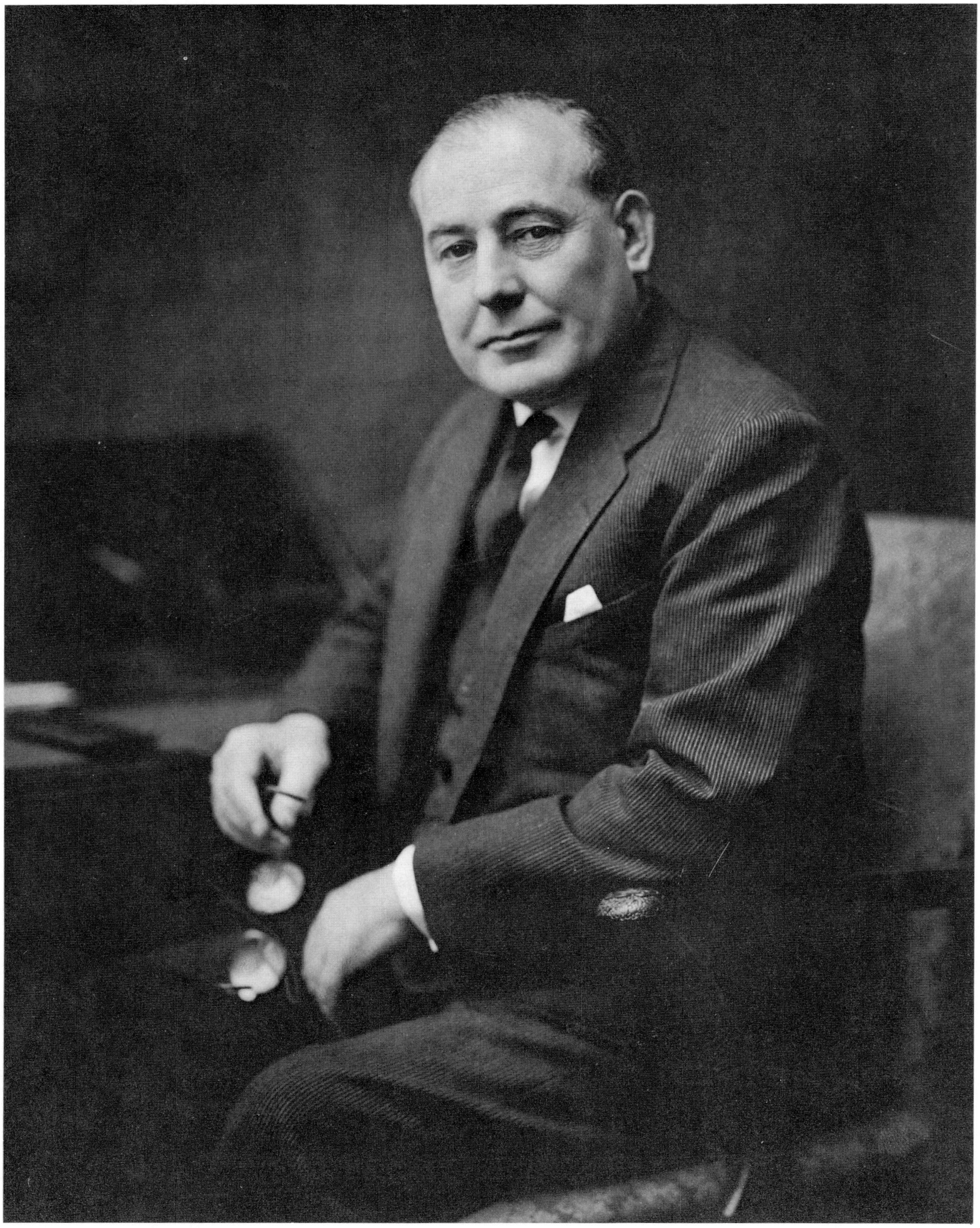

D. Drysdale, President of the Scottish Rugby Union
1951–52.

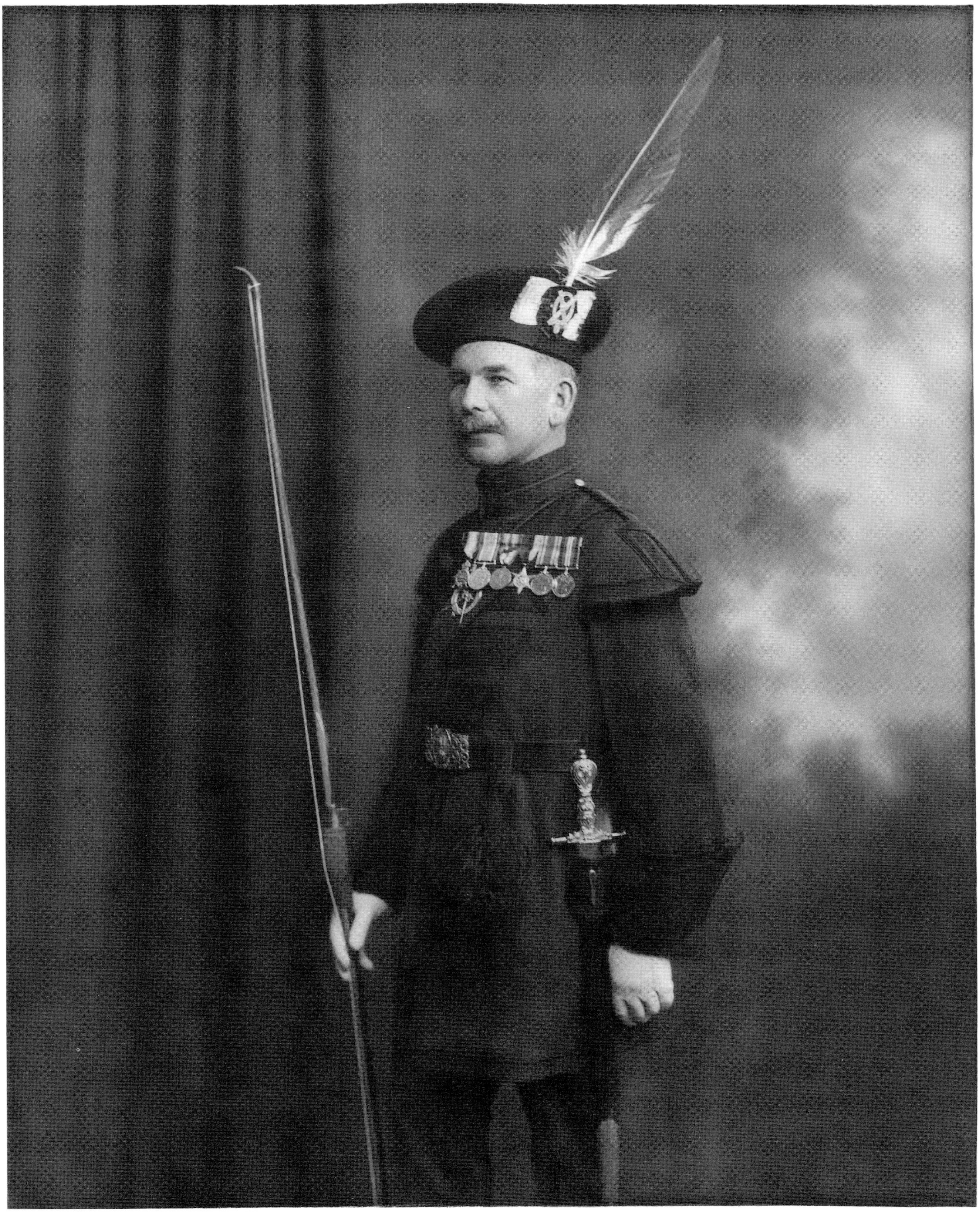

A Member of the Queen's Body Guard for Scotland (Royal Company of Archers), established 1676, by Edward R. Yerbury.

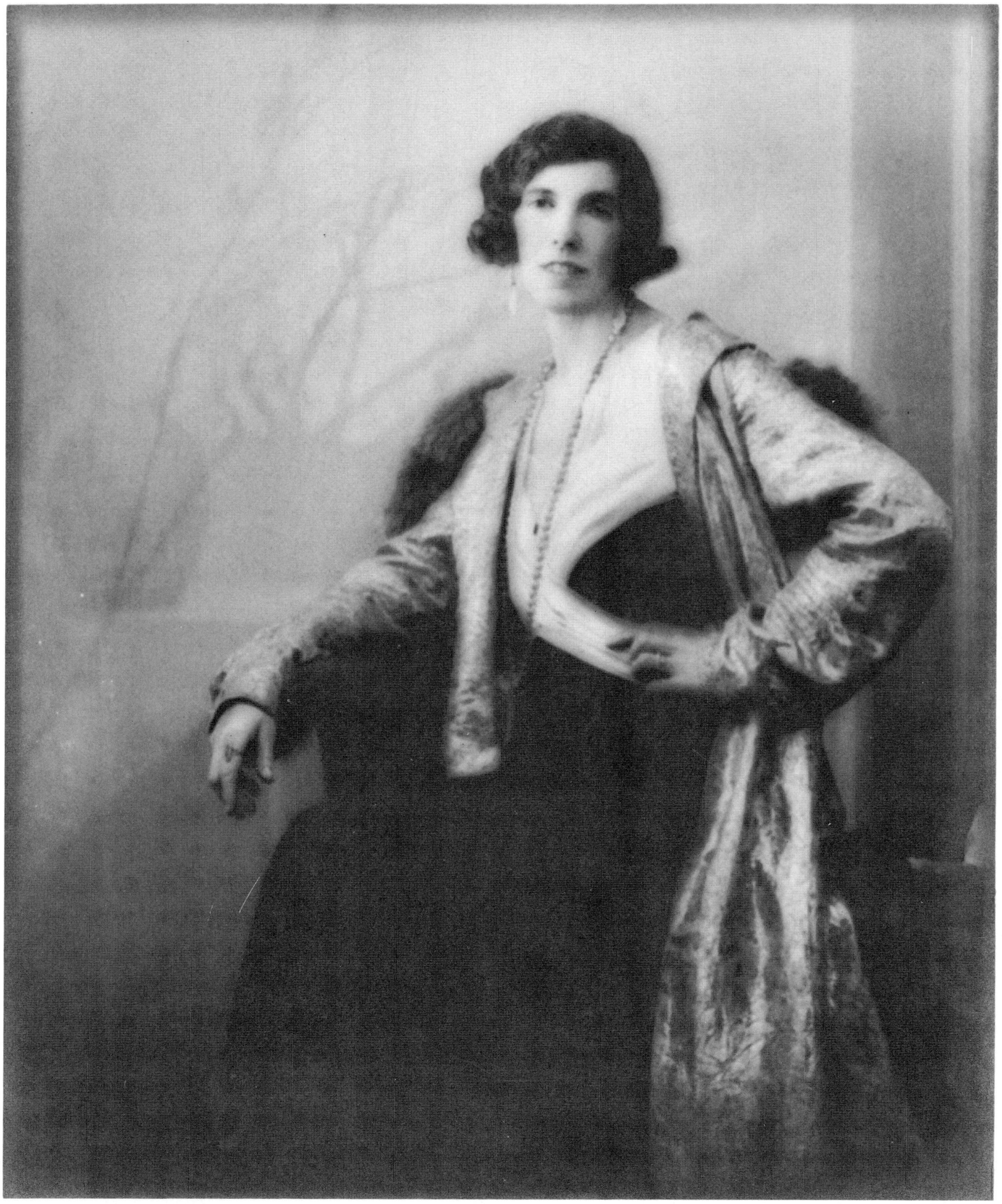

The artist's wife, Grace, by E. R. Yerbury.

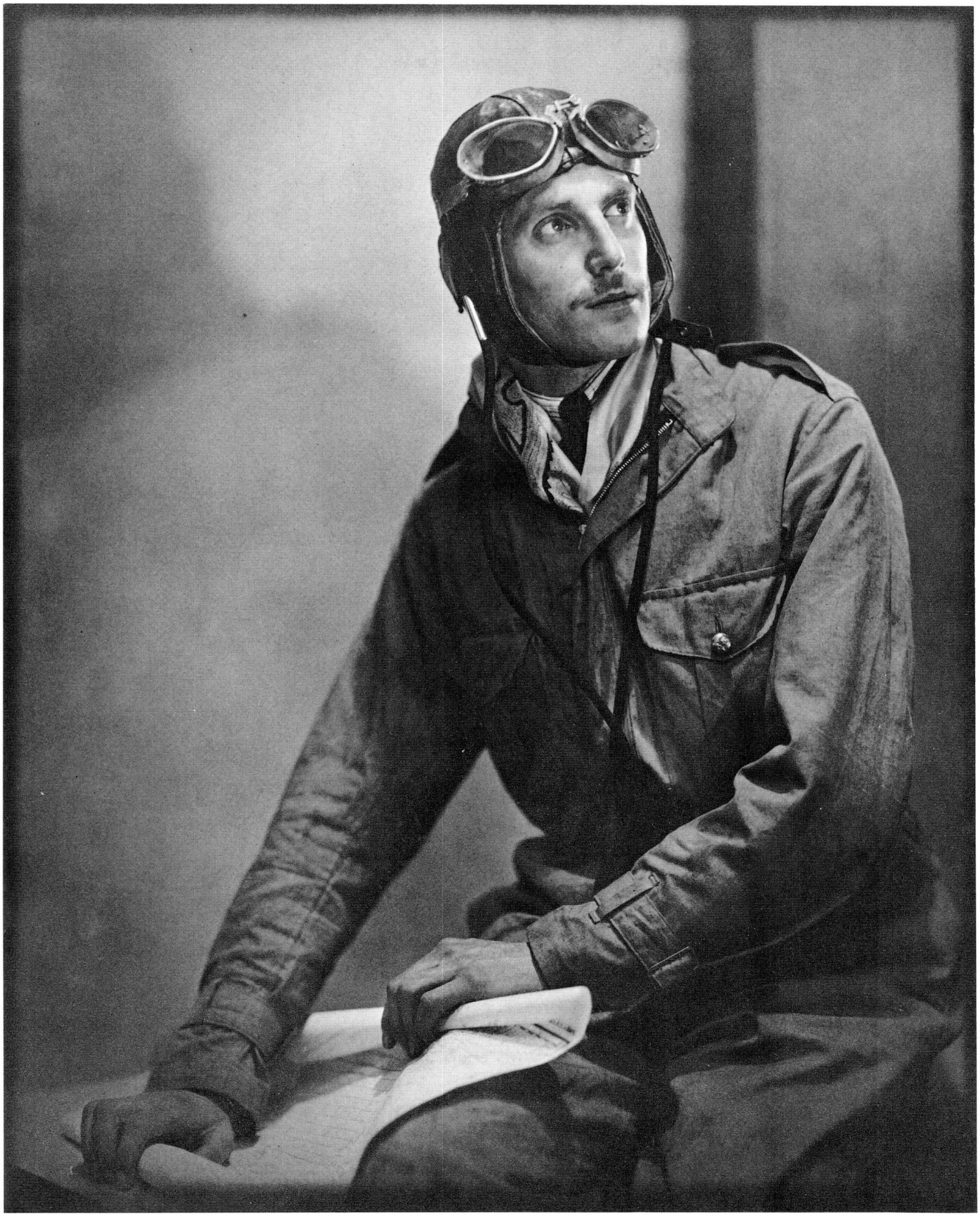

The Sky Pilot (Edward R. Yerbury) by his father, E. R. Yerbury.

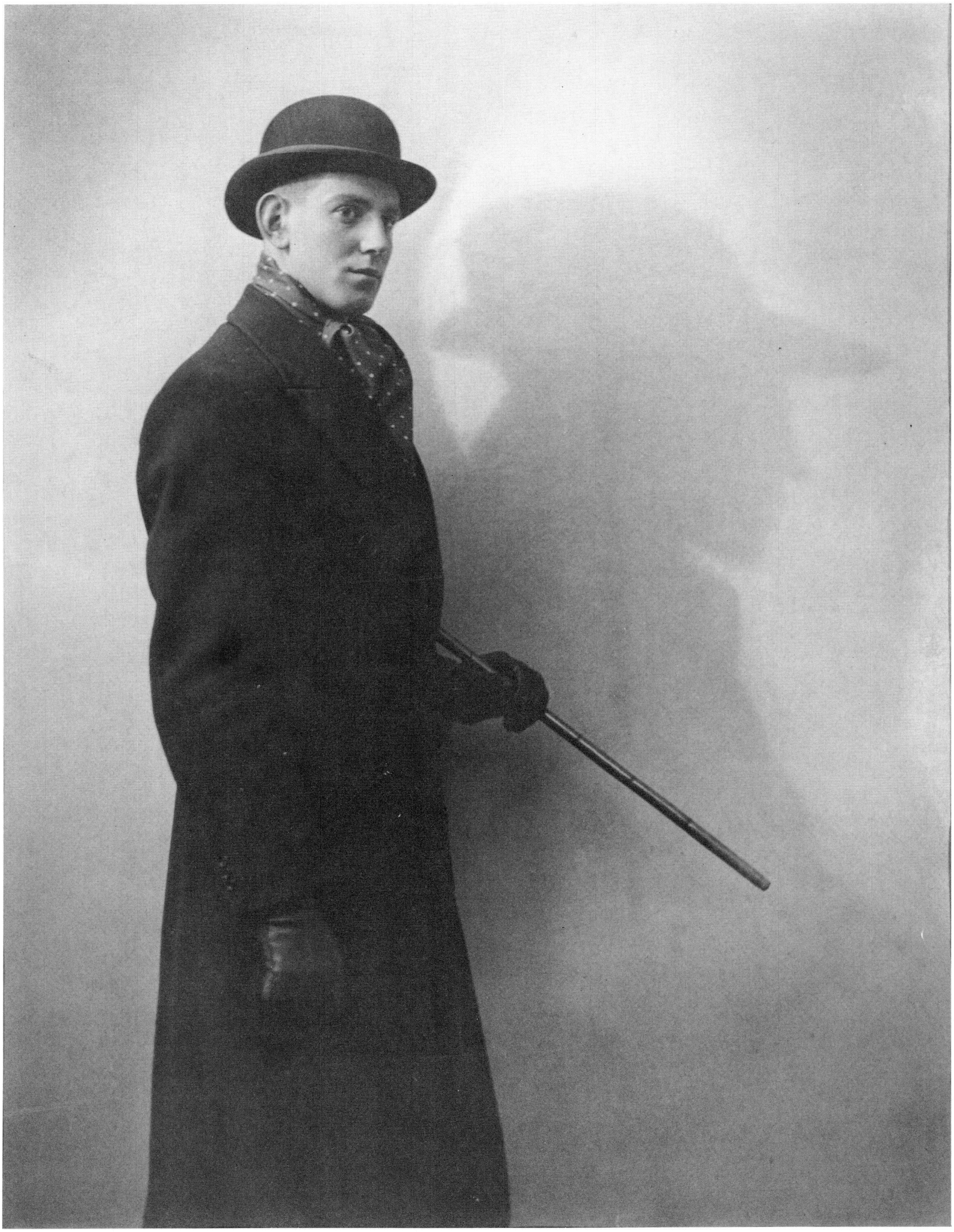

Portrait of a Young Man, by E. R. Yerbury.

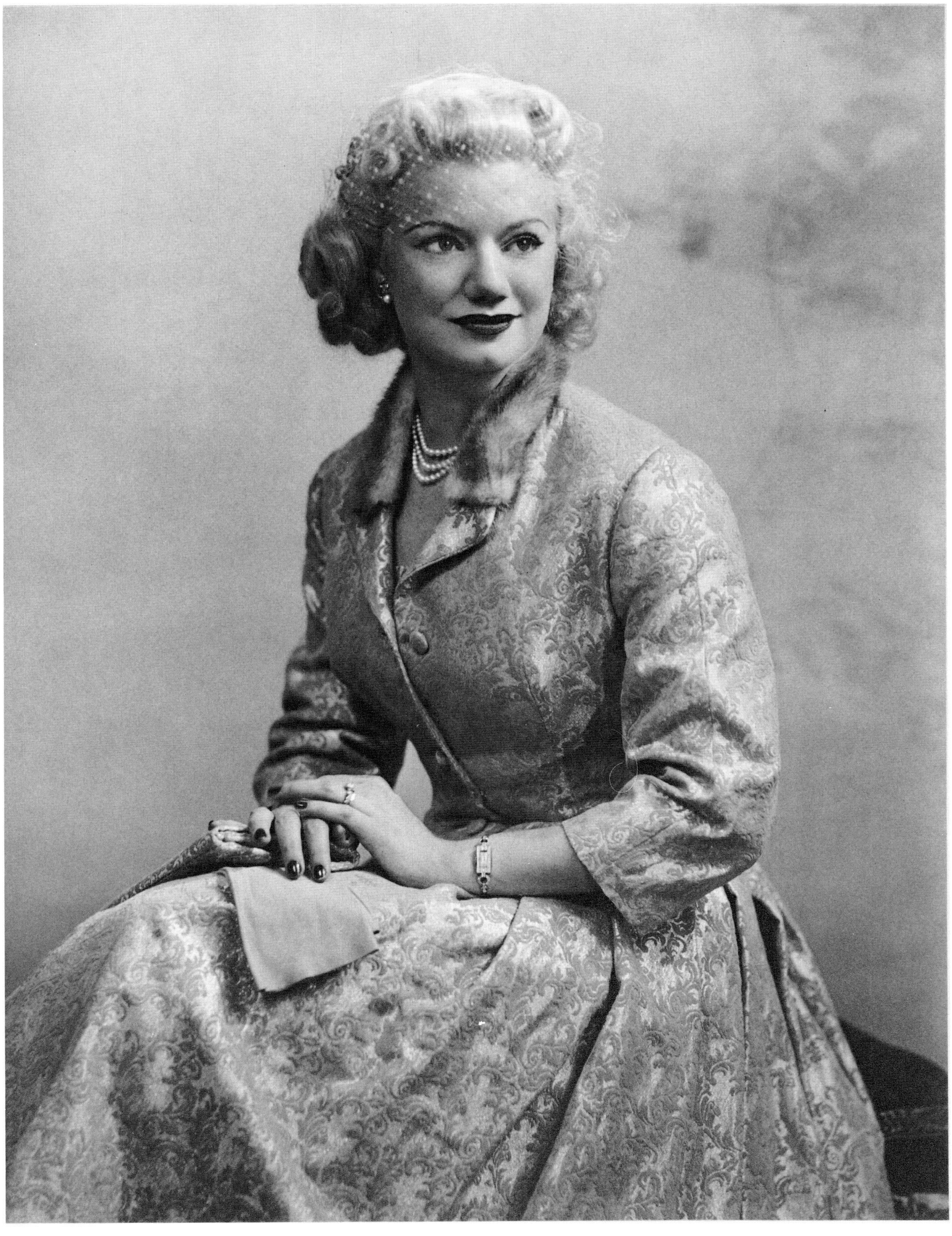

Portrait of a Young Lady.

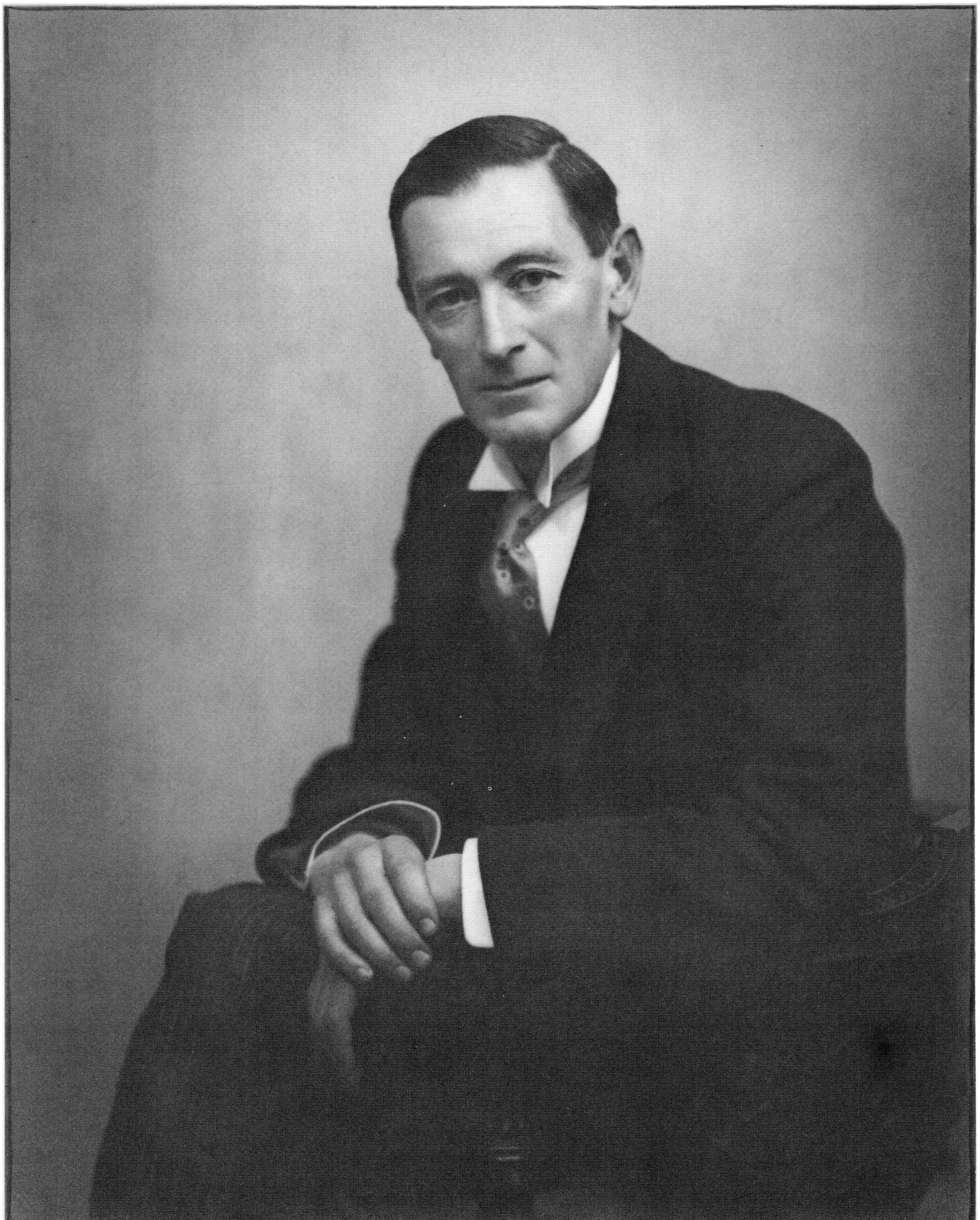

Portrait of a Gentleman, by E. R. Yerbury.

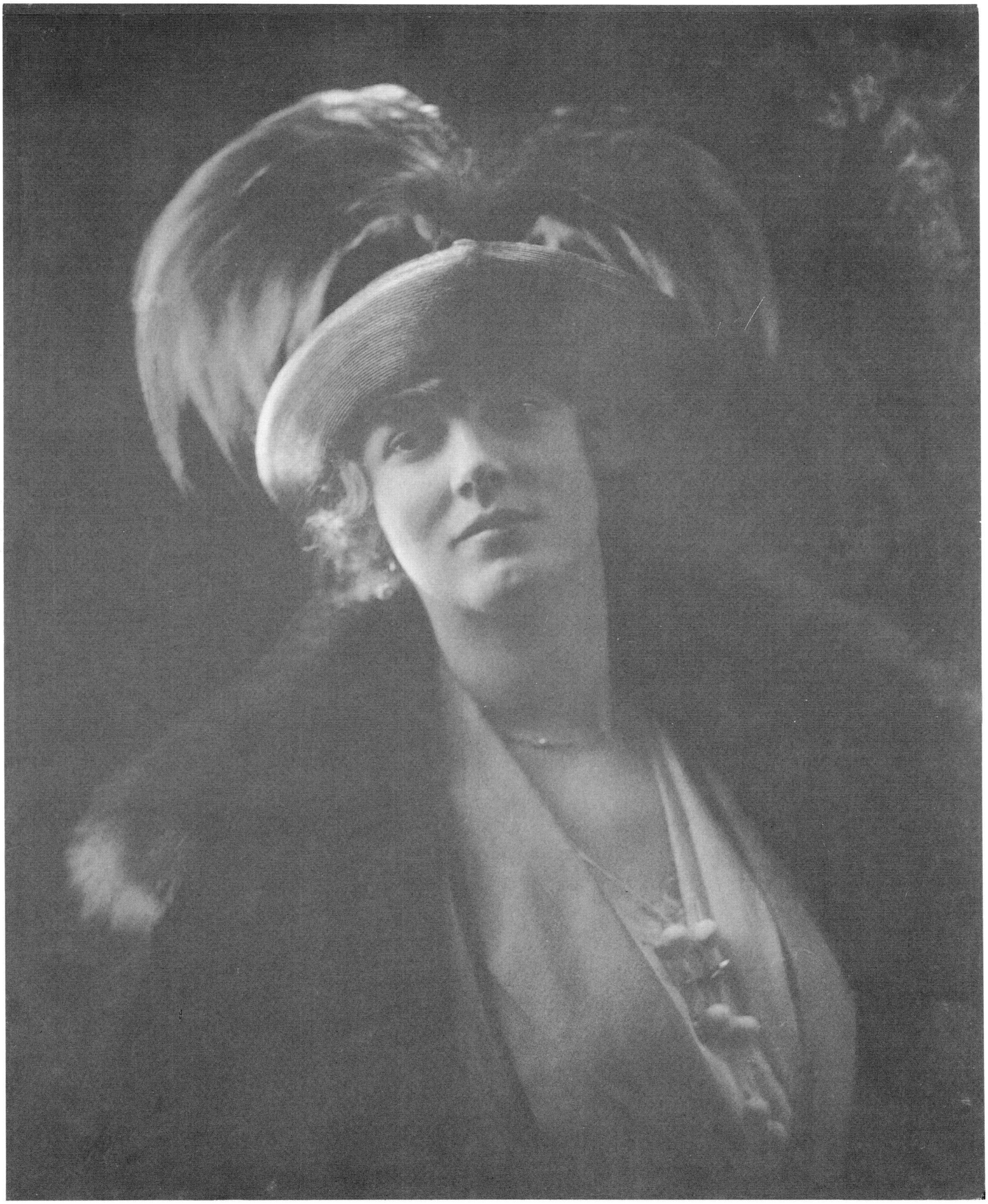

Portrait of a Lady, by W. Crooke.

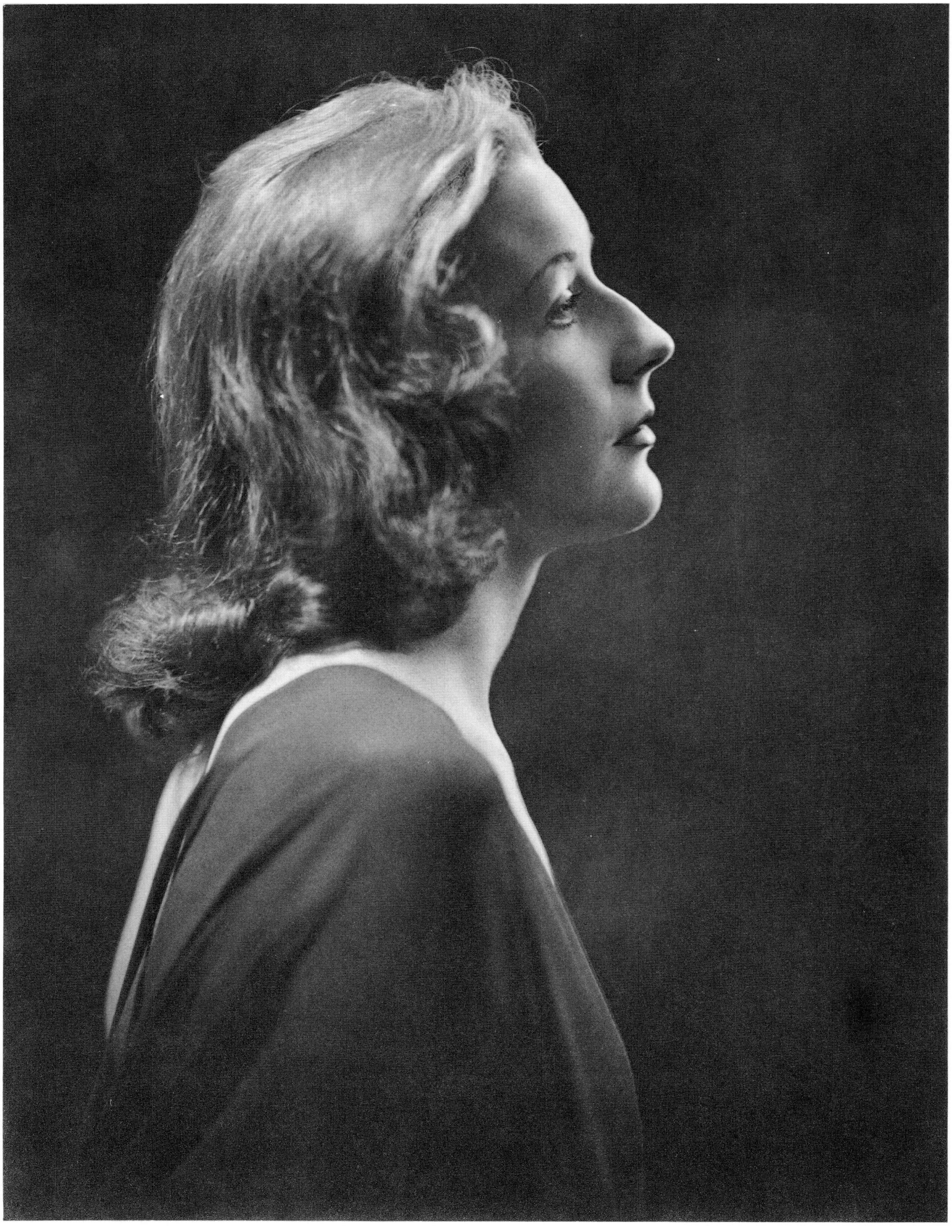

Young Lady in Profile.

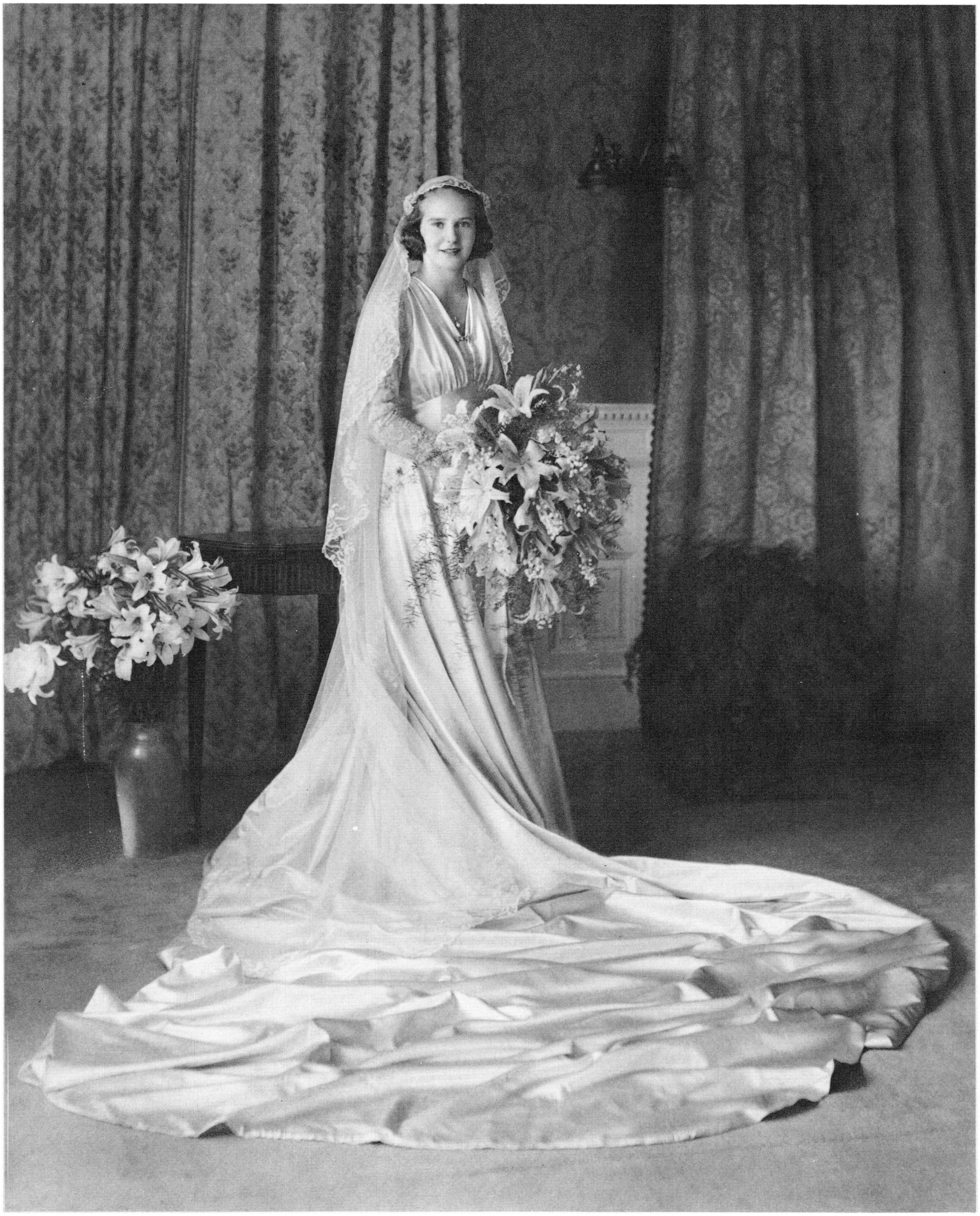

Portrait of a Bride, by E. R. Yerbury.

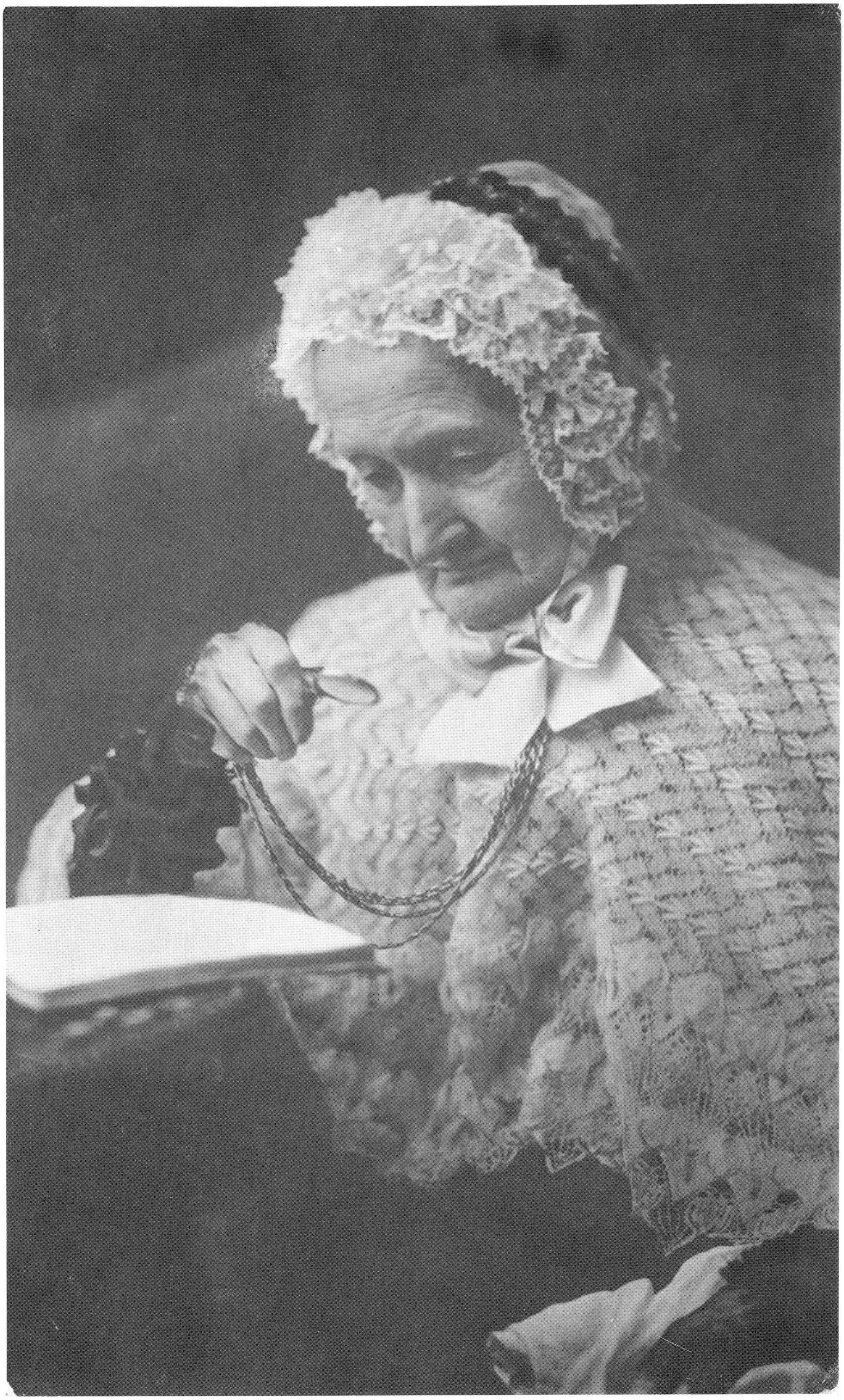

Portrait of an Old Lady.

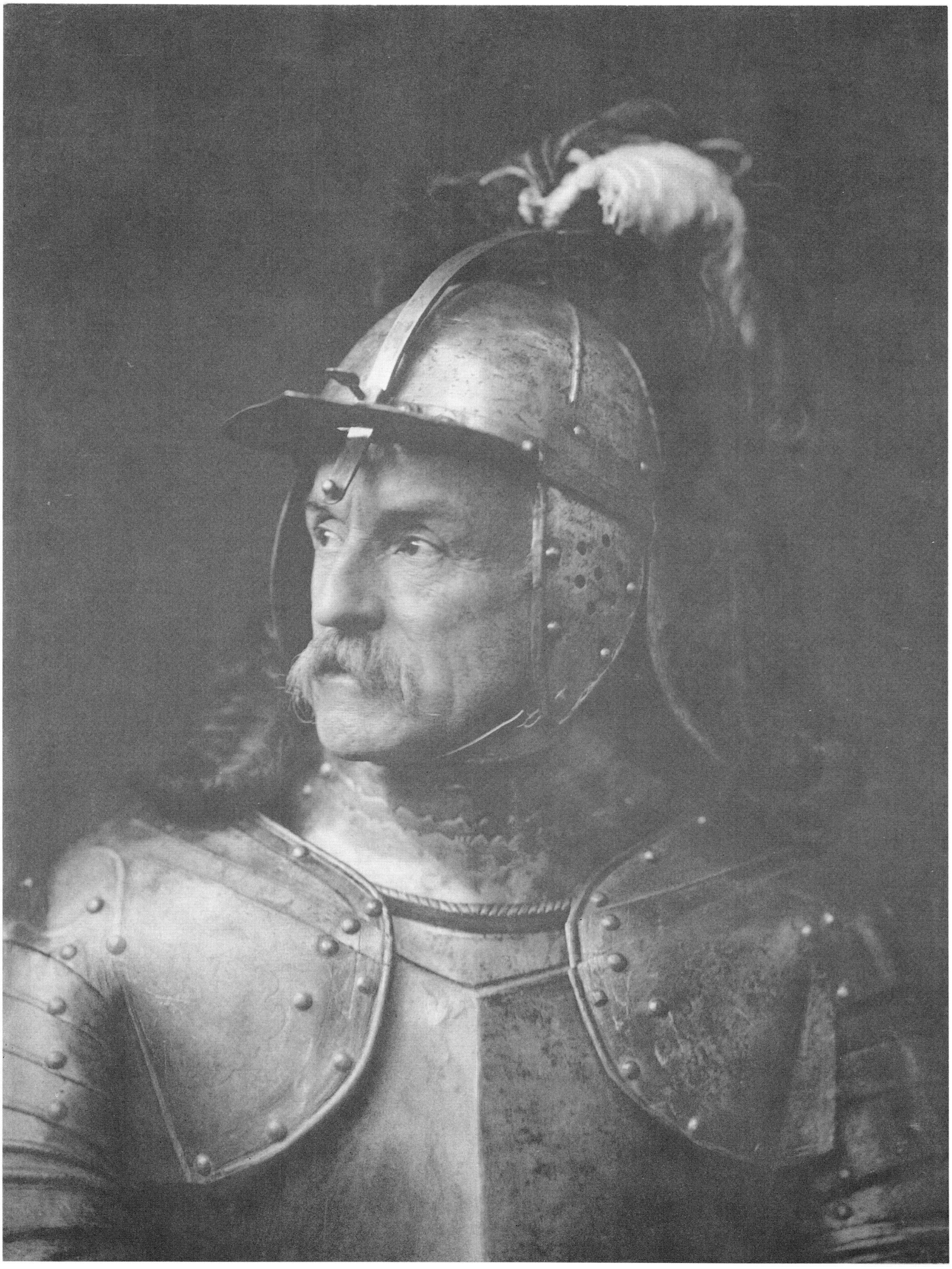

Man in Armour, by W. Crooke.

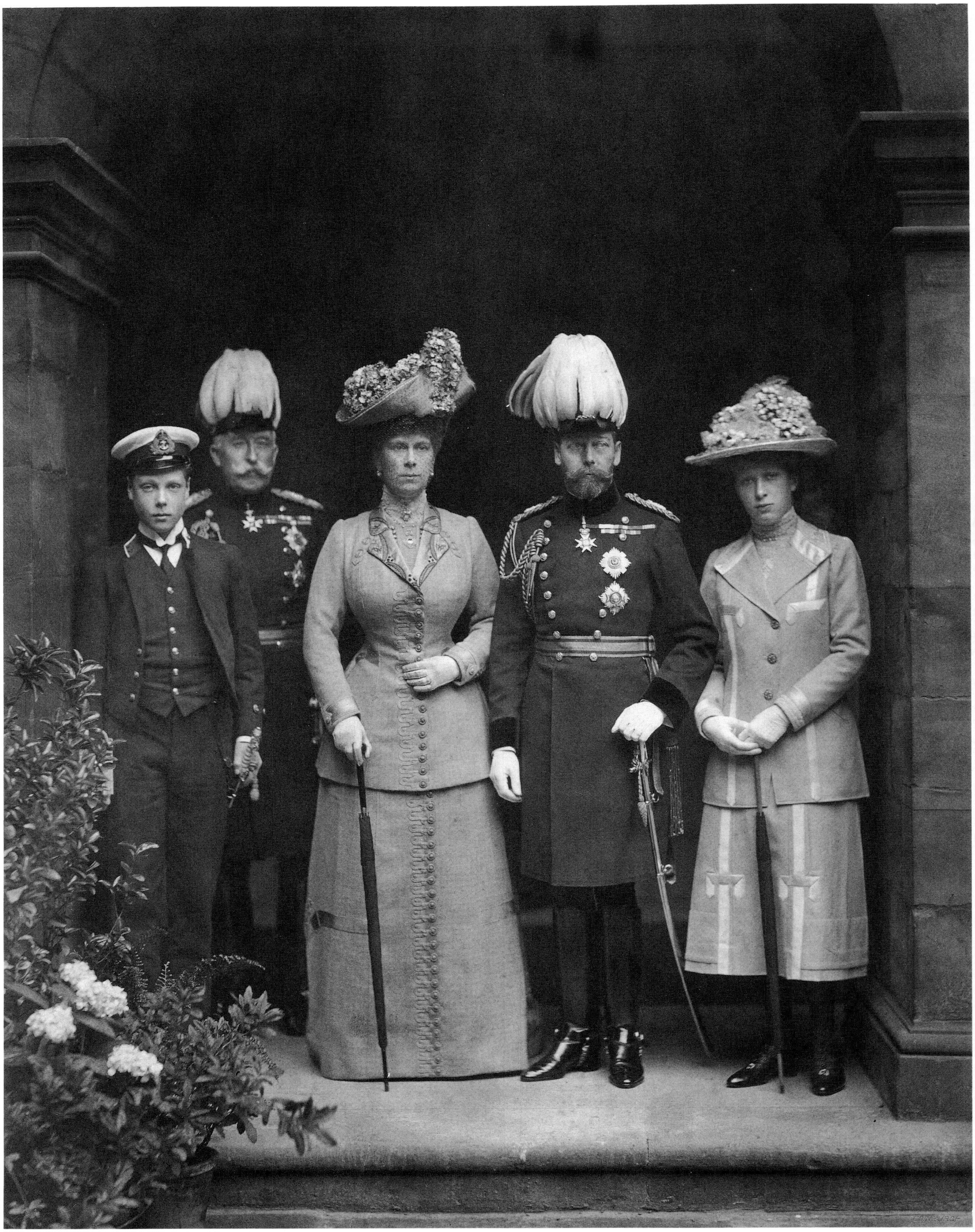

A Royal Group (left to right): Edward, Prince of Wales; Arthur, Duke of Connaught (the King's uncle); Queen Mary; King George V and Princess Mary, by W. Crooke.

HRH The Princess Royal and Officers of The Royal Scots, 1933.

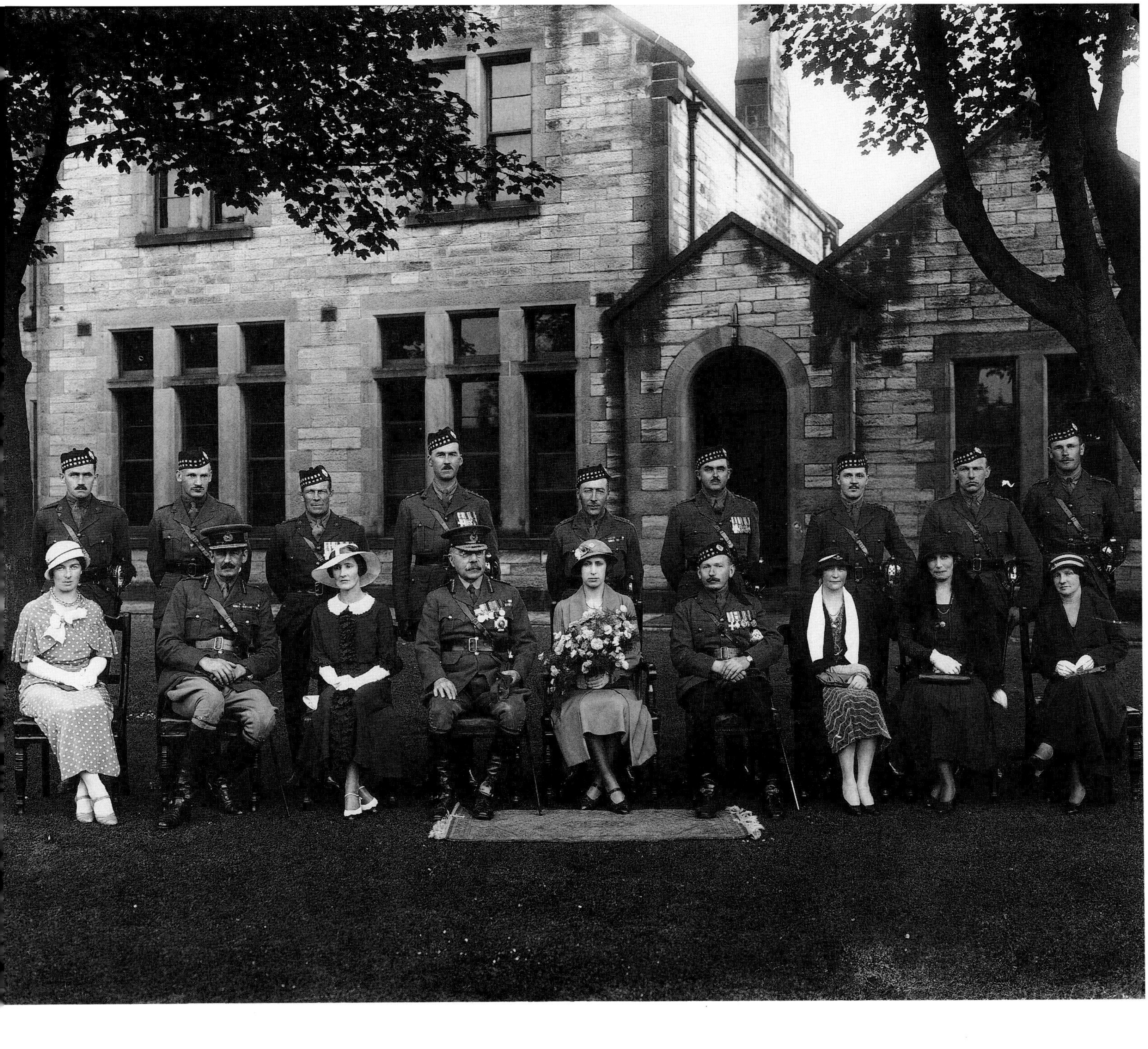

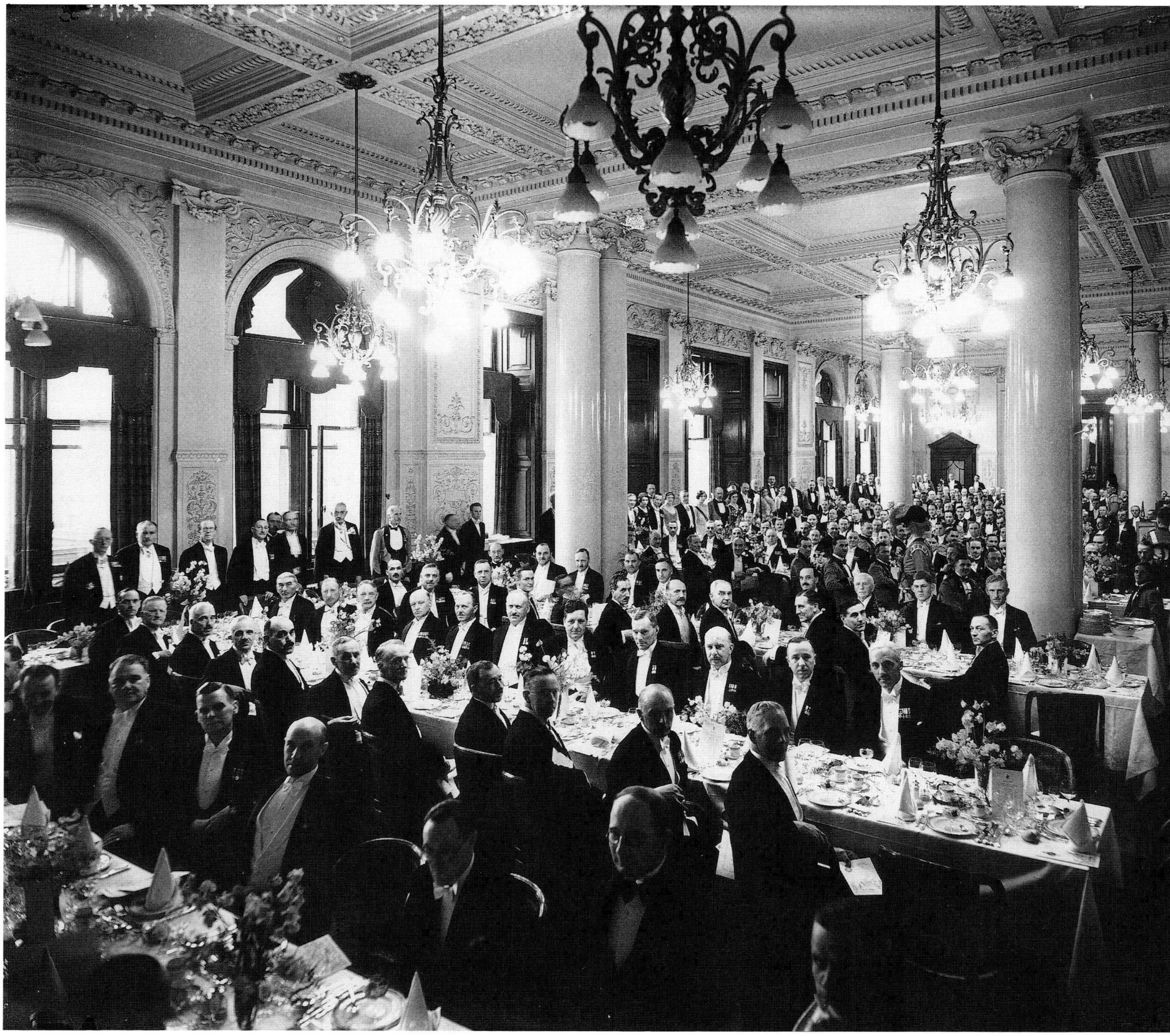

The Royal Scots Tercentenary Dinner on 23rd June
1933 at the North British Station Hotel.

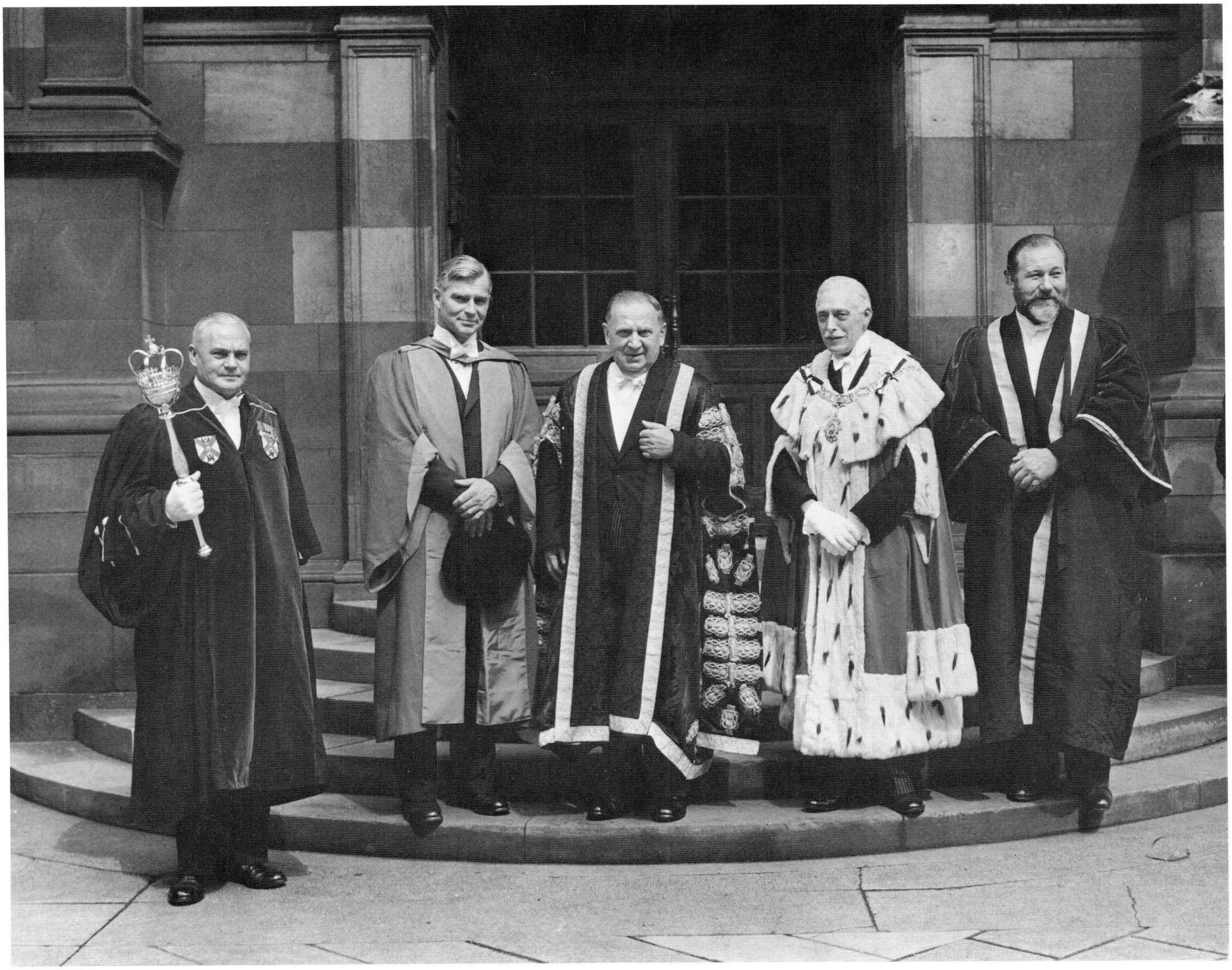

Edinburgh University Group at the McEwan Hall, 1959. The centre figure is the Vice-Chancellor, Principal Sir Edward Appleton, to the right of whom is the Lord Provost, Sir Ian Johnson Gilbert, and James Robertson Justice, who was Rector of the University in 1958 and again in 1964. On the extreme left of the picture is the Bedellus, Captain E. H. G. Elder, but unfortunately the identity of the fifth gentleman has not been established.

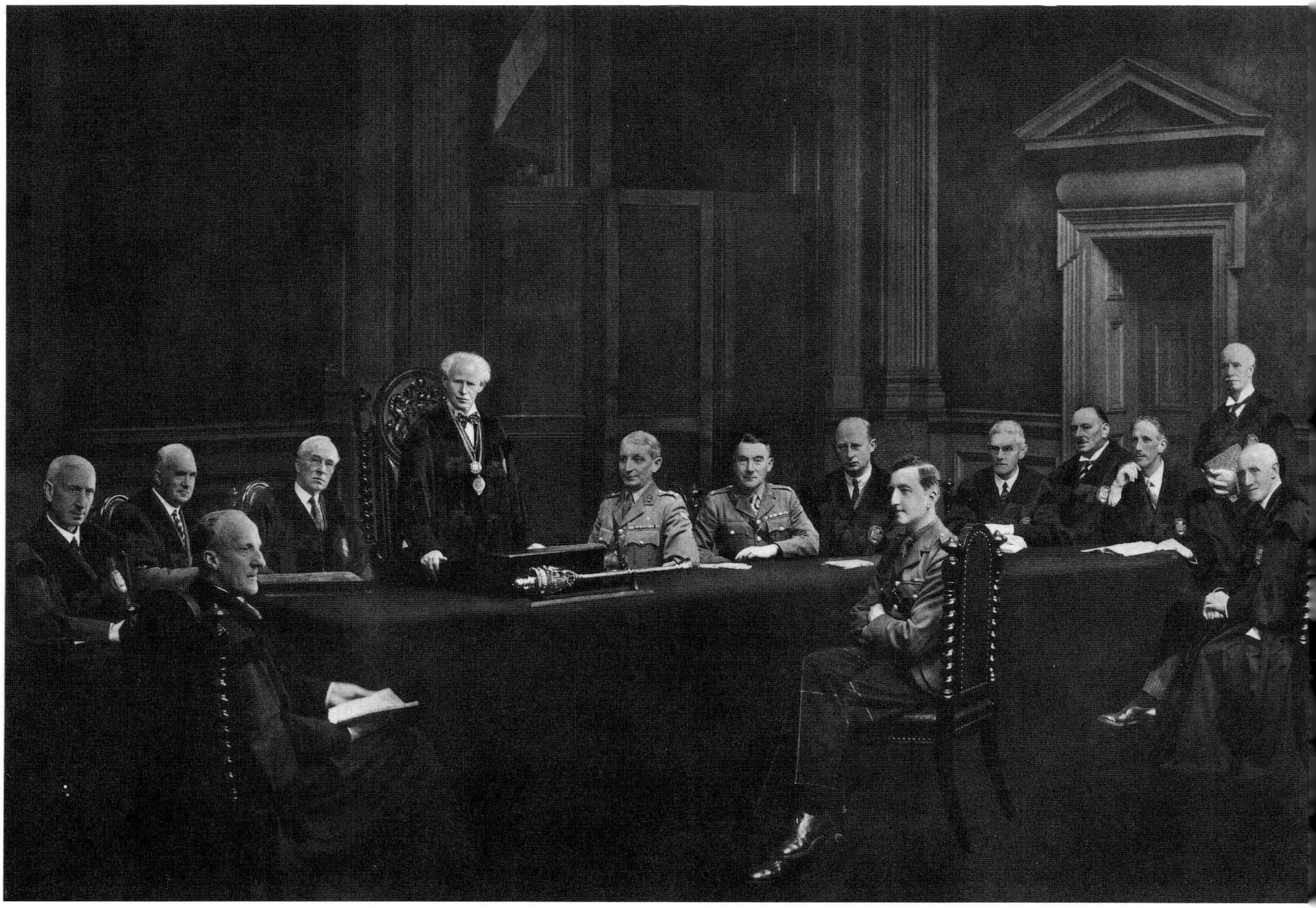

The Master, Treasurer and Assistants of the Company of Merchants of the City of Edinburgh at Merchants Hall, presided over by John G. Galloway, who was Master of the Merchant Company from 10th November 1938 to 14th November 1940, by E. R. Yerbury.

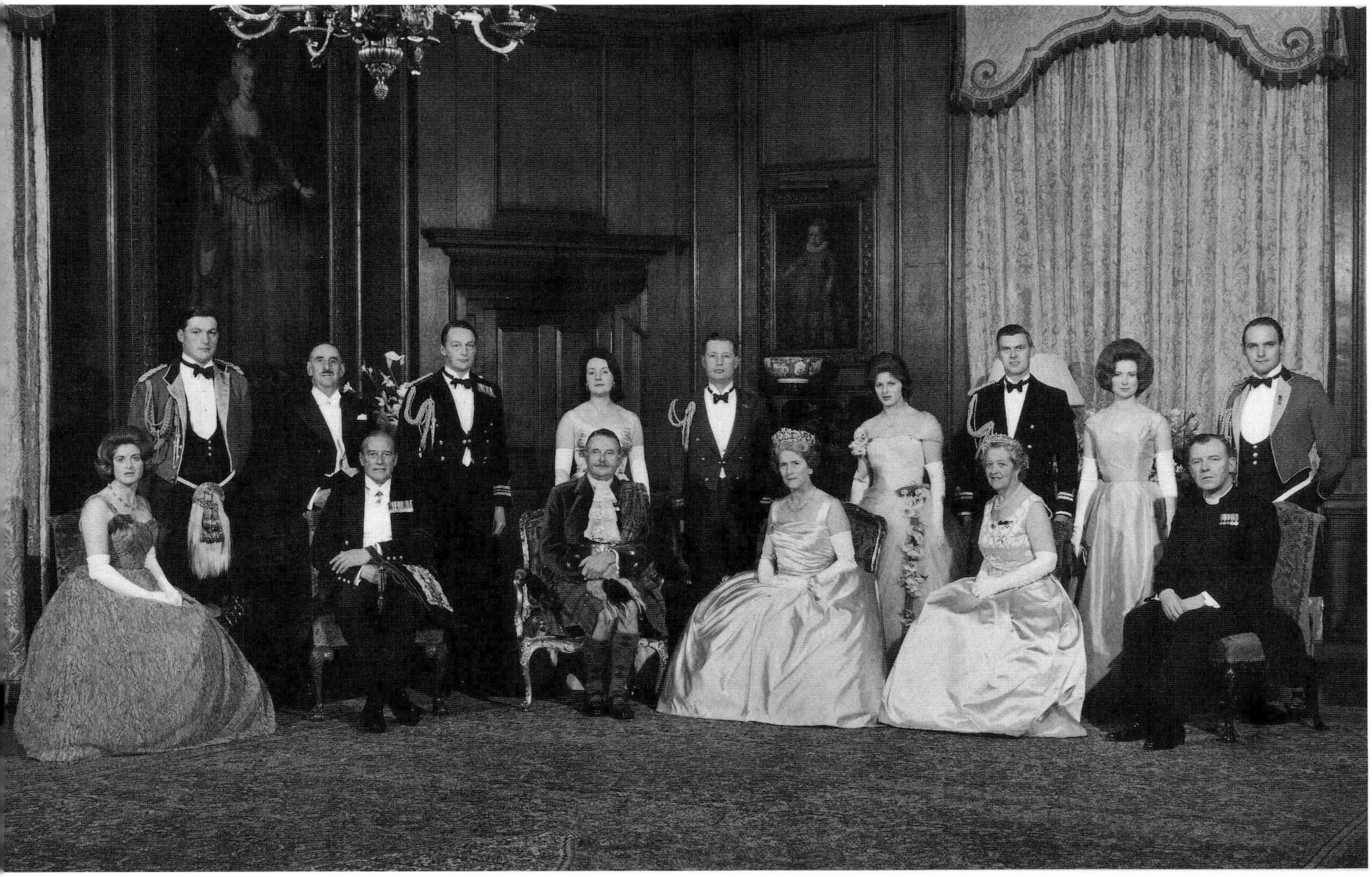

The Lord High Commissioner and Her Grace's Suite, Palace of Holyroodhouse, 1962, by E. R. Yerbury. General Assembly of the Church of Scotland, Palace of Holyroodhouse, May 1950, by E. R. Yerbury.

Admiral of the Fleet Viscount Cunningham of Hyndhope, KT, GCB, OM, DSO, Lord High Commissioner and Her Grace the Viscountess Cunningham.

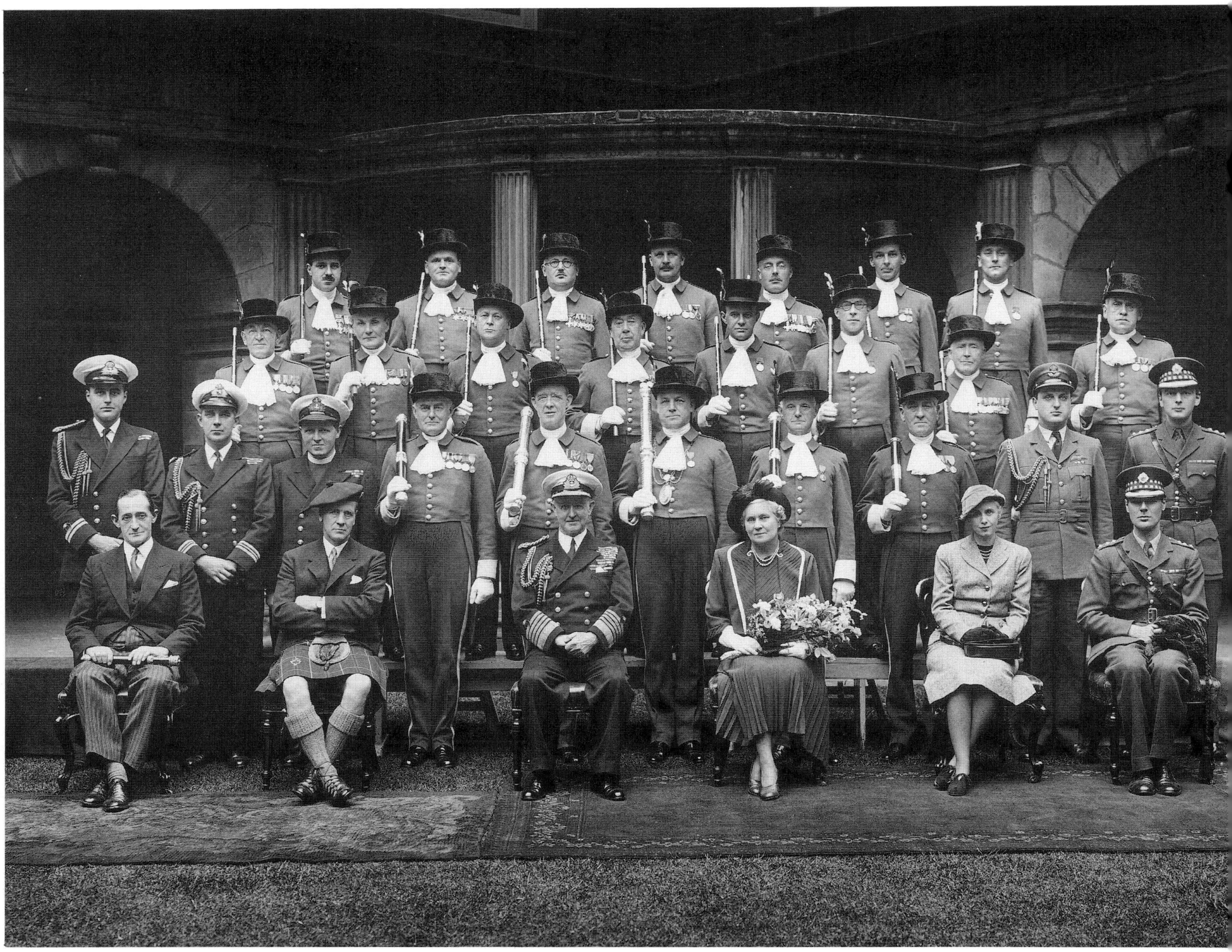

Forestry Exhibition 1884

The Prime Minister, W. E. Gladstone, and Mrs Gladstone were given a tour of the grounds of Donaldson's Hospital in Mr Binko's electric railway during their visit to the Forestry Exhibition on 29th August 1884. Photograph by J. Moffat.

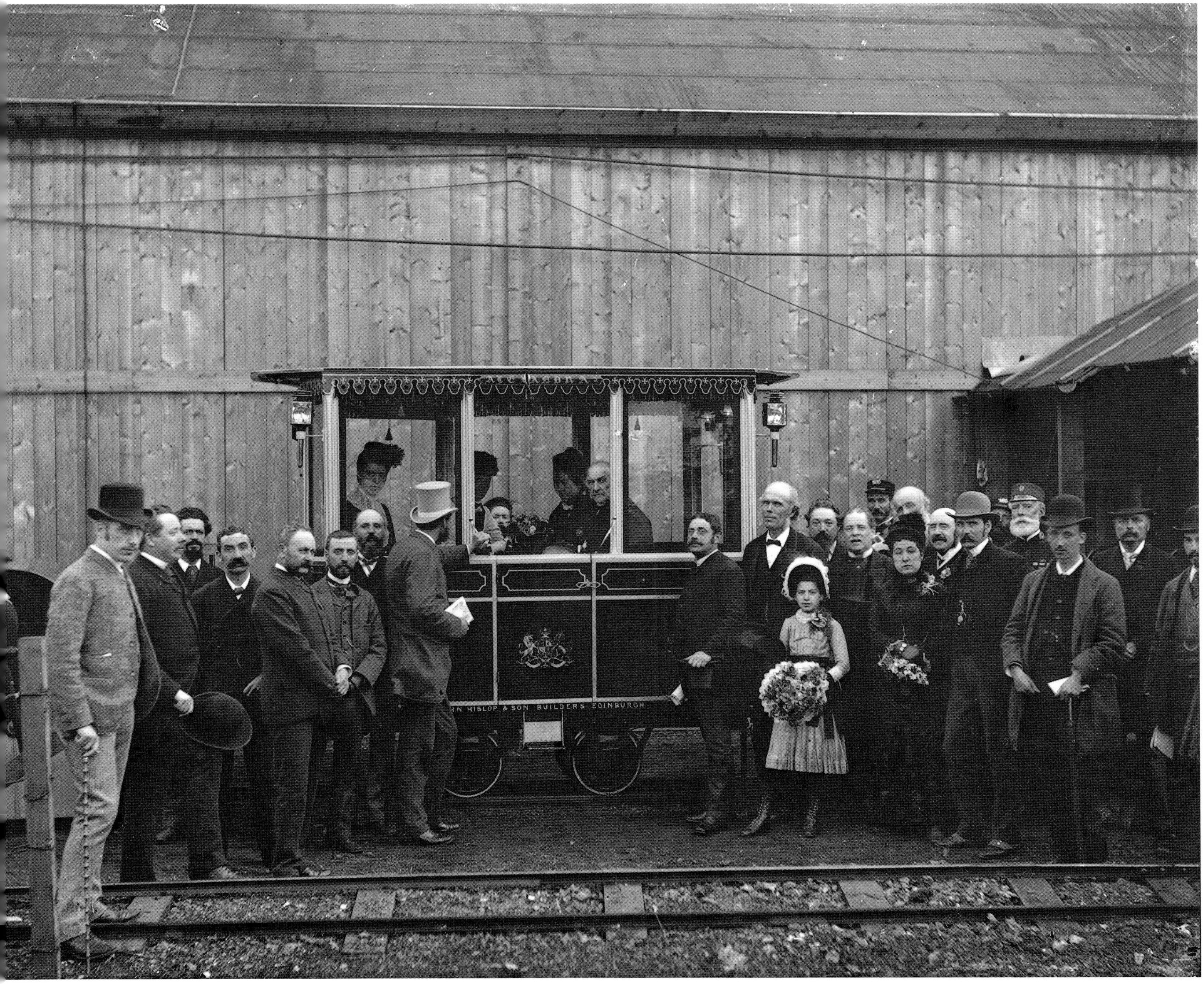

Mr and Mrs Gladstone at Dalmeny House

Mr and Mrs Gladstone visited Lord and Lady Rosebery at Dalmeny House, South Queensferry during the first Midlothian campaign in November 1879 and again during the second campaign in March 1880. The unmistakable figure of Mr Gladstone is seated, holding his hat in his left hand. Mrs Gladstone is seated at the other end of the couch and Lord Rosebery (with the bowler hat) is behind and to the right of Mrs Gladstone.

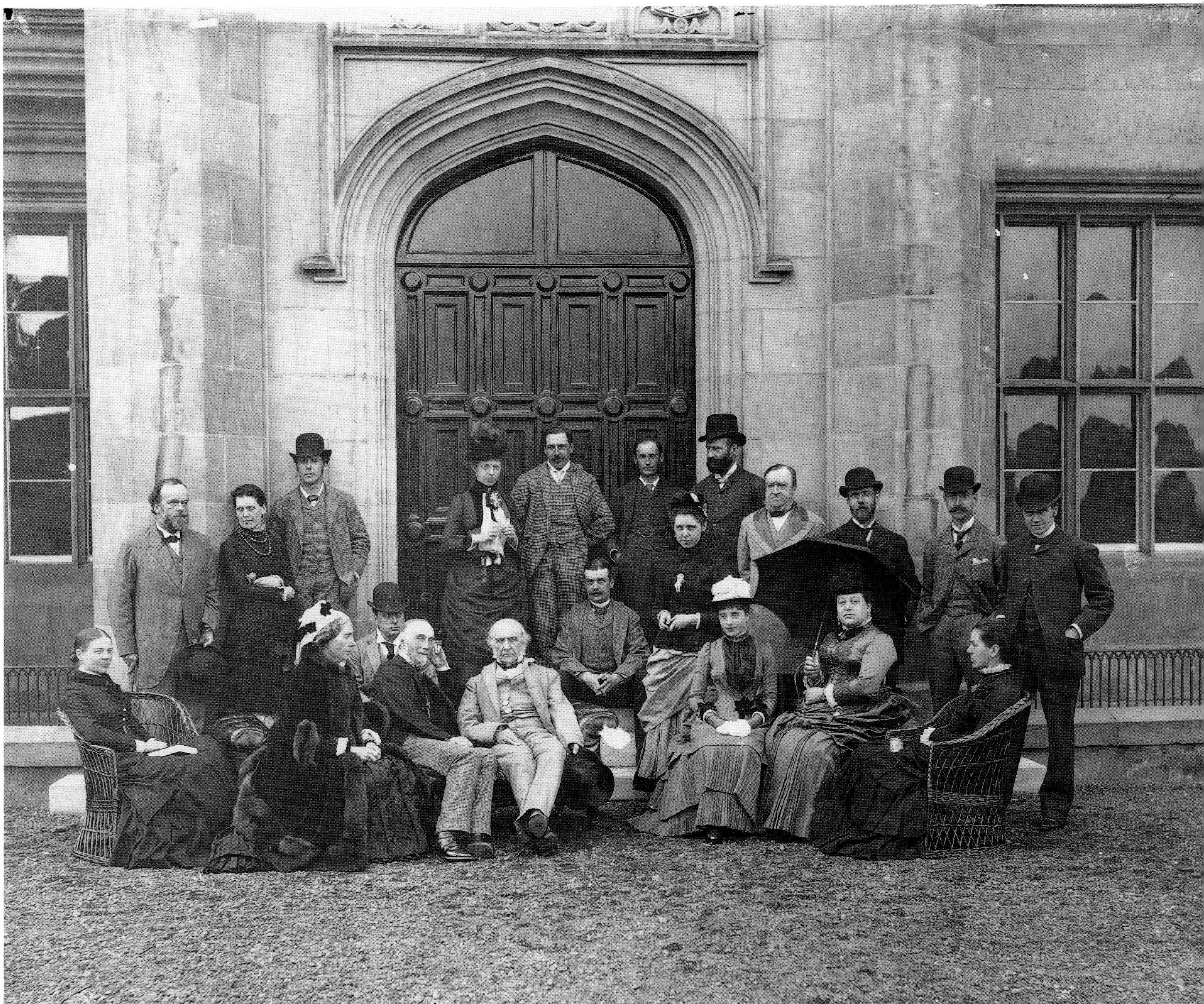

Prince of Wales at Dalmeny

Edward, Prince of Wales, is in the centre of the group at a tree-planting ceremony at Dalmeny House, South Queensferry, in August 1884. To the Prince's left is Lord Rosebery, holding his younger child The Hon. Neil Primrose. The three young children on the extreme left of the photograph are Lady Margaret Primrose, Lord Dalmeny and Lady Sybil Primrose.

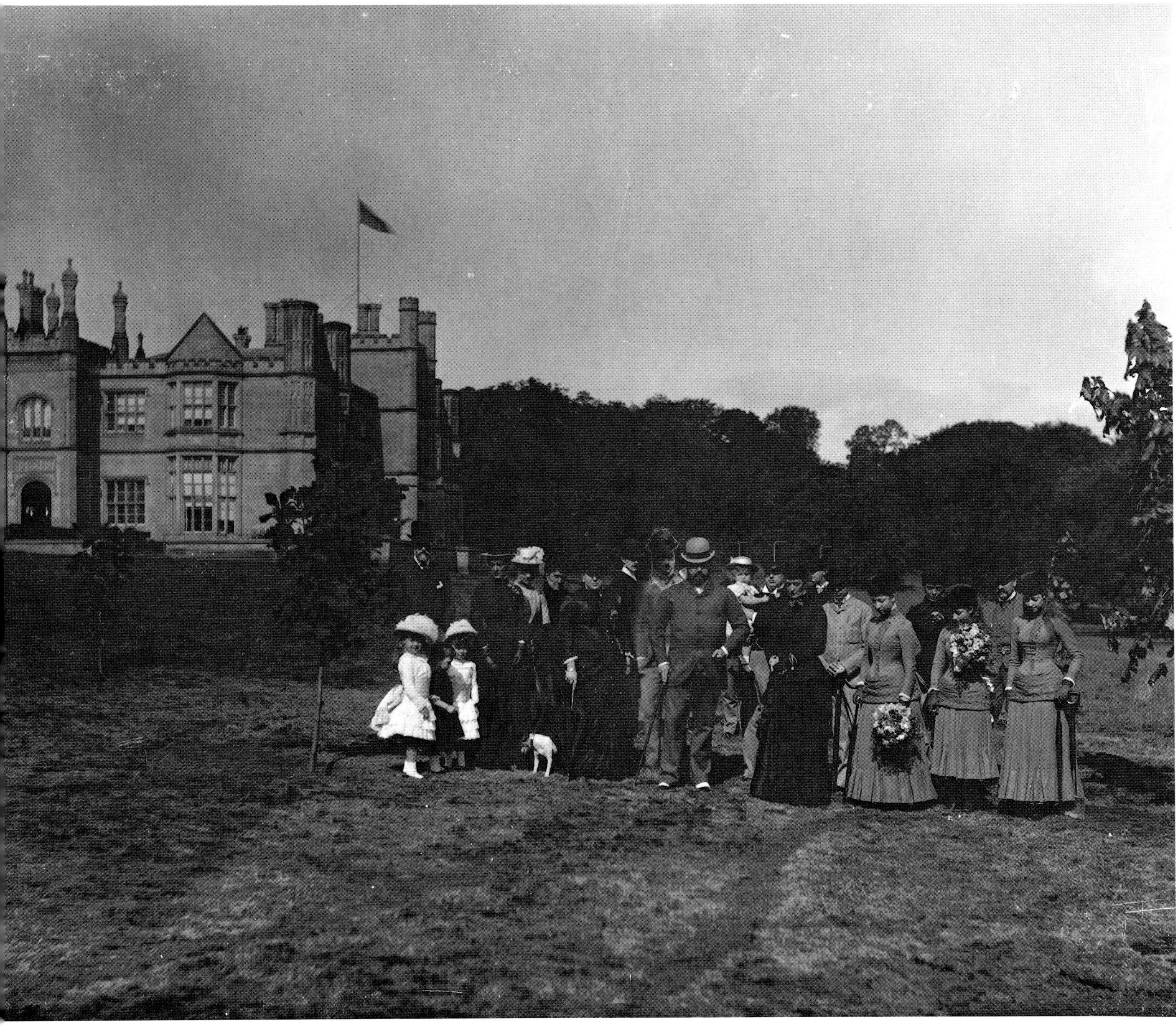

CHAPTER 9

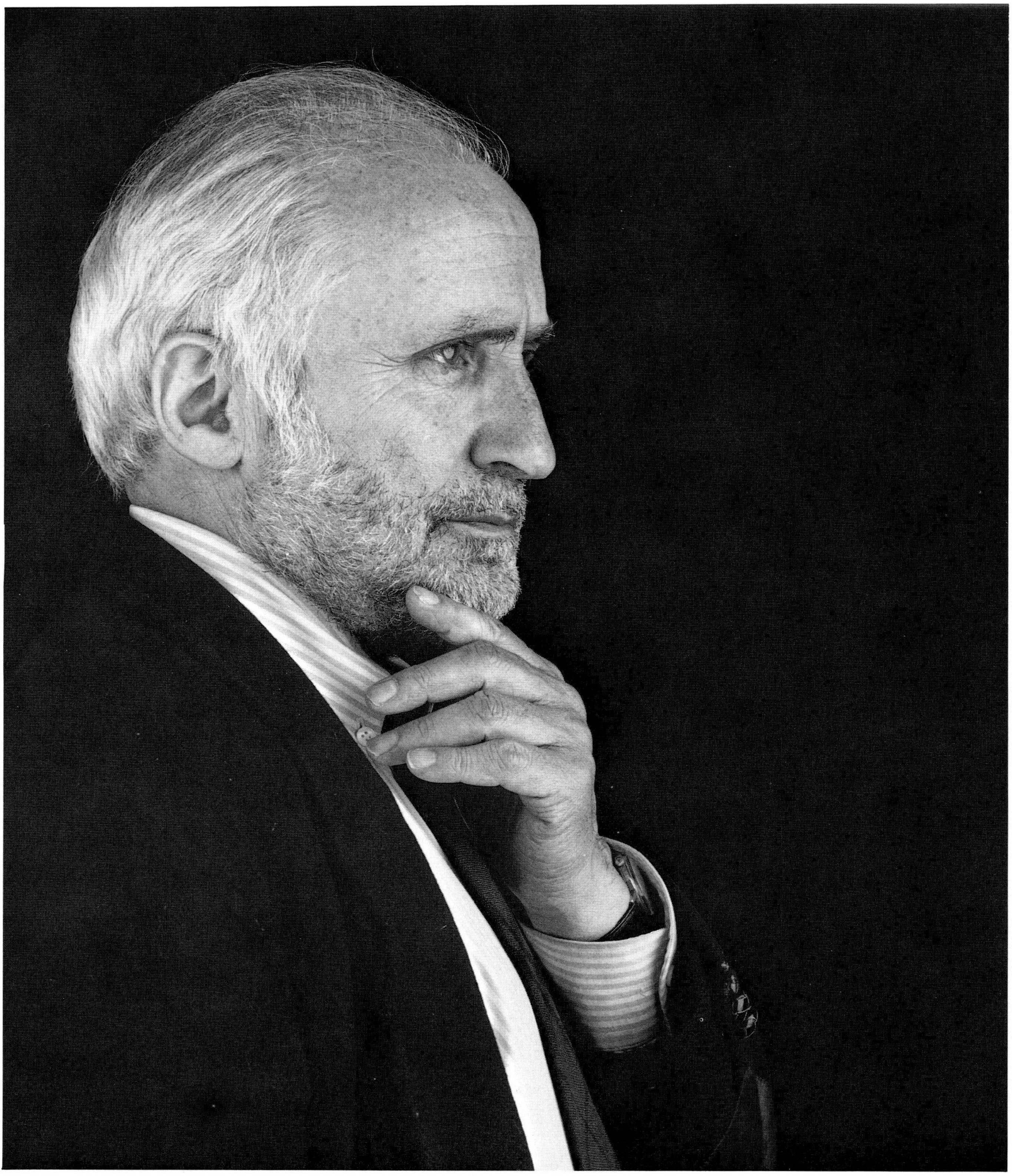

Richard Demarco

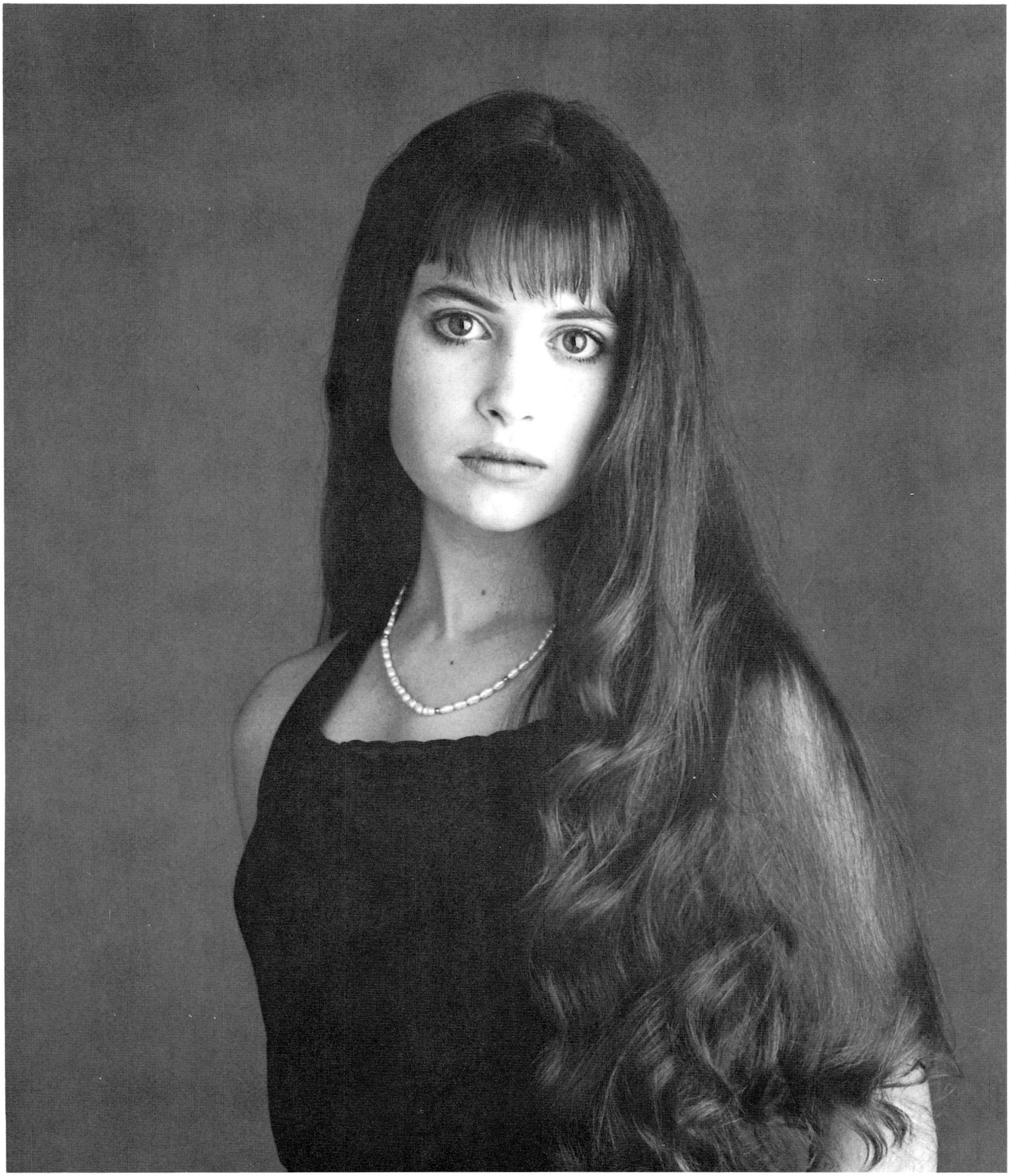

JoJo

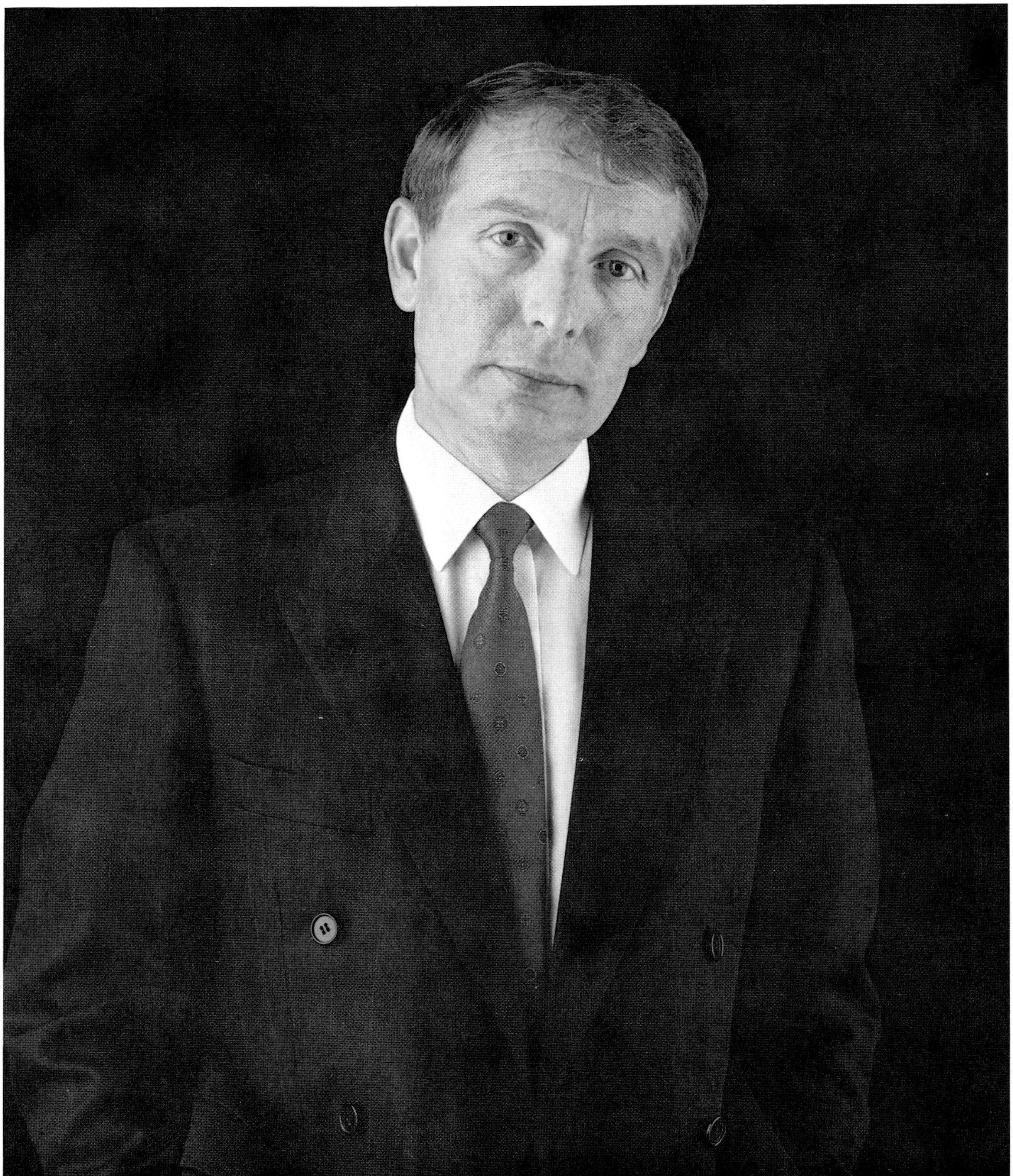

Tom Farmer

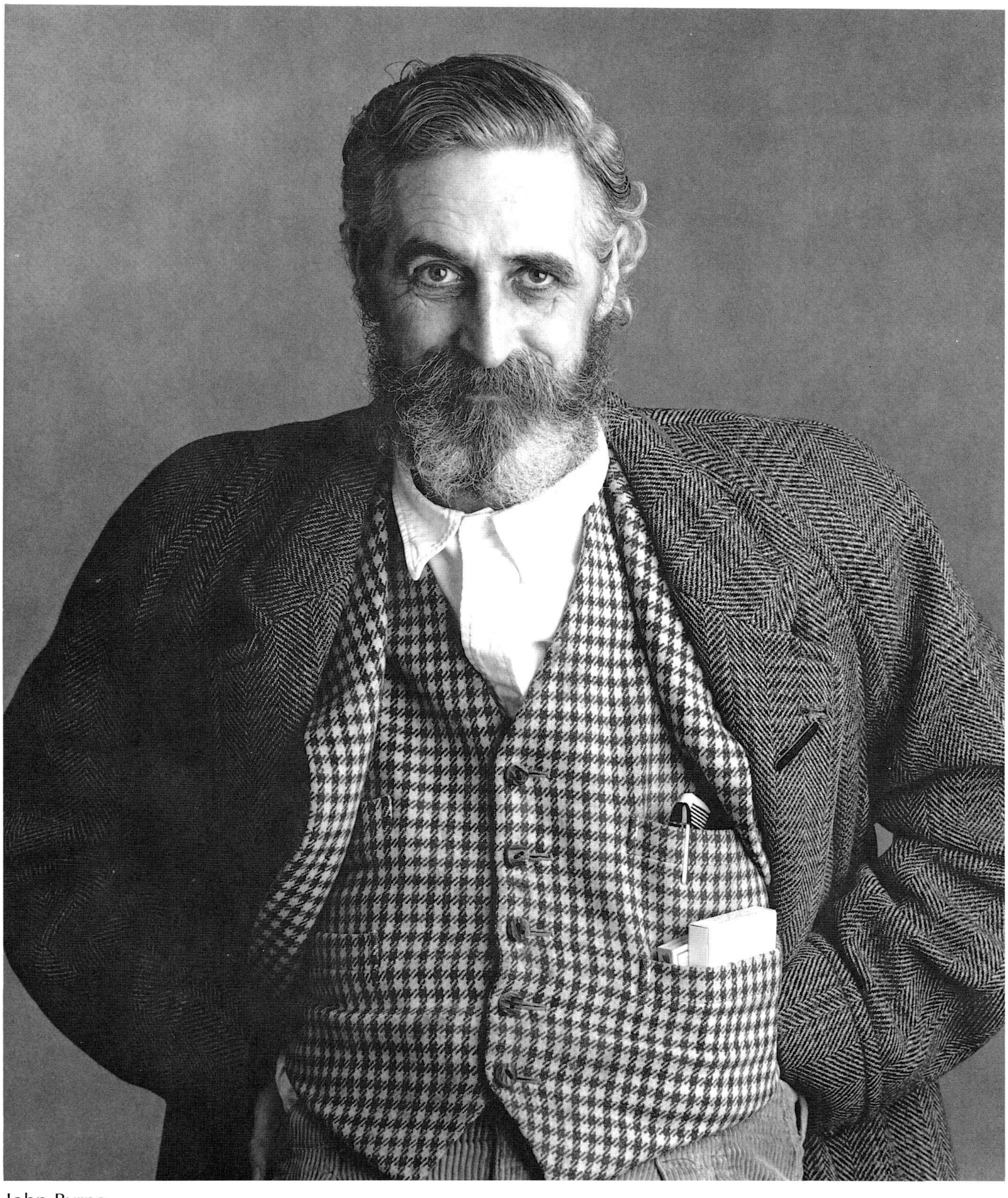

John Byrne

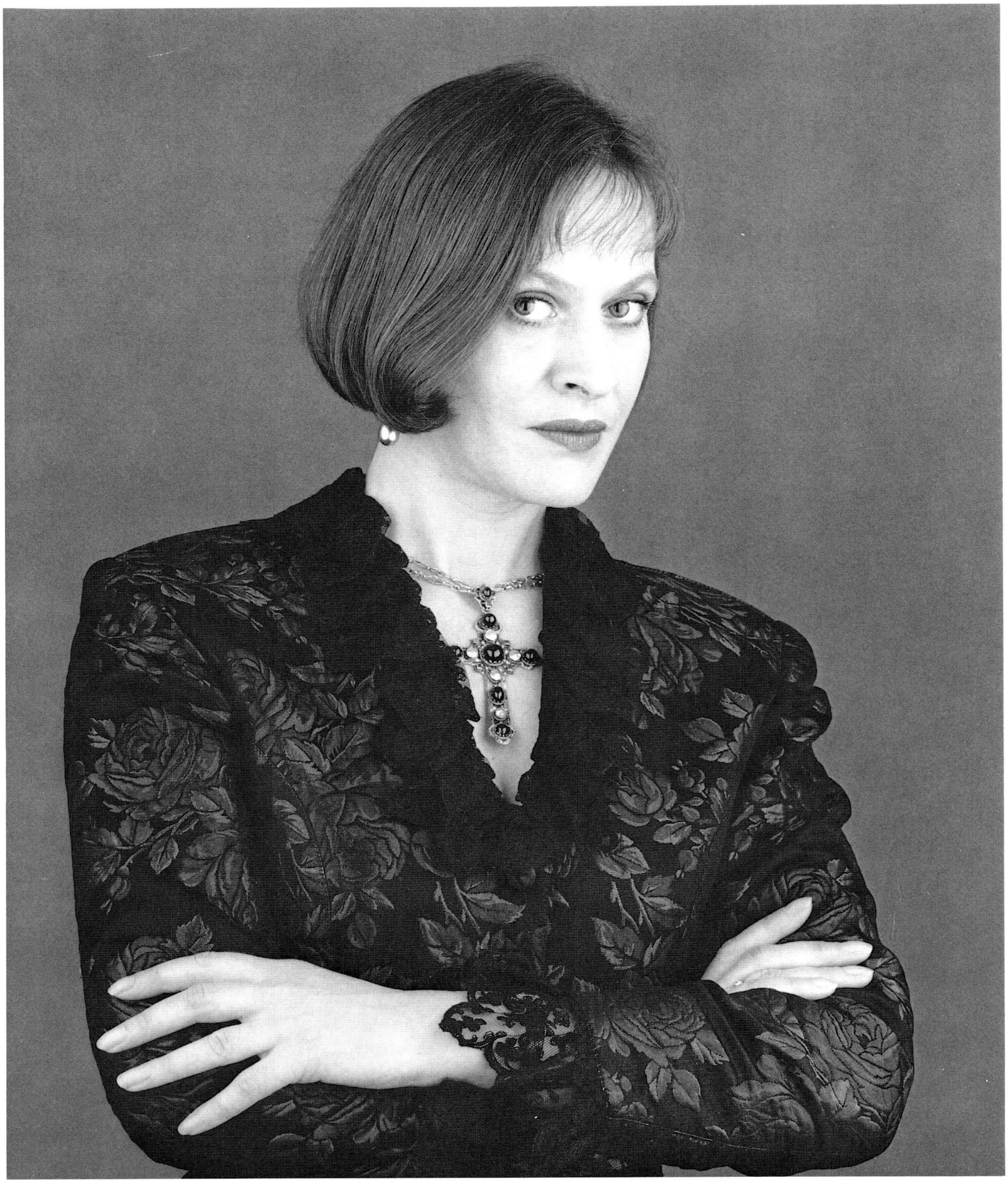

Suzy Raeburn

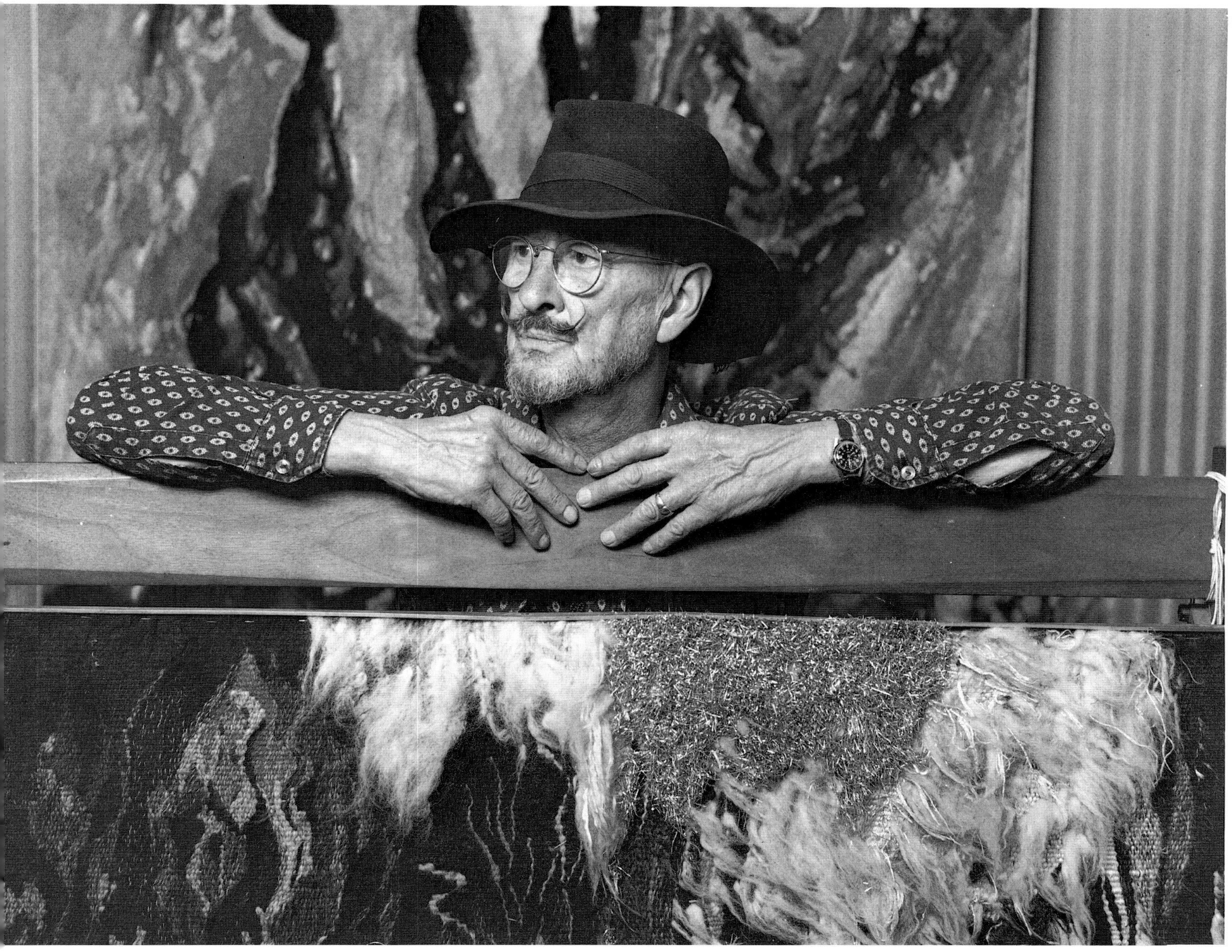

Sax Shaw

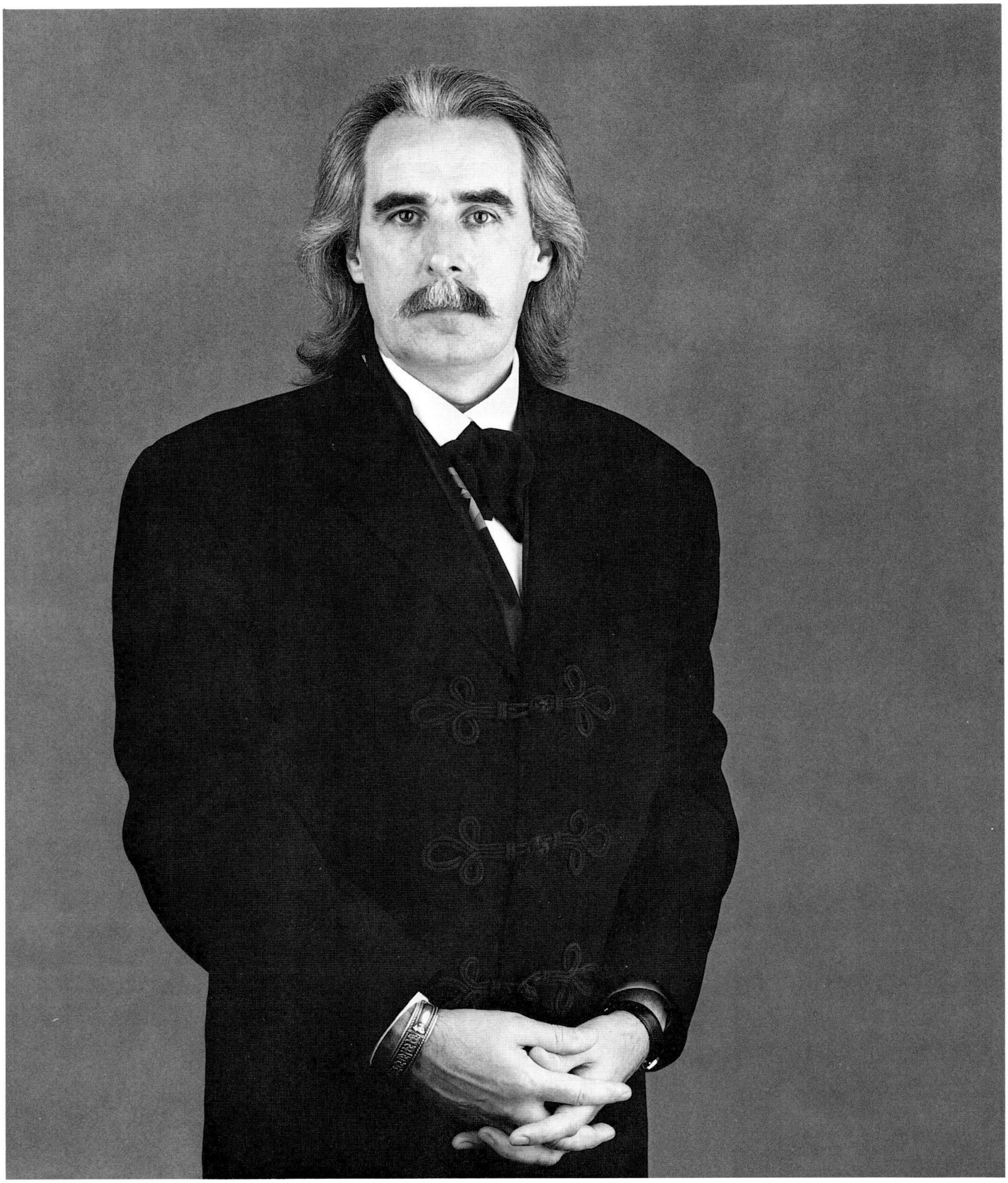

Charlie Miller

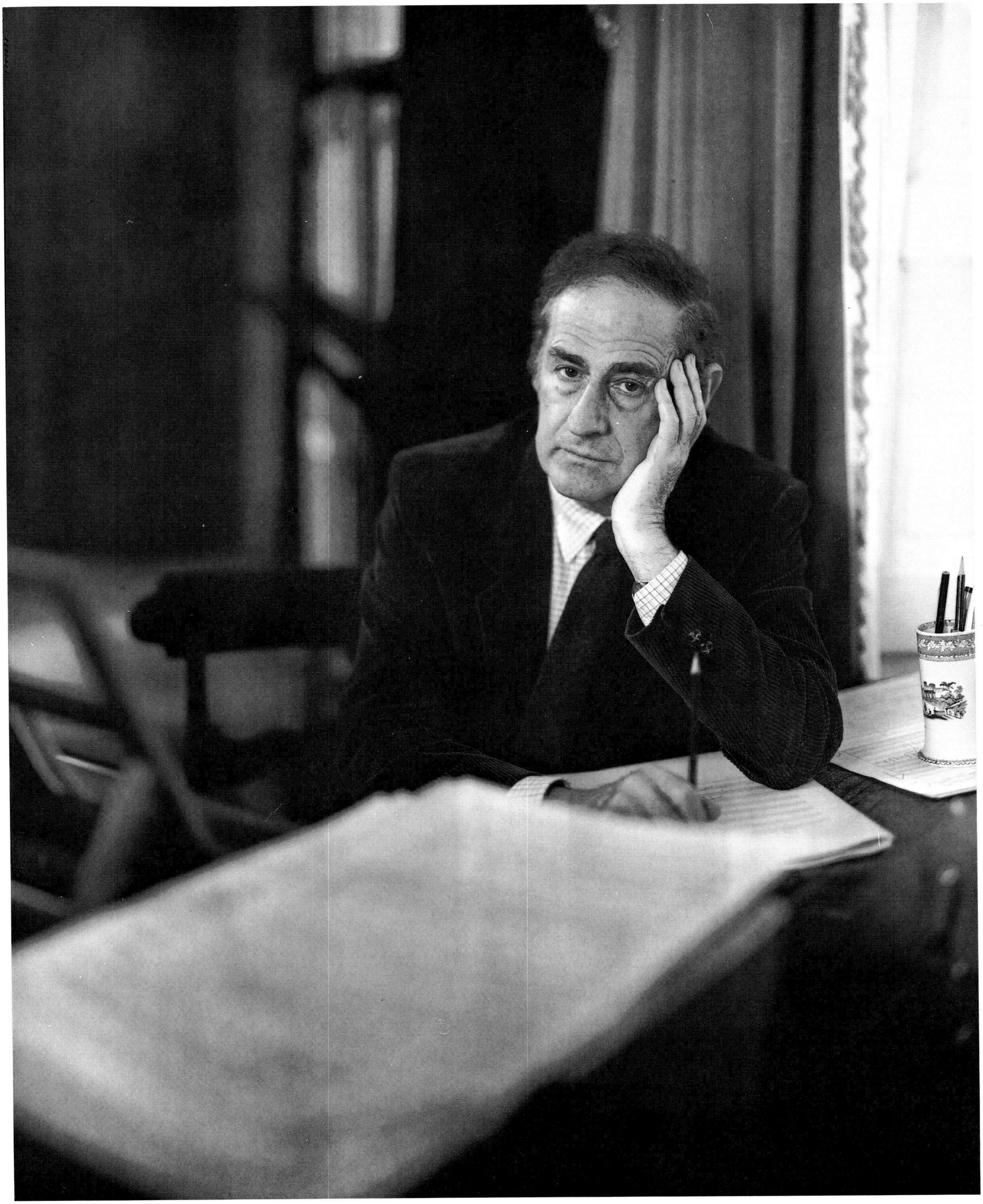

Gian Carlo Menotti

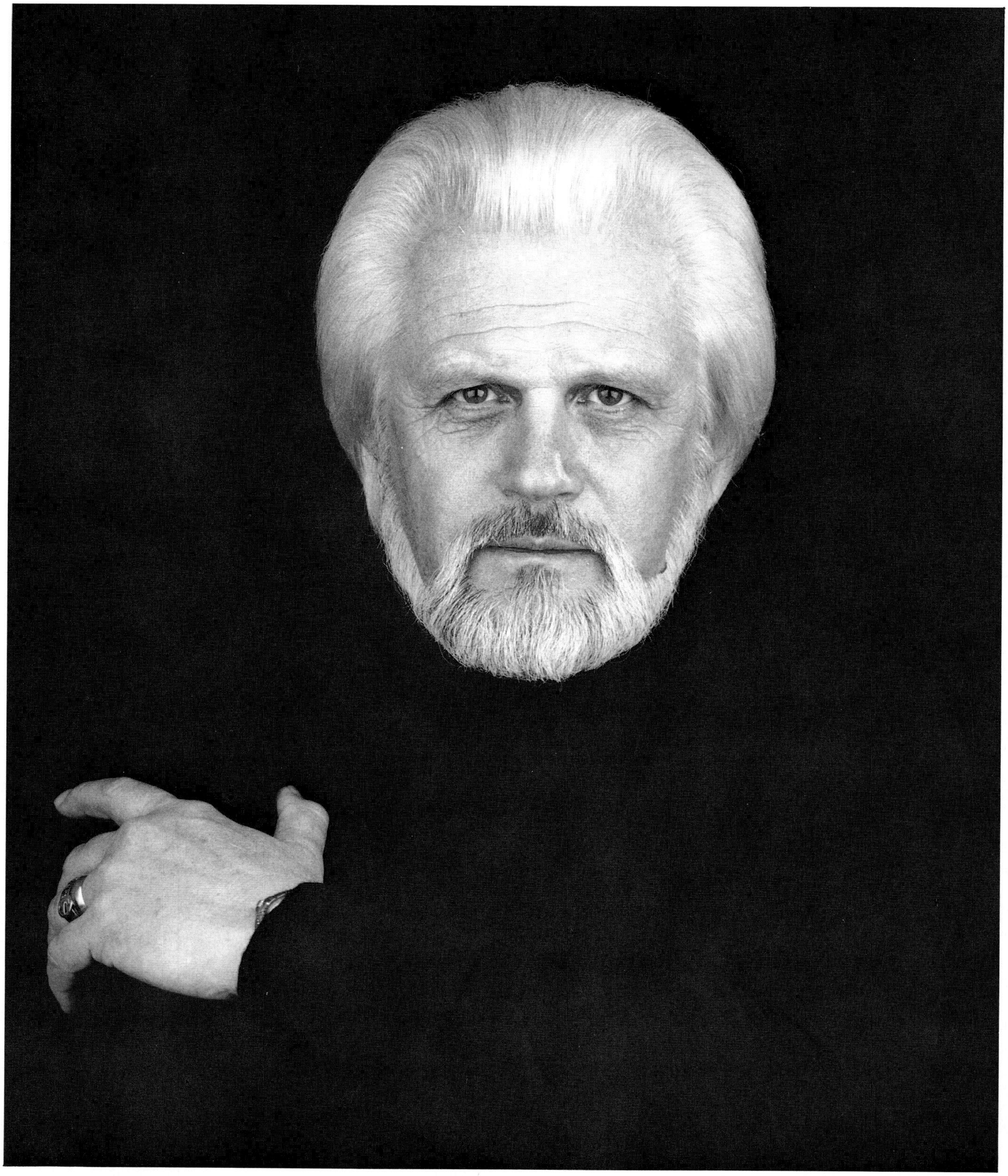

Ronnie Browne

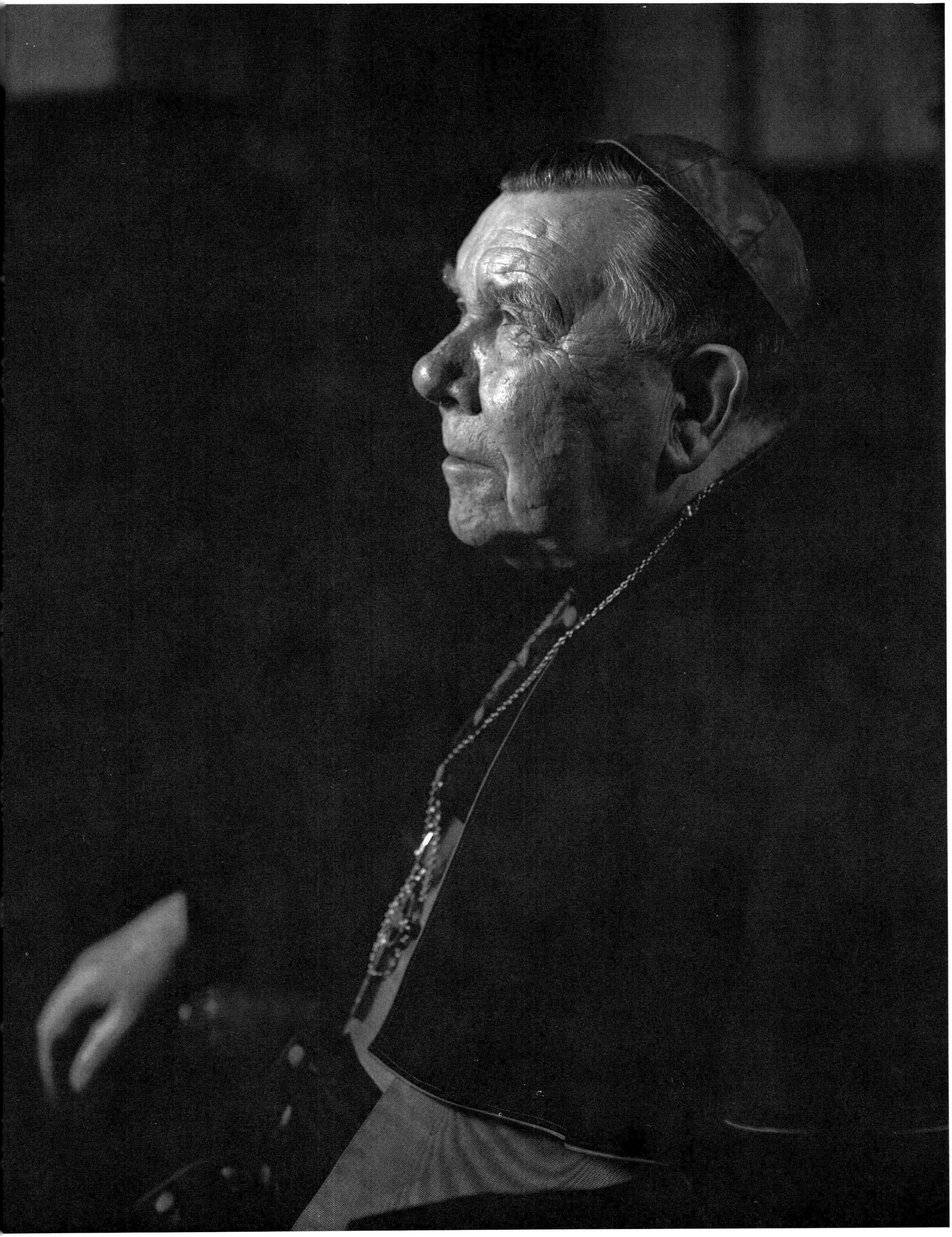

Cardinal Gray

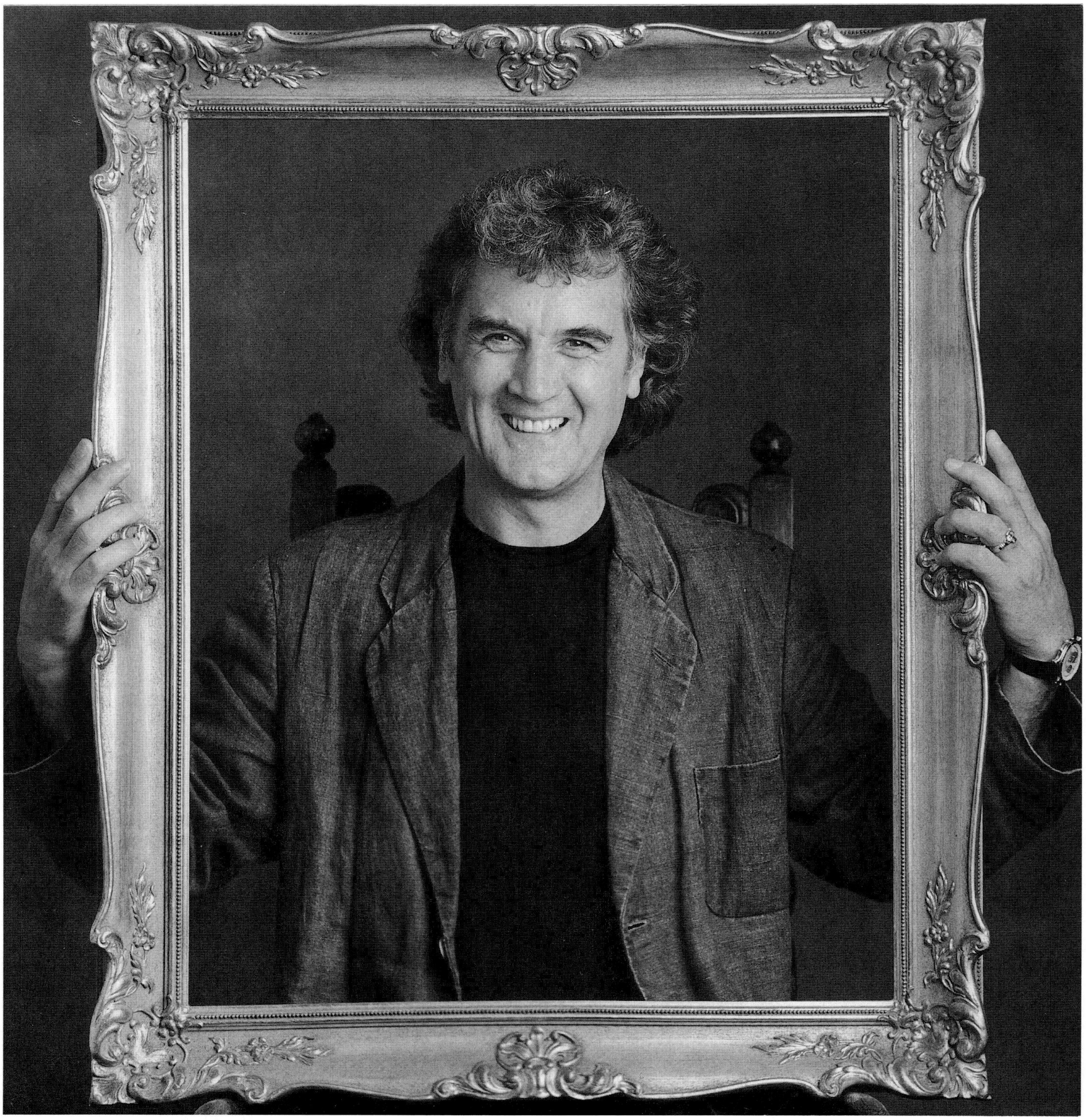

Billy Connolly

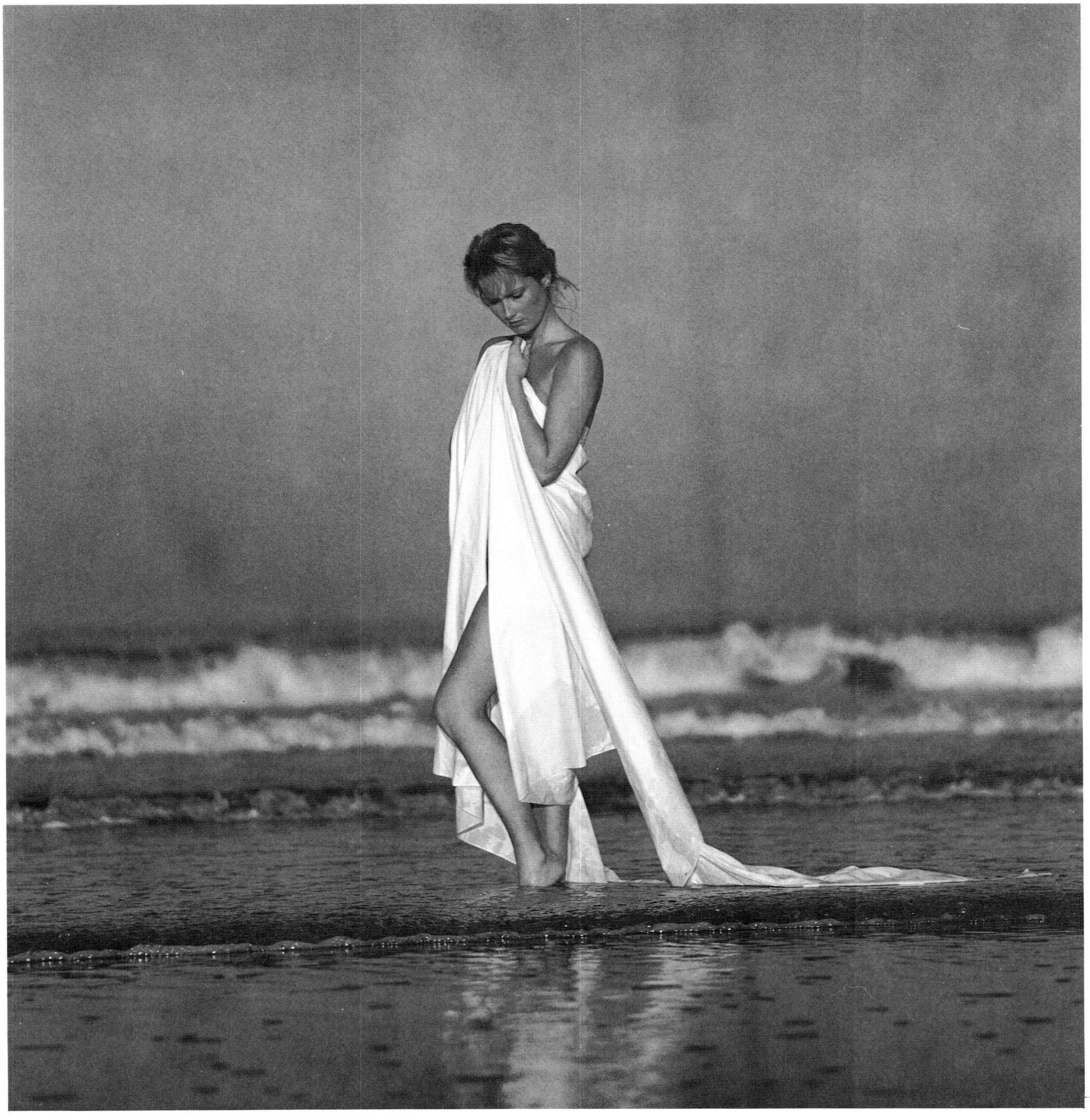

Dawn – Yellowcraigs Beach

INDEX

Titles of pictures which appear in the text are given in italic.

Aberdour, photographic outing to, 146
Adam Flockhart's Hostelry, 93
Adam, Robert, 37
Adamson's Coach Offfice, 82
Advocate's Close, 23
Anderson, Sir R. Rowand, 154
Apostolic Church, 46
Appleton, Sir Edward, 171
Architects
  Adam, Robert, 37
  Anderson, Sir R. Rowand, 37, 46
  Anderson, Sir R. Rowand, 154
  Blanc, Hippolyte J., 61, 62
  Browne, George Washington, 65
  Bryce, David, 23
  Burn, William, 61
  Graham, James Gillespie, 84
  Kemp. George Meikle, 54
  Kinnear & Peddie, 76
  Pilkington, F. T., 86
  Playfair, William H., 37, 56, 59, 68
  Raeburn, Robert Reid, 66
Argyle Place United Presbyterian Church, 66

Balmain, J. C. H., 9, 74, 79
Balmain, Mr & Mrs and the cycling party, 75
Balmoral Hotel, 42, 50, 54
Bank of Scotland, Mound, 22, 58
Barrie, Sir James M., 149
Beaton, Cardinal, 25
Bertrams Engineering, 74
Berwick Law, 135
Binn's Corner, 61
Blackford Farmhouse, 69
Blackford Glen, 71
Blackford Hill, 70
Blackford Hill Station, 69
Blanc, Hippolyte J., 61, 62
Bouch, Sir Thomas, 69
Boyd, Sir Thomas J., 76
Braid, James, 130, 132
Brandfield Street, 95
Bridewell, 47
Brown, Sir William Slater, 127
Browne, George Washington, 65
Browne, Ronnie, 186
Bruntsfield Links, 137
Bruntsfield Links Golfing Society, 134, 137
Bryce, David, 23
Burn, William, 61
Byrne, John, 181

C & A's, 118
Calton Jail, 47
Cameron Toll, 91
Cameron Toll Shopping Centre, 84
Cannonball House, 26
Cant's Close, 33
Carey, Johnny, 132
Carlton Cricket Club, 68
Carlton Cricket Club, 129
Carnegie, Sir Andrew, 39
Carnegie, Sir Andrew, 150
Castle Hill, 27
Catholic Apostolic Church, 46
Causewayside, 1850, 78
Causewayside, 1900, 80, 81
Causewayside, Nos. 200-208, 77
Causewayside at Sciennes Place, 75
Centre Court, 137
Chancelot Flour Mills, 46
Christie, William, 86
Church Hill, navvies at, 73
City Chambers, 22, 128
Clearburn House, 92
Clearburn Lodge, 92
Cockburn Street, 22
Cockle Mill, 99
Cockle Mill on the River Almond, 100
Cockles and Mussels, 38
Coconut Tam, 33
Company of Merchants of the City of Edinburgh, 172
Connolly, Billy, 188
Connolly, James, 25
Cook's Tourist Office, 54
Cowgate, 25
Craigend Cottages, 88
Craigend Dairy, 87
Craigend Park, 86
Craigend, Upper, 88
Craigmillar Castle, 89
Craigmillar Park Parish Church, 83
Cramond foreshore, 101
Cramond Heritage Trust, 101
Cramond, sailing ships at, 99
Cranston, Sir Robert, 43, 118
Cranston and Elliot salute His Majesty, 119
Crooke, William, photographer, 9
Cupar Cricket Club, 130

Dalkeith Road, 91
Darling, Sir William Young, 151
Davidson's Land, 35
Davidson's Mains, 137
Dawn –Yellowcraigs Beach, 189
de Gaulle, General, 18
de Gaulle, General, 147
Demarco, Richard, 178
Dickson's Close, 33
Drummond, Sir George, 42
Drysdale, D., 156
Duddingston Curling Club, 142
Duddingston Kirk, 143
Duddingston Loch, 142
Duddingston Loch, skaters on, 143
Duke of Wellington, statue of, 45
Duncan, Flockhart & Co., 116

East Coast Railway Companies, 52, 54
Edinburgh Castle, 61
Edinburgh Castle, the, 96
Edinburgh Castle and Princes Street Gardens, 58
Edinburgh and District Tramways Co., 95
Edinburgh Gas Light Company's Works, 39
Edinburgh and Glasgow Railway Company, 23
Edinburgh Military Tattoo, 58
Edinburgh, Perth & Dundee Railway Company, 22
Edinburgh Street Tramways Co., 95
Edinburgh University group, 171
Edinburgh University Old Quad, 37
Edward VII and Queen Alexandra, 114
Elder, Captain E. H. G., 171

Farmer, Tom, 180
Fiery, the Musselburgh Caddy, 133
Fisherrow, 110
Fisherrow, baiting the line, 109
Fisherrow Fishwives, 108
Forestry Exhibition, 1884, 175
Forman's Pub at Levenhall, 93
Fruitseller, the, 31

Galloway Saloon Steam Packet Co., 97
General Post Office, 43, 48
George IV, 97
George IV Bridge, 25
George V and Queen Mary, 126
George Watson's College, 64
George Watson's Ladies College, 64
Gilbert, Sir Ian Johnson, 171
Gilmerton Road, near Kingston Avenue, 86
Gilmour, Sir John, 89
Gilmour, Brig. – Gen. Robert Gordon, 152
Gladstone, W. E. and Mrs at Dalmeny House, 176
Golfing on the Links, 136
Gowffing in the Fifties, 134
Graham, James Gillespie, 84
Graham's Hotel, 50
Grange Loan, 67, 129
Grange Loan at Causewayside, 78
Grange Loan, at the entrance to Grange House, 68
Grange Loan Toll House, 67
Grant, Sir Francis James, 135
Gray, Cardinal, 187
Grove Works, 95

Hanover Street, 118
Hanover Street, triumphal arch at, 118
Harrison, Sir George, 71

Hatton Place, 66
Heart of Midlothian Football Club, 140
Hewit's Place, 79
High School Yards, 24
High Street, 33
Hokey Pokey Man, 32
Holyrood Curling Club, 142
Holyrood Park car rally, 138

John Knox's House, 34
Jo Jo, 179

Kemp, George Meikle, 54
King's Theatre, 39
Kinnear & Peddie, 76

Lady Road, 84
Leven Street, 39
Levenhall, horse bus at, 93
Liberton Brae, crossroads, 85
Liberton Dams, 85
Liberton Kirk, 84
Longmore Hospital, 76
Lord Aberdour, the, 96
Lord High Commissioner, 173, 174
Lothian Road, triumphal arch at, 117

McDonald, Sir Andrew, 44
Man in armour, 167
Maule's by night, 127
Maule's Corner, 60, 115
Menotti, Gian Carlo, 185
Merchant Maiden Hospital, 64
Midland Railway Company, 52, 54
Miller, Charlie, 184
Minto Street, triumphal arch at, 125
Modes, C. and A., 118
Moray–Knox Church, 34
Morningside Road, 73
Moubray House, 34
Mound, the, 57
Murrayfield Golf Club, 132
Murrayfield Tram Terminus, 94

National Gallery of Scotland, 56
New Street, Fisherrow, 110
Newhaven, 102
Newhaven, fishwives at, 103
Newington Station, 83
North Berwick, golfers at, 135
North Berwick, seaside, 112, 113
North Berwick Golf Club, 135
North Bridge, first, 42, 43
North Bridge, new, 44
North British Hotel, 39, 42, 50, 54
North British Station Hotel, 44, 54

O'Hagan the Grocer, 72
Old Town from Princes Street, 22, 23
Original Rosslyn Inn, 111

Palace of Holyroodhouse, old houses at, 36
Park, Willie Jnr., 132
Peacock Inn, 102
Peffermill Road at Peffermill House, 92
Pilkington, F. T., 86
Playfair, William H., 37, 56, 59, 68
Polly the Fortune Teller, 29
Port Edgar, fleet at, 97
Portobello Amusement Arcade, 105
Portobello Fairground, 106
Portobello Open Air Pool, 107
Portobello Pier, 104
Portrait of a bride, 165
Portrait of a gentleman, 162
Portrait of a lady, 163
Portrait of an old lady, 166
Portrait of a young lady, 161
Portrait of a young man, 160
Prince of Wales at Dalmeny, 177
Princes Street, 115, 118, 120, 122, 128
Princes Street, royal entourage at the east end of, 122
Princes Street, looking west from the Scott Monument, 56
Princes Street, triumphal arch at east end of, 123
Princes Street, triumphal arch at west end of, 116
Princes Street and Waterloo Place, 48, 49
Princes Street, looking east at Waverley Bridge, 51
Princes Street, looking west at Waverley Bridge, 50
Princes Street at Waverley Market, 53

Queen's Body Guard in Scotland, member of, 157
Queen Mary's Tree, 90

Raeburn, Robert Reid, 66
Raeburn, Suzy, 182
Ramsay, Sir James, of Banff, 153
Register House, 42, 43, 46, 54
Rosebery, Lord and Lady, 176
Royal Edinburgh Hospital for Sick Children, 65
Royal group, 168
Royal High School, 25
Royal Institution, the, 59
Royal panorama, 120, 121
Royal Scots, the, 169, 170
Royal Scottish Academy, 56, 59

St Andrews House, 47
St Cuthbert's Parish Church, 61
St Cuthbert's Parish Church Bell, 62
St George Motor Club, 145
St Giles Cathedral, 30
St James Square, looking north, 46
St John's Episcopal Church, 61, 62
St John's and St Cuthbert's, 61
St Mary's Episcopal Cathedral, 56
Salvesen, Iver R. R., 155
Scott Monument, 29
Scott Monument, 55
Scott, Sir Walter, 54
Scottish XV v England, first, 141
Shaw, Sax, 183
Silver Jubilee visit, 128
Sky Pilot, the, 159
South Queensferry, 98
Street scene in fishing community, 110
Summerhall, 74

Theatre Royal, 42, 43, 50
Transport Officials and Staff, 94
Tunny, James G., 74, 79
Tunny's Photographic Rooms, 79

Upper Bow, 27

Vardon, Harry, 130, 132
Victoria Street, 28
Victorian drawing room of the Yerbury family in the 1890s, 11

Waterloo Place, triumphal arch at, 124
Watson, George, 64
Watsonians v Crocks, 139
Waverley Bridge, 22, 52, 53
Waverley Market, 50, 52, 53, 54
Waverley Market and North British Station Hotel, 54
Waverley Market and Princes Street, 52
Waverley Station, 39, 44, 114, 125
Waverley Station and Jeffrey Street, 40, 41
West End arch, 116
West End, of Edinburgh, 63
Whitehorse Close, 35
Wilkie & Paul, 95
Wood, Sir Henry J., 148

Yerbury, Mrs Blanche, 9, 18
Yerbury, David Stenhouse, 18
Yerbury, David Stenhouse 1925-1980, 13
Yerbury, David Stenhouse at age ten, 19,
Yerbury, David Stenhouse as White Rabbit, 17
Yerbury, E. R. & Son, 118
Yerbury, E. R. & Son, premises of, 19
Yerbury, Edward Reuben b. 1816, 11
Yerbury, Edward Reuben 1843-1933, 12
Yerbury, Edward Reuben b. 1881, 13
Yerbury, Edward Reuben 1881-1952, 12
Yerbury, Edward Reuben, in the late 1930s, 20
Yerbury, Edward Reuben and Grace Stenhouse, 15
Yerbury, Edward R. – three times, 15
Yerbury, Edward Roper, 18
Yerbury, Edward Roper, 144, 145
Yerbury, Edward Roper, c.1918, 17
Yerbury, Edward Roper and David Stenhouse Yerbury, 1930, 18
Yerbury family group, 14
Yerbury, Mrs Faye, 21
Yerbury, Grace, 158
Yerbury, Grace (nee Stenhouse) with Edward and David, 16
Yerbury, Rachel, 21
Yerbury, Trevor E. R., 9
*Yerbury, Trevor E. R. 1951- *, 13
Young lady in profile, 164